DO YOU KNOW . . .

WHICH IS THE MOST CROWDED AIRPORT IN THE U.S.?

HOW MUCH A GOLF BALL WEIGHS?

HOW MANY PEOPLE GET MARRIED—AND DIVORCED—EVERY YEAR?

THE LONGEST RIVER? THE HIGHEST POINT ON EARTH?

WHERE IT IS DEADLIEST TO DRIVE A CAR?

HOW MANY PEOPLE ARE ON THE FEDERAL PAYROLL?

THE HOTTEST TEMPERATURE AND THE GREATEST ONE-MONTH SNOWFALL EVER RECORDED IN THE U.S.?

WHAT TO GIVE A COUPLE ON THEIR TWENTY-FIRST ANNIVERSARY?

ALL ABOUT THE SUN, MOON, AND PLANETS?

WHOSE FACE IS ON THE $100,000 BILL?

Now the Facts are at your fingertips!

INFORMATION PLEASE
PRESENTS

THE
BOOK OF FACTS

Prepared by the Editors of
THE INFORMATION PLEASE ALMANAC

Nicholas Swyrydenko, *Project Editor*
Harvey Wasserman, *Advising Editor*

•

A DELL BOOK

Published by
Dell Publishing Co., Inc.
1 Dag Hammarskjold Plaza
New York, New York 10017

Dell ® TM 681510, Dell Publishing Co., Inc.

ISBN: 0-440-14329-2

Printed in the United States of America

First printing—April 1979

FACT-FINDER INDEX

D

X

Y

Z

ANIMALS

What Do You Call Different Animals?

Animal	Male	Female	Young	Animal	Male	Female	Young
Ass	Jack	Jenny	Foal	Goose	Gander	Goose	Gosling
Bear	He-bear	She-bear	Cub	Horse	Stallion	Mare	Foal
Cat	Tom	Queen	Kitten	Lion	Lion	Lioness	Cub
Cattle	Bull	Cow	Calf	Rabbit	Buck	Doe	Bunny
Chicken	Rooster	Hen	Chick	Sheep	Ram	Ewe	Lamb
Deer	Buck	Doe	Fawn	Swan	Cob	Pen	Cygnet
Dog	Dog	Bitch	Pup	Swine	Boar	Sow	Piglet
Duck	Drake	Duck	Duckling	Tiger	Tiger	Tigress	Cub
Elephant	Bull	Cow	Calf	Whale	Bull	Cow	Calf
Fox	Dog	Vixen	Cub	Wolf	Dog	Bitch	Pup

Source: James Doherty, Curator of Mammals, N.Y. Zoological Society.

When Birds of a Feather Flock Together, What Are They Called?

Source: James Doherty, Curator of Mammals, N.Y. Zoological Society, and *Information Please* data.

ants: colony

bears: sleuth, sloth

bees: grist, hive, swarm

birds: flight, volery

cattle: drove

cats: clutter, clowder

chicks: brood, clutch

clams: bed

cranes: sedge, seige

crows: murder

doves: dule

ducks: brace, team

elephants: herd

elks: gang

finches: charm

fish: school, shoal, draught

foxes: leash, skulk

geese: flock, gaggle, skein

gnats: cloud, horde

goats: trip

gorillas: band

hares: down, husk

hawks: cast

hens: brood

hogs: drift

horses: pair, team

hounds: cry, mute, pack

kangaroos: troop

kittens: kindle

larks: exaltation

leopards: leap

lions: pride

locusts: plague		**rabbits:** nest	
magpies: tidings		**seals:** pod	
mules: span		**sheep:** drove, flock	
nightingales: watch		**sparrows:** host	
oxen: yoke		**storks:** mustering	
oysters: bed		**swans:** bevy, wedge	
parrots: company		**swine:** sounder	
partridges: covey		**toads:** knot	
peacocks: muster, osten-tation		**turkeys:** rafter	
pheasants: nest, bouquet		**turtles:** bale	
pigs: litter		**vipers:** nest	
ponies: string		**whales:** gam, pod	
quail: bevy, covey		**wolves:** pack, route	
		woodcocks: fall	

How Fast Can Animals Run?

Most of the following measurements are for maximum speeds over approximate quarter-mile distances. Exceptions—which are included to give a wide range of animals—are the lion and elephant, whose speeds were clocked in the act of charging; the whippet, which was timed over a 200-yard course; the cheetah over a 100-yard distance; man for a 15-yard segment of a 100-yard run; and the black mamba, six-lined race runner, spider, giant tortoise, three-toed sloth, and garden snail, which were measured over various small distances.

Animal	Speed mph	Animal	Speed mph
Cheetah	70	Reindeer	32
Pronghorn antelope	61	Giraffe	32
Wildebeest	50	White-tailed deer	30
Lion	50	Wart hog	30
Thomson's gazelle	50	Grizzly bear	30
Quarter horse	47.5	Cat (domestic)	30
Elk	45	Man	27.89
Cape hunting dog	45	Elephant	25
Coyote	43	Black mamba snake	20
Gray fox	42	Six-line race runner	18
Hyena	40	Squirrel	12
Zebra	40	Pig (domestic)	11
Mongolian wild ass	40	Chicken	9
Greyhound	39.35	Spider (Tegenearia atrica)	1.17
Whippet	35.5	Giant Tortoise	0.17
Rabbit (domestic)	35	Three-toed sloth	0.15
Mule deer	35	Garden snail	0.03
Jackal	35		

Source: *Natural History* Magazine, March 1974, copyright 1974, The American Museum of Natural History; and James Doherty, Curator of Mammals, N.Y. Zoological Society.

How Long Does It Take an Elephant to have a Baby-And How Long Will It Live?

Animal	Gestation or incubation, in days & (average)	Longevity, in years & (record exceptions)
Ass	365	18–20 (63)
Bear	180–240[1]	15–30 (47)
Cat	52–69 (63)	10–12 (26+)
Chicken	22	7–8 (14)
Cow	c. 280	9–12 (25)
Deer	197–300[1]	10–15 (26)
Dog	53–71 (63)	10–12 (24)
Duck	21–35[1] (28)	10 (15)
Elephant	510–730 (624)[1]	30–40 (71)
Fox	51–63[1]	8–10 (14)
Goat	136–160 (151)	12 (17)
Groundhog	31–32	4–9
Guinea pig	58–75 (68)	3 (6)
Hamster, golden	15–17	2 (8)
Hippopotamus	220–255 (240)	30 (49+)
Horse	264–420 (336)[2]	20–25 (50+)
Kangaroo	32–39[1]	4–6 (23)
Lion	105–113 (108)	10 (29)
Man	253–303	[3]
Monkey	139–270[1]	12–15[1] (29)
Mouse	19–31[1]	1–3 (4)
Parakeet (Budgerigar)	17–20 (18)	8 (12+)
Pig	101–130 (115)	10 (22)
Pigeon	11–19	10–12 (39)
Rabbit	30–35 (31)	6–8 (15)
Rat	21	3 (5)
Sheep	144–152 (151)[1]	12 (16)
Squirrel	44	8–9 (15)
Whale	365–547[1]	—
Wolf	60–63	10–12 (16)

1. Depending on kind. 2. Horse has the greatest variation of gestation period of any species. This is caused by seasonal or feed factors. 3. For life expectancy charts, see Index. Source: James Doherty, Curator of Mammals, N.Y. Zoological Society.

AUTOMOBILES

The Economics of Used Cars

Source: The Hertz Corporation.

Nearly three out of four U.S. passenger cars bought for personal driving are second-hand. An average of 13.5 million used autos were sold annually from 1967 to 1976. Motorists spend more than $21.3 billion a year for used cars; new car dealers account for over $14 billion of this total.

For used cars from one to four years old, purchase prices ranged from 20 to 80 percent below new car outlays. Savings on running expenses ran 10 to 50 percent under typical new car expenses.

The greatest potential savings are realized if a used car is kept at least three years, at an assumed 10,000 miles per year of travel. A three-year-old used car driven 10,000 miles a year for another three years costs half as much to run as the same car purchased new and also driven for three years.

Only about 12 percent of all new U.S. cars sold are traded after one year; another 14 percent are sold at the end of two years. In the third year, nearly 17 percent of the cars are traded; another 14.5 percent are sold after four years of operation.

After ten years of operation, 40 to 45 percent of cars are still on the road.

Automobile Expense (1978)

The American Automobile Association says the cost of owning and operating the average 1978 intermediate-size car is 19.6¢ per mile ($1,957 a year), down from 20.2¢ for the 1977-model car.

Auto Facts
(1976 estimate)

Type of vehicle	Total travel (million vehicle miles)	Number of registered vehicles (thousands)	Average miles traveled per vehicle	Fuel consumed (million gallons)	Average fuel consumption per vehicle (gallons)	Average miles per gallon
All passenger vehicles	1,102,213	115,818.9	9,517	79,703.8	688	13.83
Total personal passenger vehicles	1,096,452	115,340.6	9,506	78,739.8	683	13.93
Cars	1,074,000	110,351.4	9,733	78,290.8	709	13.72
Motorcycles	22,452	4,989.2	4,500	449.0	90	50.00
All buses	5,761	478.3	12,045	964.0	2,015	5.98
Commercial	2,899	96.8	29,948	574.1	5,931	5.05
School and other nonrevenue	2,862	381.5	7,502	389.9	1,022	7.34
All cargo vehicles	306,950	27,719.6	11,073	35,996.3	1,299	8.53
Single unit trucks	247,895	26,498.6	9,355	25,039.9	945	9.90
Combinations	59,055	1,221.0	48,366	10,956.4	8,973	5.39
All motor vehicles	1,409,163	143,538.5	9,817	115,700.1	800	12.18

Source: Department of Transportation, Federal Highway Administration.

Road Mileages Between U.S. Cities[1]

Cities	Birmingham	Boston	Buffalo	Chicago	Cleveland	Dallas	Denver
Birmingham, Ala.	—	1,194	947	657	734	653	1,318
Boston, Mass.	1,194	—	457	983	639	1,815	1,991
Buffalo, N.Y.	947	457	—	536	192	1,387	1,561
Chicago, Ill.	657	983	536	—	344	931	1,050
Cleveland, Ohio	734	639	192	344	—	1,205	1,369
Dallas, Tex.	653	1,815	1,387	931	1,205	—	801
Denver, Colo	1,318	1,991	1,561	1,050	1,369	801	—
Detroit, Mich.	754	702	252	279	175	1,167	1,301
El Paso, Tex.	1,278	2,358	1,928	1,439	1,746	625	652
Houston, Tex.	692	1,886	1,532	1,092	1,358	242	1,032
Indianapolis, Ind.	492	940	510	189	318	877	1,051
Kansas City, Mo.	703	1,427	997	503	815	508	616
Los Angeles, Calif.	2,078	3,036	2,606	2,112	2,424	1,425	1,174
Louisville, Ky.	378	996	571	305	379	865	1,135
Memphis, Tenn.	249	1,345	965	546	773	470	1,069
Miami, Fla.	777	1,539	1,445	1,390	1,325	1,332	2,094
Minneapolis, Minn.	1,067	1,402	955	411	763	969	867
New Orleans, La.	347	1,541	1,294	947	1,102	504	1,305
New York, N.Y.	983	213	436	840	514	1,604	1,780
Omaha, Neb.	907	1,458	1,011	493	819	661	559
Philadelphia, Pa.	894	304	383	758	432	1,515	1,698
Phoenix, Ariz.	1,680	2,664	2,234	1,729	2,052	1,027	836
Pittsburgh, Pa.	792	597	219	457	131	1,237	1,411
St. Louis, Mo.	508	1,179	749	293	567	638	871
Salt Lake City, Utah	1,805	2,425	1,978	1,458	1,786	1,239	512
San Francisco, Calif.	2,385	3,179	2,732	2,212	2,540	1,765	1,266
Seattle, Wash.	2,612	3,043	2,596	2,052	2,404	2,122	1,373
Washington, D.C.	751	440	386	695	369	1,372	1,635

Cities	Detroit	El Paso	Houston	Indian- apolis	Kansas City	Los Angeles	Louisville
Birmingham, Ala.	754	1,278	692	492	703	2,078	378
Boston, Mass.	702	2,358	1,886	940	1,427	3,036	996
Buffalo, N.Y.	252	1,928	1,532	510	997	2,606	571
Chicago, Ill.	279	1,439	1,092	189	503	2,112	305
Cleveland, Ohio	175	1,746	1,358	318	815	2,424	379
Dallas, Tex.	1,167	625	242	877	508	1,425	865
Denver, Colo.	1,310	652	1,032	1,051	616	1,174	1,135
Detroit, Mich.	—	1,696	1,312	290	760	2,369	378
El Paso, Tex.	1,696	—	756	1,418	936	800	1,443
Houston, Tex.	1,312	756	—	1,022	750	1,556	981
Indianapolis, Ind.	290	1,418	1,022	—	487	2,096	114
Kansas City, Mo.	760	936	750	487	—	1,609	519
Los Angeles, Calif.	2,369	800	1,556	2,096	1,609	—	2,128
Louisville, Ky.	378	1,443	981	114	519	2,128	—
Memphis, Tenn.	756	1,095	586	466	454	1,847	396
Miami, Fla.	1,409	1,957	1,237	1,225	1,479	2,757	1,111
Minneapolis, Minn.	698	1,353	1,211	600	466	2,041	716
New Orleans, La.	1,101	1,121	365	839	839	1,921	725
New York, N.Y.	671	2,147	1,675	729	1,216	2,825	785
Omaha, Neb.	754	1,015	903	590	204	1,733	704
Philadelphia, Pa.	589	2,065	1,586	647	1,134	2,743	703
Phoenix, Ariz.	1,986	402	1,158	1,713	1,226	398	1,749
Pittsburgh, Pa.	288	1,778	1,395	360	847	2,456	416
St. Louis, Mo.	529	1,179	799	239	255	1,864	264
Salt Lake City, Utah	1,721	877	1,465	1,545	1,128	728	1,647
San Francisco, Calif.	2,475	1,202	1,958	2,299	1,882	403	2,401
Seattle, Wash.	2,339	1,760	2,348	2,241	1,909	1,150	2,355
Washington, D.C.	526	1,997	1,443	565	1,071	2,680	601

1. These figures represent estimates and are subject to change.

Road Mileages Between U.S. Cities

Cities	Memphis	Miami	Minneapolis	New Orleans	New York	Omaha	Philadelphia
Birmingham, Ala.	249	777	1,067	347	983	907	894
Boston, Mass.	1,345	1,539	1,402	1,541	213	1,458	304
Buffalo, N.Y.	965	1,445	955	1,294	436	1,011	383
Chicago, Ill.	546	1,390	411	947	840	493	758
Cleveland, Ohio	773	1,325	763	1,102	514	819	432
Dallas, Tex.	470	1,332	969	504	1,604	661	1,515
Denver, Colo.	1,069	2,094	867	1,305	1,780	559	1,698
Detroit, Mich.	756	1,409	698	1,101	671	754	589
El Paso, Tex.	1,095	1,957	1,353	1,121	2,147	1,015	2,065
Houston, Tex.	586	1,237	1,211	365	1,675	903	1,586
Indianapolis, Ind.	466	1,225	600	839	729	590	647
Kansas City, Mo.	454	1,479	466	839	1,216	204	1,134
Los Angeles, Calif.	1,847	2,757	2,041	1,921	2,825	1,733	2,743
Louisville, Ky.	396	1,111	716	725	785	704	703
Memphis, Tenn.	—	1,025	854	401	1,134	658	1,045
Miami, Fla.	1,025	—	1,801	892	1,328	1,683	1,239
Minneapolis, Minn.	854	1,801	—	1,255	1,259	373	1,177
New Orleans, La.	401	892	1,255	—	1,330	1,043	1,241
New York, N.Y.	1,134	1,328	1,259	1,330	—	1,315	93
Omaha, Neb.	658	1,683	373	1,043	1,315	—	1,233
Philadelphia, Pa.	1,045	1,239	1,177	1,241	93	1,233	—
Phoenix, Ariz.	1,464	2,359	1,644	1,523	2,442	1,305	2,360
Pittsburgh, Pa.	810	1,250	876	1,118	386	932	304
St. Louis, Mo.	295	1,241	559	696	968	459	886
Salt Lake City, Utah	1,556	2,571	1,243	1,743	2,282	967	2,200
San Francisco, Calif.	2,151	3,097	1,997	2,269	3,036	1,721	2,954
Seattle, Wash.	2,363	3,389	1,641	2,606	2,900	1,705	2,818
Washington, D.C.	902	1,101	1,114	1,098	229	1,170	140

Cities	Phoenix	Pitts-burgh	St. Louis	Salt Lake City	San Francisco	Seattle	Wash-ington
Birmingham, Ala.	1,680	792	508	1,805	2,385	2,612	751
Boston, Mass.	2,664	597	1,179	2,425	3,179	3,043	440
Buffalo, N.Y.	2,234	219	749	1,978	2,732	2,596	386
Chicago, Ill.	1,729	457	293	1,458	2,212	2,052	695
Cleveland, Ohio	2,052	131	567	1,786	2,540	2,404	369
Dallas, Tex.	1,027	1,237	638	1,239	1,765	2,122	1,372
Denver, Colo.	836	1,411	871	512	1,266	1,373	1,635
Detroit, Mich.	1,986	288	529	1,721	2,475	2,339	526
El Paso, Tex.	402	1,778	1,179	877	1,202	1,760	1,997
Houston, Tex.	1,158	1,395	799	1,465	1,958	2,348	1,443
Indianapolis, Ind.	1,713	360	239	1,545	2,299	2,241	565
Kansas City, Mo.	1,226	847	255	1,128	1,882	1,909	1,071
Los Angeles, Calif.	398	2,456	1,864	728	403	1,150	2,680
Louisville, Ky.	1,749	416	264	1,647	2,401	2,355	601
Memphis, Tenn.	1,464	810	295	1,556	2,151	2,363	902
Miami, Fla.	2,359	1,250	1,241	2,571	3,097	3,389	1,101
Minneapolis, Minn.	1,644	876	559	1,243	1,997	1,641	1,114
New Orleans, La.	1,523	1,118	696	1,743	2,269	2,626	1,098
New York, N.Y.	2,442	386	968	2,282	3,036	2,900	229
Omaha, Neb.	1,305	932	459	967	1,721	1,705	1,178
Philadelphia, Pa.	2,360	304	886	2,200	2,954	2,818	140
Phoenix, Ariz.	—	2,073	1,485	651	800	1,482	2,278
Pittsburgh, Pa.	2,073	—	599	1,899	2,653	2,517	241
St. Louis, Mo.	1,485	599	—	1,383	2,137	2,164	836
Salt Lake City, Utah	651	1,899	1,383	—	754	883	2,110
San Francisco, Calif.	800	2,653	2,137	754	—	817	2,864
Seattle, Wash.	1,482	2,517	2,164	883	817	—	2,755
Washington, D.C.	2,278	241	836	2,110	2,864	2,755	—

Dangerous Driving

Country	Motor vehicles[1]	Death rate[2]	Death rate[3]
United States	670	21	32
France	450	28	63
Denmark	320	17	53
Netherlands	410	18	43
Norway	320	12	36
West Germany	360	24	67
Austria	340	28	82
Finland	300	17	57
United Kingdom	310	12	38
Italy	390	17	44
Ireland	210	17	81
Spain	210	17	82
Sweden	380	14	38
Switzerland	440	19	43
Czechoslovakia	160	18	113
East Germany	350	16	44
Hungary	140	15	108
Poland	110	17	159
Australia	490	26	54
Japan	340	11	33

1. Per 1,000 population, 1976. 2. Deaths per 100,000 population. 3. Deaths per 100,000 registered motor vehicles. *Source:* Department of Transportation, National Highway Traffic Safety Administration.

Not So Trivial

In 1977, 10,400,000 American cars of various model years were recalled, while only 9,300,000 new cars were sold.

AVIATION

Famous Aviation Firsts

1782 **First balloon flight.** Jacques and Joseph Montgolfier of Annonay, France, sent up a small smoke-filled balloon about mid-November.

1783 **First hydrogen-filled balloon flight.** Jacques A. C. Charles, Paris physicist, supervised construction by A. J. and M. N. Robert of a 13-ft diameter balloon that was filled with hydrogen. It got up to about 3,000 ft and traveled about 16 mi. in a 45-min flight (Aug. 27).
First human balloon flights. A Frenchman, Jean Pilâtre de Rozier, made the first captive-balloon ascension (Oct. 15). With the Marquis d'Arlandes, Pilâtre de Rozier made the first free flight, reaching a peak altitude of about 500 ft, and traveling about 5$\frac{1}{2}$ mi. in 20 min (Nov. 21).

1784 **First powered balloon.** Gen. Jean Baptiste Marie Meusnier developed the first propeller-driven and elliptically-shaped balloon—the crew cranking three propellers on a common shaft to give the craft a speed of about 3 mph.
First woman to fly. Mme. Thible, a French opera singer (June 4).

1793 **First balloon flight in America.** Jean Pierre Blanchard, a French pilot, made it from Philadelphia to near Woodbury, Gloucester County, N.J., in a little over 45 min (Jan. 9).

1794 **First military use of the balloon.** Jean Marie Coutelle, using a balloon built for the French Army, made two 4-hr observation ascents. The military purpose of the ascents seems to have been to damage the enemy's morale.

1797 **First parachute jump.** André-Jacques Garnerin dropped from about 6,500 ft over Monceau Park in Paris in a 23-ft diameter parachute made of white canvas with a basket attached (Oct. 22).

1843 First air transport company. In London, William S. Henson and John Stringfellow filed articles of incorporation for the Aerial Transit Company (March 24). It failed

1852 First dirigible. Henri Giffard, a French engineer, flew in a controllable (more or less) steam-engine powered balloon, 144 ft long and 39 ft in diameter, inflated with 88,000 cu ft of coal gas. It reached 6.7 mph on a flight from Paris to Trappe (Sept. 24).

1860 First aerial photographers. Samuel Archer King and William Black made two photos of Boston, still in existence.

1872 First gas-engine powered dirigible. Paul Haenlein, a German engineer, flew in a semi-rigid-frame dirigible, powered by a 4-cylinder internal-combustion engine running on coal gas drawn from the supporting bag.

1873 First transatlantic attempt. *The New York Daily Graphic* sponsored the attempt with a 400,000 cu ft balloon carrying a lifeboat. A rip in the bag during inflation brought collapse of the balloon and the project.

1897 First successful metal dirigible. An all-metal dirigible, designed by David Schwarz, a Hungarian, took off from Berlin's Tempelhof Field and, powered by a 16-hp Daimler engine, got several miles before leaking gas caused it to crash (Nov. 13).

1900 First Zeppelin flight. Germany's Count Ferdinand von Zeppelin flew the first of his long series of rigid-frame airships. It attained a speed of 18 mi. per h and got $3^1/_2$ mi. before its steering gear failed (July 2).

1903 First successful heavier-than-air machine flight. Aviation was really born on the sand dunes at Kitty Hawk, N.C., when Orville Wright crawled to his prone position between the wings of the biplane he and his brother Wilbur had built, opened the throttle of their home-made 12-hp engine and took to the air. He covered 120 ft in 12 sec. Later that day, in one of four flights, Wilbur stayed up 59 sec and covered 852 ft (Dec. 17).

1904 First airplane maneuvers. Orville Wright made the first turn with an airplane (Sept. 15); 5 days later his brother Wilbur made the first complete circle.

1905 First airplane flight over half an hour. Orville Wright kept his craft up 33 min 17 sec (Oct. 4).

1906 First European airplane flight. Alberto Santos-Dumont, a Brazilian, flew a heavier-than-air machine at Bagatelle Field, Paris (Sept. 13).

1908 **First airplane fatality.** Lt. Thomas E. Selfridge, U.S. Army Signal Corps, was in a group of officers evaluating the Wright plane at Fort Myer, Va. He was up about 75 ft with Orville Wright when the propeller hit a bracing wire and was broken, throwing the plane out of control, killing Selfridge and seriously injuring Wright (Sept. 17).

1910 **First licensed woman pilot.** Baroness Raymonde de la Roche of France, who learned to fly in 1909, received ticket No. 36 on March 8.

First flight from shipboard. Lt. Eugene Ely, USN, took a Curtiss plane off from the deck of cruiser *Birmingham* at Hampton Roads, Va., and flew to Norfolk (Nov. 14). The following January, he reversed the process, flying from Camp Selfridge to the deck of the armored cruiser *Pennsylvania* in San Francisco Bay (Jan. 18).

1911 **First U.S. woman pilot.** Harriet Quimby, a magazine writer, who got ticket No. 37.

1913 **First multi-engined aircraft.** Built and flown by Igor Ivan Sikorsky while still in his native Russia.

1914 **First aerial combat.** In August, Allied and German pilots and observers started shooting at each other with pistols and rifles—with negligible results.

1915 **First air raids on England.** German Zeppelins started dropping bombs on four English communities (Jan. 19).

1918 **First U.S. air squadron.** The U.S. Army Air Corps made its first independent raids over enemy lines, in DH-4 planes (British-designed) powered with 400-hp American-designed Liberty engines (April 8).

First regular airmail service. Operated for the Post Office Department by the Army, the first regular service was inaugurated with one round trip a day (except Sunday) between Washington, D.C., and New York City (May 15).

1919 **First transatlantic flight.** The NC-4, one of four Curtiss flying boats commanded by Lt. Comdr. Albert C. Read, reached Lisbon, Portugal, (May 27) after hops from Trepassy Bay, Newfoundland, to Horta, Azores (May 16–17), to Ponta Delgada (May 20). The Liberty-powered craft was piloted by Walter Hinton.

First nonstop transatlantic flight. Capt. John Alcock and Lt. Arthur Whitten Brown, British World War I flyers, made the 1,900 mi. from St. John's, Newfoundland, to Clifden, Ireland, in 16 h 12 min in a Vickers-Vimy bomber with two 350-hp Rolls-Royce engines (June 15–16).

First lighter-than-air transatlantic flight. The British dirigible R-34, commanded by Maj. George H. Scott, left Firth of Forth, Scotland, (July 2) and touched down at Mineola, L.I., 108 h later. The eastbound trip was made in 75 h (completed July 13).

First scheduled passenger service (using airplanes). Aircraft Travel and Transport inaugurated London-Paris service (Aug. 25). Later the company started the first trans-channel mail service on the same route (Nov. 10).

1921 **First naval vessel sunk by aircraft.** Two battleships being scrapped by treaty were sunk by bombs dropped from Army planes in demonstration put on by Brig. Gen. William S. Mitchell (July 21).

First helium balloon. The C-7, non-rigid Navy dirigible was first to use non-inflammable helium as lifting gas, making a flight from Hampton Roads, Va., to Washington, D.C. (Dec. 1).

1922 **First member of Caterpillar Club.** Lt. (later Maj. Gen.) Harold Harris bailed out of a crippled plane he was testing at McCook Field, Dayton, Ohio (Oct. 20), and became the first man to join the Caterpillar Club— those whose lives have been saved by parachute.

1923 **First nonstop transcontinental flight.** Lts. John A. Macready and Oakley Kelly flew a single-engine Fokker T-2 nonstop from New York to San Diego, a distance of just over 2,500 mi. in 26 h 50 min (May 2–3).

First autogyro flight. Juan de la Cierva, a brilliant Spanish mathematician, made the first successful flight in a rotary wing aircraft in Madrid (June 9).

1924 **First round-the-world flight.** Four Douglas Cruiser biplanes of the U.S. Army Air Corps took off from Seattle under command of Maj. Frederick Martin (April 6). 175 days later, two of the planes (Lt. Lowell Smith's and Lt. Erik Nelson's) landed in Seattle after a circuitous route—one source saying 26,345 mi., another saying 27,553 mi.

1926 **First polar flight.** Then-Lt. Cmdr. Richard E. Byrd, acting as navigator, and Floyd Bennett as pilot, flew a
trimotor Fokker from Kings Bay, Spitsbergen, over
the North Pole and back in 15½ h (May 8–9).

1927 **First solo transatlantic flight.** Charles Augustus Lindbergh
lifted his Wright-powered Ryan monoplane, *Spirit of
St. Louis,* from Roosevelt Field, L.I., to stay aloft 33
h 39 min and travel 3,600 mi. to Le Bourget Field
outside Paris (May 20–21).
First transatlantic passenger. Charles A. Levine was piloted by Clarence D. Chamberlin from Roosevelt Field,
L.I., to Eisleben, Germany, in a Wright-powered Bel-
lanca (June 4–5).

1928 **First east-west transatlantic crossing.** Baron Guenther von
Huenefeld, piloted by German Capt. Hermann Ko-
ehl and Irish Capt. James Fitzmaurice, left Dublin for
New York City (April 12) in a single-engine all-metal
Junkers monoplane. Some 37 h later, they crashed on
Greely Island, Labrador. Rescued.
First U.S.-Australia flight. Sir Charles Kingsford-Smith and
Capt. Charles T. P. Ulm, Australians, and two Ameri-
can navigators, Harry W. Lyon and James Warner,
crossed the Pacific from Oakland to Brisbane. They
went via Hawaii and the Fiji Islands in a trimotor
Fokker (May 31–June 8).
First transarctic flight. Sir Hubert Wilkins, an Australian
explorer and Carl Ben Eielson, who served as pilot,
flew from Point Barrow, Alaska, to Spitsbergen (mid-
April).

1929 **First of the endurance records.** With Air Corps Maj. Carl
Spaatz in command and Capt. Ira Eaker as chief pilot,
an Army Fokker, aided by refueling in the air, remained aloft 150 h 40 min at Los Angeles (Jan. 1–7).
First blind flight. James H. Doolittle proved the feasibili-
ty of instrument-guided flying when he took off and
landed entirely on instruments (Sept. 24).
First rocket-engine flight. Fritz von Opel, a German auto
maker, stayed aloft in his small rocket-powered craft
for 75 sec, covering nearly 2 mi. (Sept. 30).
First South Pole flight. Comdr. Richard E. Byrd, with
Bernt Balchen as pilot, Harold I. June, radio operator,
and Capt. A. C. McKinley, photographer, flew a
trimotor Fokker from the Bay of Whales, Little
America, over the South Pole and back (Nov. 28–29).

1930 **First Paris–New York nonstop flight.** Dieudonné Coste and Maurice Bellonte, French pilots, flew a Hispano-powered Breguet biplane from Le Bourget Field to Valley Stream, L.I., in 37 h 18 min. (Sept. 2–3).

1931 **First flight into the stratosphere.** Auguste Piccard, a Swiss physicist, and Charles Knipfer, ascended in a balloon from Augsburg, Germany, and reached a height of 51,793 ft in a 17-h flight that terminated on a glacier near Innsbruck, Austria (May 27).

First nonstop transpacific flight. Hugh Herndon and Clyde Pangborn took off from Sabishiro Beach, Japan, dropped their landing gear, and flew 4,860 mi. to near Wenatchee, Wash., in 41 h 13 min. (Oct. 4–5).

1932 **First woman's transatlantic solo.** Amelia Earhart, flying a Pratt & Whitney Wasp-powered Lockheed Vega, flew alone from Harbor Grace, Newfoundland, to Ireland in approximately 15 h (May 20–21).

First westbound transatlantic solo. James A. Mollison, a British pilot, took a de Havilland Puss Moth from Portmarnock, Ireland, to Pennfield, N.B. (Aug. 18).

First woman airline pilot. Ruth Rowland Nichols, first woman to hold three international records at the same time—speed, distance, altitude—was employed by N.Y.-New England Airways.

1933 **First round-the-world solo.** Wiley Post took a Lockheed Vega, *Winnie Mae*, 15,596 mi. around the world in 7 d 18 h 49¹/₂ min (July 15–22).

1937 **First successful helicopter.** Hanna Reitsch, a German pilot, flew Dr. Heinrich Focke's FW-61 in free, fully-controlled flight at Bremen (July 4).

1939 **First turbojet flight.** Just before their invasion of Poland, the Germans flew a Heinkel He-178 plane powered by a Heinkel S3B turbojet (Aug. 27).

1942 **First American jet plane flight.** Robert Stanley, chief pilot for Bell Aircraft Corp., flew the Bell XP-59 *Airacomet* at Muroc Army Base, Calif. (Oct. 1).

1947 **First piloted supersonic flight in an airplane.** Capt. Charles E. Yeager, U.S. Air Force, flew the X-1 rocket-powered research plane built by Bell Aircraft Corp., faster than the speed of sound at Muroc Air Force Base, California (Oct. 14).

1949 **First round-the-world nonstop flight.** Capt. James Gallagher and USAF crew of 13 flew a Boeing B-50A Superfortress around the world nonstop from Ft. Worth, returning to same point: 23,452 mi. in 94 h 1 min, with 4 aerial refuelings enroute (Feb. 27–March 2).

1950 **First nonstop transatlantic jet flight.** Col. David C. Schilling (USAF) flew 3,300 mi. from England to Limestone, Maine, in 10 h 1 min (Sept. 22).

1951 **First solo across North Pole.** Charles F. Blair, Jr., flew a converted P-51 (May 29).

1952 **First jetliner service.** De Havilland Comet flight inaugurated by BOAC between London and Johannesburg, South Africa (May 2). Flight, including stops, took 23 h 38 min.

   First transatlantic helicopter flight. Capt. Vincent H. McGovern and 1st Lt. Harold W. Moore piloted 2 Sikorsky H-19s from Westover, Mass., to Prestwick, Scotland (3,410 mi.). Trip was made in 5 steps, with flying time of 42 h 25 min (July 15–31).

   First transatlantic round trip in same day. British Canberra twin-jet bomber flew from Aldergrove, Northern Ireland, to Gander, Newfoundland, and back in 7 h 59 min flying time (Aug. 26).

1955 **First transcontinental round trip in same day.** Lt. John M. Conroy piloted F-86 Sabrejet across U.S. (Los Angeles –New York) and back—5,085 mi.—in 11 h 33 min 27 sec (May 21).

1957 **First round-the-world, nonstop jet plane flight.** Maj. Gen. Archie J. Old, Jr., USAF, led a flight of 3 Boeing B-52 bombers, powered with 8 10,000-lb. thrust Pratt & Whitney Aircraft J57 engines around the world in 45 h 19 min; distance 24,325 mi.; average speed 525 mph. (Completed Jan. 18.)

1958 **First transatlantic jet passenger service.** BOAC, New York to London (Oct. 4). Pan American started daily service, N.Y. to Paris (Oct. 26).

   First domestic jet passenger service. National Airlines inaugurated service between New York and Miami (Dec. 10).

1976 **First regularly-scheduled commercial supersonic transport (SST) flights begin.** Air France and British Airways inaugurate service (January 21). Air France flies the Paris-Rio de Janeiro route; B.A., the London-Bahraine. Both airlines begin SST service to Washington, D.C. (May 24).

1977 **First successful man-powered aircraft.** Paul MacCready, an aeronautical engineer from Pasadena, Calif., was awarded the Kremer Prize for creating the world's first successful man-powered aircraft. The *Gossamer Condor* was flown by Bryan Allen over the required 3-mile course on Aug. 23.

1978 **First successful transatlantic balloon flight.** Three Albuquerque, N.M., men, Ben Abruzzo, Larry Newman, and Maxie Anderson, completed the crossing (Aug. 16. Landed, Aug. 17) in their hot air balloon, *Double Eagle II.*

Passenger Traffic at Leading U.S. Airports, 1977

Airport	Passengers[1]
O'Hare; Chicago	44.2
Hartsfield International; Atlanta	29.9
International; Los Angeles	28.4
Kennedy; New York City	22.7
International; San Francisco	20.2
International; Honolulu	18.1
Dallas–Ft. Worth	17.3
Stapleton International; Denver	15.3
La Guardia; New York City	15.2
International; Miami	13.3
National; Washington, D.C.	13.2
Logan; Boston	12.1
Metro Wayne; Detroit	9.0
Pittsburgh	8.8
International; Philadelphia	8.6
Intercontinental; Houston	8.0
Las Vegas; Nev.	8.0
International; Newark, N.J.	7.4
Seattle–Tacoma; Seattle, Wash.	7.3
International; St. Louis	6.9
Hopkins; Cleveland	6.4
International; Tampa, Fla.	5.9

1. Enplaned, deplaned, and transfer, in millions. *Source:* Airport Operators Council International.

Official World Airplane Records

Source: National Aeronautic Association.

Speed Over Measured Straightaway Course

Speed (mph)	Date	Type plane	Pilot	Place
314.32	Dec. 25, 1934	Caudron	Raymond Delmotte (France)	Istres, France
352.39	Sept. 13, 1935	Hughes Special	Howard Hughes (U.S.)	Santa Ana, Calif.
379.63	Nov. 11, 1937	BF-113R	Herman Wurster (Germany)	Augsburg, Germany
469.22	April 26, 1939	ME-109R	Fritz Wendel (Germany)	Augsburg, Germany
606.25	Nov. 7, 1945	Gloster Meteor IV	Group Capt. H. Wilson (U.K.)	Herne Bay, England
615.78	Sept. 7, 1946	Gloster Meteor	Group Capt. E. M. Donalson (U.K.)	Littlehampton, England
650.80	Aug. 25, 1947	Douglas D-558	Maj. Marion Carl, USMC	Muroc AFB, Calif.
670.98	Sept. 15, 1948	North American F-86A	Maj. R. L. Johnson (USAF)	Muroc AFB, Calif.
698.51	Nov. 19, 1952	North American F-86D	Capt. James S. Nash (USAF)	Salton Sea, Calif.
755.14	Oct. 29, 1953	North American YF	Lt. Col. F. K. Everest, Jr. (USAF)	Salton Sea, Calif.
822.27	Aug. 20, 1955	North American F-100C	Col. Horace A. Hanes (U.S.)	Palmdale, Calif.
1,132.14	March 10, 1956	Fairey Delta 2	L. Peter Twiss, D.S.C. (U.K.)	Ford-Chichester, England
1,207.60	Dec. 12, 1957	McDonnell F-101A	Maj. Adrian E. Drew (USAF)	Edwards AFB, Calif.
1,404.09	May 16, 1958	Lockheed F104	Capt. Walter W. Irwin (USAF)	Edwards AFB, Calif.
1,483.85	Oct. 31, 1959	Sukhoi S-66	G. Mossolov (U.S.S.R.)	U.S.S.R.
1,525.96	Dec. 15, 1959	F-106A Delta Wing Monoplane	Maj. Joseph W. Rogers (USAF)	Edwards AFB, Calif.
1,606.32	Nov. 22, 1961	McDonnell F4H	Lt. Col. R. B. Robinson (USMC)	Edwards AFB, Calif.
1,665.89	July 7, 1962	E-166 Jet	G. Mossolov (U.S.S.R.)	U.S.S.R.
2,070.101	May 1, 1965	Lockheed YF-12A Jet	Col. R. L. Stephens (USAF)	Edwards AFB, Calif.
2,196.17	July 28, 1976	Lockheed SR-71	Capt. Eldon W. Joersz (USAF)	Beale AFB, Calif.

Fastest U.S. continental: Capt. Robert G. Sowers (USAF)—Convair B-58 "Hustler"—from Long Beach, Calif., to Kennedy International Airport, N.Y.—2,458.58 statute miles—2 h 0 min 58.71 sec—average speed, 1,214.65 mph—March 5, 1962.

Distance, Straight Line

Distance (mi.)	Date	Crew	From	To
4,911.93	Sept. 27–29, 1929	Costes & Bellonte (France)	Le Bourget, France	Manchuria
5,011.35	July 28–30, 1931	Russel N. Boardman, John Polando (U.S.)	New York	Istanbul
5,656.93	Aug. 5–7, 1933	Maurice Rossi, Paul Codos (France)	New York	Ryack, Syria
6,305.66	July 12–14, 1937	Gromov, Youmachev, Daniline (U.S.S.R.)	Moscow	San Jacinto, Calif.
7,158.44	Nov. 5–7, 1938	Sqd. Ldr. R. Kellett (U.K.)	Ismailia, Egypt	Darwin, Australia
7,916.00	Nov. 19–20, 1945	Col. C. S. Irvine & Lt. Col. G. R. Stanley (U.S.)	Guam	Washington, D. C.
11,235.60	Sept. 29–Oct. 1, 1946	Comdr. Thomas D. Davies, Comdrs. Eugene P. Rankin, Walter S. Reid, Lt. Comdr. Ray A. Tabeling (USN)	Perth, Australia	Columbus, Ohio
12,532.28	Jan. 10–11, 1962	Maj. Clyde P. Evely (USAF)	Kadena, Okinawa	Madrid

Longest light airplane (3,858–6,614 lb) distance:·Maximillian A. Conrad—U. S. Piper Comanche 250, Lycoming 0-540-AIAS (250 hp), from Casablanca, Morocco, to Los Angeles, 7,668.48 mi.—June 2–4, 1959.

Distance, Closed Course

Distance (mi.)	Date	Crew	Place
6,587.441	March 23–26, 1932	Bossoutrot & Rossi (France)	Oran
7,239.588	May 13–15, 1938	Comdr. Fujita & Sgt. Maj. Takahashi (Japan)	Kisarasu, Japan
8,037.899	July 30–Aug. 1, 1939	Angelo Tondi, Roberto Dagasso, Ferrucio Vignoli (Italy)	Rome
8,854.308	Aug. 1–2, 1947	Lt. Col. O. F. Lassiter (U.S.) Capt. W. J. Valentine (U.S.)	Tampa, Fla.
10,078.84	Dec. 13–14, 1960	Lt. Col. J. R. Grissom (USAF)	Edwards AFB, Calif.
11,336.92	June 6–7, 1962	Capt. William Stevenson (USAF)	Seymour-Johnson, N.C.

Altitude

Height (ft)	Date	Crew	Place
44,819	Sept. 28, 1933	G. Lemoine (France)	Villacoublay, France
47,352	April 11, 1934	Comdr. Renato Donati (Italy)	Rome
49,944	Sept. 28, 1936	Sqd. Ldr. F. R. D. Swain (U.K.)	South Farnborough, England
53,937	June 30, 1937	Fl. Lt. M. J. Adam (U.K.)	Farnborough, England
56,046	Oct. 22, 1938	Col. Mario Pezzi (Italy)	Montecelio
59,445[1]	March 23, 1948	John Cunningham (U.K.)	Hatfield, England
63,668[1]	May 4, 1953	Walter F. Gibb (U.K.)	Bristol, England
65,889[1]	Aug. 29, 1955	Walter F. Gibb (U.K.)	Bristol, England
70,308[1]	Aug. 28, 1957	Michael Randrup (U.K.)	Luton, England
91,243[1]	May 7, 1958	Maj. H. C. Johnson (USAF)	Palmdale, Calif.
103,389[1]	Nov. 14, 1959	Capt. Joe B. Jordan (USAF)	Edwards AFB, Calif.
314,750[2]	July 17, 1962	Maj. Robert M. White (USAF)	Edwards AFB, Calif.
118,898	July 25, 1973	Alexander Fedotov (U.S.S.R.)	U.S.S.R.
123,524	Aug. 31, 1977	Alexander Fedotov (U.S.S.R.)	U.S.S.R.

1. Jet-propelled aircraft. 2. X-15-1-rocket plane.

Air Distances Between U.S. Cities in Statute Miles

Cities	Birmingham	Boston	Buffalo	Chicago	Cleveland	Dallas	Denver
Birmingham, Ala.	—	1,052	776	578	618	581	1,095
Boston, Mass.	1,052	—	400	851	551	1,551	1,769
Buffalo, N. Y.	776	400	—	454	173	1,198	1,370
Chicago, Ill.	578	851	454	—	308	803	920
Cleveland, Ohio	618	551	173	308	—	1,025	1,227
Dallas, Tex.	581	1,551	1,198	803	1,025	—	663
Denver, Colo.	1,095	1,769	1,370	920	1,227	663	—
Detroit, Mich.	641	613	216	238	90	999	1,156
El Paso, Tex.	1,152	2,072	1,692	1,252	1,525	572	557
Houston, Tex.	567	1,605	1,286	940	1,114	225	879
Indianapolis, Ind.	433	807	435	165	263	763	1,000
Kansas City, Mo.	579	1,251	861	414	700	451	558
Los Angeles, Calif.	1,802	2,596	2,198	1,745	2,049	1,240	831
Louisville, Ky.	331	826	483	269	311	726	1,038
Memphis, Tenn.	217	1,137	803	482	630	420	879
Miami, Fla.	665	1,255	1,181	1,188	1,087	1,111	1,726
Minneapolis, Minn.	862	1,123	731	355	630	862	700
New Orleans, La.	312	1,359	1,086	833	924	443	1,082
New York, N. Y.	864	188	292	713	405	1,374	1,631
Omaha, Neb.	732	1,282	883	432	739	586	488
Philadelphia, Pa.	783	271	279	666	360	1,299	1,579
Phoenix, Ariz.	1,456	2,300	1,906	1,453	1,749	887	586
Pittsburgh, Pa.	608	483	178	410	115	1,070	1,320
St. Louis, Mo.	400	1,038	662	262	492	547	796
Salt Lake City, Utah	1,466	2,099	1,699	1,260	1,568	999	371
San Francisco, Calif.	2,013	2,699	2,300	1,858	2,166	1,483	949
Seattle, Wash.	2,082	2,493	2,117	1,737	2,026	1,681	1,021
Washington, D.C.	661	393	292	597	306	1,185	1,494

Cities	Detroit	El Paso	Houston	Indian-apolis	Kansas City	Los Angeles	Louisville
Birmingham, Ala.	641	1,152	567	433	579	1,802	331
Boston, Mass.	613	2,072	1,605	807	1,251	2,596	826
Buffalo, N.Y.	216	1,692	1,286	435	861	2,198	483
Chicago, Ill.	238	1,252	940	165	414	1,745	269
Cleveland, Ohio	90	1,525	1,114	263	700	2,049	311
Dallas, Tex.	999	572	225	763	451	1,240	726
Denver, Colo.	1,156	557	879	1,000	558	831	1,038
Detroit, Mich.	—	1,479	1,105	240	645	1,983	316
El Paso, Tex.	1,479	—	676	1,264	839	701	1,254
Houston, Tex.	1,105	676	—	865	644	1,374	803
Indianapolis, Ind.	240	1,264	865	—	453	1,809	107
Kansas City, Mo.	645	839	644	453	—	1,356	480
Los Angeles, Calif.	1,983	701	1,374	1,809	1,356	—	1,829
Louisville, Ky.	316	1,254	803	107	480	1,829	—
Memphis, Tenn.	623	976	484	384	369	1,603	320
Miami, Fla.	1,152	1,643	968	1,024	1,241	2,339	919
Minneapolis, Minn.	543	1,157	1,056	511	413	1,524	605
New Orleans, La.	939	983	318	712	680	1,673	623
New York, N.Y.	482	1,905	1,420	646	1,097	2,451	652
Omaha, Neb.	669	878	794	525	166	1,315	580
Philadelphia, Pa.	443	1,836	1,341	585	1,038	2,394	582
Phoenix, Ariz.	1,690	346	1,017	1,499	1,049	357	1,508
Pittsburgh, Pa.	205	1,590	1,137	330	781	2,136	344
St. Louis, Mo.	455	1,034	679	231	238	1,589	242
Salt Lake City, Utah	1,492	689	1,200	1,356	925	579	1,402
San Francisco, Calif.	2,091	995	1,645	1,949	1,506	347	1,986
Seattle, Wash.	1,938	1,376	1,891	1,872	1,506	959	1,943
Washington, D.C.	396	1,728	1,220	494	945	2,300	476

Source: National Geodetic Survey.

Air Distances Between U.S. Cities in Statute Miles

Cities	Memphis	Miami	Minne-apolis	New Orleans	New York	Omaha	Phila-delphia
Birmingham, Ala.	217	665	862	312	864	732	783
Boston, Mass.	1,137	1,255	1,123	1,359	188	1,282	271
Buffalo, N.Y.	803	1,181	731	1,086	292	883	279
Chicago, Ill.	482	1,188	355	833	713	432	666
Cleveland, Ohio	630	1,087	630	924	405	739	360
Dallas, Tex.	420	1,111	862	443	1,374	586	1,299
Denver, Colo.	879	1,726	700	1,082	1,631	488	1,579
Detroit, Mich.	623	1,152	543	939	482	669	443
El Paso, Tex.	976	1,643	1,157	983	1,905	878	1,836
Houston, Tex.	484	968	1,056	318	1,420	794	1,341
Indianapolis, Ind.	384	1,024	511	712	646	525	585
Kansas City, Mo.	369	1,241	413	680	1,097	166	1,038
Los Angeles, Calif.	1,603	2,339	1,524	1,673	2,451	1,315	2,394
Louisville, Ky.	320	919	605	623	652	580	582
Memphis, Tenn.	—	872	699	358	957	529	881
Miami, Fla.	872	—	1,511	669	1,092	1,397	1,019
Minneapolis, Minn.	699	1,511	—	1,051	1,018	290	985
New Orleans, La.	358	669	1,051	—	1,171	847	1,089
New York, N.Y.	957	1,092	1,018	1,171	—	1,144	83
Omaha, Neb.	529	1,397	290	847	1,144	—	1,094
Philadelphia, Pa.	881	1,019	985	1,089	83	1,094	—
Phoenix, Ariz.	1,263	1,982	1,280	1,316	2,145	1,036	2,083
Pittsburgh, Pa.	660	1,010	743	919	317	836	259
St. Louis, Mo.	240	1,061	466	598	875	354	811
Salt Lake City, Utah	1,250	2,089	987	1,434	1,972	833	1,925
San Francisco, Calif.	1,802	2,594	1,584	1,926	2,571	1,429	2,523
Seattle, Wash.	1,867	2,734	1,395	2,101	2,408	1,369	2,380
Washington, D.C.	765	923	934	966	205	1,014	123

Cities	Phoenix	Pitts-burgh	St. Louis	Salt Lake City	San Francisco	Seattle	Wash-ington
Birmingham, Ala.	1,456	608	400	1,466	2,013	2,082	661
Boston, Mass.	2,300	483	1,038	2,099	2,699	2,493	393
Buffalo, N.Y.	1,906	178	662	1,699	2,300	2,117	292
Chicago, Ill.	1,453	410	262	1,260	1,858	1,737	597
Cleveland, Ohio	1,749	115	492	1,568	2,166	2,026	306
Dallas, Tex.	887	1,070	547	999	1,483	1,681	1,185
Denver, Colo.	586	1,320	796	371	949	1,021	1,494
Detroit, Mich.	1,690	205	455	1,492	2,091	1,938	396
El Paso, Tex.	346	1,590	1,034	689	995	1,376	1,728
Houston, Tex.	1,017	1,137	679	1,200	1,645	1,891	1,220
Indianapolis, Ind.	1,499	330	231	1,356	1,949	1,872	494
Kansas City, Mo.	1,049	781	238	925	1,506	1,506	945
Los Angeles, Calif.	357	2,136	1,589	579	347	959	2,300
Louisville, Ky.	1,508	344	242	1,402	1,986	1,943	476
Memphis, Tenn.	1,263	660	240	1,250	1,802	1,867	765
Miami, Fla.	1,982	1,010	1,061	2,089	2,594	2,734	923
Minneapolis, Minn.	1,280	743	466	987	1,584	1,395	934
New Orleans, La.	1,316	919	598	1,434	1,926	2,101	966
New York, N.Y.	2,145	317	875	1,972	2,571	2,408	205
Omaha, Neb.	1,036	836	354	833	1,429	1,369	1,014
Philadelphia, Pa.	2,083	259	811	1,925	2,523	2,380	123
Phoenix, Ariz.	—	1,828	1,272	504	653	1,114	1,983
Pittsburgh, Pa.	1,828	—	559	1,668	2,264	2,138	192
St. Louis, Mo.	1,272	559	—	1,162	1,744	1,724	712
Salt Lake City, Utah	504	1,668	1,162	—	600	701	1,848
San Francisco, Calif.	653	2,264	1,744	600	—	678	2,442
Seattle, Wash.	1,114	2,138	1,724	701	678	—	2,329
Washington, D.C.	1,983	192	712	1,848	2,442	2,329	—

Source: National Geodetic Survey.

Air Distances Between World Cities in Statute Miles

Cities	Berlin	Buenos Aires	Cairo	Calcutta	Cape Town	Caracas	Chicago
Berlin	—	7,402	1,795	4,368	5,981	5,247	4,405
Buenos Aires	7,402	—	7,345	10,265	4,269	3,168	5,598
Cairo	1,795	7,345	—	3,539	4,500	6,338	6,129
Calcutta	4,368	10,265	3,539	—	6,024	9,605	7,980
Cape Town, South Africa	5,981	4,269	4,500	6,024	—	6,365	8,494
Caracas, Venezuela	5,247	3,168	6,338	9,605	6,365	—	2,501
Chicago	4,405	5,598	6,129	7,980	8,494	2,501	—
Hong Kong	5,440	11,472	5,061	1,648	7,375	10,167	7,793
Honolulu, Hawaii	7,309	7,561	8,838	7,047	11,534	6,013	4,250
Istanbul	1,078	7,611	768	3,638	5,154	6,048	5,477
Lisbon	1,436	5,956	2,363	5,638	5,325	4,041	3,990
London	579	6,916	2,181	4,947	6,012	4,660	3,950
Los Angeles	5,724	6,170	7,520	8,090	9,992	3,632	1,745
Manila	6,132	11,051	5,704	2,203	7,486	10,620	8,143
Mexico City	6,047	4,592	7,688	9,492	8,517	2,232	1,691
Montreal	3,729	5,615	5,414	7,607	7,931	2,449	744
Moscow	1,004	8,376	1,803	3,321	6,300	6,173	4,974
New York	3,965	5,297	5,602	7,918	7,764	2,132	713
Paris	545	6,870	1,995	4,883	5,807	4,736	4,134
Rio de Janeiro	6,220	1,200	6,146	9,377	3,773	2,810	5,296
Rome	734	6,929	1,320	4,482	5,249	5,196	4,808
San Francisco	5,661	6,467	7,364	7,814	10,247	3,904	1,858
Shanghai, China	5,218	12,201	5,183	2,117	8,061	9,501	7,061
Stockholm	504	7,808	2,111	4,195	6,444	5,420	4,278
Sydney, Australia	10,006	7,330	8,952	5,685	6,843	9,513	9,272
Tokyo	5,540	11,408	5,935	3,194	9,156	8,799	6,299
Warsaw	320	7,662	1,630	4,048	5,958	5,517	4,667
Washington, D.C.	4,169	5,218	5,800	8,084	7,901	2,059	597

Cities	Hong Kong	Honolulu	Istanbul	Lisbon	London	Los Angeles	Manila
Berlin	5,440	7,309	1,078	1,436	579	5,724	6,132
Buenos Aires	11,472	7,561	7,611	5,956	6,916	6,170	11,051
Cairo	5,061	8,838	768	2,363	2,181	7,520	5,704
Calcutta	1,648	7,047	3,638	5,638	4,947	8,090	2,203
Cape Town, South Africa	7,375	11,534	5,154	5,325	6,012	9,992	7,486
Caracas, Venezuela	10,167	6,013	6,048	4,041	4,660	3,632	10,620
Chicago	7,793	4,250	5,477	3,990	3,950	1,745	8,143
Hong Kong	—	5,549	4,984	6,853	5,982	7,195	693
Honolulu, Hawaii	5,549	—	8,109	7,820	7,228	2,574	5,299
Istanbul	4,984	8,109	—	2,012	1,552	6,783	5,664
Lisbon	6,853	7,820	2,012	—	985	5,621	7,546
London	5,982	7,228	1,552	985	—	5,382	6,672
Los Angeles, Calif.	7,195	2,574	6,783	5,621	5,382	—	7,261
Manila	693	5,299	5,664	7,546	6,672	7,261	—
Mexico City	8,782	3,779	7,110	5,390	5,550	1,589	8,835
Montreal	7,729	4,910	4,789	3,246	3,282	2,427	8,186
Moscow	4,439	7,037	1,091	2,427	1,555	6,003	5,131
New York	8,054	4,964	4,975	3,364	3,458	2,451	8,498
Paris	5,985	7,438	1,400	904	213	5,588	6,677
Rio de Janeiro	11,021	8,285	6,389	4,796	5,766	6,331	11,259
Rome	5,768	8,022	843	1,161	887	6,732	6,457
San Francisco	6,897	2,393	6,703	5,666	5,357	347	6,967
Shanghai, China	764	4,941	4,962	6,654	5,715	6,438	1,150
Stockholm	5,113	6,862	1,348	1,856	890	5,454	5,797
Sydney, Australia	4,584	4,943	9,294	11,302	10,564	7,530	3,944
Tokyo	1,794	3,853	5,560	6,915	5,940	5,433	1,866
Warsaw	5,144	7,355	863	1,715	899	5,922	5,837
Washington, D.C.	8,147	4,519	5,215	3,562	3,663	2,300	8,562

Source: Encyclopaedia Britannica.

Air Distances Between World Cities in Statute Miles

Cities	Mexico City	Montreal	Moscow	New York	Paris	Rio de Janeiro	Rome
Berlin	6,047	3,729	1,004	3,965	545	6,220	734
Buenos Aires	4,592	5,615	8,376	5,297	6,870	1,200	6,929
Cairo	7,688	5,414	1,803	5,602	1,995	6,146	1,320
Calcutta	9,492	7,607	3,321	7,918	4,883	9,377	4,482
Cape Town, South Africa	8,517	7,931	6,300	7,764	5,807	3,773	5,249
Caracas, Venezuela	2,232	2,449	6,173	2,132	4,736	2,810	5,196
Chicago	1,691	744	4,974	713	4,134	5,296	4,808
Hong Kong	8,782	7,729	4,439	8,054	5,985	11,021	5,768
Honolulu	3,779	4,910	7,037	4,964	7,438	8,285	8,022
Istanbul	7,110	4,789	1,091	4,975	1,400	6,389	843
Lisbon	5,390	3,246	2,427	3,364	904	4,796	1,161
London	5,550	3,282	1,555	3,458	213	5,766	887
Los Angeles	1,589	2,427	6,003	2,451	5,588	6,331	6,732
Manila	8,835	8,186	5,131	8,498	6,677	11,259	6,457
Mexico City	—	2,318	6,663	2,094	5,716	4,771	6,366
Montreal	2,318	—	4,386	320	3,422	5,097	4,080
Moscow	6,663	4,386	—	4,665	1,544	7,175	1,474
New York	2,094	320	4,665	—	3,624	4,817	4,281
Paris	5,716	3,422	1,544	3,624	—	5,699	697
Rio de Janeiro	4,771	5,097	7,175	4,817	5,699	—	5,684
Rome	6,366	4,080	1,474	4,281	697	5,684	—
San Francisco	1,887	2,539	5,871	2,571	5,558	6,621	6,240
Shanghai, China	8,022	7,053	4,235	7,371	5,754	11,336	5,677
Stockholm	5,959	3,667	762	3,924	958	6,651	1,234
Sydney, Australia	8,052	9,954	9,012	9,933	10,544	8,306	10,136
Tokyo	7,021	6,383	4,647	6,740	6,034	11,533	6,135
Warsaw	6,365	4,009	715	4,344	849	6,467	817
Washington, D.C.	1,887	488	4,858	205	3,829	4,796	4,434

Cities	San Francisco	Shanghai	Stockholm	Sydney	Tokyo	Warsaw	Washington
Berlin	5,661	5,218	504	10,006	5,540	320	4,169
Buenos Aires	6,467	12,201	7,808	7,330	11,408	7,662	5,218
Cairo	7,364	5,183	2,111	8,952	5,935	1,630	5,800
Calcutta	7,814	2,117	4,195	5,685	3,194	4,048	8,084
Cape Town, South Africa	10,247	8,061	6,444	6,843	9,156	5,958	7,901
Caracas, Venezuela	3,904	9,501	5,420	9,513	8,799	5,517	2,059
Chicago	1,858	7,061	4,278	9,272	6,299	4,667	597
Hong Kong	6,897	764	5,113	4,584	1,794	5,144	8,147
Honolulu	2,393	4,941	6,862	4,943	3,853	7,355	4,519
Istanbul	6,703	4,962	1,348	9,294	5,560	863	5,215
Lisbon	5,666	6,654	1,856	11,302	6,915	1,715	3,562
London	5,357	5,715	890	10,564	5,940	899	3,663
Los Angeles	347	6,438	5,454	7,530	5,433	5,922	2,300
Manila	6,967	1,150	5,797	3,944	1,866	5,837	8,562
Mexico City	1,887	8,022	5,959	8,052	7,021	6,365	1,887
Montreal	2,539	7,053	3,667	9,954	6,383	4,009	488
Moscow	5,871	4,235	762	9,012	4,647	715	4,858
New York	2,571	7,371	3,924	9,933	6,740	4,344	205
Paris	5,558	5,754	958	10,544	6,034	849	3,829
Rio de Janeiro	6,621	11,336	6,651	8,306	11,533	6,467	4,796
Rome	6,240	5,677	1,234	10,136	6,135	817	4,434
San Francisco	—	6,140	5,361	7,416	5,135	5,841	2,442
Shanghai, China	6,140	—	4,825	9,696	1,097	4,951	7,448
Stockholm	5,361	4,825	—		5,051	501	4,123
Sydney, Australia	7,416	4,899	9,696	—	4,866	9,696	9,758
Tokyo	5,135	1,097	5,051	4,866	—	5,249	6,772
Warsaw	5,841	4,951	501	9,696	5,249	—	4,457
Washington, D.C.	2,442	7,448	4,123	9,758	6,772	4,457	—

Source: Encyclopedia Britannica.

CANADA

Area: 3,851,809 sq mi. (9,976,139 sq km)
Population (est. 1978): 23,445,200 (British, 44.6%; French, 28.7%; other
European, 23%; Indian and Eskimo, 1.4%)
Capital: Ottawa, Ont.
Largest cities (1976 census): Montreal, Que., 1,080,546; Toronto, Ont.,
633,318; Winnipeg, Man., 560,874; Calgary, Alta., 469,917; Edmonton, Alta.,
461,361; Vancouver, B.C., 410,188; Hamilton, Ont., 312,003; Ottawa, Ont.,
304,462; London, Ont., 240,392; Windsor, Ont., 196,526; Quebec, Que.,
177,082; Regina, Sask., 149,593
Monetary Unit: Canadian dollar
Languages: English, French
Religions: Roman Catholic, 46.2%; United Church, 17.5%; Anglican, 11.8%;
Presbyterian, 4%; Lutheran, 3.3%; Baptist, 3.1%; others, 14.1%
Gross national product (1976): $1,707 billion

Geography. Covering most of the northern part of the
North American continent and with an area larger than
that of the United States, Canada has an extremely varied
topography. The northeastern region, including most of
Quebec, northern Ontario and Manitoba, and the Northwest Territories, with Hudson Bay in the center, is an important source of minerals, wood pulp, and water power.
In the east the mountainous maritime provinces have an
irregular coast line on the Gulf of St. Lawrence and the
Atlantic. The St. Lawrence plain, covering most of southern Quebec and Ontario, and the interior continental
plain, covering southern Manitoba and Saskatchewan and
most of Alberta, are the principal cultivable areas. They
are separated by a forested plateau rising from lakes Superior and Huron. Westward toward the Pacific, most of
British Columbia, Yukon, and part of western Alberta are
covered by parallel mountain ranges including the Rock-
ies. The Pacific border of the coast range is ragged with
fiords and channels. The highest point in Canada is Mt.
Logan (19,850 ft; 6,050 m), which is in the Yukon.

Canada has an abundance of large and small lakes. In
addition to the Great Lakes on the U.S. border, there are
9 others that are more than 100 miles long and 35 that are
more than 50 miles long.

The two principal river systems are the Mackenzie and
the St. Lawrence. The St. Lawrence, with its tributaries, is
navigable for over 1,900 miles (3,058 km).

Provinces and Territories of Canada

Province, territory, or district	Date of admission or creation	Legislative process
Ontario	July 1, 1867	Act of Imperial Parliament—The
Quebec	July 1, 1867	British North America Act, 1867
Nova Scotia	July 1, 1867	(Br. Stat 1867, c. 3) and Imperial
New Brunswick	July 1, 1867	Order in Council, May 22, 1867
Manitoba	July 15, 1870	Manitoba Act, 1870 (SC 1870, C. 3) and Imperial Order in Council, June 23, 1870
British Columbia	July 20, 1871	Imperial Order in Council, May 16, 1871
Prince Edward Island	July 1, 1873	Imperial Order in Council, June 26, 1873
Saskatchewan	Sept. 1, 1905	Saskatchewan Act, 1905 (SC 1905, C. 42)
Alberta	Sept. 1, 1905	Alberta Act, 1905 (SC 1905, C. 3)
Newfoundland	March 31, 1949	The British North America Act, 1949 (Br. Stat. 1949, c. 22)
Northwest Territories	July 15, 1870	Act of Imperial Parliament—Rupert's Land Act, 1868 (Br. Stat. 1868, c. 105) and Imperial Order in Council, June 23, 1870
Mackenzie	Jan. 1, 1920	
Keewatin	Jan. 1, 1920	Order in Council, March 16, 1918
Franklin	Jan. 1, 1920	
Yukon Territory	June 13, 1898	Yukon Territory Act, 1898 (SC 1898, c. 6)

Population of Canada by Provinces and Territories

Province	1978 (Estimate)	1971 (Census)
Alberta	1,948,000	1,627,874
British Columbia	2,530,100	2,184,621
Manitoba	1,036,000	988,247
New Brunswick	693,200	634,557
Newfoundland	565,200	522,104
Nova Scotia	840,700	788,960
Ontario	8,460,900	7,703,106
Prince Edward Island	122,200	111,641
Quebec	6,290,000	6,027,764
Saskatchewan	945,600	926,242
Northwest Territories	43,700	34,807
Yukon Territory	22,100	18,388
Total	23,497,700	21,568,311
Rural	—	5,157,525
Urban	—	16,410,785

Land and Fresh Water Areas of Canada

Province, territory, or district	Land sq miles	Fresh water sq miles	Total sq miles	Percent of total area
Alberta	248,800	6,485	255,285	6.6
British Columbia	359,279	6,976	366,255	9.5
Manitoba	211,775	39,225	251,000	6.5
New Brunswick	27,835	519	28,354	0.7
Newfoundland	143,045	13,140	156,185	4.1
Nova Scotia	20,402	1,023	21,425	0.6
Ontario	344,092	68,490	412,582	10.7
Prince Edward Island	2,184	—	2,184	0.1
Quebec	523,860	71,000	594,860	15.4
Saskatchewan	220,182	31,518	251,700	6.5
Northwest Territories	1,253,438	51,465	1,304,903	33.9
Franklin	541,753	7,500	549,253	14.3
Keewatin	218,460	9,700	228,160	5.9
Mackenzie	493,225	34,265	527,490	13.7
Yukon Territory	205,346	1,730	207,076	5.4
Totals	**3,560,238**	**291,571**	**3,851,809**	**100.0**

Highest Elevations in Canada

Province or territory	Height in feet
Alberta—Mount Columbia	12,294
British Columbia—Mt. Fairweather	15,300
Manitoba—Baldy Mountain	2,729
New Brunswick—Mount Carleton	2,690
Newfoundland—Cirque Mt., Labrador Penin.	5,160
Nova Scotia—North Barren Mt., Cape Breton Island	1,747
Ontario—Ogidaki Mt.	2,183
Prince Edward Island—highest point Queens County	465
Quebec—Mt. Jacques Cartier, Gaspé Penin.	4,160
Saskatchewan—Cypress Hills	4,546
Northwest Territories—Mt. Sir James MacBrien	9,062
Yukon Territory—Mount Logan	19,850

DISASTERS

Earthquakes and Volcanic Eruptions

A.D. 79 **Aug. 24, Italy:** eruption of Mt. Vesuvius buried cities of Pompeii and Herculaneum, killing thousands.

1556 **Jan. 24, Shensi Province, China:** most deadly earthquake in history; 830,000 killed.

1755 **Nov. 1, Portugal:** one of the most severe of recorded earthquakes leveled Lisbon and was felt as far away as southern France and North Africa; 10,000–20,000 killed in Lisbon.

1883 **Aug. 26–28, Netherlands Indies:** eruption of Krakatoa; violent explosions destroyed two thirds of island. Sea waves occurred as far away as Cape Horn, and possibly England. Estimated 36,000 dead.

1902 **May 8, Martinique, West Indies:** Mt. Pelée erupted and wiped out city of St. Pierre; 40,000 dead.

1906 **April 18, San Francisco:** earthquake accompanied by fire razed more than 4 sq mi.; more than 500 dead or missing; property damage about $250–300 million.

1908 **Dec. 28, Messina, Sicily:** about 85,000 killed and city totally destroyed.

1920 **Dec. 16, Kansu Province, China:** earthquake killed 200,000.

1923 **Sept. 1, Japan:** earthquake destroyed third of Tokyo and most of Yokohama; more than 140,000 killed.

1935 **May 31, India:** earthquake at Quetta killed an estimated 50,000.

1939 **Jan. 24, Chile:** earthquake razed 50,000 sq mi.; about 30,000 killed.

Dec. 27, Northern Turkey: severe quakes destroyed city of Erzingan; about 100,000 casualties.

1949 **Aug. 5, Ecuador:** earthquake killed about 6,000 and razed 50 towns.

1950 **Aug. 15, India:** earthquake affected 30,000 sq mi. in Assam; 20,000–30,000 believed killed.

1960 **May 21–22, 27–29, Chile:** 5,700 dead in earthquakes.

1962 **Sept. 1, Northwest Iran:** more than 10,000 killed in earthquakes.

1963 **July 26, Skoplje, Yugoslavia:** four fifths of city destroyed; 1,011 dead, 3,350 injured.

1964 **March 27, Alaska:** strongest earthquake ever to strike North America hits 80 miles east of Anchorage; followed by seismic wave 50 feet high that traveled 8,445 miles at 450 miles per hour; 131 killed and damage in Alaska and West Coast $500–750 million.

1970 **May 31, Peru:** earthquake left 50,000 dead, 17,000 missing.

1971 **Feb. 9, Los Angeles:** earthquake rocked San Fernando Valley. Death toll 64, damage $1 billion.

1972 **April 10, Iran:** 5,000 killed in earthquake 600 miles south of Teheran.
Dec. 22, Managua, Nicaragua: earthquake devastated city, leaving up to 12,000 dead.

1974 **Dec. 28, Pattan, Pakistan:** earthquake affecting 1,000 sq mi. in northern section killed over 5,000.

1976 **Feb. 4, Guatemala:** earthquake left over 23,000 dead.
June 26, Irian-Jaya, Indonesia: earthquake and landslides killed over 3,000, with another 3,000 missing.
July 28, Tangshan, China: earthquake devastated 20-sq-mi. area of city leaving estimated 655,000 dead.
Aug. 17, Mindanao, Philippines: earthquake and tidal wave left up to 8,000 dead or missing.

1977 **March 4, Bucharest:** earthquake razed most of downtown Bucharest; 1,541 reported dead, over 11,000 injured.

Floods, Avalanches, and Tidal Waves

1228 **Holland:** 100,000 persons reputedly drowned by sea flood in Friesland.

1642 **China:** rebels destroyed Kaifeng seawall; 300,000 drowned.

1887 **China:** hundreds of thousands of lives lost in Honan province in overflow of Hwang Ho River.

1889 **Pennsylvania:** more than 2,000 died in Johnstown flood.

1896 **Japan:** earthquake and tidal wave at Sanriku killed 27,-000.

1913 **Ohio and Indiana:** floods of Ohio and Indiana rivers took 730 lives.

1927 **Mississippi Valley:** floods inundated 20,000 sq mi.; 700,-000 left homeless.

1939 **China:** floods in north; casualties estimated at 10 million homeless, starved, or drowned.

1950 China: floods in eastern and southern China left 1 million homeless and killed 500.

1953 Northwest Europe: storm followed by floods devastated North Sea coastal areas. Netherlands was hardest hit with 1,794 dead.

1955 Northern California and Oregon: rains caused $150 million damage, 74 deaths.

1959 Dec. 2, Frejus, France: flood caused by collapse of Malpasset Dam left 412 dead.

1960 Agadir, Morocco: 10,000–12,000 dead as earthquake set off tidal wave and fire, destroying most of city.

1962 Jan. 10, Peru: avalanche down Huascaran, extinct Andean volcano, killed more than 3,000 persons.

1963 Oct. 9, Italy: landslide collapsed Valont Dam; flood killed about 2,000.

1966 Oct. 21, Aberfan, Wales: avalanche of coal, waste, mud, and rocks killed 144 persons, including 116 children in school.

1969 Jan. 18–26, Southern California: floods and mudslides from heavy rains caused widespread property damage; at least 100 dead. Another downpour (Feb. 23–26) caused further floods and mudslides; at least 18 dead.

1970 Nov. 13, East Pakistan: 200,000 killed by cyclone-driven tidal wave from Bay of Bengal. Over 100,000 missing.

1971 Sept. 29, Orissa State, India: cyclone and tidal wave off Bay of Bengal killed as many as 10,000.

1972 Feb. 26, Man, W. Va.: more than 118 died when slag-pile dam collapsed under pressure of torrential rains and flooded 17-mile valley.

June 9–10, Rapid City, S.D.: flash flood caused 237 deaths and $160 million in damage.

June 20, Eastern Seaboard: tropical storm Agnes, in 10-day rampage, caused widespread flash floods. Death toll was 129, 115,000 were left homeless, and damage estimated at $3.5 billion.

1976 Aug. 1, Loveland, Colo.: Flash flood along Route 34 in Big Thompson Canyon left 139 dead.

1977 Nov. 6, Toccoa, Ga.: rupture of Kelly Barnes Dam left 39 dead.

Nov. 19, Andhra Pradesh State, India: cyclone and flood from Bay of Bengal left 7,000–10,000 dead.

Storms and Weather

1864 **Oct. 5, India:** most of Calcutta denuded by cyclone; 70,-000 killed.

1876 **Oct. 31, India:** cyclone and tidal wave swept 3,000 sq mi.; 215,000 killed.

1882 **June 6, India:** cyclone and tidal wave killed 100,000 in Bombay.

1884 **Feb. 19, U.S.:** Tornadoes killed 800 from Mississippi through Indiana.

1900 **Aug. 27-Sept. 15, U.S.:** Hurricane winds of 120 mph and storm waves inundated Galveston, Texas; 6,000 deaths resulted.

1906 **China:** typhoon at Hong Kong killed about 10,000.

1925 **March 18, U.S.:** Tornadoes killed 792; Missouri and Illinois hardest hit.

1928 **Sept. 6-20, U.S.:** Hurricane in southern Florida caused Lake Okeechobee to overflow; 1,836 killed.

1930 **Sept. 3. Santo Domingo:** hurricane killed about 2,000 and injured 6,000.

1934 **Sept. 21, Japan:** hurricane killed more than 4,000 on Honshu.

1936 **April 5-6, U.S.:** 498 killed in tornadoes that hit southern states.

1938 **Sept. 10-22, U.S.:** Unusually destructive hurricane killed 600 in Long Island and southern New England.

1942 **Oct. 16, India:** cyclone devastated Bengal; about 40,000 lives lost.

1963 **May 28–29, East Pakistan:** cyclone killed about 22,000 along coast.

Oct. 2–7, Caribbean: Hurricane Flora killed up to 7,000 in Haiti and Cuba.

1965 **April 11-12, U.S.:** 47 tornadoes in Midwest killed 257; $200 million in property damages.

May 11–12 and June 1–2, East Pakistan: cyclones killed about 47,000.

Dec. 15, Karachi, Pakistan: cyclone killed about 10,000.

1969 **Aug. 14-22, U.S.:** Hurricane Camille killed 256 from Mississippi through West Virginia; one of the most destructive killer storms ever to hit U.S.

1970 **July 23-Aug. 5, U.S.:** Hurricane Celia hit Texas coast with winds of 161 mph; costliest storm in Texas history with $453.8 million in damages.

1972 **June 14-23, U.S.:** Hurricane Agnes killed 117 from Florida to New York; over 3 billion in damages.

1974 **April 3-4, U.S.:** 144 tornadoes swept through 13 states in East, South, and Midwest; resulted in 307 deaths and over $500 million in damages.

Sept. 20, Honduras: Hurricane Fifi strikes northern section of country, leaving 8,000 dead, 100,000 homeless.

Dec. 25, Darwin, Australia: cyclone destroys nearly the entire city, causing mass evacuation.

Fires and Explosions

1666 **Sept. 2, England:** "Great Fire of London" destroyed St. Paul's Church, etc. Damage 10 million.

1812 **Sept. 14, Russia:** fire started by Russians in Moscow after French occupation destroyed 30,800 houses.

1835 **Dec. 16, New York City:** 530 buildings destroyed by fire.

1871 **Oct. 8, Chicago:** the "Chicago Fire" burned 17,450 buildings, killed 250 persons; $196 million damage.

Oct. 8, Peshtigo, Wis.: over 1,200 lives lost; 2 billion trees burned.

1872 **Nov. 9, Boston:** fire destroyed 800 buildings; $75-million damage.

1876 **Dec. 5, New York City:** fire in Brooklyn Theater killed more than 300.

1881 **Dec. 8, Vienna:** at least 620 died in fire at Ring Theatre.

1900 **May 1, Scofield, Utah:** explosion of blasting powder in coal mine killed 1,200.

1903 **Dec. 30, Chicago:** Iroquois Theatre fire killed 602.

1904 **Feb. 7, Baltimore:** business section burned; estimated $125-million damage.

1906 **March 10, France:** explosion in coal mine in Courrières killed 1,060.

1909 **Nov. 13, Cherry, Ill.:** explosion in coal mine killed 259.

1911 **March 25, New York City:** fire in Triangle Shirtwaist Factory fatal to 145.

1913 **Oct. 22, Dawson, N.M.:** coal mine explosion left 263 dead.

1917 **Dec. 6, Canada:** explosion and fire at Halifax when ammunition ship collided with a vessel; 1,500 dead.

1930 **April 21, Columbus, Ohio:** fire in Ohio State Penitentiary killed 322 convicts.

1937 **March 18, New London, Tex.:** explosion destroyed schoolhouse; 294 killed.

1942 **April 26, Manchuria:** explosion in Honkeiko Colliery killed 1,549.

Nov. 28, Boston: Cocoanut Grove nightclub fire killed 498.

1944 **July 6, Hartford, Conn.:** fire and ensuing stampede in main tent of Ringling Brothers Circus killed 168, injured 487.

July 17, Port Chicago, Calif.: 300 killed as ammunition ships explode.

1946 **Dec. 7, Atlanta:** fire in Winecoff Hotel killed 119.

1947 **April 16–18, Texas City, Tex.:** most of city destroyed, 516 dead following explosion on ship.

1949 **Sept. 2, China:** fire on Chungking waterfront killed 1,-700.

1953 **Oct. 16, Boston:** explosion and fire aboard U.S.S. *Leyte* killed 37.

1954 **May 26, off Quonset Point, R.I.:** explosion and fire aboard aircraft *Bennington* killed 103 crewmen.

1955 **June 11, France:** crash and explosion of racing car into crowd during Grand Prix race, Le Mans, killed 82.

1956 **Aug. 7, Colombia:** about 1,100 reported killed when seven army ammunition trucks exploded at Cali.

Aug. 8, Belgium: 262 died in coal mine fire at Marcinelle.

1958 **Dec. 1, Chicago:** fire at Our Lady of the Angels school killed 96.

1960 **Jan. 21, Coalbrook, South Africa:** coal mine explosion killed 437.

Nov. 13, Syria: 152 children killed in movie-house fire.

Dec. 19. Brooklyn, N.Y.: blaze on aircraft carrier *Constellation* killed 49 workmen.

1961 **Dec. 17, Niteroi, Brazil:** circus fire fatal to 323.

1962 **Feb. 7, Saarland, West Germany:** coal mine gas explosion killed 298.

1963 **Nov. 9, Japan:** explosion in coal mine at Omuta killed 447.

1965 **May 28, India:** coal mine fire in state of Bihar killed 375.

June 1, near Fukuoka, Japan: coal mine explosion killed 236.

1966 **Oct. 17, New York City:** 12 firemen were killed in sudden collapse of burning building.

Oct. 26, off South Vietnam: fire on U.S. carrier *Oriskany* killed 43.

1967 **May 22, Brussels:** fire in L'Innovation, major department store, left 322 dead.

1969 **Jan. 14, Pearl Harbor, Hawaii:** nuclear aircraft carrier *Enterprise* ripped by explosions; 27 dead, 82 injured.
April 6, New Orleans: Taiwanese freighter and string of oil-loaded barges collided in fiery explosion on Mississippi River; 25 dead.

1970 **Nov. 1, Saint-Laurent-du-Pont, France:** fire in dance hall killed 146 young people.
Dec. 30, Wooten, Ky.: coal-dust explosion in coal mine killed 38.

1972 **May 2, Kellogg, Idaho:** fire in Sunshine silver mine killed 91 miners; two men survived.
May 13, Osaka, Japan: 118 people died in fire in nightclub on top floor of Sennichi department store.
June 6, Wankie, Rhodesia: explosion in coal mine killed 427.

1973 **Nov. 29, Kumamoto, Japan:** fire in Taiyo department store killed 101.

1974 **Feb. 1, Sao Paulo, Brazil:** fire in upper stories of bank building killed 189 persons, many of whom leaped to death.

1975 **Dec. 27, Dhanbad, India:** explosion in coal mine followed by flooding from nearby reservoir left 372 dead.

1977 **Feb. 25, Moscow:** fire in 6,000-bed Hotel Rossiya fatal to at least 45 guests.
May 28, Southgate, Ky.: fire in Beverly Hills Supper Club; 167 dead.
June 26, Columbia, Tenn.: fire believed set by inmate is fatal to 42 prisoners and visitors at Maury County Jail.
Dec. 22, Westwego, La.: explosion destroyed Continental Grain Company plant, killing 35.

Shipwrecks

1833 **May 11, *Lady of the Lake:*** bound from England to Quebec, struck iceberg; 215 perished.

1853 **Sept. 29 *Annie Jane:*** emigrant vessel off coast of Scotland; 348 died.

1865 **April 27, *Sultana:*** boiler explosion on Mississippi River steamboat near Memphis, 1,450 killed.

1904 **June 15, *General Slocum:*** excursion steamer burned in New York Harbor; 1,021 perished.

1912 **March 5, *Principe de Asturias:*** Spanish steamer struck rock off Sebastien Point; 500 drowned.
April 15, *Titanic:* sank after colliding with iceberg; 1,513 died.

1914 May 29, *Empress of Ireland:* sank after collision in St. Lawrence River; 1,024 perished.

1915 July 24, *Eastland:* Great Lakes excursion steamer overturned in Chicago River; 812 died.

1928 Nov. 12, *Vestris:* British steamer sank in gale off Virginia; 110 died.

1931 June 14: French excursion steamer overturned in gale off St. Nazaire; approximately 450 died.

1934 Sept. 8, *Morro Castle:* about 130 killed in fire off Asbury Park, N.J.

1939 May 23, *Squalus:* submarine with 59 men sank off Hampton Beach, N.H.; 33 saved.
June 1, Submarine *Thetis:* sank in Liverpool Bay, England; 99 perished.

1942 Oct. 2, *Queen Mary:* rammed and sank a British cruiser; 338 aboard the cruiser died.

1945 April 9: U.S. ship, loaded with aerial bombs, exploded at Bari, Italy; at least 360 killed.

1948 Dec. 3, *Kiangya:* Chinese refugee ship wrecked in explosion; about 1,000 believed dead.

1949 Sept. 17, *Noronic:* Canadian Great Lakes cruise ship burned at Toronto dock; about 130 died.

1951 April 16, *Affray:* British submarine sank in English Channel; 75 dead.

1952 April 26, *Hobson:* minesweeper collided with aircraft carrier *Wasp* and sank during night maneuvers in mid-Atlantic; 176 persons lost.

1953 Jan. 9, *Chang Tyong-Ho:* South Korean ferry foundered off Pusan; 249 reported dead.
Jan. 31, *Princess Victoria:* British ferry sank in Irish Sea; 133 lost.

1956 July 25, *Andrea Doria:* Italian liner collided with Swedish liner *Stockholm* off Nantucket Island, Mass., sinking next day; 52, mostly passengers on Italian ship, dead or unaccounted for; over 1,600 rescued.

1962 April 8, *Dara,* British liner, exploded and sank in Persian Gulf; 236 persons dead. Caused by time bomb.

1963 April 10, *Thresher:* atomic-powered submarine sank in North Atlantic; 129 dead.
May 4: U.A.R. ferry capsized and sank in upper Nile; over 200 died.

1964 Nov. 26, *Shalom:* Israeli liner collided with Norwegian tanker *Stolt Dagali* off New Jersey coast; 19 of tanker's crew dead.

1965 Nov. 13, *Yarmouth Castle:* cruise ship burned and sank 60 miles northeast of Nassau en route from Miami to Bahamas; 90 dead.

1968 Late May, *Scorpion:* nuclear submarine sank in Atlantic 400 miles S.W. of Azores; 99 dead. (Located Oct. 31.)

1970 Aug. 1: ferry between Basseterre, St. Kitts, and Charlestown, Nevis, capsized in Caribbean; 125 believed lost.

Dec. 15: ferry in Korean Strait capsized; 261 lost.

1976 Oct. 20, Luling, La.: *George Prince,* Mississippi River ferry, rammed by Norwegian tanker *Frosta;* 77 dead.

Aircraft Accidents

1921 Aug. 24, England: *ZR-2* British dirigible, broke in two on trial trip near Hull; 62 died.

1925 Sept. 3, Caldwell, Ohio: U.S. dirigible *Shenandoah* broke apart; 14 dead.

1933 April 4, New Jersey Coast: U.S. dirigible *Akron* crashed; 73 died.

1937 May 6, Lakehurst, N.J.: German zeppelin *Hindenburg* destroyed by fire at tower mooring; 36 killed.

1945 July 28, New York City: U.S. Army bomber crashed into Empire State Building; 13 dead.

1946 May 20, New York City: U.S. Army plane crashed into Manhattan Company building; five dead.

1949 Nov. 1, Washington, D.C.: fighter plane rammed airliner, killing 55.

1951 Dec. 16, Elizabeth, N.J.: nonscheduled airliner crash killed 56.

1952 Jan. 22, Elizabeth, N.J.: 29 killed, including former Secretary of War Robert P. Patterson, when airliner hit apartments; seven of dead were on ground.

Feb. 11, Elizabeth, N.J.: third major air disaster in Elizabeth within two months fatally injured 33.

1953 June 18, near Tokyo: crash of U.S. Air Force "Globemaster" killed 129 servicemen.

1955 Nov. 1, near Longmont, Colo.: time bomb hidden in luggage destroyed airliner in flight, killing 44.

1956 June 30, Grand Canyon, Ariz.: 128 died in collision of TWA Super Constellation and United Airlines DC-7.

1957 March 17, near Cebu City, Philippines: President Ramón Magsaysay and 24 others killed in crash.

1959 Feb. 3, New York City: American Airlines Lockheed Electra turboprop plane crashed in East River; 65 dead.

1960 **Feb. 25, Rio de Janeiro:** U.S. Navy plane, flying Navy musicians to perform at dinner given by visiting President Eisenhower, collided with Brazilian airliner, killing 61.

Sept. 19, near Guam: crash shortly after take-off of World Airways plane took 78 lives.

Oct. 4, Boston Harbor: Eastern Airlines plane sank; 61 dead.

Dec. 16, New York City: United and Trans World planes collided in fog, crashed in two boroughs, killing 134 in air and on ground.

1961 **Feb. 15, near Brussels:** 72 on board and farmer on ground killed in crash of Sabena plane; U.S. figure skating team wiped out.

1962 **March 1, New York City:** American Airlines jetliner crashed into Jamaica Bay, near Idlewild Airport, killing all 95 on board.

June 3, Paris: chartered Air France Boeing Jet 707 crashed at Orly Airport; 130 dead.

June 22, Grande-Teree Island, Guadeloupe: Air France Boeing 707 crashed, killing all 113 aboard.

1965 **Feb. 8, New York City:** Eastern Airlines DC-7B went down in Atlantic shortly after take-off from Kennedy International Airport; 84 dead.

1966 **Jan. 24, Mont Blanc:** Indian airliner crashed into mountain in fog; 117 dead.

March 5, Japan: British airliner caught fire and crashed into Mt. Fuji; 124 dead.

Dec. 24, Binh Thai, South Vietnam: crash of military-chartered plane into village killed 129.

1967 **April 20, Nicosia, Cyprus:** crash of chartered Swiss Turbo-prop killed 126.

July 19, near Hendersonville, N.C.: Piedmont Airlines Boeing 727 collided with private plane; 82 dead.

1968 **May 3, near Dawson, Tex.:** Braniff airliner crashed; 85 dead.

1969 **March 16, Maracaibo, Venezuela:** Venezuelan jetliner crashed and exploded; 84 crew members and passengers died and 71 were killed on ground.

Sept. 9, Shelbyville, Ind.: Allegheny Airlines jetliner and single-engine plane flown by student pilot collided in air and crashed; 83 dead.

Dec. 8, Keratea, Greece: rain and hurricane winds caused Greek airliner to crash into 2,000-foot mountain while approaching Athens; 90 dead.

1970 **Feb. 15, Santo Domingo, Dominican Republic:** Dominican Republic jetliner plunged into Caribbean on takeoff; 102 dead.

July 4, Arbucias, Spain: British Comet crashed into mountains while coming in for landing at Barcelona; 112 dead.

July 5, Toronto: Canadian jetliner crashed on landing approach; 109 dead.

Aug. 9, Cuzco, Peru: Peruvian turboprop, with 51 teenage U.S. students among passengers, crashed shortly after takeoff; 99 dead.

Nov. 13, Huntington, W. Va.: chartered plane carrying 43 players and coaches of Marshall University football team crashed; 75 dead.

1971 **June 6, near Los Angeles:** Air West DC-9 and Navy F-4 fighter collided over San Gabriel Canyon; 49 killed; one Navy crewman parachuted to safety.

July 30, Morioka, Japan: Japanese Boeing 727 and F-86 fighter collided in mid-air; toll was 162.

Sept. 4, near Juneau, Alaska: Alaska Airlines Boeing 727 crashed into Chilkoot Mountains; 109 killed.

1972 **May 5, Palermo, Sicily:** Alitalia DC-8 hit mountain, killing 115.

June 18, London: B.E.A. Trident jetliner plunged into field minutes after take-off from Heathrow Airport; all 118 aboard dead.

Aug. 14, East Berlin, East Germany: Soviet-built East German Ilyushin plane crashed, killing 156.

Oct. 13, Moscow: 176 died when Soviet Ilyushin airliner crashed.

Dec. 3, Santa Cruz de Tenerife, Canary Islands: Spanish charter jet carrying West German tourists crashed on take-off; all 155 aboard killed.

Dec. 30, Miami, Fla.: Eastern Airlines Lockheed 1011 TriStar Jumbo jet crashed into Everglades; 101 killed, 75 survived.

1973 **Jan. 22, Kano, Nigeria:** 171 Nigerian Moslems returning from Mecca and five crewmen died in crash.

April 10, Hochwald, Switzerland: British airliner carrying tourists to Swiss fair crashed in blizzard; 106 dead.

July 11, Paris: Boeing 707 of Varig Airlines, en route to Rio de Janeiro, crashed near airport, killing 122 of 134 passengers.

July 31, Boston: Delta Airlines jet crashed in heavy fog in landing at Logan International Airport killing 88 of 89 aboard.

1974 **Jan. 31, Pago Pago, Samoa:** Pan American 707 crashed while landing; 97 of 101 persons aboard killed.

March 3, Paris: Turkish DC-10 jumbo jet crashed in forest shortly after take-off; all 346 passengers and crew killed in worst single-plane disaster to date.

Dec. 1, Upperville, Va.: all 92 aboard killed in crash of TWA 727 into wooded area.

Dec. 4, Colombo, Sri Lanka: Dutch DC-8 carrying Moslems to Mecca crashed on landing approach, killing all 191 persons aboard.

1975 **April 4, near Saigon, Vietnam:** Air Force Galaxy C-58 crashed after take-off, killing 172, mostly Vietnamese children.

June 24, New York City: Eastern Airlines Boeing 727, arriving from New Orleans, crashed at Kennedy International Airport, killing 113 in highest single-aircraft toll in U.S. to date.

Aug. 3, Agadir, Morocco: Chartered Boeing 707, returning Moroccan workers home after vacation in France, plunged into mountainside; all 188 aboard killed.

Aug. 20, Damascus, Syria: Czech airliner crashed while landing, killing 126 of 128 persons aboard.

1976 **Sept. 10, Zagreb, Yugoslavia:** midair collision between British Airways Trident and Yugoslav charter DC-9 fatal to all 176 persons aboard; worst mid-air collision on record.

1977 **March 27, Santa Cruz de Tenerife, Canary Islands:** Pan American and KLM Boeing 747s collided on runway. All 249 on KLM plane and 333 of 394 aboard Pan Am jet killed. Total of 582 is highest for any type of aviation disaster.

1978 **Jan. 1, Bombay:** Air India 747 with 213 aboard explodes and plunges into sea minutes after takeoff.

Sept. 25, San Diego: All 135 on Pacific Southwest jet liner approaching San Diego dead in mid-air collision with private plane. Two in small plane and people on ground also killed, bringing toll to 144.

Railroad Accidents

1864 June 29, near Beloeil, Canada: about 90 killed when train ran through open switch.

1879 Dec. 28, Dundee, Scotland: train blown off Tay bridge; 73 drowned.

1881 June 24, near Cuartla, Mexico: about 200 died when train fell into river.

1882 July 13, near Tcherny, Russia: more than 150 killed in derailment.

1891 June 14, near Basel, Switzerland: about 100 killed in collision.

1915 May 22, Gretna, Scotland: two passenger trains and troop train collided; 227 killed.

1917 Dec. 12, Modane, France: nearly 550 killed in derailment of troop train near mouth of Mt. Cenis tunnel.

1939 Dec. 22, near Magdeburg, Germany: more than 125 killed in collision; 99 killed in another wreck near Friedrichshafen.

1943 Dec. 16, near Rennert, N.C.: 72 killed in derailment and collision of two Atlantic Coast Line trains.

1944 March 2, near Salerno, Italy: 521 suffocated when Italian train stalled in tunnel.

Dec. 31, near Ogden, Utah: 48 killed in collision of two sections of Southern Pacific's Pacific Limited.

1946 April 25, Naperville, Ill.: at least 47 killed in collision of two trains of Burlington Railroad.

1949 Oct. 22, near Nowy Dwor, Poland: more than 200 reported killed in derailment of Danzig-Warsaw express.

1950 Feb. 17, Rockville Centre, N.Y.: head-on crash of two Long Island R.R. commuter trains killed 30.

Nov. 22, Richmond Hill, N.Y.: 79 died when one Long Island Rail Road commuter train crashed into rear of another.

1951 Feb. 6, Woodbridge, N.J.: 85 died when Pennsylvania Railroad commuter train plunged through temporary overpass.

1952 Oct. 8, Harrow-Wealdstone, England: two express trains crashed into commuter train; 112 dead.

1953 Dec. 24, near Sakvice, Czechoslovakia: two trains crashed; over 100 dead.

1956 Sept. 2, near Mahbubnagar, India: at least 120 killed when bridge collapsed under train.

1957 Sept. 1, near Kendal, Jamaica: about 175 killed when train plunged into ravine.

Sept. 29, near Montgomery, West Pakistan: express train crashed into standing oil train; nearly 300 killed.

Dec. 4, St. John's, England: 92 killed, 187 injured as one commuter train crashed into another in fog.

1958 Sept. 15, near Bayonne, N.J.: over 40 killed when Central Railroad of New Jersey train went through open drawbridge.

1960 Nov. 14, Pardubice, Czechoslovakia: two trains collided; 110 dead, 106 injured.

1962 May 3, near Tokyo: 163 killed and 400 injured when train crashed into wreckage of collision between inbound freight train and outbound commuter train.

1963 Nov. 9, near Yokohama, Japan: two passenger trains crashed into derailed freight, killing 162.

1964 July 26, Custoias, Portugal: passenger train derailed; 94 dead.

1970 Feb. 4, near Buenos Aires: 236 killed when express train crashed into standing commuter train.

1972 July 21, Seville, Spain: head-on crash of two passenger trains killed 76.

Oct. 6, near Saltillo, Mexico: train carrying religious pilgrims derailed and caught fire, killing 204 and injuring over 1,000.

Oct. 30, Chicago: two Illinois Central commuter trains collided during morning rush hour; 45 dead and over 200 injured.

1974 Aug. 30, Zagreb, Yugoslavia: train entering station derailed, killing 153 and injuring over 60.

1977 Feb. 4, Chicago: 11 killed and over 180 injured when elevated train hit rear of another, sending two cars to street.

ECONOMIC FACTS

How Many People Work At . . . Employment by Major Occupations, 1977
(in thousands)

Occupations	Total employed	Percent distribution Female	Percent distribution Black and other
White-collar workers	45,187	51.3	7.7
Professional and technical	13,692	42.6	8.4
Accountants	868	27.5	6.8
Architects	58	3.4	5.2
Computer programmers	221	26.2	6.3
Computer systems analysts	129	20.2	5.4
Engineers	1,267	2.7	5.5
Aeronautical and astronautical engineers	54	1.9	3.7
Civil engineers	171	1.2	7.6
Electrical and electronic engineers	324	2.8	5.9
Industrial engineers	214	7.0	4.2
Mechanical engineers	215	.9	5.6
Lawyers and judges	462	9.5	3.2
Librarian, archivists, and curators	208	79.8	9.1
Life and physical scientists	275	15.6	8.7
Biological scientists	55	36.4	12.7
Chemists	124	13.7	10.5
Operations and systems researchers and analysts	122	20.5	4.1
Personnel and labor relations workers	370	43.5	11.9
Dentists	105	2.9	5.7
Pharmacists	138	17.4	4.3
Physicians, medical and osteopathic	403	11.2	9.2
Registered nurses	1,063	96.7	11.3
Therapists	178	68.5	9.6

Occupations	Total employed	Percent distribution Female	Percent distribution Black and other
Health technologists and technicians	462	71.4	12.1
Religious workers	347	13.0	8.6
Economists	106	17.9	4.7
Psychologists	92	41.3	2.2
Social workers	325	61.2	19.1
Recreation workers	119	59.7	19.3
Teachers, college and university	562	31.7	7.5
Teachers, except college and university	3,024	70.9	9.8
Engineering and science technicians	892	14.9	7.0
Airplane pilots	64	—	1.6
Vocational and educational counselors	175	49.1	14.3
Writers, artists, and entertainers	1,141	35.5	5.4
Athletes and kindred workers	105	41.9	6.7
Designers	146	24.0	2.7
Editors and reporters	185	44.9	4.9
Musicians and composers	154	31.2	9.7
Painters and sculptors	177	44.6	4.5
Photographers	81	13.6	3.7
Public relations specialists and publicity writers	120	38.3	5.0
Managers and administrators, except farm	9,662	22.3	4.8
Bank officials and financial managers	543	27.3	4.4
Buyers and purchasing agents	372	28.0	3.8
Buyers, wholesale and retail trade	162	37.0	4.3
Credit and collection managers	54	33.3	1.9
Health administrators	175	45.1	5.1
Officials and administrators, public administration n.e.c.	401	24.9	8.5
Officials of lodges, societies, and unions	118	24.6	5.9
Restaurant, cafeteria, and bar managers	548	34.7	8.9
Sales managers and department heads, retail trade	345	36.2	5.2
Sales managers, except retail trade	321	3.7	7.9
School administrators, college	126	29.4	2.5
School administrators, elementary and secondary	265	36.2	7.9
Sales workers	5,728	43.3	4.5
Insurance agents, brokers, and underwriters	500	16.6	5.4

Occupations	Total employed	Percent distribution Female	Percent distribution Black and other
Real estate agents and brokers	502	43.8	2.0
Stock and bond sales agents	98	13.3	2.0
Sales representatives, manufacturing industries	336	13.1	3.6
Sales representatives, wholesale trade	850	7.6	2.6
Sales clerks, retail trade	2,316	70.4	5.8
Sales workers, except clerks, retail trade	486	14.6	2.9
Sales workers, services and construction	154	35.1	4.5
Clerical workers	16,106	78.9	9.8
Bank tellers	408	90.0	7.6
Billing clerks	156	87.8	5.8
Bookkeepers	1,726	90.0	4.4
Cashiers	1,326	87.0	8.8
File clerks	274	84.7	20.4
Insurance adjusters, examiners, and investigators	168	50.6	10.1
Library attendants and assistants	142	80.3	16.2
Mail carriers, post office	242	9.5	10.3
Office machine operators	759	73.8	14.9
Computer and peripheral equipment operators	302	54.6	11.6
Key punch operators	280	93.2	17.9
Postal clerks	267	31.8	26.2
Receptionists	531	96.8	8.1
Secretaries	3,421	99.1	5.4
Statistical clerks	357	75.6	11.2
Stenographers	83	91.6	12.0
Stock clerks and storekeepers	497	30.8	12.3
Teachers aides, except school monitors	320	93.4	16.9
Telephone operators	342	95.3	14.0
Typists	1,006	96.3	14.5
Blue-collar workers	30,211	17.7	12.2
Craft and kindred workers	11,881	5.0	7.4
Carpenters	1,171	.9	4.4
Brickmasons and stonemasons	177	—	18.1
Electricians	588	.2	4.8
Excavating, grading, and road machinery operators	406	.2	9.6
Painters, construction and maintenance	461	3.3	10.2
Plumbers and pipefitters	429	.5	8.2
Blue-collar worker supervisors, n.e.c.	1,554	9.0	7.4

Occupations	Total employed	Percent distribution Female	Black and other
Machinists and job setters	576	2.6	8.0
Metal craft workers, excluding mechanics, machinists, and job setters	653	3.1	6.7
Mechanics, automobiles	1,161	.9	8.0
Mechanics, except automobiles	2,019	1.6	6.1
Printing craft workers	389	22.4	8.0
Telephone installers and repairers	279	5.0	6.5
Operatives, except transport	10,354	39.6	14.3
Assemblers	1,136	50.3	15.7
Garage workers and gas station attendants	427	5.2	8.9
Packers and wrappers, excluding meat and produce	610	63.6	17.4
Precision machine operatives	372	10.2	8.3
Sewers and stitchers	820	95.2	18.8
Transport equipment operatives	3,476	6.8	14.6
Truck drivers	1,898	1.3	14.3
Nonfarm laborers	4,500	9.4	18.1
Service workers	12,392	62.0	19.8
Private households	1,158	97.0	35.8
Service workers, except private households	11,234	58.3	18.1
Cleaning workers	2,363	34.9	28.9
Bartenders	272	41.9	6.6
Cooks	1,106	56.3	20.6
Waiters	1,310	90.4	7.6
Health service workers	1,747	89.2	22.7
Dental assistants	123	98.4	5.7
Health aides and trainees, excluding nursing	245	84.5	18.0
Nursing aides, orderlies, and attendants	1,008	86.3	26.5
Practical nurses	371	96.8	21.6
Personal service workers	1,705	74.0	13.6
Fire fighters	225	.4	7.1
Guards	490	10.2	18.0
Police	498	3.8	9.2
Farm workers	2,756	17.2	7.7
Farm laborers, wage workers	936	17.0	17.2
Total employed	90,546	40.5	10.8

NOTE: n.e.c. — "not elsewhere classified" and designates broad categories of occupations that cannot be more specifically identified. *Source:* Department of Labor, Bureau of Labor Statistics.

Employment and Unemployment
(in millions of persons)

Category[1]	1978[2]	1970	1950	1941	1932
EMPLOYMENT STATUS[1]					
Total noninstitutional population	161.1	140.2	106.6	101.5	—
Total labor force	102.7	85.9	63.9	57.5	51.3
Percent of population	63.8	61.3	59.9	56.7	—
Civilian labor force	100.6	82.7	62.2	55.9	51.0
Employed	94.4	78.6	58.9	50.4	38.9
Agriculture	3.4	3.5	7.2	9.1	10.2
Nonagricultural industries	91.0	75.2	51.8	41.3	28.8
Unemployed	6.2	4.1	3.3	5.6	12.1
Percent of labor labor	6.2	4.9	5.3	9.9	23.6
Not in labor force	58.4	54.3	42.8	44.0	—
INDUSTRY					
Total nonagricultural employment	86.0	70.9	45.2	36.6	23.6
Goods-producing industries	25.6	23.5	18.5	15.9	8.6
Mining	0.9	0.6	0.9	1.0	0.7
Contract construction	4.4	3.5	2.3	1.8	1.0
Manufacturing: Durable goods	12.1	11.2	8.1	7.0	—
Nondurable goods	8.2	8.2	7.1	6.2	—
Services-producing industries	60.4	47.7	26.7	20.6	15.0
Transportation and public utilities	4.7	4.5	4.0	3.3	2.8
Trade: Wholesale	4.6	3.8	2.5	1.9	—
Retail	14.5	11.2	6.9	5.4	—
Finance, insurance, real estate	4.8	3.7	1.9	1.5	1.3
Services	16.1	11.6	5.4	3.9	2.9
Federal government	2.8	2.7	1.9	1.3	0.6
State and local government	12.9	9.8	4.1	3.3	2.7

1. For 1932–41, figures on labor force status relate to persons 14 years and over; beginning 1950, 16 years and over. 2. July, seasonally adjusted (preliminary). NOTE: Figures may not add to totals due to rounding. *Source:* Department of Labor, Bureau of Labor Statistics.

Median Family Income

Year	Median family income	Annual percent gain or loss	Year	Median family income	Annual percent gain or loss
1970	$14,465	—	1974	$14,891	3.5
1971	14,457	−0.1	1975	14,510	−2.6
1972	15,126	4.7	1976	14,958	3.1
1973	15,437	2.1	1977	16,010	7.0

Source: Department of Commerce, Bureau of the Census.

Federal Individual Income Tax Returns, 1975

(in millions of dollars, except percent)

Source of income	Adjusted gross income classes							Total income[3]
	Under $5,000	$5,000-$9,999	$10,000-$14,999	$15,000-$49,999	$50,000-$499,999	$500,000 and over	Total[2]	
Adjusted gross income	$27,425	$130,817	$182,732	$474,858	$79,260	$4,630	$899,723	$953,764
Salaries, gross	23,562	111,735	164,574	409,964	40,807	684	751,327	793,884
Percent of gross income	85.9	85.4	90.1	86.3	51.5	14.8	83.5	83.2
Dividends[4]	414	1,400	1,583	7,604	8,248	1,488	20,736	21,782
Interest	2,006	7,143	6,411	17,497	5,311	313	38,682	42,905
Rents and royalties, net	164	747	487	1,846	1,806	182	5,234	5,595
Business or profession, net[5]	463	3,400	4,361	20,287	9,368	268	38,145	41,025
Farm,[5] net	-13	103	421	3,483	1,129	-13	5,111	5,628
Partnership, net	-186	561	912	5,468	5,798	152	12,705	12,971
Sales of capital assets, net	304	847	1,153	4,463	4,271	1,215	12,263	13,062
Sales of property other than capital assets, net	10	26	29	225	98	26	415	386
Pensions and annuities, taxable portion	946	5,887	4,184	7,035	591	7	18,649	20,812
Other sources[6]	248	1,028	1,383	3,014	-1,833	-310	3,534	8,589

1. Includes a small number of taxable returns with no adjusted gross income. 2. Income from sources subject to tax, less certain exclusions. 3. Excludes returns with no adjusted gross income. 4. Dividends in adjusted gross income. 5. Business profit and loss without deduction for net operating loss. 6. Comprises income or loss from alimony, state income tax refunds, small business corporations, estate or trust, and other income sources, less statutory adjustments. *Source:* Department of the Treasury, Internal Revenue Service, preliminary report, *Statistics of Income, 1975, Individual Income Tax Returns.*

IRS Informers

In the year ending Sept. 30, 1977, the Internal Revenue Service paid out $360,304 to 483 informers (an average of $745.97 per informant) for tips on which were based $14.9 million worth of tax assessments.

Taxes, Taxes, Taxes

The Internal Revenue Service mailed out about 45.5 million 1040 forms and 37.7 million 1040-A forms and instructions for the 1977 tax year. The 83.2 million total is about 2.9 million more than the number mailed the year before.

Total Family Income
(figures in percent)

Family income	White		Black and other races	
	1977	1965	1977	1965
Families (thousands)[1]	50,530	43,497	6,685	4,782
Under $3,000	2.8	5.1	9.6	14.6
$3,000 to $4,999	4.8	6.2	13.2	15.3
$5,000 to $6,999	6.6	7.1	12.4	15.3
$7,000 to $9,999	10.5	12.1	14.2	18.0
$10,000 to $11,999	7.1	9.9	7.9	9.1
$12,000 to $14,999	11.5	15.5	10.0	10.3
$15,000 to $24,999	33.0	31.3	22.0	14.3
$25,000 and over	23.9	12.8	10.8	3.0
Median Income (1977 dollars)	$16,740	$13,927	$10,142	$7,670

1. As of March 1978. *Source:* Department of Commerce, Bureau of the Census.

Strikes and Lockouts

Year	Strikes and lockouts	Workers involved (thousands)	Man-days idle (thousands)
1900	1,839	568	n.a.
1920	3,411	1,463	n.a.
1930	637	183	3,320
1940	2,508	577	6,700
1950	4,843	2,410	38,800
1960	3,333	1,320	19,100
1970	5,716	3,305	66,414
1977	5,600	2,300	36,000

NOTE: n.a. = not available. *Source:* Department of Labor, Bureau of Labor Statistics.

More Women Run Homes

The Census Bureau reports that, in 1978, about 11% of the country's 76 million households were headed by a woman, with no husband present. This represents an increase of 2.5 million woman-run households. The report also indicated that the average size of U.S. households declined from 3.1 persons in 1970 to 2.8 persons in 1978.

Where Does Our Energy Come From?

Fuel	1978	1977
Imported oil	25.8%	20.3%
Domestic oil	22.8	26.7
Natural gas	25.9	27.0
Coal	18.8	19.2
Hydroelectric and geothermal	3.2	4.1
Nuclear fuels	3.5	2.7
Total	100.0	100.0

Source: Department of Energy, Energy Information Administration.

Where Does Our Energy Go To?

Type	1978	1977
Household and commercial	37.0%	37.3%
Industry	36.8	37.0
Transportation	26.2	25.7
Total	100.0	100.0

Source: Department of Energy, Energy Information Administration.

Where Do People Consume The Most Energy?
(10 highest per capita consumers)

Country	kwh per capita[1]	Population (thousands)	Production plus net import[2]
Norway	18,769	4,026	75,565
Panama Canal Zone	16,250	40	650
Canada	12,278	23,143	284,153
New Caledonia	11,844	135	1,599
Luxembourg	11,682	358	4,182
Guam	11,183	93	1,040
Iceland	11,027	220	2,426
Sweden	10,766	8,222	88,518
United States	9,911	215,118	2,132,018
Christmas Island	9,333	3	28
World	1,720	—	—

1. Production plus net imports divided by total population.
2. In million kilowatt hours. NOTE: Data on consumption are derived from the formula "production plus imports minus exports." Accordingly, apparent consumption may occasionally be only an indication of the magnitude of actual gross inland availability. Where relatively small populations are involved, large fluctuations in per capita consumption series may derive from small quantitative variations. *Source:* United Nations, *World Energy Supplies, 1972–76.*

World's Ten Largest Electric Energy Producers, 1976

(in million kilowatt hours)

| Country | Production | | | |
	Hydro	Nuclear	Thermal	Total
United States	290,499	191,108	1,641,799	2,123,406
USSR	135,735	14,000[2]	961,685[2]	1,111,420
Japan	88,741[1]	34,079	388,956	511,776
West Germany	14,052	24,262	295,337	333,651
Canada	213,049	16,430	63,888	293,367
United Kingdom	5,121	36,155	235,700	276,976
France	49,287	15,763	138,044	203,094
Italy	43,466[1]	3,807	116,277	163,550
China	37,500[2]	—	100,500[2]	138,000[2]
Poland	2,098	—	102,003	104,101
Sub-total	879,548	335,604	4,044,189	5,259,341
All others	576,608	62,165	1,018,540	1,657,313
World total	1,456,156	397,769	5,062,729	6,916,654

1. Production from geothermal sources included. 2. Estimate. *Source:* United Nations, *World Energy Supplies, 1972–1976.*

Money in Circulation by Denomination[1]

(in millions)

Denomination	1977[2]	1970	1960	1950	1939
Coin	$ 9,876	$ 6,281	$ 2,427	$ 1,554	$ 590
$1[4]	2,835	2,310	1,533	1,113	559
$2	636	136	88	64	36
$5	3,816	3,161	2,246	2,049	1,019
$10	10,552	9,170	6,591	5,998	1,772
$20	31,060	18,581	10,536	8,529	1,576
$50	9,520	4,896	2,815	2,422	460
$100	29,155	12,084	5,954	5,043	919
$500	170	215	249	368	191
$1,000	197	252	316	588	425
$5,000	2	3	3	4	20
$10,000	4	4	10	12	32
Total[5]	97,823	57,093	32,869	27,741	7,598

1. End of year unless otherwise noted. 2. Sept. 30. 3. Paper currency only. $1 coins reported under coin. 4. Includes unassorted currency. *Source:* Department of the Treasury, Bureau of Government Financial Operations.

Portraits and Designs of U.S. Paper Currency[1]

Currency	Portrait	Design on back
$1	Washington	ONE between obverse and reverse of Great Seal of U.S.
$2[2]	Jefferson	Monticello
$2[3]	Jefferson	"The Signing of the Declaration of Independence"
$5	Lincoln	Lincoln Memorial
$10	Hamilton	U.S. Treasury Building
$20	Jackson	White House
$50	Grant	U.S. Capitol
$100	Franklin	Independence Hall
$500	McKinley	Ornate FIVE HUNDRED
$1,000	Cleveland	Ornate ONE THOUSAND
$5,000	Madison	Ornate FIVE THOUSAND
$10,000	Chase	Ornate TEN THOUSAND
$100,000[4]	Wilson	Ornate ONE HUNDRED THOUSAND

1. Denominations of $500 and higher were discontinued in 1969. 2. Discontinued in 1966. 3. New issue, April 13, 1976. 4. For use only in transactions between Federal Reserve System and Treasury Department.

How Consumers Spend Their Dollar
(in billions)

	1977	1977 % of total
Food	$217.0	17.9
Tobacco	16.5	1.4
Alcohol	28.2	2.3
Clothing, accessories, and jewelry	95.6	7.9
Personal care	16.7	1.4
Housing	184.6	15.3
Household operation	176.9	14.7
Medical care	118.0	9.8
Personal business	60.4	5.0
Transportation	172.1	14.3
Recreation	81.2	6.7
Private education and research	18.8	1.6
Religious and welfare activities	15.4	1.3
Foreign travel and other	5.1	0.4
Total	1,206.5	100.0

Source: Department of Commerce, Bureau of Economic Analysis.

Federal Consumer Offices

The federal government publishes a *Directory of Federal Consumer Offices.* This directory lists the addresses and phone numbers of federal offices and agencies that deal with a variety of areas of interest to consumers. It is arranged by subject. A free copy of the complete directory may be obtained by writing to the Consumer Information Center, Pueblo, Colo. 81009. Following are some selected offices:

Advertising: Director, Bureau of Consumer Protection, Federal Trade Commission, Washington, D.C. 20580

Air Travel—Routes and Service: Director, Office of the Consumer Advocate, Civil Aeronautics Board, Washington, D.C. 20423

Alcoholism, Drug Abuse, and Mental Illness: Office of Public Affairs, Alcohol, Drug Abuse, and Mental Health Service, 5600 Fishers Lane, Rockville, Md. 20857

Auto Safety and Highways: Director, Office of Public and Consumer Affairs, Transportation Department, Washington, D.C. 20590, *and* National Highway Traffic Safety Administration, toll-free hotline, 800–424–9393

Children and Youth: Director of Public Information, Office of Human Development Services, Department of Health, Education, and Welfare, Washington, D.C. 20201

Consumer Affairs—Complaints: Director, Office of Consumer Affairs, Department of Health, Education, and Welfare, 621 Reporters Bldg., Washington, D.C. 20201. This office serves as a clearinghouse for complaints from consumers. Complaints not handled directly are referred to appropriate federal, state, or local offices.

Credit: Director, Bureau of Consumer Protection, Federal Trade Commission, Washington, D.C. 20850

Crime Insurance: Federal Crime Insurance, Department of Housing and Urban Development, P.O. Box 41033, Washington, D.C. 20014

Drugs and Cosmetics: Consumer Inquiry Section, Food and Drug Administration, 5600 Fishers Lane, Rockville, Md. 20852

Energy: Director for Consumer Affairs, Department of Energy, Washington, D.C. 20461

Food: Assistant Secretary for Food and Consumer Services, U.S. Department of Agriculture, Washington, D.C. 20205 *and* Consumer Inquiry Section, Food and Drug Administration, 5600 Fishers Lane, Rockville, Md. 20852

Handicapped: Director, Division of Public Information, Office of Human Development Services, Department of Health, Education, and Welfare, Washington, D.C. 20201

Housing: Assistant Secretary for Neighborhoods, Voluntary Associations, and Consumer Protection, Department of Housing and Urban Development, Washington, D.C. 20410.

Mail: Check with your local postal inspector about problems relating to mail fraud and undelivered merchandise, or contact the Chief Postal Inspector, U.S. Postal Service, Washington, D.C. 20260

Medicaid-Medicare: Health Care Financing Administration, Department of Health, Education, and Welfare, Washington, D.C. 20201

Moving: Interstate Commerce Commission, toll-free hotline, 800–424–9312

Pensions: Office of Communications, Pension Benefit Guaranty Corporation, 2020 K St., N.W., Washington, D.C. 20006 *and* Labor Management Standards Administration, Department of Labor, Washington, D.C. 20210

Runaway Children: The National Runaway Hotline, toll-free, 800–621–4000

Travel Information: U.S. Travel Service, Department of Commerce, Washington, D.C. 20230

Wages and Working Conditions: Employment Standards Administration, Department of Labor, Washington, D.C. 20210

ENTERTAINMENT

TOP MONEY-MAKING FILMS[2]

1.	Star Wars (1977)	$127,000,000
2.	Jaws (1975)	121,356,000
3.	The Godfather (1972)	86,112,947
4.	The Exorcist (1973)	82,200,000
5.	The Sound of Music (1965)	78,662,000
6.	The Sting (1973)	78,090,000
7.	Gone With the Wind (1939)	76,700,000
8.	One Flew Over the Cuckoo's Nest (1975)	58,300,000
9.	Rocky (1976)	54,000,000
10.	Love Story (1970)	50,000,000
11.	Towering Inferno (1975)	50,000,000
12.	The Graduate (1968)	49,078,000
13.	American Graffiti (1973)	47,308,000
14.	Doctor Zhivago (1965)	46,550,000
15.	Butch Cassidy and the Sundance Kid (1969)	46,039,000
16.	Airport (1970)	45,300,000
17.	The Ten Commandments (1956)	43,000,000
18.	Mary Poppins (1964)	42,250,000
19.	The Poseidon Adventure (1972)	42,000,000
20.	Smokey and the Bandit (1977)	39,744,000
21.	A Star Is Born (1976)	37,100,000
22.	M*A*S*H (1970)	36,720,000
23.	Ben-Hur (1959)	36,650,000
24.	Earthquake (1974)	36,094,000
25	King Kong (1976)	35,851,283

1. As of Sept. 10, 1978. M = musical. Years are those of opening and closing. 2. Figures are rentals collected by film distributors in the U.S. and Canada as of Jan. 1, 1977.

LONGEST BROADWAY RUNS[1]

1. Fiddler on the Roof (M) (1964–72)	3,242
2. Life With Father (1939–47)	3,224
3. Tobacco Road (1933–41)	3,182
4. Hello, Dolly! (M) (1964–71)	2,844
5. Grease (M) (1972–)	2,720
6. My Fair Lady (M) (1956–62)	2,717
7. Man of La Mancha (M) (1965–71)	2,329
8. Abie's Irish Rose (1922–27)	2,327
9. Oklahoma! (M) (1943–48)	2,212
10. South Pacific (M) (1949–54)	1,925
11. Pippin (M) (1972–77)	1,908
12. Harvey (1944–49)	1,775
13. The Magic Show (1974–)	1,765
14. Hair (M) (1968–72)	1,742
15. Born Yesterday (1946–49)	1,642
16. Mary, Mary (1961–64)	1,572
17. Voice of the Turtle (1943–48)	1,557
18. Barefoot in the Park (1963–67)	1,532
19. The Wiz (M) (1975–)	1,512
20. Mame (M) (1966–70)	1,503
21. Same Time, Next Year (1975–)	1,455
22. Arsenic and Old Lace (1941–44)	1,444
23. Sound of Music (M) (1959–63)	1,443
24. How to Succeed in Business Without Really Trying (M) (1961–65)	1,417
25. Hellzapoppin' (M) (1938–41)	1,404

Motion Picture Academy Awards (Oscars)

	Best Picture	Director	Actress	Actor
1928	Wings, Paramount	Frank Borzage, Seventh Heaven; Lewis Milestone, Two Arabian Nights	Janet Gaynor, Seventh Heaven, Street Angel, Sunrise	Emil Jannings, The Way of All Flesh, The Last Command
1929	The Broadway Melody, M-G-M	Frank Lloyd, The Divine Lady	Mary Pickford, Coquette	Warner Baxter, In Old Arizona
1930	All Quiet on the Western Front, Universal	Lewis Milestone, All Quiet on the Western Front	Norma Shearer, The Divorce	George Arliss, Disraeli
1931	Cimarron, RKO Radio	Norman Taurog, Skippy	Marie Dressler, Min and Bill	Lionel Barrymore, A Free Soul
1932	Grand Hotel, M-G-M	Frank Borzage, Bad Girl	Helen Hayes, The Sin of Madelon Claudet	Frederic March, Dr. Jekyll and Mr. Hyde, and Wallace Beery, The Champ
1933	Cavalcade, Fox	Frank Lloyd, Cavalcade	Katharine Hepburn, Morning Glory	Charles Laughton, The Private Life of Henry VIII
1934	It Happened One Night, Columbia	Frank Capra, It Happened One Night	Claudette Colbert It Happened One Night	Clark Gable, It Happened One Night
1935	Mutiny on the Bounty, M-G-M	John Ford, The Informer	Bette Davis, Dangerous	Victor McLaglen, The Informer
1936	The Great Ziegfeld, M-G-M	Frank Capra, Mr. Deeds Goes to Town	Luise Rainer, The Great Ziegfeld	Paul Muni, The Story of Louis Pasteur
1937	The Life of Emile Zola, Warner Bros.	Leo McCarey, The Awful Truth	Luise Rainier The Good Earth	Spencer Tracy, Captains Courageous
1938	You Can't Take It with You, Columbia	Frank Capra, You Can't Take It with You	Bette Davis, Jezebel	Spencer Tracy, Boys Town

Year	Best Picture	Best Director	Best Actress	Best Actor
1939	Gone with the Wind, Selznick-M-G-M	Victor Fleming, Gone with the Wind	Vivien Leigh, Gone with the Wind	Robert Donat, Goodbye, Mr. Chips
1940	Rebecca, Selznick-UA	John Ford, The Grapes of Wrath	Ginger Rogers, Kitty Foyle	James Stewart, The Philadelphia Story
1941	How Green Was My Valley, 20th Century-Fox	John Ford, How Green Was My Valley	Joan Fontaine, Suspicion	Gary Cooper, Sergeant York
1942	Mrs. Miniver, M-G-M	William Wyler, Mrs. Miniver	Greer Garson, Mrs. Miniver	James Cagney, Yankee Doodle Dandy
1943	Casablanca, Warner Bros.	Michael Curtiz, Casablanca	Jennifer Jones, The Song of Bernadette	Paul Lukas, Watch on the Rhine
1944	Going My Way, Paramount	Leo McCarey, Going My Way	Ingrid Bergman, Gaslight	Bing Crosby, Going My Way
1945	The Lost Weekend, Paramount	Billy Wilder, The Lost Weekend	Joan Crawford, Mildred Pierce	Ray Milland, The Lost Weekend
1946	The Best Years of Our Lives, Goldwyn-RKO Radio	William Wyler, The Best Years of Our Lives	Olivia de Havilland, To Each His Own	Fredric March, The Best Years of Our Lives
1947	Gentleman's Agreement, 20th Century-Fox	Elia Kazan, Gentleman's Agreement	Loretta Young, The Farmer's Daughter	Ronald Colman, A Double Life
1948	Hamlet, Rank-Two Cities-U-I	John Huston, Treasure of Sierra Madre	Jane Wyman, Johnny Belinda	Laurence Olivier, Hamlet
1949	All the King's Men, Rossen-Columbia	Joseph L. Mankiewicz, A Letter to Three Wives	Olivia de Havilland, The Heiress	Broderick Crawford, All the King's Men
1950	All About Eve, 20th Century-Fox	Joseph L. Mankiewicz, All About Eve	Judy Holliday, Born Yesterday	José Ferrer, Cyrano de Bergerac
1951	An American in Paris, M-G-M	George Stevens, A Place in the Sun	Vivien Leigh, A Streetcar Named Desire	Humphrey Bogart, The African Queen
1952	The Greatest Show on Earth, DeMille-Paramount	John Ford, The Quiet Man	Shirley Booth, Come Back, Little Sheba	Gary Cooper, High Noon

	Best Picture	Director	Actress	Actor
1953	From Here to Eternity, Columbia	Fred Zinnemann, From Here to Eternity	Audrey Hepburn, Roman Holiday	William Holden, Stalag 17
1954	On the Waterfront, Horizon-American Corp., Columbia	Elia Kazan, On the Waterfront	Grace Kelley, The Country Girl	Marlon Brando, On the Waterfront
1955	Marty, Hecht and Lancaster, United Artists	Delbert Mann, Marty	Anna Manani, The Rose Tatoo	Ernest Borgnine, Marty
1956	Around the World in 80 Days, the Michael Todd Co., Inc.-UA	George Stevens, Giant	Ingrid Bergman, Anastasia	Yul Bryner, The King and I
1957	The Bridge on the River Kwai, Horizon Picture, Columbia	David Lean, The Bridge on the River Kwai	Joanne Woodward, The Three Faces of Eve	Alec Guiness, The Bridge on the River Kwai
1958	Gigi, Arthur Freed Productions, Inc., M-G-M	Vincente Minelli, Gigi	Susan Hayward, I Want to Live!	David Niven, Separate Tables
1959	Ben-Hur, M-G-M Mirisch Co., Inc., United Artist	William Wyler, Ben-Hur	Simone Signoret, Room at the Top	Charlton Heston, Ben-Hur
1960	The Apartment, Mirisch Co., Inc., United Artists	Billy Wilder, The Apartment	Elizabeth Taylor, Butterfield 8	Burt Lancaster, Elmer Gantry
1961	West Side Story, Mirisch Pictures, Inc., and B and P Enterprises, Inc., United Artists	Robert Wise and Jerome Robbins, West Side Story	Sophia Loren, Two Women	Maximillian Schell, Judgment at Nuremberg
1962	Lawrence of Arabia, Horizon Pictures, Ltd.-Columbia	David Lean, Lawrence of Arabia	Anne Bancroft, The Miracle Worker	Gregory Peck, To Kill a Mockingbird

Year	Picture	Director	Actress	Actor
1963	*Tom Jones*, A Woodfall Production, UA-Lopert Pictures	Tony Richardson, *Tom Jones*	Patricia Neal, *Hud*	Sidney Poitier, *Lilies of the Field*
1964	*My Fair Lady*, Warner Bros.	George Cukor, *My Fair Lady*	Julie Andrews, *Mary Poppins*	Rex Harrison, *My Fair Lady*
1965	*The Sound of Music*, Argyle Enterprises Production, 20th Century-Fox	Robert Wise, *The Sound of Music*	Julie Christie, *Darling*	Lee Marvin, *Cat Ballou*
1966	*A Man for All Seasons*, Highland Films, Ltd., Production, Columbia	Fred Zinnemann, *A Man for All Seasons*	Elizabeth Taylor, *Who's Afraid of Virginia Woolf?*	Paul Scofield, *A Man for All Seasons*
1967	*In the Heat of the Night*, Mirisch Corp. Production, United Artists	Mike Nichols, *The Graduate*	Katharine Hepburn, *Guess Who's Coming to Dinner*	Rod Steiger, *In the Heat of the Night*
1968	*Oliver!*, Columbia Pictures	Sir Carol Reed, *Oliver!*	Katharine Hepburn, *The Lion in Winter*, and Barbara Streisand, *Funny Girl*	Cliff Robertson, *Charly*
1969	*Midnight Cowboy*, Jerome Hellman-John Schlesinger Production, United Artists	John Schlesinger, *Midnight Cowboy*	Maggie Smith, *The Prime of Miss Jean Brodie*	John Wayne, *True Grit*
1970	*Patton*, Frank McCarthy-Franklin J. Schaffner Production, 20th Century-Fox	Franklin J. Schaffner, *Patton*	Glenda Jackson, *Women in Love*	George C. Scott, *Patton*
1971	*The French Connection*, D'Antoni Productions, 20th Century-Fox	William Friedkin, *The French Connection*	Jane Fonda, *Klute*	Gene Hackman, *The French Connection*
1972	*The Godfather*, Albert S. Ruddy Production, Paramount	Bob Fosse, *Cabaret*	Liza Minelli, *Cabaret*	Marlon Brando, *The Godfather*

	Best Picture	Director	Actress	Actor
1973	*The Sting,* Universal-Bill Phillips-George Roy Hill Production, Universal	George Roy Hill, *The Sting*	Glenda Jackson, *A Touch of Class*	Jack Lemmon, *Save the Tiger*
1974	*The Godfather, Part II,* Coppola Co. Production, Paramount	Francis Ford Coppola, *The Godfather, Part II*	Ellen Burstyn, *Alice Doesn't Live Here Anymore*	Art Carney, *Harry and Tonto*
1975	*One Flew Over the Cuckoo's Nest,* Fantasy Films Production, United Artists	Milos Forman, *One Flew Over the Cuckoo's Nest*	Louise Fletcher, *One Flew Over the Cuckoo's Nest*	Jack Nicholson, *One Flew Over the Cuckoo's Nest*
1976	*Rocky,* Robert Chartoff-Irwin Winkler Production, United Artists	John G. Avidsen, *Rocky*	Faye Dunaway, *Network*	Peter Finch, *Network*
1977	*Annie Hall,* Jack Rollins-Charles H. Joffee Production, United Artists	Woody Allen, *Annie Hall*	Diane Keaton, *Annie Hall*	Richard Dreyfuss, *The Goodbye Girl*

GEOGRAPHY

Explorations and Discoveries
(All years are A.D. unless B.C. is specified.)

Country or place	Explorer or discover	Date
AFRICA		
Sierra Leone	Hanno, Carthaginian seaman	c. 520 B.C.
Congo River	Diogo Cão, Protuguese	c. 1484
Cape of Good Hope	Bartholomeu Diaz, Portuguese	1488
Gambia River	Mungo Park, Scottish explorer	1795
Sahara Desert	Dixon Denham and Hugh Clapperton, English explorers	1822–23
Zambezi River	Davis Livingstone, Scottish explorer	1851
Sudan	Heinrich Barth, German explorer	1852–55
Victoria Falls	Livingstone	1855
Lake Tanganyika	Richard Burton and John Speke, British explorers	1858
Congo River	Sir Henry M. Stanley, British explorer	1877
ASIA		
Punjab (India)	Alexander the Great	327 B.C.
China	Marco Polo, Italian traveler	c. 1272
Tibet	Odoric of Pordenone, Italian monk	c. 1325
Southern China	Niccolò dei Conti, Venetian traveler	c. 1440
India	Vasco da Gama, Portuguese navigator	1498
Japan	St. Francis Xavier of Spain	1549
Arabia	Carsten Niebuhr, German explorer	1762
China	Ferdinand Richthofen, German scientist	1868
Mongolia	Nikolai M. Przhevalsky, Russian explorer	1870–73
Central Asia	Sven Hedin, Swedish scientist	1890–1908
EUROPE		
Shetland Islands	Pytheas of Massilia (Marseille)	c. 325 B.C.
North Cape	Ottar, Norwegian explorer	c. 870
Iceland	Norwegian noblemen	c. 890–900

Country or place	Explorer or discover	Date
NORTH AMERICA		
Greenland	Eric the Red, Norwegian	c. 985
Labrador; Nova Scotia (?)	Leif Ericson, Norse explorer	1000
West Indies	Christopher Columbus, Italian	1492
North America	Giovanni Caboto (John Cabot), for British	1497
Pacific Ocean	Vasco Núñez de Balboa, Spanish explorer	1513
Florida	Ponce de León, Spanish explorer	1513
Mexico	Hernando Cortés, Spanish adventurer	1519–21
St. Lawrence River	Jacques Cartier, French navigator	1534
Southwest U. S.	Francisco Coronado, Spanish explorer	1540–42
Colorado River	Hernando de Alarcón, Spanish explorer	1540
Mississippi River	Hernando de Soto, Spanish explorer	1541
Frobisher Bay	Martin Frobisher, English seaman	1576
Maine Coast	Samuel de Champlain, French explorer	1604
Jamestown, Va.	John Smith, English colonist	1607
Hudson River	Henry Hudson, English navigator	1609
Hudson Bay (Canada)	Henry Hudson	1610
Baffin Bay	William Baffin, English navigator	1616
Lake Michigan	Jean Nicolet, French explorer	1634
Arkansas River	Jacques Marquette and Louis Jolliet, French explorers	1673
Mississippi River	Sieur de La Salle, French explorer	1682
Bering Strait	Vitus Bering, Danish explorer	1728
Alaska	Vitus Bering	1741
Mackenzie River (Canada)	Sir Alexander Mackenzie, Scottish-Canadian explorer	1789
Northwest U. S.	Meriwether Lewis and William Clark	1804–06
Northeast Passage (Arctic Ocean)	Nils Nordenskjöld, Swedish explorer	1879
Greenland	Robert Peary, American explorer	1892
Northwest Passage	Roald Amundsen, Norwegian explorer	1906
SOUTH AMERICA		
Continent	Columbus, Italian	1498
Brazil	Pedro Alvarez Cabral, Portuguese	1500
Peru	Francisco Pizarro, Spanish explorer	1532–33
Amazon River	Francisco Orellana, Spanish explorer	1541
Cape Horn	Willem C. Schouten, Dutch navigator	1615

Country or place	Explorer or discover	Date
OCEANIA		
New Guinea	Jorge de Menezes, Portuguese explorer	1526
Australia	Abel Janszoon Tasman, Dutch navigator	1642
Tasmania		
Australia	John McDouall Stuart, English explorer	1828
Australia	Robert Burke and William Wills, Australian explorers	1861
New Zealand	Abel Janszoon Tasman	1642
New Zealand	James Cook, English navigator	1769
ARCTIC, ANTARCTIC, AND MISCELLANEOUS		
Ocean exploration	Magellan's ships circled globe	1519–22
Galápagos Islands	Diego de Rivadeneira, Spanish captain	1535
Spitsbergen	Willem Barents, Dutch navigator	1596
Antarctic Circle	James Cook, English navigator	1773
Antarctica	Nathaniel Palmer, U. S. whaler (archipelago) and Fabian Gottlieb von Bellingshausen, Russian admiral (mainland)	1820–21
Antarctica	Charles Wilkes, American explorer	1840
North Pole	Robert E. Peary, American explorer	1909
South Pole	Roald Amundsen, Norwegian explorer	1911

Water Supply of the World[1]

The Antarctic Icecap is the largest supply of fresh water, nearly 2 percent of the world's total of fresh and salt water. As can be seen from the table below, the amount of water in our atmosphere is over ten times as large as the water in all the rivers taken together. The fresh water actually available for human use in lakes and rivers and the accessible ground water amounts to only about one third of one percent of the total.

	Surface area (square miles)	Volume (cubic miles)	Percentage of total
Salt Water			
The oceans	139,500,000	317,000,000	97.2
Inland seas and saline lakes	270,000	25,000	0.008
Fresh Water			
Freshwater lakes	330,000	30,000	0.009
All rivers (average level)	—	300	0.0001
Antarctic Icecap	6,000,000	6,300,000	1.9
Arctic Icecap and glaciers	900,000	680,000	0.15
Water in the atmosphere	197,000,000	3,100	0.001
Ground water within half a mile from surface	—	1,000,000	0.31
Deep-lying ground water	—	1,000,000	0.31
Total (rounded)	—	326,000,000	100.00

1. All figures are estimated. *Source:* Department of the Interior, Geological Survey.

Highest, Lowest, and Mean Altitudes in the United States

State	Altitude, ft[1]	Highest point	Altitude, ft	Lowest point	Altitude, ft
Alabama	500	Cheaha Mountain	2,407	Gulf of Mexico	Sea level
Alaska	1,900	Mount McKinley	20,320	Pacific Ocean	Sea level
Arizona	4,100	Humphreys Peak	12,633	Colorado River	70
Arkansas	650	Magazine Mountain	2,753	Ouachita River	55
California	2,900	Mount Whitney	14,494	Death Valley	282[2]
Colorado	6,800	Mount Elbert	14,433	Arkansas River	3,350
Connecticut	500	Mount Frissell, on south slope	2,380	Long Island Sound	Sea level
Delaware	60	On Ebright Road	442	Atlantic Ocean	Sea level
D. C.	150	Tenleytown, northwest part	410	Potomac River	1
Florida	100	Sec. 30, T6N, R20W[3]	345	Atlantic Ocean	Sea level
Georgia	600	Brasstown Bald	4,784	Atlantic Ocean	Sea level
Hawaii	3,030	Mauna Kea	13,796	Pacific Ocean	Sea level
Idaho	5,000	Borah Peak	12,662	Snake River	710
Illinois	600	Charles Mound	1,235	Mississippi River	279
Indiana	700	Franklin Township, Wayne County	1,257	Ohio River	320
Iowa	1,100	Sec. 29, T100N, R41W[4]	1,670	Mississippi River	480
Kansas	2,000	Mount Sunflower	4,039	Verdigris River	680
Kentucky	750	Black Mountain	4,145	Mississippi River	257
Louisiana	100	Driskill Mountain	535	New Orleans	5[2]
Maine	600	Mount Katahdin	5,268	Atlantic Ocean	Sea level
Maryland	350	Backbone Mountain	3,360	Atlantic Ocean	Sea level
Massachusetts	500	Mount Greylock	3,491	Atlantic Ocean	Sea level
Michigan	900	Mount Curwood	1,980	Lake Erie	572
Minnesota	1,200	Eagle Mountain	2,301	Lake Superior	602
Mississippi	300	Woodall Mountain	806	Gulf of Mexico	Sea level

State	Approximate mean altitude[1]	Highest point	Elevation	Lowest point	Elevation
Missouri	800	Taum Sauk Mountain	1,772	St. Francis River	230
Montana	3,400	Granite Peak	12,799	Kootenai River	1,800
Nebraska	2,600	Johnson Township, Kimball County	5,426	Southeast corner of state	840
Nevada	5,500	Boundary Peak	13,143	Colorado River	470
New Hampshire	1,000	Mount Washington	6,288	Atlantic Ocean	Sea level
New Jersey	250	High Point	1,803	Atlantic Ocean	Sea level
New Mexico	5,700	Wheeler Peak	13,161	Red Bluff Reservoir	2,817
New York	1,000	Mount Marcy	5,344	Atlantic Ocean	Sea level
North Carolina	700	Mount Mitchell	6,684	Atlantic Ocean	Sea level
North Dakota	1,900	White Butte	3,506	Red River	750
Ohio	850	Campbell Hill	1,550	Ohio River	433
Oklahoma	1,300	Black Mesa	4,973	Little River	287
Oregon	3,300	Mount Hood	11,235	Pacific Ocean	Sea level
Pennsylvania	1,100	Mount Davis	3,213	Delaware River	Sea level
Rhode Island	200	Jerimoth Hill	812	Atlantic Ocean	Sea level
South Carolina	350	Sassafras Mountain	3,560	Atlantic Ocean	Sea level
South Dakota	2,200	Harney Peak	7,242	Big Stone Lake	962
Tennessee	900	Clingmans Dome	6,643	Mississippi River	182
Texas	1,700	Guadalupe Peak	8,751	Gulf of Mexico	Sea level
Utah	6,100	Kings Peak	13,528	Beaverdam Creek	2,000
Vermont	1,000	Mount Mansfield	4,393	Lake Champlain	95
Virginia	950	Mount Rogers	5,729	Atlantic Ocean	Sea level
Washington	1,700	Mount Rainier	14,410	Pacific Ocean	Sea level
West Virginia	1,500	Spruce Knob	4,863	Potomac River	240
Wisconsin	1,050	Timms Hill	1,952	Lake Michigan	581
Wyoming	6,700	Gannett Peak	13,804	Belle Fourche River	3,100
United States	2,500	Mount McKinley (Alaska)	20,320	Death Valley (California)	282[2]

1. Approximate mean altitude. 2. Below sea level. 3. Walton County. 4. Osceola County. *Source:* Department of the interior, U.S. Geological Survey.

The United States

Source: Department of the Interior, U.S. Geological Survey.

Highest point: Mount McKinley,
  Alaska   20,320 ft (6,193 m)
Lowest point: Death Valley,
  Calif.   282 ft (86 m) below sea level
Approximate mean altitude   2,500 ft (762 m)
Points farthest apart (50 states):
  Log Point, Elliot Key, Fla.,
  and Kure Island, Hawaii   5,852 mi. (9,418 km)
Geographic center (50 states):
  In Butte County, S.D.
  (west of Castle Rock) 44° 58' N. lat.   103° 46' W. long.
Geographic center (48 conterminous states):
  In Smith County, Kan.
  (near Lebanon)   39° 50' N. lat.   98° 35' W. long.
Boundaries:
  Between Alaska and Canada   1,538 mi. (2,475 km)
  Between the 48
  conterminous states and Canada
  (incl. Great Lakes)   3,987 mi. (6,416 km)
  Between the United States
  and Mexico   1,933 mi. (3,111 km)

Extreme Points of the United States (50 States)

Extreme point	Latitude	Longitude	Distance[1] mi.	km
Northernmost point:				
Point Barrow, Alaska	71°23' N	156°29' W	2,502	4,027
Easternmost point:				
West Quoddy Head, Me.	44°49' N	66°57' W	1,785	2,873
Southernmost point:				
Ka Lae (South Cape), Hawaii	18°56' N	155°41' W	3,456	5,562
Westernmost point:				
Cape Wrangell, Alaska (Attu Island)	52°55' N	172°27' E	3,620	5,826

1. From geographic center of United States (incl. Alaska and Hawaii), west of Castle Rock, S.D., 44°58' N. lat., 103°46' W long.

The Continents

A continent is defined as a large unbroken land mass completely surrounded by water, although in some cases continents are (or were in part) connected by land bridges.

The hypothesis first suggested late in the 19th century was that the continents consist of lighter rocks that rest on heavier crustal material in about the same manner that icebergs float on water. That the rocks forming the continents are lighter than the material below them and under the ocean bottoms is now established. As a consequence of this fact, Alfred Wegener (for the first time in 1912) suggested that the continents are slowly moving, at a rate of about one yard per century, so that their relative positions are not rigidly fixed. Many geologists that were originally skeptical have come to accept this theory of Continental Drift.

When describing a continent, it is important to remember that there is a fundamental difference between a deep ocean, like the Atlantic, and shallow seas, like the Baltic and most of the North Sea, which are merely flooded portions of a continent. Another and entirely different point to remember is that political considerations have often overridden geographical facts when it came to naming continents.

Geographically speaking, Europe, including the British Isles, is a large western peninsula of the continent of Asia; and many geographers, when referring to Europe and Asia, speak of the Eurasian Continent. But traditionally, Europe is counted as a separate continent, with the Ural and the Caucasus mountains forming the line of demarcation between Europe and Asia.

To the south of Europe, Asia has an odd-shaped peninsula jutting westward, which has a large number of political subdivisions. The northern section is taken up by Turkey; to the south of Turkey there are Syria, Iraq, Israel, Jordan, Saudi Arabia, and a number of smaller Arab countries. All this is part of Asia. Traditionally, the island of Cyprus in the Mediterranean is also considered to be part of Asia, while the island of Crete is counted as European.

The large islands of Java, Borneo, and Sumatra and the smaller islands near them are counted as part of "tropical Asia," while New Guinea is counted as related to Australia.

In the case of the Americas, the problem arises as to whether they should be considered one or two continents. There are good arguments on both sides, but since there is now a land bridge between North and South America (in the past it was often flooded) and since no part of the sea east of the land bridge is deep ocean, it is more logical to consider the Americas as one continent.

Politically, based mainly on history, the Americas are divided into North America (from the Arctic to the Mexican border), Central America (from Mexico to Panama, with the Caribbean islands), and South America. Greenland is considered a section of North America, while Iceland is traditionally counted as a European island because of its political ties with the Scandinavian countries.

The island groups in the Pacific are often called "Oceania," but this name does *not* imply that scientists consider them the remains of a continent.

Oceans and Seas

Name	Area	Average depth	Greatest known depth	Place greatest known depth
Pacific Ocean	64,000,000	13,215	37,782	Mindanao Deep
Atlantic Ocean	31,815,000	12,880	30,246	Puerto Rico Trough
Indian Ocean	25,300,000	13,002	24,460	Sunda Trench
Arctic Ocean	5,440,200	3,953	18,456	77° 45′ N; 175° W
Mediterranean Sea[1]	1,145,100	4,688	15,197	Off Cape Matapan, Greece
Caribbean Sea	1,049,500	8,685	22,788	Off Cayman Islands
South China Sea	895,400	5,419	16,456	West of Luzon
Bering Sea	884,900	5,075	15,659	Off Buldir Island
Gulf of Mexico	615,000	4,874	12,425	Sigsbee Deep
Okhotsk Sea	613,800	2,749	12,001	146° 10′ E; 46° 50′ N
East China Sea	482,300	617	9,126	25° 16′ N; 125° E
Hudson Bay	475,800	420	600	Near entrance
Japan Sea	389,100	4,429	12,276	Central Basin
Andaman Sea	308,100	2,854	12,392	Off Car Nicobar Island
North Sea	222,100	308	2,165	Skagerrak
Red Sea	169,100	1,611	7,254	Off Port Sudan
Baltic Sea	163,000	180	1,380	Off Gotland

1. Includes Black Sea and Sea of Azov. NOTE: For Caspian Sea, *see* Ten Largest Lakes of World.

Ten Longest Rivers of the World

River	Source	Outflow	Approx. length miles
Nile	Tributaries of Lake Victoria, Africa	Mediterranean Sea	4,180
Amazon	Glacier-fed lakes, Peru	Atlantic Ocean	3,912
Mississippi-Missouri-Red Rock	Source of Red Rock, Montana	Gulf of Mexico	3,741
Yangtze Kiang	Tibetan plateau, China	China Sea	3,602
Ob	Altai Mts., U.S.S.R.	Gulf of Ob	3,459
Yellow (Hwang Ho)	Eastern part of Kunlan Mts., west China	Gulf of Chihli	2,900
Yenisei	Tannu-Ola Mts., western Tuva, U.S.S.R.	Arctic Ocean	2,800
Paraná	Confluence of Paranaiba and Grande rivers	Río de la Plata	2,795
Irtish	Altai Mts., U.S.S.R.	Ob River	2,758
Congo	Confluence of Lualaba and Luapula rivers, Zaire	Atlantic Ocean	2,716

Ten Highest Mountain Peaks of the World

Mountain peak	Range	Location	Height feet
Everest[1]	Himalayas	Nepal-Tibet	29,028
Godwin Austen (K-2)	Karakoram	India	28,741
Kanchenjunga	Himalayas	Nepal-Sikkim	28,208
Lhotse	Himalayas	Nepal-Tibet	27,890
Makalu	Himalayas	Tibet-Nepal	27,790
Dhaulagiri I	Himalayas	Nepal	26,810
Manaslu	Himalayas	Nepal	26,760
Cho Oyu	Himalayas	Nepal	26,750
Nanga Parbat	Himalayas	India	26,660
Annapurna I	Himalayas	Nepal	26,504

1. The U. S. Air Force Planning Charts list the height of Mt. Everest as 29,141 ft.

The Continental Divide

The Continental Divide is a ridge of high ground which runs irregularly north and south through the Rocky Mountains and separates eastward-flowing from westward-flowing streams. The waters which flow eastward empty into the Atlantic Ocean, chiefly by way of the Gulf of Mexico; those which flow westward empty into the Pacific.

Ten Largest Lakes of the World

Name and location	Area sq mi.	Length mi.	Maximum depth feet
Caspian Sea, U.S.S.R.-Iran[1]	152,239	745	3,104
Superior, U.S.-Canada	31,820	383	1,333
Victoria, Tanzania–Uganda	26,828	200	82
Aral, U.S.S.R.	25,659	266	223
Huron, U.S.-Canada	23,010	247	750
Michigan, U.S.	22,400	321	923
Tanganyika, Tanzania-Zaire	12,700	420	4,708
Baikal, U.S.S.R.	12,162	395	5,712
Great Bear, Canada	12,000	232	270
Nyasa, Malawi-Mozambique-Tanzania	11,600	360	2,316

1. The Caspian Sea is called "sea" because the Romans, finding it salty, named it *Mare Caspium*. Many geographers, however, consider it a lake because it is land-locked.

Ten Greatest Man-Made Lakes

Name of dam	Location	Millions of cubic meters	Year completed
Owen Falls	Uganda	204,800	1954
Bratsk	U.S.S.R.	169,270	1964
High Aswan	Egypt	169,000	1970
Kariba	Rhodesia-Zambia	160,368	1958
Akosombo	Ghana	148,000	1965
Daniel Johnson	Canada	141,852	1968
Krasnoyarsk	U.S.S.R.	73,300	1972
W. A. C. Bennett	Canada	70,309	1967
Zeya	U.S.S.R.	68,400	1975
Cabora Bassa	Mozambique	64,000	1974

Source: Department of the Interior, Bureau of Reclamation.

Ten Largest Islands of the World

Island	Location and status	Area sq mi.
Greenland	North Atlantic (Danish)	839,999
New Guinea	Southwest Pacific (Irian Jaya, Indonesian, west part; Papua New Guinea, east part)	316,615
Borneo	West mid-Pacific (Indonesian, south part; British protectorate, and Malaysian, north part)	286,914
Madagascar	Indian Ocean (Malagasy Republic)	226,657
Baffin	North Atlantic (Canadian)	183,810
Sumatra	Northeast Indian Ocean (Indonesian)	182,859
Honshu	Sea of Japan-Pacific (Japanese)	88,925
Great Britain	Off coast of NW Europe (England, Scotland, and Wales)	88,758
Ellesmere	Arctic Ocean (Canadian)	82,119
Victoria	Arctic Ocean (Canadian)	81,930

Principal Deserts of the World

Desert	Location	Approximate size	Approx. elevation, ft
Atacama	North Chile	400 mi. long	7,000–13,500
Black Rock	Northwest Nevada	About 1,000 sq mi.	2,000–8,500
Colorado	Southeast California from San Gorgonio Pass to Gulf of California	200 mi. long and a maximum width of 50 mi.	Few feet above to 250 below sea level
Dasht-e-Kavir	Southeast of Caspian Sea, Iran	—	2,000
Dasht-e-Lut	Northeast of Kerman, Iran	—	1,000
Gobi (Shamo)	Covers most of Mongolia	500,000 sq mi.	3,000–5,000
Great Arabian	Most of Arabia	1,500 mi. long	
Great Australian	Western portion of Australia	About one half the continent	600–1,000
Great Salt Lake	West of Great Salt Lake to Lake to Nevada–Utah boundary	About 110 mi. by 50 mi.	4,500
Kalahari	South Africa—South-West Africa	About 120,000 sq mi.	Over 3,000
Kara Kum (Desert of Kiva)	Southwest Turkmen, U.S.S.R.	115,000 sq mi.	—
Kyzyl Kum	Uzbek and Kazakh, U.S.S.R.	Over 100,000 sq mi.	160–2,000
Libyan	Libya, Egypt, Sudan	Over 500,000 sq mi.	—
Mojave	North of Colorado Desert and south of Death Valley, southeast California	15,000 sq mi.	2,000
Nubian	From Red Sea to great west bend of the Nile, Sudan	—	2,500
Painted Desert	Northeast Arizona	Over 7,000 sq mi.	High plateau, 5,000
Sahara	North Africa to about lat. 15°N and from Red Sea to Atlantic Ocean	3,200 mi. greatest length along lat. 20°N; area over 3,500,000 sq mi.	440 below sea level to 11,000 above; avg elevation, 1,400–1,600
Takla Makan	South central Sinkiang, China	Over 100,000 sq mi.	
Thar (Indian)	Pakistan-India	Nearly 100,000 sq mi.	Over 1,000

Ten Highest Waterfalls of the World

Waterfall	Location	River	Height feet
Angel	Venezuela	Tributary of Caroní	3,281
Tugela	Natal, South Africa	Tugela	3,000
Cuquenán	Venezuela	Cuquenán	2,000
Sutnerland	South Island, N.Z.	Arthur	1,904
Takkakaw	British Columbia	Tributary of Yoho	1,650
Ribbon (Yosemite)	California	Creek flowing into Yosemite	1,612
Upper Yosemite	California	Yosemite Creek, tributary of Merced	1,430
Gavarnie	Southwest France	Gave de Pau	1,384
Vettisfoss	Norway	Mörkedola	1,200
Widows' Tears (Yosemite)	California	Tributary of Merced	1,170

NOTE: Niagara Falls (New York-Ontario), though of great volume, has parallel drops of only 158 and 167 feet.

Table of Geological Periods

It is now generally assumed that planets are formed by the accretion of gas and dust in a cosmic cloud, but there is no way of estimating the length of this process. Our earth acquired its present size, more or less, between 4,000 and 5,000 million years ago. Life on earth originated about 2,000 million years ago, but there are no good fossil remains from periods earlier than the Cambrian, which began about 550 million years ago. The largely unknown past before the Cambrian Period is referred to as the Pre-Cambrian and is subdivided into the Lower (or older) and Upper (or younger) Pre-Cambrian—also called the Archaeozoic and Proterozoic Eras.

The known geological history of the earth since the beginning of the Cambrian Period is subdivided into three "eras," each of which comprises a number of "periods." They, in turn, are subdivided into "subperiods." In a subperiod, a certain section may be especially well known because of rich fossil finds. Such a section is called a "formation," and it is usually identified by a place name.

Paleozoic Era

This era began 550 million years ago and lasted for 355 million years. The name was compounded from Greek *palaios* (old) and *zoön* (animal).

Period	Duration[1]	Subperiods	Events
Cambrian (from *Cambria*, Latin name for Wales)	70	Lower Cambrian Middle Cambrian Upper Cambrian	Invertebrate sea life of many types, proliferating during this and the following period
Ordovician (from Latin *Ordovices*, people of early Britain)	85	Lower Ordovician Upper Ordovician	First known fishes; gigantic sea scorpions
Silurian (from Latin *Silures*, people of early Wales)	40	Lower Silurian Upper Silurian	Proliferation of fishes and other forms of sea life; land still largely lifeless
Devonian (from Devonshire in England)	50	Lower Devonian Upper Devonian	
Carboniferous (from Latin *carbo* = coal + *fero* = to bear)	85	Lower or Mississippian Upper or Pennsylvanian	Period of maximum coal formation in swampy forests; early insects and first known amphibians
Permian (from district of Perm in Russia)	25	Lower Permian Upper Permian	Early reptiles and mammals; earliest form of turtles

1. In millions of years.

Mesozoic Era

This era began 195 million years ago and lasted for 135 million years. The name was compounded from Greek *mesos* (middle) and *zoön* (animal). Popular name: Age of Reptiles.

Period	Duration[1]	Subperiods	Events
Triassic (from *trias* = triad)	35	Lower or Buntsandstein (from German *bunt* = colorful + *Sandstein* = sandstone) Middle or Muschelkalk (from German *Muschel* = clam + *Kalk* = limestone) Upper or Keuper (old miners' term)	Early saurians
Jurassic (from Jura Mountains)	35	Lower or Black Jurassic, or Lias (from French *lias* = hard stone) Middle or Brown Jurassic, or Dogger (old provincial English for ironstone) Upper or White Jurassic, or Malm (Middle English for sand)	Many sea-going reptiles; early large dinosaurs; somewhat later, flying reptiles (pterosaurs), earliest known birds
Cretaceous (from Latin *creta* = chalk)	65	Lower Cretaceous Upper Cretaceous	Maximum development of dinosaurs; birds proliferating; opossum-like mammals

1. In millions of years.

Cenozoic Era

This era began 60 million years ago and includes the geological present. The name was compounded from Greek *kainos* (new) and *zoön* (animal). Popular name: Age of Mammals.

Period	Duration[1]	Subperiods	Events
Tertiary (originally thought to be the third of only three periods)	c. 60	Paleocene (from Greek *palaios* = old + *kainos* = new)	First mammals other than marsupials
		Eocene (from Greek *eos* = dawn + *kainos* = new)	Formation of amber; rich insect fauna; early bats
		Oligocene (from Greek *oligos* = few + *kainos* = new)	Steady increase of large mammals
		Miocene (from Greek *meios* = less + *kainos* = new)	
		Pliocene (from Greek *pleios* = more + *kainos* = new)	Mammals closely resembling present types; protohumans
Pleistocene (from Greek *pleistos* = most + *kainos* = new) (popular name: Ice Age)	1	Four major glaciations, named Günz, Mindel, Riss, and Würm, originally the names of rivers. Last glaciation ended 10,000 to 15,000 years ago	Various forms of early man
Holocene (from Greek *holos* = entire + *kainos* = new)		The present	The last 3,000 years are called "history"

1. In millions of years.

MILITARY

U.S. Armed Services
Source: Department of Defense.

U.S. Army

On June 14, 1775, the Continental Congress "adopted" the New England Army—a mixed force of militia and volunteers besieging the British in Boston—by appointing a committee to draft "Rules and regulations for the government of the Army" and voting to raise 10 rifle companies as a reinforcement. The next day, it appointed Washington commander-in-chief of the "Continental forces to be raised for the defense of liberty," and he took command at Boston on July 3, 1775. The Continental Army that fought the Revolution was our first national military organization, and hence the Army is the senior service. After the war, the Continental Army was radically reduced but enough survived to form a small Regular Army of about 700 men under the Constitution in 1789, a nucleus for expansion in the 1970s to successfully meet threats from the Indians and from France. From these humble beginnings, the U.S. Army has developed, normally expanding rapidly by absorbing citizen soldiers in wartime and contracting just as rapidly after each war.

U.S. Navy

The antecedents of the U.S. Navy go back to September 1775, when Gen. Washington commissioned 7 schooners and brigantines to prey on British supply vessels bound for the Colonies or Canada. In Oct. 1775, a motion in the Continental Congress called for the construction of 2 vessels for the purpose of intercepting enemy transports. With its passage a Naval Committee of 7 men was formed, and they rapidly obtained passage of legislation calling for construction of additional vessels. The Continental Navy was supplemented by privateers and ships operated as state navies, but soon after the British surrender it was disestablished.

In 1794, because of dissatisfaction with the payment of tribute to the Barbary pirates, Congress authorized construction of 6 frigates. The first, *United States*, was launched May 10, 1797, but the Navy still remained under the control of the Secretary of War until April 1798, when the Secretary of the Navy was given full Cabinet rank and the U.S. Navy came into its own.

U.S. Air Force

Until creation of the National Military Establishment in September 1947, which united the services under one department, military aviation was a part of the U.S. Army. In the Army, aeronautical operations came under the Signal Corps from 1907 to 1918, when the U.S. Air Service was established. In 1926, the U.S. Air Corps came into being and remained until 1942, when the Army Air Forces succeeded it as the Army's air arm. In 1947, the U.S. Air Force was established as an independent military service under the National Military Establishment. At that time, the name "Army Air Forces" was abolished.

U.S. Coast Guard

Our country's oldest continuous seagoing service, the U.S. Coast Guard, traces its history back to 1790, when the first Congress authorized the construction of ten vessels for the collection of revenue. Known first as the Revenue Marine, and later as the Revenue Cutter Service, the Coast Guard received its present name in 1915 under an act of Congress combining the Revenue Cutter Service with the Life-Saving Service. In 1939, the Lighthouse Service was also consolidated with this unit. The Bureau of Marine Inspection and Navigation was transferred temporarily to the Coast Guard in 1942, permanently in 1946. Through its antecedents, the Coast Guard is one of the oldest organizations under the federal government and, until the Navy Department was established in 1798, served as the only U.S. armed force afloat. In times of peace, it operates under the Department of Transportation, serving as the nation's primary agency for promoting marine safety and enforcing federal maritime laws. In times of war, or on direction of the President, it is attached to the Navy Department.

U.S. Marine Corps

Founded in 1775 and observing its official birthday on Nov. 10, the U.S. Marine Corps was developed to serve on land, on sea, and in the air.

Marines have fought in every U.S. war. From an initial two battalions in the Revolution, the Corps reached a peak strength of six divisions and five aircraft wings in World War II. Its present strength is three active divisions and aircraft wings and a Reserve division/aircraft wing team. In 1947, the National Security Act set Marine Corps strength at not less than three divisions and three aircraft wings.

Budget Outlays for National Defense
(in billions of dollars, except as indicated)

item	1977	1975	1970
Defense Dept., military	98.0	85.0	77.2
Military personnel	26.2	25.0	23.0
Percent of military	26.7	29.4	29.9
Active forces	24.3	23.2	22.0
Reserve forces	1.9	1.7	1.1
Military retirees	8.2	6.2	2.8
Operation, maintenance	31.1	26.3	21.6
Procurement[1]	18.7	16.0	21.6
Army	2.6	2.5	5.2
Navy[2]	8.9	8.1	7.9
Air Force	7.0	5.3	8.4
Research and develop	10.9	8.9	7.2
Military construction	2.1	1.5	1.2
Family housing	1.4	1.1	.6
Civil defense	.1	.1	.1
Other[3]	.1	—.1	—1.0
Military assistance	.2	1.0	.7
Atomic energy activities[4]	1.8	1.5	1.4
Defense-related activities	—.1	—.9	—
Total	100.1	86.6	79.3

1. Includes other defense agencies not shown separately. 2. Includes Marine Corps. 3. Revolving and management funds, trust funds, special foreign currency program, allowances, and offsetting receipts. 4. Defense activities only. NOTE: Through 1976, for year ending June 30, except as noted; 1977 year ending Sept. 30, 1977, data are estimates. *Source:* Office of Management and Budget.

U.S. Military Actions Other Than Declared Wars

Hawaii (1893): U.S. Marines, ordered to land by U.S. Minister John L. Stevens, aided the revolutionary Committee of Safety in overthrowing the native government. Stevens then proclaimed Hawaii a U.S. protectorate. Annexation, resisted by the Democratic administration in Washington, was not formally accomplished until 1898.

China (1900): Boxers (a group of Chinese revolutionists) occupied Peking and laid siege to foreign legations. U.S. troops joined an international expedition which relieved the city.

Panama (1903): After Colombia had rejected a proposed agreement for relinquishing sovereignty over the Panama Canal Zone, revolution broke out, aided by promoters of the Panama Canal Co. Two U.S. warships were standing by to protect American privileges. The U.S. recognized the Republic of Panama on November 6.

Dominican Republic (1904): When the Dominican Republic failed to meet debts owed to the U.S. and foreign creditors, President Theodore Roosevelt declared the U.S. intention of exercising "international police power" in the Western Hemisphere whenever necessary. The U.S. accordingly administered customs and managed debt payments of the Dominican Republic from 1905 to 1907.

Nicaragua (1911): The possibility of foreign control over Nicaragua's canal route led to U.S. intervention and agreement. The U.S. landed Marines in Nicaragua (Aug. 14, 1912) to protect American interests there. A small detachment remained until 1933.

Mexico (1914): Mexican dictator Victoriano Huerta, opposed by President Woodrow Wilson, had the support of European governments. An incident involving unarmed U.S. sailors in Tampico led to the landing of U.S. forces on Mexican soil. Veracruz was bombarded by the Navy to prevent the landing of munitions from a German vessel. At the point of war, both powers agreed to mediation by Argentina, Brazil, and Chile. Huerta abdicated, and Venustiano Carranza succeeded to the presidency.

Haiti (1915): U.S. Marines imposed a military occupation. Haiti signed a treaty making it a virtual protectorate of the U.S. until troops were withdrawn in 1934.

Mexico (1916): Raids by Pancho Villa cost American lives on both sides of the border. President Carranza consented to a punitive expedition led by Gen. John J. Pershing, but antagonism grew in Mexico. Wilson withdrew the U.S. force when war with Germany became imminent.

Dominican Republic (1916): Renewed intervention in the Dominican Republic with internal administration by U.S. naval officers lasted until 1924.

Korea (1950): In this undeclared war, which terminated with the July 27, 1953, truce at Panmunjom and the establishment of a neutral nations' supervisory commission, the U.S. and 15 member-nations of the U.N. came to the aid of the Republic of South Korea, whose 38th-parallel border was crossed by the invading Russian Communist-controlled North Koreans, who were later joined by the Chinese Communists.

Lebanon (1958): Fearful of the newly formed U.A.R. abetting the rebels of his politically and economically torn country, President Camille Chamoun appealed to the U.S. for military assistance. U.S. troops landed in Beirut in mid-July and left before the end of the year, after internal and external quiet were restored.

Dominican Republic (1965): On April 28, when a political coup-turned-civil war endangered the lives of American nationals, President Lyndon B. Johnson rushed 400 marines into Santo Domingo, the beginning of an eventual U.S. peak-commitment of 30,000 troops, constituting the preponderant military strength of the OAS-created Inter-American Peace Force, and 6,500 troops, including 5,000 Americans, remained until after the peaceful inauguration of President Joaquín Balaguer on July 1, 1966, and the entire force left the country on September 20.

Vietnam: This longest war in U.S. history began with economic and technical assistance after 1954 Geneva accords ending the Indochinese War. By 1964 it had escalated into a major conflict.

This involvement spanning the administrations of five Presidents led to domestic discontent in the late 1960s. By April 1969, U.S. troop strength reached a peak of 543,400. Peace negotiations began in Paris in 1968 but proved fruitless. Finally, on Jan. 27, 1973, a peace accord was signed in Paris by the U.S., North and South Vietnam, and the Vietcong. Within 60 days, U.S. POWs were returned, and the U.S. withdrew all military forces from South Vietnam.

U.S. Casualties in Major Wars

War	Branch of service	Numbers engaged	Battle deaths	Other deaths	Total deaths	Wounds not mortal	total[1]
Revolutionary War 1775 to 1783	Army	n.a.	4,044	n.a.	n.a.	6,004	n.a.
	Navy	n.a.	342	n.a.	n.a.	114	n.a.
	Marines	n.a.	49	n.a.	n.a.	70	n.a.
	Total	**n.a.**	**4,435**	**n.a.**	**n.a.**	**6,188**	**n.a.**
War of 1812 1812 to 1815	Army	n.a.	1,950	n.a.	n.a.	4,000	n.a.
	Navy	n.a.	265	n.a.	n.a.	439	n.a.
	Marines	n.a.	45	n.a.	n.a.	66	n.a.
	Total	**286,730**	**2,260**	**n.a.**	**n.a.**	**4,505**	**n.a.**
Mexican War 1846 to 1848	Army	n.a.	1,721	11,550	13,271	4,102	17,373
	Navy	n.a.	1	n.a.	n.a.	3	n.a.
	Marines	n.a.	11	n.a.	n.a.	47	n.a.
	Total	**78,718**	**1,733**	**n.a.**	**n.a.**	**4,152**	**n.a.**
Civil War[2] 1861 to 1865	Army	2,128,948	138,154	221,374	359,528	280,040	639,568
	Navy	84,415	2,112	2,411	4,523	1,710	6,233
	Marines		148	312	460	131	591
	Total	**2,213,363**	**140,414**	**224,097**	**364,511**	**281,881**	**646,392**
Spanish-American War 1898	Army	280,564	369	2,061	2,430	1,594	4,024
	Navy	22,875	10	0	10	47	57
	Marines	3,321	6	0	6	21	27
	Total	**306,760**	**385**	**2,061**	**2,446**	**1,662**	**4,108**

World War I 1917 to 1918	Army	4,057,101	50,510	55,868	106,378	193,663	300,041
	Navy	599,051	431	6,856	7,287	819	8,106
	Marines	78,839	2,461	390	2,851	9,520	12,371
	Total	**4,734,991**	**53,402**	**63,114**	**116,516**	**204,002**	**320,518**
World War II 1941 to 1946	Army[3]	11,260,000	234,874	83,400	318,274	565,861	884,135
	Navy	4,183,466	36,950	25,664	62,614	37,778	100,392
	Marines	669,100	19,733	4,778	24,511	67,207	91,718
	Total	**16,112,566**	**291,557**	**113,842**	**405,399**	**670,846**	**1,076,245**
Korean War 1950 to 1953	Army	2,834,000	27,704	9,429	37,133	77,596	114,729
	Navy	1,177,000	458	4,043	4,501	1,576	6,077
	Marines	424,000	4,267	1,261	5,528	23,744	29,272
	Air Force	1,285,000	1,200	5,884	7,084	368	7,452
	Total	**5,720,000**	**33,629**	**20,617**	**54,246**	**103,284**	**157,530**
War in Southeast Asia[4]	Army	4,386,000	30,717	7,194	37,911	201,536	239,447
	Navy[5]	1,842,000	1,535	909	2,444	10,078	12,522
	Marines	794,000	13,025	1,680	14,705	88,633	103,338
	Air Force	1,740,000	1,339	603	1,942	3,457	5,399
	Total	**8,744,000**	**46,616**	**10,386**	**57,002**	**303,704**	**360,706**

1. Excludes captured or interned and missing in action who were subsequently returned to military control. 2. Union forces only. Totals should probably be somewhat larger as data or disposition of prisoners are far from complete. Final Confederate deaths, based on incomplete returns, were 133,821, to which should be added 26,000–31,000 personnel who died in Union prisons. 3. Army data include Air Force. 4. As of Sept. 30, 1977. 5. Includes a small number of Coast Guard. NOTE: All data are subject to revision. For wars before World War I, information represents best data from available records. However, due to incomplete records and possible difference in usage of terminology, reporting systems, etc., figures should be considered estimates. n.a. = not available. *Source:* Department of Defense.

NUTRITION AND HEALTH

Recommended Daily Dietary Allowances[1]

Designed for the maintenance of good nutrition of practically all healthy persons in the U.S. (revised 1974)

Vitamins

| | | | | Water-Soluble Vitamins | | | | | | |
Persons	Age (years)	Wgt. (lbs)	Hgt. (in.)	Ascorbic Acid (mg)	Folacin[3] (μg)	Niacin[4] (mg)	Riboflavin (mg)	Thiamin (mg)	Vitamin B_6 (mg)	Vitamin B_{12} (μg)
Infants	0.0–0.5	14	24	35	50	5	0.4	0.3	0.3	0.3
	0.5–1.0	20	28	35	50	8	0.6	0.5	0.4	0.3
Children	1–3	28	34	40	100	9	0.8	0.7	0.6	1.0
	4–6	44	44	40	200	12	1.1	0.9	0.9	1.5
	7–10	66	54	40	300	16	1.2	1.2	1.2	2.0
Males	11–14	97	63	45	400	18	1.5	1.4	1.6	3.0
	15–18	134	69	45	400	20	1.8	1.5	2.0	3.0
	19–22	147	69	45	400	20	1.8	1.5	2.0	3.0
	23–50	154	69	45	400	18	1.6	1.4	2.0	3.0
	51+	154	69	45	400	16	1.5	1.2	2.0	3.0
Females	11–14	97	62	45	400	16	1.3	1.2	1.6	3.0
	15–18	119	65	45	400	14	1.4	1.1	2.0	3.0
	19–22	128	65	45	400	14	1.4	1.1	2.0	3.0
	23–50	128	65	45	400	13	1.2	1.0	2.0	3.0
	51+	128	65	45	400	12	1.1	1.0	2.0	3.0
Pregnant	—	—	—	60	800	+2	+0.3	+0.3	2.5	4.0
Lactating	—	—	—	80	600	+4	+0.5	+0.3	2.5	4.0

				Fat-Soluble Vitamins		
Persons	Age (years)	Wgt. (lbs)	Hgt. (in.)	Vitamin A Activity (IU)	Vitamin D (IU)	Vitamin E Activity[2] (IU)
Infants	0.0–0.5	14	24	1,400	400	4
	0.5–1.0	20	28	2,000	400	5
Children	1–3	28	34	2,000	400	7
	4–6	44	44	2,500	400	9
	7–10	66	54	3,500	400	10
Males	11–14	97	63	5,000	400	12
	15–18	134	69	5,000	400	15
	19–22	147	69	5,000	400	15
	23–50	154	69	5,000	—	15
	51+	154	69	5,000	—	15
Females	11–14	97	62	4,000	400	12
	15–18	119	65	4,000	400	12
	19–22	128	65	4,000	400	12
	23–50	128	65	4,000	—	12
	51+	128	65	4,000	—	12
Pregnant	—	—	—	5,000	400	15
Lactating	—	—	—	6,000	400	15

Minerals

				Minerals					
Persons	Age (years)	Wgt. (lbs)	Hgt. (in.)	Calcium (mg)	Phosphorus (mg)	Iodine (μg)	Iron (mg)	Magnesium (mg)	Zinc (mg)
Infants	0.0–0.5	14	24	360	240	35	10	60	3
	0.5–1.0	20	28	540	400	45	15	70	5
Children	1–3	28	34	800	800	60	15	150	10
	4–6	44	44	800	800	80	10	200	10
	7–10	66	54	800	800	110	10	250	10
Males	11–14	97	63	1,200	1,200	130	18	350	15
	15–18	134	69	1,200	1,200	150	18	400	15
	19–22	147	69	800	800	140	10	350	15
	23–50	154	69	800	800	130	10	350	15
	51+	154	69	800	800	110	10	350	15

Minerals

Persons	Age (years)	Wgt. (lbs)	Hgt. (in.)	Calcium (mg)	Phosphorus (mg)	Iodine (µg)	Iron (mg)	Magnesium (mg)	Zinc (mg)
Females	11–14	97	62	1,200	1,200	115	18	300	15
	15–18	119	65	1,200	1,200	115	18	300	15
	19–22	128	65	800	800	100	18	300	15
	23–50	128	65	800	800	100	18	300	15
	51+	128	65	800	800	80	10	300	15
Pregnant	—	—	—	1,200	1,200	125	18+[5]	450	20
Lactating	—	—	—	1,200	1,200	150	18	450	25

1. Allowances provide for individual variances among most normal persons living in the United States under usual environmental stresses. 2. Total vitamin E activity, estimated to be 80 percent as *a*-tocopherol and 20 percent other tocopherols. 3. Pure forms of folacin may be effective in doses of less than one-fourth. 4. Although expressed as niacin, the average 1 mg. of niacin is derived from each 60 mg. of dietary tryptophan. 5. Cannot be met by ordinary diets; use of supplemental iron is recommended. NOTE: mg—milligram; µ g—microgram; IU—International Units; Lbs—Pounds; Wgt.—Weight; Hgt.—Height. *Source:* Food and Nutrition Board, National Academy of Sciences—National Research Council.

Teen-Agers' Diet

A *Scholastic* magazine survey shows that 42% of U.S. teenagers prefer to make a meal of pizza, 19% choose steak, and 10% like hamburger.

Cigarette Smoking

In 1975, Americans smoked 603 billion cigarettes, 9 billion more than they did in 1974. The Federal Trade Commission reported that in 1975 an average of 11.2 cigarettes a day was produced for every person in the nation over 18 years of age. These figures do not include the number of cigarettes smoked by children *under* 18.

Each American over 18 smoked, on average, 4,095 cigarettes in 1975.

Desirable Weights[1]

Men Age 25 and Over

Height (with shoes on— 1-inch heels) feet	inches	Small frame	Medium frame	Large frame
5	2	112–120	118–129	126–141
5	3	115–123	121–133	129–144
5	4	118–126	124–136	132–148
5	5	121–129	127–139	135–152
5	6	124–133	130–143	138–156
5	7	128–137	134–147	142–161
5	8	132–141	138–152	147–166
5	9	136–145	142–156	151–170
5	10	140–150	146–160	155–174
5	11	144–154	150–165	159–179
6	0	148–158	154–170	164–184
6	1	152–162	158–175	168–189
6	2	156–167	162–180	173–194
6	3	160–171	167–185	178–199
6	4	164–175	172–190	182–204

Women Age 25 and Over[2]

Height (with shoes on— 2-inch heels) feet	inches	Small frame	Medium frame	Large frame
4	10	92–98	96–107	104–119
4	11	94–101	98–110	106–122
5	0	96–104	101–113	109–125
5	1	99–107	104–116	112–128
5	2	102–110	107–119	115–131
5	3	105–113	110–122	118–134
5	4	108–116	113–126	121–138
5	5	111–119	116–130	125–142
5	6	114–123	120–135	129–146
5	7	118–127	124–139	133–150
5	8	122–131	128–143	137–154
5	9	126–135	132–147	141–158
5	10	130–140	136–151	145–163
5	11	134–144	140–155	149–168
6	0	138–148	144–159	153–173

1. Weight in pounds according to frame (in indoor clothing). 2. For girls between 18 and 25, subtract 1 pound for each year under 25. *Source:* Metropolitan Life Insurance Company.

Major Nutrients and Where to Find Them.

Nutrient[1][2]	What they do	Where found
Protein	Keeps body processes working. Carries oxygen into blood stream. Produces antibodies in blood stream that fight off disease and infection. Builds muscle tissue.	Meat, poultry, fish, milk, cheese, eggs, bread, cereal, and vegetables (soybeans, dry beans, and peanuts).
Fats	Provide energy. Some contain vitamins A,D,E, and K. Protect vital organs by providing a cushion around them.	Butter, margarine, shortening, salad oils and dressings, cream, moist cheeses, mayonnaise, nuts, and bacon.
Carbohydrates	Major source of energy. Help body make best use of other nutrients.	Wheat, oats, corn and rice and foods made from them, such as bread and pasta. Potatoes, sweet potatoes, peas, dry beans, peanuts, and soybeans. Dried fruits.
Minerals Calcium	Builds bones and teeth. Aids blood clotting and heart function. Aids nervous system.	Milk and cheese. Dark green leafy vegetables (collards, mustard or turnip greens). Salmon and sardine bones.
Iron	Combines with protein to make hemoglobin. Needed to prevent iron deficiency anemia.	Liver, heart, kidney, shellfish (especially oysters). Enriched bread and cereals. Dark leafy green vegetables.

Iodine	Assists thyroid gland function. Prevents goiter.	Iodized salt and seafood.
Vitamins		
Vitamin A (retinol)	Needed for normal vision. Protects against night blindness. Keeps skin and mucous membranes resistant to infection.	Spinach, beet and turnip greens, carrots, squash, sweet potatoes. Yellow peaches, apricots, cantaloupe, and papayas also help. Liver and whole milk.
Vitamin B_1 (thiamin)	Promotes normal appetite and digestion. Necessary for a healthy nervous system.	Lean pork, dry beans, some of the organ meats, some nuts. Enriched or whole-grain breads and cereals. Meats, milk, whole grain or enriched breads and cereals: Green leafy vegetables.
Vitamin B_2 (riboflavin)	Helps cells use oxygen. Helps maintain good vision. Needed for good skin.	
Vitamin B_6 and B_{12}, Folacin	Maintain normal hemoglobin (carry oxygen to tissues).	Occur in foods of animal origin, brown rice, bananas, pears.
Vitamin C (ascorbic acid)	Maintains cementing material that holds body cells together. Needed for healthy gums. Aids body to resist infection.	Citrus fruits and juices, potatoes, sweet potatoes, tomatoes, peppers, green vegetables (broccoli, turnip greens, raw cabbage, and collards.)
Vitamin D	Builds strong bones and teeth. Aids calcium absorption.	Milk fortified with vitamin D, egg yolk, fish liver, liver, oils. Sunlight.
Vitamin E	Not fully understood.	Abundant in vegetable oils and margarines. Wheat germ and lettuce.
Vitamin K	Aids blood clotting.	Green and leafy vegetables, tomatoes, cauliflower, egg yolks, soybean oil, and liver.

1. The body also requires zinc, copper, sodium, potassium, magnesium and phosphorus. These show up in most foods of the above. Magnesium abounds in nuts, whole grain products, dry beans and dark green vegetables. Phosphorus is in the same foods that supply you with protein and calcium. 2. The B-Vitamins should be taken together because an inadequate intake of one may impair the utilization of the other. *Source:* Department of Agriculture, Science and Education Administration.

Calories, Minerals, and Vitamins of Selected Foods

Food and amount	Energy (calories)	Nutrients		Minerals		A (IU)	Vitamins			C ascorbic acid (mg)
		Protein (gm)	Fat (gm)	Calcium (mg)	Iron (mg)		B₁ thiamin (mg)	B₂ riboflavin (mg)	Niacin (mg)	
Apple, 1 medium, raw	80	—	1	10	.4	120	.04	.03	.1	6
Applesauce, 1 cup, canned, unsweetened	100	—	—	10	1.2	100	.05	.02	.1	2
Bacon, 2 slices, crisp	85	4	8	2	.5	—	.08	.05	.8	—
Banana, 1 medium	100	1	—	10	.8	230	.06	.07	.8	12
Beans, snap green, 1 cup cooked	30	2	—	63	.8	680	.09	.11	.6	15
Beans, red kidney, 1 cup canned	230	15	1	74	4.6	10	.13	.10	1.5	—
Beans, baked, pork and molasses, 1 cup	385	16	12	161	5.9	—	.15	.10	1.3	—
Beef cuts, cooked: Chuck, boned, 3 ounces	245	23	16	10	2.9	30	.04	.18	3.6	—
Hamburger, 3 ounces	235	20	17	9	2.6	30	.07	.17	4.4	—
Rib roast, 3 ounces boned	375	17	33	8	2.2	70	.05	.13	3.1	—
Round, 3 ounces boned	220	24	12	10	3.0	20	.07	.19	4.8	—
Sirloin, 3 ounces boned	330	20	27	9	2.5	50	.05	.15	4.0	—
Beef stew with vegetables, 1 cup	220	16	11	29	2.9	2,400	.15	.17	4.7	17
Beets, 1 cup cooked	55	2	—	24	.9	30	.05	.07	.5	10
Breads: Cracked wheat, ½-inch slice	65	2	1	22	.5	—	.08	.06	.8	—
Italian, average slice, enriched	85	3	—	5	.7	—	.12	.07	1.0	—
Raisin, ½-inch slice, enriched	65	2	1	18	.6	—	.09	.06	.6	—
Rye (American), ½-inch slice	60	2	—	19	.5	—	.07	.05	.7	—
White, ½-inch slice enriched	70	2	1	21	.6	—	.10	.06	.8	—
Whole wheat, ½-inch slice	65	3	1	24	.8	—	.09	.03	.8	—

Food	Calories	Protein (g)	Fat (g)	Calcium (mg)	Iron (mg)	Vitamin A (I.U.)	Thiamine (mg)	Riboflavin (mg)	Niacin (mg)	Ascorbic Acid (mg)
Butter, 1 tbsp.	100	—	12	3	—	430	—	—	—	—
Cabbage, 1 cup, raw, coarsely shredded	15	1	—	34	.3	90	.04	.04	.2	33
Cake: Sponge, average slice	195	5	4	20	1.1	300	.09	.14	.6	—
Pound, average slice	160	2	10	6	.5	80	.05	.06	.4	—
Candies: Caramels, 1 ounce	115	1	3	42	.4	—	.01	.05	.1	—
Chocolate, milk, 1 ounce	145	2	9	65	.3	80	.02	.10	.1	—
Cantaloup, ½ melon	80	2	—	38	1.1	9,240	.11	.08	1.6	90
Carrot, raw, 1 average size	30	1	—	27	.5	7,930	.04	.04	.4	6
Catsup, 1 tbsp.	15	—	—	3	.1	210	.01	.01	.2	2
Cheese: Cheddar, 1 ounce	115	7	9	204	.2	300	.01	.11	—	—
Cottage, creamed, 1 cup	235	28	10	135	.3	370	.05	.37	.3	—
Cottage, uncreamed, 1 cup	125	25	1	46	.3	40	.04	.21	.2	—
Cream cheese, 1 ounce	100	2	10	23	.3	400	—	.06	—	—
Swiss, natural, 1 ounce	105	8	8	272	—	240	.01	.10	—	—
Swiss, process, 1 ounce	95	7	7	219	.2	230	—	.08	—	—
Chicken, broiled, 3 ounces	115	20	3	8	1.4	80	.05	.16	7.4	—
Chicken, fried, ½ breast, 3.3 ounces	160	26	5	9	1.3	70	.04	.17	11.6	—
Chicken, canned, boned, 3 ounces	170	18	10	18	1.3	200	.03	.11	3.7	3
Clams, raw, 3 ounces	65	11	1	59	5.2	90	.08	.15	1.1	8
Cocoa, 1 cup, homemade	220	9	9	298	.8	320	.10	.44	.4	2
Coffee; black, 1 cup	—	—	—	—	—	—	—	—	—	—
Cola, carbonated, 12 ounces	145	—	—	—	—	—	—	—	—	—
Corn, average ear	70	2	1	2	.5	310	.09	.08	1.1	7
Corn flakes, 1 cup	95	2	—	3	.6	1,180	.29	.35	2.9	9
Crabmeat, canned, 3 ounces	85	15	2	38	.7	—	.07	.07	1.6	—
Crackers, Graham, 4	110	2	3	11	1.0	—	.04	.16	1.0	—
Saltines, 4	50	1	1	2	.5	—	.05	.05	.4	—

Food and amount	Energy (calories)	Protein (gm)	Fat (gm)	Calcium (mg)	Iron (mg)	A (IU)	B_1 thiamin (mg)	B_2 riboflabin (mg)	Niacin (mg)	C ascorbic acid (mg)
Cream: Light, table, 1 cup	470	6	46	231	.1	1,730	.08	.36	.1	2
Heavy, whipping, 1 cup	820	5	88	154	.1	3,500	.05	.26	.1	1
Sour, 1 cup	495	7	48	268	.1	1,820	.08	.34	.2	2
Whipped topping (pressurized), 1 cup	155	2	13	61	—	550	.02	.04	—	—
Doughnut, 1 plain	100	1	5	10	.4	20	.05	.05	.4	—
Egg: Raw or cooked in shell, 1	80	6	6	28	1.0	260	.04	.14	—	—
Omelet, scrambled, 1	95	6	7	47	.9	310	.04	.16	—	—
Frankfurter, 1	170	7	15	3	.8	—	.08	.11	1.4	—
Fruit cocktail, 1 cup canned	195	1	—	23	1.0	360	.05	.03	1.0	5
Grapefruit: Raw, ½	45	1	—	19	.5	10	.05	.02	.2	44
Canned, syrup, 1 cup	180	2	—	33	.8	30	.08	.05	.5	76
Juice, fresh, 1 cup	95	1	—	22	.5	20	.10	.05	.5	93
Haddock, breaded, fried, 3 ounces	140	17	5	34	1.0	—	.03	.06	2.7	2
Honey, strained, 1 tbsp.	65	—	—	1	.1	—	—	.01	.1	—
Ice cream, 1 cup	270	5	14	176	.1	540	.05	.33	.1	1
Jellies, 1 tbsp.	50	—	—	4	.3	—	—	.01	—	1
Lamb: Rib chop, boned, 4 ounces	400	25	33	10	1.5	—	.14	.25	5.6	—
Leg roast, 3 ounces, boned	235	22	16	9	1.4	—	.13	.23	4.7	—
Lemon, 1 medium	20	1	—	19	.4	10	.03	.01	.1	39
Liver: Beef, fried, 2 ounces	130	15	6	6	5.0	30,280	.15	2.37	9.4	15
Luncheon meat: Boiled ham, 2 ounces	135	11	10	6	1.6	—	.25	.09	1.5	—
Canned, spiced or unspiced, 2 ounces	165	8	14	5	1.2	—	.18	.12	1.6	—
Macaroni, enriched, 1 cup	155	5	1	11	1.3	—	.20	.11	1.5	—
Macaroni and cheese, 1 cup	430	17	22	362	1.8	860	.20	.40	1.8	—
Margarine, 1 tbsp.	100	—	12	3	—	470	—	—	—	—

Food										
Mayonnaise, 1 tbsp.	100		11	3		40		.01		
Milk: Whole, 1 cup	150	8	8	291	.1	310	.09	.40	.2	2
Skim (non-fat), 1 cup	85	8		302	.1	500	.09	.34	.2	2
Buttermilk, 1 cup	100	8	2	285	.1	80	.08	.38	.1	2
Mushrooms, canned, 1 cup	40	5		15	1.2		.04	.60	4.8	4
Nuts: Almonds, 1 cup shelled	850	26	77	332	6.7		.34	1.31	5.0	
Peanuts, roasted, 1 cup	840	37	72	107	3.0		.46	.19	24.8	
Oatmeal, 1 cup cooked	130	5	2	22	1.4		.19	.05	.2	
Oils, salad, cooking, 1 tbsp.	120		14							
Orange, 1 medium	65	1		54	.5	260	.13	.05	.5	66
Orange juice, fresh, 1 cup	110	2		27	.5	500	.22	.07	1.0	124
Frozen, diluted with 3 parts water, 1 cup	120	2		25	.2	540	.23	.03	.9	120
Oysters, raw, 1 cup	160	20	4	226	13.2	740	.34	.43	6.0	
Pancake, wheat, 1 average	60	2	2	27	.4	30	.06	.07	.5	
Peach, raw, 1 medium	40	1		9	.5	1,330	.02	.05	1.0	7
Peanut butter, 1 tbsp.	95	4	8	9	.3		.02	.02	2.4	
Peas, green, 1 cup	115	9	1	37	2.9	860	.45	.18	3.7	32
Pie: Apple, 4-inch wedge	345	3	15	11	.9	40	.15	.11	1.3	2
Cherry, 4-inch wedge	350	4	15	19	.9	590	.16	.12	1.4	
Lemon meringue, 4-inch wedge	305	4	12	17	1.0	200	.09	.12	.7	4
Pineapple, raw, 1 cup diced	80			26	.8	110	.14	.05	.3	26
Pineapple juice, canned, 1 cup	140	1		38	.8	130	.13	.05	.5	23
Pizza (cheese), 4¾-inch wedge	145	6	4	86	1.1	230	.16	.18	1.6	4
Pork: Roast, 3 ounces	310	21	24	9	2.7		.78	.22	4.8	
Chop, with bone, 2.7 ounces	305	19	25	9	2.7		.75	.22	4.5	
Potatoes: Baked, 1 medium	145	4		14	1.1		.15	.07	2.7	31
French fried, deep fat, 10 pieces	135	2	7	8	.7		.07	.04	1.6	11

Food and amount	Energy (calories)	Protein (gm)	Fat (gm)	Calcium (mg)	Iron (mg)	A (IU)	B₁ thiamin (mg)	B₂ riboflavin (mg)	Niacin (mg)	C ascorbic acid (mg)
		Nutrients		Minerals			Vitamins			
Mashed with milk, 1 cup	135	4	2	50	.8	40	.17	.11	2.1	21
Potato chips, 10	115	1	8	8	.4	—	.04	.01	1.0	3
Prune juice, 1 cup canned	195	1	—	36	1.8	—	.03	.03	1.0	5
Rice: White, enriched, 1 cup cooked	225	4	—	21	1.8	—	.23	.02	2.1	—
Puffed, 1 cup	60	1	—	3	.3	—	.07	.01	.7	—
Salad dressings: Mayonnaise type, 1 tbsp.	65	—	6	2	.1	30	—	—	—	—
French, 1 tbsp.	65	—	6	2	.1	—	—	—	—	—
French, low calorie, 1 tbsp.	15	—	1	2	.1	—	—	—	—	—
Salmon: Canned, 3-ounces	120	17	5	167	.7	60	.03	.16	6.8	—
Sardines, canned, 3 ounces	175	20	9	372	2.5	190	.02	.17	4.6	—
Spaghetti, 1 cup cooked	155	5	1	11	1.3	—	.20	.11	1.5	—
Spinach, 1 cup cooked	40	5	1	167	4.0	14,580	.13	.25	.9	50
Sugar, 1 teaspoon	15	—	—	—	—	—	—	—	—	—
Tomato juice, canned, 1 cup	45	2	—	17	2.2	1,940	.12	.07	1.9	39
Tuna fish, 3 ounces	170	24	7	7	1.6	70	.04	.10	10.1	—
Veal, 3-ounce cutlet	185	23	9	9	2.7	—	.06	.21	4.6	—
Yogurt, from lowfat milk, 8-oz. container, plain	145	12	4	415	.2	150	.10	.49	.3	2

NOTE: Gm—gram; Mg—milligram; IU—International Unit. A dash in a column indicates little or no basis for assigning value. *Source:* Department of Agriculture, Science and Education Administration.

The Orthodox, Catholic, Apostolic Church is the direct descendant of the Byzantine State Church and consists of a series of independent national churches that are united by Doctrine, Liturgy, and Hierarchical organization (deacons and priests, who may either be married or be monks before ordination, and bishops, who must be celebates). The heads of these Churches are patriarchs or metropolitans; the Patriarch of Constantinople is only "first among equals." Rivalry between the Pope of Rome and the Patriarch of Constantinople, aided by differences and misunderstandings that existed for centuries between the Eastern and Western parts of the Empire, led to a schism in 1054. Repeated attempts at reunion have failed in past centuries. The mutual excommunication pronounced in that year was lifted in 1965, however, and because of greater interaction in theology between Orthodox Churches and those in the West, a climate of better understanding has been created in the 20th century. First contacts were with Anglicans and Old Catholics. Orthodox Churches belong to the World Council of Churches.

The Eastern Orthodox Churches recognize only the canons of the seven Ecumenical Councils (325–787) as binding for faith and they reject doctrines that have been added in the West.

The central worship service is called the Liturgy, which is understood as representation of God's acts of salvation. Its center is the celebration of the Eucharist, or Lord's Supper.

In their worship *icons* (sacred pictures) are used that have a sacramental meaning as representation. The Mother of Christ, angels, and saints are highly venerated.

The number of sacraments in the Orthodox Church is the same as in the Western Catholic Church.

Orthodox Churches are found in the Balkans and the Soviet Union also, since the 20th century, in Western Europe and other parts of the world, particularly in America.

Eastern Orthodoxy also includes the Uniate Churches that recognize the authority of the Pope but keep their own traditional liturgies and those Churches dating back to the 5th century that emancipated themselves from the Byzantine State Church: the Nestorian Church in the Near East and India with approximately half a million members and the Monophysite Churches with some 17 million members (Coptic, Ethiopian, Syrian, Armenian, and the Mar Thoma Church in India).

Roman Catholicism

Roman Catholicism comprises the belief and practice of the Roman Catholic Church. The Church stands under the authority of the Bishop of Rome, the Pope, and is ruled by him and bishops who are held to be, through ordination, successors of Peter and the Apostles, respectively. Fundamental to the structure of the Church is the juridical aspect: doctrine and sacraments are bound to the power of jurisdiction and consecration of the hierarchy. The Pope, as the head of the hierarchy of archbishops, bishops, priests, and deacons, has full ecclesiastical power, granted him by Christ, through Peter. As successor to Peter, he is the Vicar of Christ. The powers that others in the hierarchy possess are delegated.

Roman Catholics believe their Church to be the one, holy, catholic, and apostolic Church, possessing all the properties of the one, true Church of Christ.

The faith of the Church is understood to be identical with that taught by Christ and his Apostles and contained in Bible and Tradition, i.e. the original deposit of faith, to which nothing new may be added. New definitions of doctrines, such as the Immaculate Conception of Mary (1854) and the bodily Assumption of Mary (1950), have been declared by Popes, however, in accordance with the principle of development (implicit-explicit doctrine).

At Vatican Council I (1870) the Pope was proclaimed "endowed with infallibility, *et cathedra*, i.e., when exercising the office of Pastor and Teacher of all Christians."

The center of Roman Catholic worship is the Sacrament of the Mass, which is the commemoration of Christ's sacrificial death and of his resurrection. Other sacraments are Baptism, Confirmation, Confession, Matrimony, Ordination, and Extreme Unction, seven in all. The Virgin Mary and saints, and their relics, are highly venerated and prayers are made to them to intercede with God, in whose presence they are believed to dwell.

The Roman Catholic Church is the largest Christian organization in the world, found in most countries. Some 8 million belong to the Uniate rites, the vast majority to the Latin rite.

Since Vatican Council II (1962–65), and the effort to "update" the Church, many interesting changes and developments have been taking place.

Protestantism

Protestantism comprises the Christian churches that separated from Rome during the Reformation in the 16th century, initiated by an Augustinian monk, Martin Luther. "Protestant" was originally applied to followers of Luther, who protested at the Diet of Spires (1529) against the decree which prohibited all further ecclesiastical reforms. Subsequently, Protestantism came to mean rejection of attempts to tie God's revelation to earthly institutions, and a return to the Gospel and the Word of God as sole authority in matters of faith and practice. Central in the biblical message is the justification of the sinner by faith alone. The Church is understood as a fellowship and the priesthood of all believers stressed.

The Augsburg Confession (1530) was the principal statement of Lutheran faith and practice. It became a model for other Confessions of Faith, which in their turn had decisive influence on Church polity. Major Protestant denominations are the Lutheran, Reformed (Calvinist), Presbyterian, and Anglican (Episcopal). Smaller ones are the Mennonite. Schwenkfeldians, and Unitarians. In Great Britain and America there are the Congregationalists, Baptists, Quakers, Methodists, and other free church types of communities. (In regarding themselves as being faithful to original biblical Christianity, these Churches differ from such religious bodies as Unitarians, Mormons, Jehovah's Witnesses, and Christian Scientists, who either teach new doctrines or reject old ones.)

Since the latter part of the 19th century, national councils of churches have been established in many countries, e.g. the Federal Council of Churches of Christ in America in 1908. Denominations across countries joined in federations and world alliances, beginning with the Anglican Lambeth Conference in 1867.

Protestant missionary activity, particularly strong in the last century, resulted in the founding of many younger churches in Asia and Africa. The Ecumenical Movement, which originated with Protestant missions, aims at unity among Christians and churches.

Islam

Islam is the religion founded in Arabia by Mohammed between 610 and 632. Its 400 million adherents are found in countries stretching from Morocco in the West to Indonesia in the East.

Mohammed was born in A.D. 570 at Mecca and belonged to the Quraysh tribe, which was active in caravan trade. At the age of 25 he joined the caravan trade from Mecca to Syria in the employment of a rich widow, Khadiji, whom he married. Critical of the idolatry of the inhabitants of Mecca, he began to lead a contemplative life in the deserts. There he received a series of revelations. Encouraged by Khadiji, he gradually became convinced that he was given a God-appointed task to devote himself to the reform of religion and society. Idolatry was to be abandoned.

The *Hegira (Hijra)* (migration) of Mohammed from Mecca, where he was not honored, to Medina, where he was well received, occurred in 622 and marks the beginning of the Muslim era. In 630 he marched on Mecca and conquered it. He died at Medina in 632. His grave there has since been a place of pilgrimage.

Mohammed's followers, called Moslems, revered him as the prophet of *Allah* (God), beside whom there is no other God. Although he had no close knowledge of Judaism and Christianity, he considered himself succeeding and completing them as the seal of the Prophets. Sources of the Islamic faith are the *Qur'an,* regarded as the uncreated, eternal Word of God, and Tradition *(hadith)* regarding sayings and deeds of the prophet.

Islam means surrender to the will of *Allah.* He is the all-powerful, whose will is supreme and determines man's fate. Good and evil deeds will be rewarded at the Last Judgment in paradise or in hell.

The Five Pillars, primary duties, of Islam are: witness; confessing the oneness of God and of Mohammed, his prophet; prayer, to be performed five times a day; almsgiving to the poor and the mosque (house of worship); fasting during daylight hours in the month of Ramadan; and pilgrimage to Mecca at least once in the Moslem's lifetime.

The practice of Holy War *(jihad),* at first responsible for the rapid growth of the new religion, could not be maintained. Mohammed curtailed the practice of polygamy by limiting it to four wives. In modern times the position of women has improved, due to Western influence. The eating of pork and drinking of intoxicants is forbidden.

Islam, upholding the law of brotherhood, succeeded in uniting an Arab world that had disintegrated into tribes and castes. Disagreements concerning the succession of the prophet caused a great division in Islam between *Sunnis* and *Shias*. Among these, other sects arose *(Wahhabi)*. Doctrinal issues also led to the rise of different schools of thought in theology. Nevertheless, since Arab armies turned against Syria and Palestine in 635, Islam has expanded successfully under Mohammed's successors. Its rapid victorious conquests in Asia and Africa are unsurpassed in history. Turning against Europe, Moslems conquered Spain in 713. In 1453 Constantinople fell into their hands and in 1529 Moslem armies besieged Vienna. Since then, Islam has lost its foothold in Europe.

In modern times it has made great gains in Africa.

Hinduism

In India alone there are more than 300 million adherents of Hinduism. In contrast to other religions, it has no founder. Considered the oldest religion in the world, it dates back, perhaps, to prehistoric times.

Hinduism is hard to define, there being no common creed, no one doctrine to bind Hindus together. Intellectually there is complete freedom of belief, and one can be monotheist, polytheist, or atheist. What matters is the social system: a Hindu is one born into a caste.

As a religion, Hinduism is founded on the sacred scriptures, written in Sanskrit and called the *Vedas* (*Veda*-knowledge). There are four Vedic books, among which the *Rig Veda* is the most important. It speaks of many gods and also deals with questions concerning the universe and creation. The dates of these works are unknown (1000 B.C.?).

The *Upanishads* (dated 1000–300 B.C.), commentaries on the Vedic texts, have philosophical speculations on the origin of the universe, the nature of deity, of *atman* (the human soul), and its relationship to *Brahman* (the universal soul).

Brahman is the principle and source of the universe who can be indicated only by negatives. As the divine intelligence, he is the ground of the visible world, a presence that pervades all beings. Thus the many Hindu deities came to be understood as manifestations of the one *Brahman* from whom everything proceeds and to whom everything ultimately returns. The religio-social system of Hinduism is based on the concept of reincarnation and transmigration in which all living beings, from plants below to gods above, are caught in a cosmic system that is an everlasting cycle of becoming and perishing.

Life is determined by the law of *karma,* according to which rebirth is dependent on moral behavior in a previous phase of existence. The doctrine of transmigration thus provides a rationale for the caste system. In this view, life on earth is regarded as transient *(maya)* and a burden. The goal of existence is liberation from the cycle of rebirth and redeath and entrance into the indescribable state of what in Buddhism is called *nirvana* (extinction of passion).

Further important sacred writings are the Epics *(puranas),* which contain legendary stories about gods and men. They are the *Mahabharata* (composed between 200 B.C. and A.D. 200) and the *Ramayana.* The former includes the *Bhagavad-Gita* (Song of the Lord), its most famous part, that tells of devotion to *Krishna* (Lord), who appears as an *avatar* (incarnation) of the god *Vishnu,* and of the duty of obeying caste rules. The work begins with a praise of the *yoga* (discipline) system.

The practice of Hinduism consists of rites and ceremonies, performed within the framework of the caste system and centering on the main socio-religious occasions of birth, marriage, and death. There are many Hindu temples, which are dwelling places of the deities and to which people bring offerings. There are also places of pilgrimages, the chief one being Benares on the Ganges, most sacred among the rivers in India.

In modern times work has been done to reform and revive Hinduism. One of the outstanding reformers was Ramakrishna (1836-86), who inspired many followers, one of whom founded the Ramakrishna mission, which seeks to convert others to its religion. The mission is active both in India and in other countries.

Buddhism

Founded in the 6th century B.C. in northern India by Gautama Buddha, who was born in southern Nepal as son to a king. His birth is surrounded by many legends, but Western scholars agree that he lived from 563–483 B.C. Warned by a sage that his son would become an ascetic or a universal monarch, the king confined him to his home.

He was able to escape and began the life of a homeless wanderer in search of peace, passing through many disappointments until he finally came to the Tree of Enlightenment, under which he lived in meditation till enlightenment came to him and he became a Buddha (enlightened one).

Now he understood the origin of suffering, summarized in the *Four Noble Truths,* which constitutes the foundation of Buddhism. The Four are the truth of suffering, which all living beings must endure; of the origin of suffering, which is craving and which leads to rebirth; that it can be destroyed; and of the way that leads to cessation of pain, i.e., the *Noble Eightfold Way,* which is the rule of practical Buddhism: right views, right intention, right speech, right action, right livelihood, right effort, right concentration, and right ecstasy.

Nirvana is the goal of all existence, the state of complete redemption, into which the redeemed enters. Buddha's insight can free every man from the law of reincarnation through complete emptying of the self.

The nucleus of Buddha's church or association was originally formed by monks and lay-brothers, whose houses gradually became monasteries used as places for religious instruction. The worship service consisted of a sermon, expounding of Scripture, meditation, and confession. At a later stage pilgrimages to the holy places associated with the Buddha came into being, as well as veneration of relics.

In the 3rd century B.C., King Ashoka made Buddhism the State religion of India but, as centuries passed, it gradually fell into decay through splits, persecutions, and the hostile Brahmans. Buddhism spread to countries outside India, however.

At the beginning of the Christian era, there occurred a split that gave rise to two main types: *Hinayana* (Little Vehicle), or southern Buddhism, and *Mahayana* (Great Vehicle), or northern Buddhism. The former type, more individualistic, survived in Ceylon and southern Asia. Hinayana retained more closely the original teachings of the Buddha, which did not know of a personal god or soul. *Mahayana,* more social, polytheistic, and developing a pluralistic pompous cult, was strong in the Himalayas, Tibet, Mongolia, China, Korea, and Japan.

In the present century, Buddhism has found believers

also in the West and Buddhist associations have been established in Europe and the U. S.

Confucianism

Confucius (K'ung Fu-tzu), born in the state of Lu (northern China), lived from 551–479 B.C. Tradition, exaggerating the importance of Confucius in life, has depicted him as a great statesman but, in fact, he seems to have been a private teacher. Anthologies of ancient Chinese classics, along with his own Analects *(Lun Yu),* became the basis of Confucianism. These Analects were transmitted as a collection of his sayings as recorded by his students, with whom he discussed ethical and social problems. They developed into men of high moral standing, who served the State as administrators.

In his teachings, Confucius emphasized the importance of an old Chinese concept *(li)* , which has the connotation of proper conduct. There is some disagreement as to the religious ideas of Confucius, but he held high the concepts handed down from centuries before him. Thus he believed in Heaven *(T'ien)* and sacrificed to his ancestors. Ancestor worship he indeed encouraged as an expression of filial piety, which he considered the loftiest of virtues.

Piety to Confucius was the foundation of the family as well as the State. The family is the nucleus of the State, and the "five relations," between king and subject, father and son, man and wife, older and younger brother, and friend and friend, are determined by the virtues of love of fellow men, righteousness, and respect.

An extension of ancestor worship may be seen in the worship of Confucius, which became official in the 2nd century B.C. when the emperor, in recognition of Confucius' teachings, as supporting the imperial rule, offered sacrifices at his tomb.

Mencius (Meng Tse), who lived around 400 B.C., did much to propagate and elaborate Confucianism in its concern with ordering society. Thus, for two millennia, Confucius' doctrine of State, with its emphasis on ethics and social morality, rooted in ancient Chinese tradition and developed and continued by his disciples, has been standard in China and the Far East.

With the revolution of 1911 in China, however, students, burning Confucius in effigy, called for the removel of "the old curiosity shop."

Shintoism

Shinto, the Chinese term for the Japanese *Kami no Michi*, i.e., the Way of the Gods, comprises the religious ideas and cult indigenous to Japan. *Kami*, or gods, considered divine forces of nature that are worshipped, may reside in rivers, trees, rocks, mountains, certain animals, or, particularly, in the sun and moon. The worship of ancestors, heroes, and deceased emperors was incorporated later.

After Buddhism had come from Korea, Japan's native religion at first resisted it. Then there followed a period of compromise and amalgamation with Buddhist beliefs and ceremonies, resulting, since the 9th century A.D., in a syncretistic religion, a Twofold Shinto. Buddhist deities came to be regarded as manifestations of Japanese deities and Buddhist priests took over most of the Shinto shrines.

In modern times Shinto regained independence from Buddhism. Under the reign of the Emperor Meiji (1868–1912) it became the official State religion, in which loyalty to the emperor was emphasized. The line of succession of emperors is traced back to the first Emperor Jimmu (660 B.C.) and beyond him to the Sun-goddess *Amaterasuomikami*.

The centers of worship are the shrines and temples in which the deities are believed to dwell and believers approach them through *torii* (gateways). Most important among the shrines is the imperial shrine of the Sun-goddess at Ise, where state ceremonies were once held in June and December. The *Yasukuni* shrine of the war dead in Tokyo is also well known.

Acts of worship consist of prayers, clapping of hands, acts of purification, and offerings. On feast days processions and performances of music and dancing take place and priests read prayers before the gods in the shrines, asking for good harvest, the well-being of people and emperor, etc. In Japanese homes there is a god-shelf, a small wooden shrine that contains the tablets bearing the names of ancestors. Offerings are made and candles lit before it.

After World War II the Allied Command ordered the disestablishment of State Shinto. To be distinguished from State Shinto is Sect Shinto, consisting of 13 recognized sects. These have arisen in modern times, gaining large followings. Most important among them is *Tenrikyo* in Tenri City (Nara), in which healing by faith plays a central role.

Taoism

Taoism, a religion of China, was, according to tradition, founded by Lao Tse, a Chinese philosopher, long considered one of the prominent religious leaders from the 6th century B.C.

Data about him are for the most part legendary, however, and the *Tao Te Ching* (the classic of the Way and of its Power), traditionally ascribed to him, is now believed by many scholars to have originated in the 3rd century B.C. The book is composed in short chapters, written in aphoristic rhymes. Central are the word *Tao,* which means way or path and, in a deeper sense, signifies the principle that underlies the reality of this world and manifests itself in nature and in the lives of men, and the word *Te* (power).

The virtuous man draws power from being absorbed in *Tao,* the ultimate reality within an everchanging world. By non-action and keeping away from human striving it is possible for man to live in harmony with the principles that underlie and govern the universe. *Tao* cannot be comprehended by reason and knowledge, but only by inward quiet.

Besides the *Tao Te Ching,* dating from approximately the same period, are two Taoist works, written by Chuang Tse and Lieh Tse.

Theoretical Taoism of this classical philosophical movement of the 4th and 3rd centuries B.C. in China differed from popular Taoism, into which it gradually degenerated. The standard of theoretical Taoism was maintained in the classics, of course, and among the upper classes it continued to be alive until modern times.

Religious Taoism is a form of religion dealing with deities and spirits, magic and soothsaying. In the 2nd century A.D. it was organized with temples, cult, priests, and monasteries and was able to hold its own in the competition with Buddhism that came up at the same time.

After the 7th century A.D., however, Taoist religion further declined. Split into numerous sects which often operate like secret societies, it has become a syncretistic folk religion in which some of the old deities and saints live on.

Estimated Membership of the Principal Religions of the World

Statistics of the world's religions are only very rough approximations. Aside from Christianity, few religions, if any, attempt to keep statistical records; and even Protestants and Catholics employ different methods of counting members. All persons of whatever age who have received baptism in the Catholic Church are counted as members, while in most Protestant Churches only those who "join" the church are numbered. The compiling of statistics is further complicated by the fact that in China one may be at the same time a Confucian, a Taoist, and a Buddhist. In Japan, one may be both a Buddhist and a Shintoist.

Religion	North America[1]	South America	Europe	Asia	Africa	Oceania[2]	Total
Total Christian	231,099,700	158,980,000	348,059,300	89,909,000	137,460,300	18,112,600	983,620,900
Roman Catholic	131,631,500	147,280,000	182,514,300	47,046,000	53,740,000	4,475,000	566,686,800
Eastern Orthodox	4,189,000	552,000	50,545,000	1,894,000	15,255,000	380,000	72,815,000
Protestant	95,279,200	11,148,000	115,000,000	40,969,000	68,465,300	13,257,600	344,119,100
Jewish[3]	6,641,118	727,000	4,082,400	3,203,460	294,400	84,000	15,032,378
Moslem	249,200	238,300	8,283,500	433,001,000	134,285,200	103,000	576,160,200
Zoroastrian	250	2,000	6,000	224,700	600	—	233,550
Shinto	60,000	92,000	—	55,004,000	—	—	55,156,000
Taoist	16,000	12,000	—	31,088,100	—	—	31,116,100
Confucian	96,100	85,150	25,000	173,940,250	500	42,200	174,189,200
Buddhist	155,250	195,300	200,000	260,117,000	2,000	16,000	260,685,550
Hindu	81,000	782,300	260,000	515,449,500	483,650	841,000	517,897,450
Total	238,398,618	161,114,050	360,916,200	1,561,937,010	272,526,650	19,198,800	2,614,091,328

1. Includes Central America and West Indies. 2. Includes Australia and New Zealand, as well as islands of the South Pacific. 3. Includes total Jewish population, whether or not related to the synagogue. NOTE: Because of war and persecution, there are about 18,000,000 refugees throughout the world who are not integrated into religious statistics of land of their temporary residence. Source: Britannica Book of the Year, 1978.

SCIENCE

Scientific Inventions, Discoveries, and Theories

Most inventions are the results of the discoveries, theories, experiments, and improvements of many people. This list tries to suggest the development of certain particularly important ideas. In some instances, it tries to connect the fundamental theory with the ultimate practical invention.

Abacus: *See* Calculating machine
Adding machine: *See* Calculating machine; Computer
Adrenaline: (isolation of) Jokichi Takamine, U.S., 1901
Air brake: George Westinghouse, U.S., 1868
Air conditioning: Willis Carrier, U.S., 1911
Airplane: (first powered, sustained, controlled flight) Orville and Wilbur Wright, U.S., 1903. *See also* Jet propulsion, aircraft
Airship: (non-rigid) Henri Giffard, France, 1852; (rigid) Ferdinand von Zeppelin, Germany, 1900
Aluminum manufacture: (by electrolytic action) Charles M. Hall, U.S., 1866
Anesthetic: (first use of anesthetic—ether—on man) Crawford W. Long, U.S., 1842
Antibiotics: (first demonstration of antibiotic effect) Louis Pasteur, Jules-François Joubert, France, 1887; (penicillin, first modern antibiotic) Alexander Fleming, England, 1928
Antiseptic: (surgery) Joseph Lister, England, 1867
Antitoxin, diphtheria: Emil von Behring, Germany, 1890
Atomic theory: (ancient) Leucippus, Democritus, Greece, c.500 B.C.; Lucretius, Rome, c.100 B.C.; (modern) John Dalton, England, 1808
Automobile: (first with internal combustion engine, 250 rpm) Karl Benz, Germany, 1885; (first with practical high-speed internal combustion engine, 900 rpm) Gottlieb Daimler, Germany, 1885; (first true automobile, not carriage with motor) René Panhard, Emile Lavassor, France, 1891; (carburator, spray) Charles E. Duryea, U.S., 1892

Bacteria: Anton van Leeuwenhoek, The Netherlands, 1683

Bakelite: *See* Plastics

Balloon, hot-air: Joseph and Jacques Montgolfier, France, 1783

Ball-point pen: *See* Pen

Barometer: Evangelista Torricelli, Italy, 1643

Bicycle: Karl D. von Sauerbronn, Germany, 1816; (first modern model) James Starley, England, 1884

Bifocal lens: *See* Lens, bifocal

Blood, circulation of: William Harvey, England, 1628

Braille: Louis Braille, France, 1829

Bullet: (conical) Claude Minié, France, 1849

Calculating machine: (Abacus) China, c.190; (logarithms: made multiplying easier and thus calculators practical) John Napier, Scotland, 1614; (slide rule) William Oughtred, England, 1632; (digital calculator) Blaise Pascal, 1642; (multiplication machine) Gottfried Leibnitz, Germany, 1671; (important 19th-century contributors to modern machine) Frank S. Baldwin, Jay R. Monroe, Dorr E. Felt, W. T. Ohdner, William Burroughs, all U.S.; ("analytical engine" design, included concepts of programming, taping) Charles Babbage, England, 1835. *See also* Computer

Camera: (hand-held) George Eastman, U.S., 1888; (Polaroid Land) Edwin Land, U.S., 1948. *See also* Photography

Carburator: *See* Automobile

Celanese: *See* Fibers, man-made

Celluloid: *See* Plastics

Classification of plants and animals: (by genera and species) Carolus Linnaeus, Sweden, 1737–53

Clock, pendulum: Christian Huygens, The Netherlands, 1656

Combustion: (nature of) Antoine Lavoisier, France, 1777

Computer: (differential analyzer, mechanically operated) Vannevar Bush, U.S., 1928; (Mark I, first information-processing digital computer) Howard Aiken, U.S., 1944; (ENIAC, Electronic Numerical Integrator and Calculator, first all-electronic) J. Presper Eckert, John W. Mauchly, U.S., 1946; (stored-program concept) John von Neumann, U.S., 1947

Conditioned reflex: Ivan Pavlov, Russia, c.1910

Converter, Bessemer: William Kelly, U.S., 1851

Cosmetics: Egypt, c.4000 B.C.

Cotton gin: Eli Whitney, U.S., 1793

Crossbow: China, c.300 B.C.

Cyclotron: Ernest O. Lawrence, U.S., 1931

Deuterium: (heavy hydrogen) Harold Urey, U.S., 1931

DNA: (deoxyribonucleic acid) Friedrich Meischer, Germany, 1869; (determination of double-helical structure) F. H. Crick, England, James D. Watson, U.S., 1953

Dynamite: Alfred Nobel, Sweden, 1867

Electric generator (dynamo): (laboratory model) Michael Faraday, England, 1832; Joseph Henry, U.S., c.1832; (hand-driven model) Hippolyte Pixii, France, 1833; (alternating-current generator) Nikola Tesla, U.S., 1892

Electric lamp: (arc lamp) Sir Humphrey Davy, England, 1801; (fluorescent lamp) A. E. Becquerel, France, 1867; (incandescent lamp) Sir Joseph Swann, England, Thomas A. Edison, U.S., contemporaneously, 1870s; (carbon arc street lamp) Charles F. Brush, U.S., 1879; (first widely marketed incandescent lamp) Thomas A. Edison, U.S., 1879; (mercury vapor lamp) Peter Cooper Hewitt, U.S., 1903; (neon lamp) Georges Claude, France, 1911; (tungsten filament) Irving Langmuir, U.S., 1915

Electric motor: *See* Motor

Electromagnet: William Sturgeon, England, 1823

Electron: Sir Joseph J. Thompson, England, 1897

Elevator, passenger: (safety device permitting use by passengers) Elisha G. Otis, U.S., 1852; (elevator utilizing safety device) 1857

$E = mc^2$: (equivalence of mass and energy) Albert Einstein, Switzerland, 1905

Engine, internal combustion: No single inventor. Fundamental theory established by Sadi Carnot, France, 1824; (two-stroke) Étienne Lenoir, France, 1860; (ideal operating cycle for four-stroke) Alphonse Beau de Rochet, France, 1862; (operating four-stroke) Nikolaus Otto, Germany, 1876; (diesel) Rudolf Diesel, Germany, 1892; (rotary) Felix Wankel, Germany, 1956. *See also* Automobile

Engine, steam: *See* Steam engine

Evolution: (by natural selection) Charles Darwin, England, 1859

Falling bodies, law of: Galileo Galilei, Italy, 1590

Fermentation: (micro-organisms as cause of) Louis Pasteur, France, c,1860

Fibers, man-made: (nitrocellulose fibers treated to change flammable nitrocellulose to harmless cellulose, precursor of rayon) Sir Joseph Swann, England, 1883; (rayon) Count Hilaire de Chardonnet, France, 1889; (Celanese) Henry and Camille Dreyfuss, U.S., England, 1921; (research on polyesters and polyamides, basis for modern man-made fibers) U.S., England, Germany, 1930s; (nylon) Wallace H. Carothers, U.S., 1935

Fountain pen: *See* Pen

Geometry, elements of: Euclid, Alexandria, Egypt, c.300 B.C.

Gravitation, law of: Sir Isaac Newton, England, c.1665 (published 1687)

Gunpowder: China, c.700

Gyrocompass: Elmer A. Sperry, U.S., 1905

Gyroscope: Léon Foucault, France, 1852

Helicopter: Igor Sikorsky, U.S., 1939

Helium first observed on sun: Sir Joseph Lockyer, England, 1868

Heredity, laws of: Gregor Mendel, Austria, 1865

Induction, electric: Joseph Henry, U.S., 1828

Insulin: Sir Frederick G. Banting, J. J. R. MacLeod, Canada, 1922

Intelligence testing: Alfred Binet, Theodore Simon, France, 1905

Isotopes: (concept of) Frederick Soddy, England, 1912; (stable isotopes) J. J. Thompson, England, 1913; (existence demonstrated by mass spectrography) Francis W. Ashton, 1919

Jet propulsion, aircraft: Sir Frank Whittle, England, 1930

Laser: (theoretical work on) Charles H. Townes, Arthur L. Schawlow, U.S., N. Basov, A. Prokhorov, U.S.S.R., 1958; (first working model) T. H. Maiman, U.S., 1960

Lens, bifocal: Benjamin Franklin, U.S., c.1760

Light, nature of: (wave theory) Christian Huygens, Denmark, 1678; (electromagnetic theory) James Clerk Maxwell, England, 1873

Light, speed of: (theory that light has finite velocity) Olaus Roemer, Denmark, 1675

Lightning rod: Benjamin Franklin, U.S., 1752

Linotype: *See* Printing

Lithography: *See* Printing

Locomotive: (steam-powered) Richard Trevithick, England, 1804; (first practical, due to multiple-fire-tube boiler) George Stephenson, England, 1829; (largest steam-powered) Union Pacific's "Big Boy," U.S., 1941

Logarithms: *See* Calculating machine

Loom: (horizontal, two-beamed) Egypt, c.4400 B.C.; (Jacquard drawloom, pattern controlled by punch cards) Jacques de Vaucanson, France, 1745; Joseph-Marie Jacquard, 1801; (flying shuttle) John Kay, England, 1733; (power-driven loom) Edmund Cartwright, England, 1785

Machine gun: James Puckle, England, 1718; Richard J. Gatling, U.S., 1861

Match: (phosphorus) François Derosne, France, 1816; (friction) Charles Sauria, France, 1831; (safety) J. E. Lundstrom, Sweden, 1855

Mendelian law: *See* Heredity

Microscope: (compound) Zacharias Janssen, The Netherlands, 1590; (electron) Vladimir Zworykin et al., U.S., Canada, Germany, 1932–1939

Motion pictures: Thomas A. Edison, U.S., 1893

Motion pictures, sound: Product of various inventions. First picture with synchronized musical score: *Don Juan*, 1926; with spoken dialogue: *The Jazz Singer,* 1927; both Warner Bros.

Motor, electric: Michael Faraday, England, 1822; (alternating-current) Nikola Tesla, U.S., 1892

Motor, gasoline: *See* Engine, internal combustion

Motorcycle: (motor tricycle) Edward Butler, England, 1884; (gasoline-engine motorcycle) Gottieb Daimier, Germany, 1885

Neptunium: (first transuranic element, synthesis of) Edward M. McMillan, Philip H. Abelson, U.S., 1940

Neutron: James Chadwick, England, 1832

Neutron-induced radiation: Enrico Fermi et al., Italy, 1934

Nitroglycerin: Ascanio Sobrero, Italy, 1846

Nuclear fission: Otto Hahn, Fritz Strassmann, Germany, 1938

Nuclear reactor: Enrico Fermi et al., U.S., 1942

Nylon: *See* Fibers, man-made

Ohm's law: (relationship between strength of electric current, electromotive force, and circuit resistance) Georg S. Ohm, Germany, 1827

Ozone: Christian Schönbein, Germany, 1839

Paper: China, c.100 B.C.

Parachute: Louis S. Lenormand, France, 1783

Pen: (fountain) Lewis E. Waterman, U.S., 1884; (ball-point, for marking on rough surfaces) John H. Loud, U.S., 1888; (ball-point, for handwriting) Lazlo Biro, Argentina, 1944

Penicillin: *See* Antibiotics

Periodic law: (that properties of elements are functions of their atomic weights) Dmitri Mendeleev, Russia, 1869

Periodic table: (arrangement of chemical elements based on periodic law) Dmitri Mendeleev, Russia, 1869

Phonograph: Thomas A. Edison, U.S., 1877

Photography: (first paper negative, first photograph, on metal) Joseph Nicéphore Niepce, France, 1816–1827; (discovery of fixative powers of hyposulfite of soda) Sir John Herschel, England, 1819; (first direct positive image on silver plate, the daguerreotype) Louis Daguerre, based on work with Niepce, France, 1839; (first paper negative from which a number of positive prints could be made) William Talbot, England, 1841. Work of these four men, taken together, forms basis for all modern photography. (First color images) Alexandre Becquerel, Claude Niepce de Saint-Victor, France, 1848–60; (commercial color film with three emulsion layers, Kodachrome) U.S., 1935. *See also* Camera

Plastics: (first material, nitrocellulose softened by vegetable oil, camphor, precursor to Celluloid) Alexander Parkes, England, 1855; (Celluloid, involving recognition of vital effect of camphor) John W. Hyatt, U.S., 1869; (Bakelite, first completely synthetic plastic) Leo H. Baekeland, U.S., 1910; (theoretical background of macromolecules and process of polymerization on which modern plastics industry rests) Hermann Staudinger, Germany, 1922. *See also* Fibers, man-made

Plow, forked: Mesopotamia, before 3000 B.C.

Plutonium, synthesis of: Glenn T. Seaborg, Edwin M. McMillan, Arthur C. Wahl, Joseph W. Kennedy, U.S., 1941

Polaroid Land camera: *See* Camera

Polio, vaccine against: (vaccine made from dead virus strains) Jonas E. Salk, U.S., 1955; (vaccine made from live virus strains) Albert Sabin, U.S., 1960

Positron: Carl D. Anderson, U.S., 1932

Pressure cooker: (early version) Denis Papin, France, 1679

Printing: (block) Japan, c.700; (movable type) Korea, c.1400; Johann Gutenberg, Germany, c.1450 (lithography, offset) Aloys Senefelder, Germany, 1796; (rotary press) Richard Hoe, U.S., 1844; (linotype) Ottman Mergenthaler, U.S. 1884

Programming, information: *See* Calculating machine

Propeller, screw: Sir Francis P. Smith, England, 1836; John

Ericsson, England, worked independently of and simultaneously with Smith, 1837

Proton: Ernest Rutherford, England, 1919

Psychoanalysis: Sigmund Freud, Austria, c.1904

Quantum theory: Max Planck, Germany, 1901

Rabies immunization: Louis Pasteur, France, 1885

Radar: (limited to one-mile range) Christian Hulsmeyer, Germany, 1904; (pulse modulation, used for measuring height of ionosphere) Gregory Breit, Merle Tuve, U.S., 1925; (first practical radar—radio detection and ranging) Sir Robert Watson-Watt, England, 1934–35

Radio: (electromagnetism, theory of) James Clerk Maxwell, England, 1873; (spark coil, generator of electromagnetic waves) Heinrich Hertz, Germany, 1886; (first practical system of wireless telegraphy) Guglielmo Marconi, Italy, 1895; (vacuum electron tube, basis for radio telephony) Sir John Fleming, England, 1904; (triode amplifying tube) Lee de Forest, U.S., 1906; (regenerative circuit, allowing long-distance sound reception) Edwin H. Armstrong, U.S., 1912; (frequency modulation—FM) Edwin H. Armstrong, U.S., 1933

Radioactivity: (X-rays) William K. Roentgen, Germany, 1895; (radioactivity of uranium) Henri Becquerel, France, 1896; (radioactive elements, radium and polonium in uranium ore) Marie Sklodowska-Curie, Pierre Curie, France, 1898; (classification of alpha and beta particle radiation) Pierre Curie, France, 1900; (gamma radiation) Paul-Ulrich Villard, France, 1900; (carbon dating) Willard F. Libby et al., U.S., 1955

Rayon: *See* Fibers, man-made

Reaper: Cyrus McCormick, U.S., 1834

Relativity: (special and general theories of) Albert Einstein, Switzerland, Germany, U.S., 1905–53

Revolver: Samuel Colt, U.S., 1835

Rifle: (muzzle-loaded) Italy, Germany, c.1475; (breech-loaded) England, France, Germany, U.S., c.1866; (bolt-action) Paul von Mauser, Germany, 1889; (automatic) John Browning, U.S., 1918

Roller bearing: (wooden for cartwheel) Germany or France, c.100 B.C.

Rubber: (vulcanization process) Charles Goodyear, U.S., 1839

Safety match: *See* Match

Solar system, universe: (sun-centered universe) Nicolaus Copernicus, Warsaw, 1543; (establishment of planetary orbits as elliptical) Johannes Kepler, Germany, 1609; (infinity of universe) Giordano Bruno, Italian monk, 1584

Spectrum: (heterogeneity of light) Sir Isaac Newton, England, 1665–66

Spermatozoa: Anton van Leeuwenhoek, The Netherlands, 1683

Spinning: (spinning wheel) India, introduced to Europe in Middle Ages; (Saxony wheel, continuous spinning of wool or cotton yarn) England, c.1500–1600; (spinning jenny) James Hargreaves, England, 1764; (spinning frame) Sir Richard Arkwright, England, 1769; (spinning mule, completed mechanization of spinning, permitting production of yarn to keep up with demands of modern looms) Samuel Crompton, England, 1779

Steam engine: (first commercial version based on principles of French physicist Denis Papin) Thomas Savery, England, 1639; (atmospheric steam engine) Thomas Newcomen, England, 1705; (steam engine for pumping water from collieries) Savery, Newcomen, 1725; (modern condensing, double-acting) James Watt, England, 1782

Steam engine, railroad: *See* Locomotive

Steamship: Claude de Jouffroy d'Abbans, France, 1783; James Rumsey, U.S., 1787; John Fitch, U.S., 1790. All preceded Robert Fulton, U.S., 1807, credited with launching first commercially successful steamship

Sulfa drugs: (parent compound, para-aminobenzenesulfanomide) Paul Gelmo, Austria, 1908; (antibacterial activity) Gerhard Domagk, Germany, 1935

Syphilis, test for: *See* Wasserman test

Tank, military: Sir Ernest Swinton, England, 1914

Telegraph: Samuel F. B. Morse, U.S., 1837

Telephone: Alexander Graham Bell, U.S., 1876

Telescope: Hans Lippershey, The Netherlands, 1608

Television: (mechanical disk-scanning method) successfully demonstrated by J. L. Baird, England, C. F. Jenkins, U.S., 1926; (electronic scanning method) Vladimir K. Zworykin, U.S., 1928; (color, all-electronic) Zworykin, 1925; (color, mechanical disk) Baird, 1928; (color, compatible with black and white) George Valensi, France, 1938; (color, sequential rotating filter) Peter Goldmark, U.S., first introduced, 1951; (color, compatible with black and white) commercially introduced in U.S., National Television Systems Committee, 1953

Thermometer: (open-column) Galileo Galilei, c.1593; (clinical) Santorio Santorio, Padua, c.1615; (mercury, also Fahrenheit scale) Gabriel D. Fahrenheit, Germany, 1714; (centigrade scale) Anders Celsius, Sweden, 1742; (absolute-temperature, or Kelvin, scale) William Thompson, Lord Kelvin, England, 1848

Tire, pneumatic: Robert W. Thompson, England, 1845; (bicycle tire) John B. Dunlop, Northern Ireland, 1888

Toilet, flush: Product of Minoan civilization, Crete, c.2000 B.C. Alleged invention by "Thomas Crapper" is untrue.

Tractor: Benjamin Holt, U.S., 1900

Transformer, electric: William Stanley, U.S., 1885

Transistor: John Bardeen, William Shockley, Walter Brattain, U.S., 1948

Uncertainty principle: (that position and velocity of an object cannot both be measured exactly, at the same time) Werner Heisenberg, Germany, 1927

Vaccination: Edward Jenner, England, 1796

Vacuum tube: *See* Radio

Van Allen (radiation) Belt: (around the earth) James Van Allen, U.S., 1958

Vitamins: (hypothesis of disease deficiency) Sir F. G. Hopkins, Casimir Funk, England, 1912; (vitamin A) Elmer V. McCollum, M. Davis, U.S., 1912–14; (vitamin B) Elmer V. McCollum, U.S., 1915–16; (thiamin, B_1) Casimir Funk, England, 1912; (riboflavin, B_2) D. T. Smith, E. G. Hendrick, U.S., 1926; (niacin) Conrad Elvehjem, U.S., 1937; (B_6) Paul Gyorgy, U.S., 1934; (vitamin C) C. A. Holst, T. Froelich, Norway, 1912; (vitamin D) Elmer V. McCollum, U.S., 1922; (folic acid) Lucy Wills, England, 1933

Wassermann test: (for syphilis) August von Wassermann, Germany, 1906

Weaving, cloth: *See* Loom

Wheel: (cart, solid wood) Mesopotamia, c.3800–3600 B.C.

Windmill: Persia, c.600

X-ray: *See* Radioactivity

Xerography: Chester Carlson, U.S., 1938

Zero: Mayas, Central America, c.325; India, c.600; (absolute zero, cessation of all molecular energy) William Thompson, Lord Kelvin, England, 1848

Data for Sun, Moon, and Planets

	Mean distance from Sun in millions of miles	Period of revolution around the Sun	Diameter (miles)	Period of rotation on axis	Surface gravity (earth = 1)	Density H_2O = 1	Number of satellites
Sun	—	—	865,400	24d.64[2]	28	1.4	0
Moon	—	(27d.322)[1]	2,160	27d.322	0.16	3.3	0
Mercury	36.00	87d.969	3,100	58.66d	0.28	3.8	0
Venus	67.27	224d.701	7,700	243.2d	0.85	5.1	0
Earth	93.00	365d.256	7,927[3]	23h56m	1.00	5.5	1
Mars	141.71	1y.881	4,200	24h37m	0.38	4.0	2
Jupiter	483.88	11y.862	88,700[3]	9h50m [2]	2.6	1.3	13[4]
Saturn	887.14	29y.458	75,100[3]	10h14m [2]	1.2	0.7	10
Uranus	1783.98	84y.013	32,000	10¾	1.1	1.3	5
Neptune	2795.46	164y.794	27,700	15h.8	1.4	2.2	2
Pluto	3675.27	248h.430	1,500(?)	6d8h(?)	—	1.0	1

1. Period of revolution around the earth. 2. At the equator. 3. The equatorial diameters of the earth, Jupiter, and Saturn are given; polar diameters are: earth, 7,900.0 mi., Jupiter 82,789 mi., Saturn 67,170 mi. 4. Recent analysis indicates the presence of a fourteenth satellite. OTHER DATA ON THE EARTH: Equatorial circumference, 24,902.4 mi.; total area, 196,949,970 sq mi.; mass, 6.6 sextillion tons; mean diameter, 7,917.8 mi.

Formation of the Solar System

The Sun, like other stars, seems to have been formed 4.6 billion years ago from a cloud of hydrogen mixed with small amounts of other substances that had been manufactured in the bodies of other stars before the Sun was born. This was the parent cloud of the solar system. The dense hot gas at the center of the cloud gave rise to the Sun; the outer regions of the cloud—cooler and less dense—gave birth to the planets.

Our solar system consists of one star (the Sun), nine planets and all their moons, several thousand minor planets called asteroids or planetoids, and an equally large number of comets.

The Sun

All the stars, including our Sun, are gigantic balls of superheated gas, kept hot by atomic reactions in their centers. In our Sun, this atomic reaction is hydrogen fusion: four hydrogen atoms are combined to form one helium atom. The temperature at the core of our Sun must be 20 million degrees centigrade, the surface temperature is around 6,000 degrees centigrade, or about 11,000 degrees Fahrenheit. The diameter of the sun is 865,400 miles, and its surface area is approximately 12,000 times that of the Earth. Compared with other stars, our Sun is just a bit below average in size and temperature. Its fuel supply (hydrogen) is estimated to last for another 5 billion years.

Our Sun is not motionless in space; in fact it has two proper motions. One is a seemingly straight-line motion in the direction of the constellation Hercules at the rate of about 12 miles per second. But since the Sun is a part of the Milky Way system and since the whole system rotates slowly around its own center, the Sun also moves at the rate of 175 miles per second as part of the rotating Milky Way system.

In addition to this motion, the Sun rotates on its axis. Observing the motion of sun spots (darkish areas which look like enormous whirling storms) and solar flares, which are usually associated with sun spots, has shown that the rotational period of our Sun is just short of 25 days. But this figure is valid for the Sun's equator only; the sections near the Sun's poles seem to have a rotational period of 34 days. Naturally, since the Sun generates its own heat and light, there is no temperature difference between poles and equator.

What we call the Sun's "surface" is technically known as the photosphere. Since the whole Sun is a ball of very hot gas, there is really no such thing as a surface; it is a question of visual impression. The next layer outside the photosphere is known as the chromosphere, which extends several thousand miles beyond the photosphere. It is in steady motion, and often enormous prominences can be seen to burst from it, extending as much as 100,000 miles into space. Outside the chromosphere is the corona. The corona consists of very tenuous gases (essentially hydrogen) and makes a magnificent sight when the Sun is eclipsed.

The Moon

Mercury and Venus do not have any moons. Therefore, the Earth is the planet nearest the Sun to be orbited by a moon.

The next planet farther out, Mars, has two very small moons. Jupiter has four major moons and nine or ten minor ones. Saturn, the ringed planet, has ten known moons, of which one (Titan) is larger than the planet Mercury. Uranus has five known moons (four of them large) as well as rings, while Neptune has one large and one small moon. Pluto has one moon, discovered in 1978. Some astronomers still consider Pluto to be a "runaway moon" of Neptune.

Our own Moon, with a diameter of 2,160 miles, is one of the larger moons in our solar system and is especially large when compared with the planet that it orbits. In fact, the common center of gravity of the Earth-Moon system is only about 1,000 miles below the Earth's surface. The closest our Moon can come to us (its perigee) is 221,463 miles; the farthest it can go away (its apogee) is 252,710 miles. The period of rotation of our Moon is equal to its period of revolution around the Earth. Hence from Earth we can see only one hemisphere of the Moon. Both periods are 27 days, 7 hours, 43 minutes and 11.47 seconds. But while the rotation of the Moon is constant, its velocity in its orbit is not, since it moves more slowly in apogee than in perigee. Consequently, some portions near the rim which are not normally visible will appear briefly. This phenomenon is called "libration," and by taking advantage of the librations, astronomers have succeeded in mapping approximately 59% of the lunar surface. The other 41% can never be seen from the earth but has been mapped by American and Russian Moon-orbiting spacecraft.

Though the Moon goes around the Earth in the time mentioned, the interval from new Moon to new Moon is 29 days, 12 hours, 44 minutes and 2.78 seconds. This delay of nearly two days is due to the fact that the Earth is moving around the Sun, so that the Moon needs two extra days to reach a spot in its orbit where no part is illuminated by the Sun, as seen from Earth.

If the plane of the Earth's orbit around the Sun (the ecliptic) and the plane of the Moon's orbit around the Earth were the same, the Moon would be eclipsed by the Earth every time it is full, and the Sun would be eclipsed by the Moon every time the Moon is "new" (it would be better to call it the "black Moon" when it is in this position). But because the two orbits do not coincide, the Moon's shadow normally misses the Earth and the Earth's shadow misses the Moon. The inclination of the two orbital planes to each other is 5 degrees. The tides are, of course, caused by the Moon with the help of the Sun, but in the open ocean they are surprisingly low, amounting to about one yard. The very high tides which can be observed near the shore in some places are due to funnelling effects of the shorelines. At new Moon and at full Moon the tides raised by the Moon are reinforced by the Sun; these are the "spring tides." If the Sun's tidal power acts at right angles to that of the Moon (quarter moons) we get the low "neap tides."

Our Planet Earth

The Earth, circling the Sun at an average distance of 93 million miles, is the fifth largest planet and the third from the Sun. It orbits the Sun at a speed of 67,000 miles per hour, making one revolution in 365 days, 5 hours, 48 minutes, and 45.51 seconds. The Earth completes one rotation on its axis every 23 hours, 56 minutes, and 4.09 seconds. Actually a bit pear-shaped rather than a true sphere, the Earth has a diameter of 7,927 miles at the Equator and a few miles less at the poles. It has an estimated mass of about 6.6 sextillion tons, with an average density of 5.52 grams per cubic centimeter. The Earth's surface area encompasses 196,949,970 square miles, of which about three-fourths is water.

Origin of the Earth. The Earth, along with the other planets, is believed to have been born 4.6 billion years ago as a solidified cloud of dust and gases left over from the creation of the Sun. For perhaps 500 million years, the interior of the Earth stayed solid and relatively cool, perhaps 2000° F. The main ingredients, according to the best available evidence, were iron and silicates, with small amounts of other elements, some of them radioactive. As millions of years passed, energy released by radioactive decay—mostly of uranium, thorium, and potassium—gradually heated the Earth, melting some of its constituents. The iron melted before the silicates, and, being heavier, sank toward the center. This forced upward the silicates that it found there. After many years, the iron reached the center, almost 4,000 miles deep, and began to accumulate. No eyes were around at that time to view the turmoil which must have taken place on the face of the Earth—gigantic heaves and bubbling of the surface, exploding volcanoes, and flowing lava covering everything in sight. Finally, the iron in the center accumulated as the core. Around it, a thin but fairly stable crust of solid rock formed as the Earth cooled. Depressions in the crust were natural basins in which water, rising from the interior of the planet through volcanoes and fissures, collected to form the oceans. Slowly the Earth acquired its present appearance.

The Earth Today. As a result of radioactive heating over millions of years, the Earth's molten *core* is probably fairly hot today, around 11,000° F. By comparison, lead melts at around 800° F. Most of the Earth's 2,100-mile-thick core is liquid, but there is evidence that the center of the core is solid. The liquid outer portion, about 95% of the core, is constantly in motion, causing the Earth to have a magnetic field that makes compass needles point north and south. The details are not known, but the latest evidence suggests that planets which have a magnetic field probably have a solid core or a partially liquid one.

Outside the core is the Earth's *mantle,* 1,800 miles thick, and extending nearly to the surface. The mantle is composed of heavy silicate rock, similar to that brought up by volcanic eruptions. It is somewhere between liquid and solid, slightly yielding, and therefore contributing to an active, moving Earth. Most of the Earth's radioactive material is in the thin *crust* which covers the mantle, but some is in the mantle and continues to give off heat. The crust's thickness ranges from 5 to 25 miles.

Continental Drift. A great deal of recent evidence confirms the long-disputed theory that the continents of the Earth, made mostly of relatively light granite, float in the slightly yielding mantle, like logs in a pond. For many years it had been noticed that if North and South America could be pushed toward western and southern Europe and western Africa, they would fit like pieces in a jigsaw puzzle. Today, there is little question—the continents have drifted widely and continue to do so.

In 10 million years, the world as we know it may be unrecognizable, with California drifting out to sea, Florida joining South America, and Africa moving farther away from Europe and Asia.

The Earth's Atmosphere. The thin blanket of atmosphere that envelops the Earth extends several hundred miles into space. From sea level—the very bottom of the ocean of air—to a height of about 60 miles, the air in the atmosphere is made up of the same gases in the same ratio: about 78% nitrogen, 21% oxygen, and the remaining 1% being a mixture of argon, carbon dioxide, and tiny amounts of neon, helium, krypton, xenon, and other gases. The atmosphere becomes less dense with increasing altitude: more than three-fourths of the Earth's huge envelope is concentrated in the first 5 to 10 miles above the surface. At sea level, a cubic foot of the atmosphere weighs about an ounce and a quarter. The entire atmosphere weighs 5,700,000,000,-000,000 tons, and the force with which gravity holds it in place causes it to exert a pressure of nearly 15 pounds per square inch. Going out from the Earth's surface, the atmosphere is divided into five regions. The regions, and the heights to which they extend, are: *Troposphere,* 0 to 7 miles (at middle latitudes); *stratosphere,* 7 to 30 miles; *mesosphere,* 30 to 50 miles; *thermosphere,* 50 to 400 miles; and *exosphere,* above 400 miles. The boundaries between each of the regions are known respectively as the *tropopause, stratopause, mesopause,* and *thermopause.* Alternate terms often used for the layers above the troposphere are *ozonosphere* (for stratosphere) and *ionosphere* for the remaining upper layers.

The Seasons. Seasons are caused by the 23.4 degree tilt of the Earth's axis, which alternately turns the North and South Poles toward the Sun. Times when the Sun's apparent path crosses the Equator are known as *equinoxes.* Times when the Sun's apparent path is at the greatest distance from the Equator are known as *solstices.* The lengths of the days are most extreme at each solstice. If the Earth's axis were perpendicular to the plane of the Earth's orbit around the Sun, there would be no seasons, and the days always would be equal in length. Since the Earth's axis is at an angle, the Sun strikes the Earth directly at the Equator only twice a year: in March (vernal equinox) and September (autumnal equinox). In the Northern Hemisphere, spring begins at the vernal equinox, summer at the summer solstice, fall at the autumnal equinox, and winter at the winter solstice. The situation is reversed in the Southern Hemisphere.

Mercury

Mercury is the planet nearest the Sun. Appropriately named for the wing-footed Roman messenger of the gods, Mercury whizzes around the Sun at a speed of 30 miles per second, completing one circuit in 88 days. The planet rotates on its axis over a period of nearly 59 days. Daytime on cratered Mercury is hot, about 800 degrees F., although at night the temperature may fall to room temperature. Mercury has no moons, but it does have a trace of atmosphere and a weak magnetic field, according to findings of Mariner 10. Until this spacecraft flew by Mercury in 1974 and 1975, very little was known about the planet, primarily because of its short angular distance from the Sun as seen from Earth, which puts it too close to the Sun to be easily observed.

• Mercury is a naked eye object at morning or evening twilight, when it is at greatest elongation.

Venus

Although Venus is Earth's nearest neighbor, little is known about this planet because it is permanently covered by thick clouds. In 1962, Soviet and American space probes, coupled with Earth-based radar and infrared spectroscopy, began slowly unraveling some of the mystery surrounding Venus. According to these results, Venus' atmosphere is nearly 100% carbon dioxide, exerting a pressure at the surface 100 times greater than Earth's. Walking on Venus would be as difficult as walking a half-mile beneath the ocean. Because of the thick blanket of carbon dioxide, a "greenhouse effect" exists on Venus: Venus intercepts twice as much of the Sun's light as does the Earth. The light enters freely through carbon dioxide gas and is changed to heat radiation in molecular collisions. But carbon dioxide prevents the heat from escaping. Consequently, the temperature of the surface of Venus is nearly 800 degrees F., hot enough to melt lead. Radar bounced off the planet recently revealed what appear to be large craters. In 1978, NASA launched a multi-probe spacecraft toward Venus to conduct a detailed scientific examination of this enigmatic planet. Unlike other planets, Venus rotates in retrograde (clockwise) motion. Reason is not known.

• Venus is the brightest of all the planets and is often visible in the morning or evening, when it is frequently referred to as the Morning Star or Evening Star. At its brightest, it can sometimes be seen with the naked eye in full daylight, if one knows where to look.

Mars

Mars, on the other side of the Earth from Venus, is Venus' direct opposite in terms of physical properties. Its atmosphere is cold, thin, and transparent, and readily permits observation of the planet's features. We know more about Mars than any other planet except Earth. Mars is a forbidding, rugged planet with huge volcanoes and deep chasms. The largest volcano, Nix Olympia, rises 78,000 feet above the surface, higher than Mount Everest. The plains of Mars are pockmarked by the hits of thousands of meteors over the years. Most of our information about Mars comes from the Mariner 9 spacecraft, which orbited the planet in 1971. Mariner 9, photographing 100% of the planet, uncovered spectacular geological formations, including a Martian Grand Canyon that dwarfs the one on Earth. The spacecraft's cameras also recorded what appeared to be dried riverbeds, suggesting the onetime presence of water on the planet. The latter idea gives encouragement to scientists looking for life on Mars, for where there is water, there may be life. However, by 1978, no evidence of life has been found. Temperatures near the equator range from -17 degrees F. in the daytime to -130 degrees F. at night. Mars rotates upon its axis in nearly the same period as Earth—24 hours, 37 minutes—so that a Mars day is almost identical to an Earth day. Mars takes 687 days to make one trip around the Sun. Because of its eccentric orbit Mars' distance from the Sun can vary by about 36 million miles. Its distance from Earth can vary by as much as 200 million miles. The atmosphere of Mars is much thinner than Earth's; atmospheric pressure is about 1% that of our planet. Its gravity is one-third of Earth's. Major constituents are carbon dioxide and nitrogen. Water vapor and oxygen are minor constituents. Mars' polar caps, composed mostly of carbon dioxide, recede and advance according to the Martian seasons. Mars was named for the Roman god of war, because when seen from Earth its distinct red color reminded the ancient people of blood. We know now that the reddish hue reflects the oxidized (rusted) iron in the surface material. The landing of two robot Viking spacecraft on the surface of Mars in 1976 provided more information about Mars in a few months than in all the time that has gone before.

• Mars becomes especially bright when nearest to us because we then see its daylight side fully illuminated by the Sun. This happens roughly every two years and two months. The last time was in December 1975.

Jupiter

Jupiter, with an equatorial diameter of 88,000 miles, is the largest of a group of planets which differ markedly from the terrestrial planets. The others in the group are Saturn, Uranus and Neptune. All are large, with very dense atmospheres, and indeed may be giant balls of gas without any perceptible surfaces. They all whirl rapidly around their axes, but more slowly around the Sun, resulting in short days and long years. They have many moons. Majestic Jupiter, named for the king of the Roman gods, rotates so fast that it is greatly flattened at the poles. According to Pioneers 10 and 11, which flew past Jupiter in 1974 and 1975, this planet is a whirling ball of liquid hydrogen with perhaps an Earth-sized iron core. Other atmospheric constituents are helium, methane, and ammonia. Its clouds are probably ammonia ice crystals, becoming ammonia droplets deeper towards the "surface." Temperatures range from perhaps minus 300 degrees F. at the tops of the cloud decks to 100,000 degrees F. or more deep down at the center. The pressure at the center of the planet is estimated to be a crushing 10 million pounds per square inch. The most prominent feature on Jupiter is the Great Red Spot, the size of four Earths. According to Pioneer scientists, the Red Spot is the vortex of a huge 25,000-mile-wide hurricane which has been raging for at least 379 years, since Galileo first saw it through his telescope. Jupiter has possibly 14 satellites, more than any other planet. The four largest moons, called Galilean moons, are Europa, Ganymede, Io, and Callisto.

• Even when nearest the Earth, Jupiter is still almost 400 million miles away. But because of its size, it may rival Venus in brilliance when near. Jupiter's four large moons may be seen through field glasses, moving rapidly around Jupiter and changing their position from night to night.

Saturn

Saturn, one of the giant planets in the solar system, is also the least dense. It would float in an ocean if there were one big enough to hold it. Aside from its rings, Saturn is very similar to Jupiter except that it is probably colder, being twice as far from the Sun. Recent radar observations of Saturn's rings indicate that they are no more than 10 miles thick, and probably composed of chunks of rock and ice averaging a meter in size. There are four rings. The system begins about 7000 miles from the planet's disk, and extends out to about 35,000 miles. Saturn has 10 satellites. The U.S. launched two Voyager spacecraft to Jupiter in August and September 1977. After flying past Jupiter in 1981, taking pictures and making measurements, the spacecraft will go on to Saturn and possibly Uranus.

• Saturn is the last of the planets visible to the naked eye. Saturn is never an object of overwhelming brilliance, but it looks like a bright star. The rings can be seen with a small telescope.

Uranus and Neptune

Little is known about the distant giant planets Uranus and Neptune, but they are believed to be similar to Saturn and Jupiter. Being twice as far from the Sun as Saturn, Uranus must be a grim frozen world, and Neptune, 11 A.U. beyond Uranus, must be even colder and darker. The axis of Uranus is tilted at 98 degrees, so it goes around the Sun nearly lying on its side. In 1977, American astronomers made the startling discovery that Uranus has rings, like Saturn. The first Voyager to Uranus may take pictures of the rings in 1986. Uranus has five known moons; Neptune, two. Neptune's Triton, Jupiter's Ganymede and Callisto, and Saturn's Titan are the four largest moons in the solar system.

• Uranus and Neptune can—on rare occasion—become bright enough to be seen with the naked eye, if one knows exactly where to look; normally, they are objects for good field glasses or small portable telescopes.

Pluto

Pluto, the outermost and smallest planet in the solar system, looks more like a terrestrial planet than a gaseous planet. But so little is known about it, that it is difficult to classify. Appropriately named for the Roman god of the underworld, it must be frozen, dark and dead.

In 1978, light curve studies gave evidence of a moon revolving around Pluto with the same period as Pluto's rotation. Therefore, it stays over the same point on Pluto's surface. In addition, it keeps the same face toward the planet. The discovery of this moon of 500–600 miles in diameter reduces the previously estimated diameter of Pluto to little more than 1,500 miles, making the pair more like a double planet than any other in the solar system. Previously, the Earth-Moon system held this distinction. The density of Pluto is slightly greater than that of water.

Pluto was predicted by calculation when Percival Lowell noticed irregularities in the orbits of Uranus and Neptune. Clyde Tombaugh discovered the planet in 1930, precisely where Lowell predicted it would be. The name Pluto was chosen because the first two letters represent the initials of Percival Lowell.

• Pluto has the most eccentric orbit in the solar system, bringing it at times closer to the Sun than Neptune. Pluto is now approaching the perihelion of its orbit, and for the rest of this century will be closer to the Sun than Neptune. Even then, it can be seen only with a large telescope.

21 Famous Comets

Year and no.	Name of comet	Period (years)
1744	De Chéseaux's Comet	—
1806	Biela's Comet	6.7
1811 I	Great Comet of 1811	3000
1812	Di Vico's Comet	70.7
1815	Olbers' Comet	74.0
1819 I	Encke's Comet	3.3
1819	Pons-Winnecke Comet	6.0
1835 III	Halley's Comet	76.3
1843 I	Great Comet of 1843	512.4
1844 II	Great Comet of 1844	102,050
1858 VI	Donati's Comet	2,040(?)
1864 II	Great Comet of 1864	2,800,000
1871 III	Tuttle's Comet	13.8
1874 III	Coggia's Comet	6,000(?)
1879	Brorsen's Comet	5.6
1881 II	Tebbutt's Comet	—
1889 VI	Swift's 2nd Comet	7.0
1892 III	Holmes' Comet	6.9
1923	d'Arrest's Comet	6.6
1925 II	Comet Schwassman-Wachmann	16.2
1973 I	Comet Kohoutek	75,000(?)

The 88 Recognized Constellations

In astronomical works, the Latin names of the constellations are used. The letter N or S following the Latin name indicates whether the constellation is located to the north or south of the Zodiac. The letter Z indicates that the constellation is within the Zodiac.

Latin name	Letter	English version
Andromeda	N	Andromeda
Antlia	S	Airpump
Apus	S	Bird of Paradise
Aquarius	Z	Water Bearer
Aquila	N	Eagle
Ara	S	Altar
Aries	Z	Ram
Auriga	N	Charioteer
Boötes	N	Herdsmen
Caelum	S	Sculptor's Tool
Camelopardalis	N	Giraffe
Cancer	Z	Crab
Canes Venatici	N	Hunting Dogs
Canis Major	S	Great Dog
Canis Minor	S	Little Dog
Capricornus	Z	Goat (or Sea-Goat)
Carina	S	Keel (of Argo)[1]
Cassiopeia	N	Cassiopeia
Centaurus	S	Centaur
Cepheus	N	Cepheus
Cetus	S	Whale
Chamaeleon	S	Chameleon
Circinus	S	Compasses
Columba	S	Dove
Coma Berenices	N	Berenice's Hair
Corona Australis	S	Southern Crown
Corona Borealis	N	Northern Crown
Corvus	S	Crow (Raven)
Crater	S	Cup
Crux	S	Southern Cross
Cygnus	N	Swan
Delphinus	N	Dolphin
Dorado	S	Swordfish (Goldfish)
Draco	N	Dragon
Equuleus	N	Filly
Eridanus	S	Eridanus (river)
Fornax	S	Furnace
Gemini	Z	Twins
Grus	S	Crane
Hercules	N	Hercules
Horologium	S	Clock
Hydra	N	Sea Serpent
Hydrus	S	Water Snake
Indus	S	Indian
Lacerta	N	Lizard
Leo	Z	Lion

Latin name	Letter	English version
Leo Minor	N	Little Lion
Lepus	S	Hare
Libra	Z	Scales
Lupus	S	Wolf
Lynx	N	Lynx
Lyra	N	Lyre (Harp)
Mensa	S	Table (mountain)
Microscopium	S	Microscope
Monoceros	S	Unicorn
Musca	S	Southern Fly
Norma	S	Rule (straightedge)
Octans	S	Octant
Ophiuchus	N	Serpent-Bearer
Orion	S	Orion
Pavo	S	Peacock
Pegasus	N	Pegasus
Perseus	N	Perseus
Phoenix	S	Phoenix
Pictor	S	Painter (or his Easel)
Pisces	Z	Fishes
Piscis Austrinus	S	Southern Fish
Puppis	S	Poop (of Argo)[1]
Pyxis	S	Mariner's Compass
Reticulum	S	Net
Sagitta	N	Arrow
Sagittarius	Z	Archer
Scorpius	Z	Scorpion
Sculptor	S	Sculptor
Scutum	N	Shield
Serpens	N	Serpent
Sextans	S	Sextant
Taurus	Z	Bull
Telescopium	S	Telescope
Triangulum	N	Triangle
Triangulum Australe	S	Southern Triangle
Tucana	S	Toucan
Ursa Major	N	Big Dipper
Ursa Minor	N	Little Dipper
Vela	S	Sail (of Argo)[1]
Virgo	Z	Virgin
Volans	S	Flying Fish
Vulpecula	N	Fox

1. The original constellation Argo Navis (the Ship Argo) has been divided into Carina, Puppis, and Vela. Normally the brightest star in each constellation is designated by alpha, the first letter of the Greek alphabet, the second brightest by beta, the second letter of the Greek alphabet, and so forth. But the Greek letters run through Carina, Puppis, and Vela as if it were still one constellation.

The Names of the Days

Latin	Saxon	English	Spanish	German
Dies Solis	Sun's Day	Sunday	domingo	Sonntag
Dies Lunae	Moon's Day	Monday	lunes	Montag
Dies Martis	Tiw's Day	Tuesday	martes	Dienstag
Dies Mercurii	Woden's Day	Wednesday	miércoles	Mittwoch
Dies Jovis	Thor's Day	Thursday	jueves	Donnerstag
Dies Veneris	Frigg's Day	Friday	viernes	Freitag
Dies Saturni	Seterne's Day	Saturday	sábado	Sonnabend

NOTE: The Romans gave one day of the week to each planet known, the Sun and Moon being considered planets in this connection. The Saxon names are a kind of translation of the Roman names: Tiw was substituted for Mars, Woden (Wotan) for Mercury, Thor for Jupiter (Jove), Frigg for Venus, and Seterne for Saturn. The English names are adapted Saxon. The Spanish names, which are normally not capitalized, are adapted Latin. The German names follow the Saxon pattern with two exceptions: Wednesday is Mittwoch (Middle of the Week), and Saturday is Sonnabend (Sunday's Eve).

The Names of the Months

January: named after Janus, protector of the gateway to heaven

February: named after Frebrualia, a time period when sacrifices were made to atone for sins

March: named after Mars, the god of war, presumably signifying that the campaigns interrupted by the winter could be resumed

April: from *aperire,* Latin for "to open" (buds)

May: named after Maia, the goddess of growth of plants

June: from *juvenis,* Latin for "youth."

July: named after Julius Caesar

August: named after Augustus, the first Roman Emperor

September: from *septem,* Latin for "seven"

October: from *octo,* Latin for "eight"

November: from *novem,* Latin for "nine"

December: from *decem,* Latin for "ten"

NOTE: The earliest Latin calendar was a 10-month one; thus September was the seventh month, October, the eighth, etc. July was originally called Quintilis, as the fifth month; August was originally called Sextilis, as the sixth month.

Astronomical Constants

Light-year (distance traveled by light in one year)	5,880,000,000,000 mi.
Parsec (parallax of one second for stellar distances)	3.259 light-yrs.
Velocity of light	186,281.7 mi./sec.
Astronomical unit (A.U.), or mean distance earth-to-sun	ca. 93,000,000 mi.[1]
Mean distance, earth to moon	238,860 mi.
General precession	50".26
Obliquity of the ecliptic	23° 27' 8".26–0".4684(t – 1900)[2]
Equatorial radius of the earth	3963.34 statute mi.
Polar radius of the earth	3949.99 statute mi.
Earth's mean radius	3958.89 statute mi.
Oblateness of the earth	1/297
Equatorial horizontal parallax of the moon	57' 2".70
Earth's mean velocity in orbit	18.5 mi./sec.
Sidereal year	365d.2564
Tropical year	365d.2422
Sidereal month	27d.3217
Synodic month	29d.5306
Mean sidereal day	23 56 4 .091 of mean solar time
Mean solar day	24 3 56 .555 of sidereal time

1. Actual mean distance derived from radar bounces: 92,935,700 mi. The value of 92,897,400 mi. (based on parallax of 8".80) is used in calculations.
2. *t* refers to the year in question, for example, 1980.

How Old Is Man?

Paleoanthropologists (anthropologists who specialize in the study of fossil man) disagree on when humans first were differentiated from their pre-human ancestors. Estimates range from 2 to 3.8 million years ago, based on such criteria as brain size, knee joints indicating an ability to walk on two legs, and tool-making ability.

The old concept of a single line of development from ape to man has been replaced by the generally accepted theory that there were at least three different forms of early man and near man in Africa, where most scientists agree humans first emerged.

Atomic Energy

Just as the Space Age is said to have started with the orbiting of Sputnik I, the Atomic Age is said to have started with the explosion of a test bomb on July 16, 1945, near Alamogordo, N.M., at 5:30 A.M. local time. The bomb was placed on top of a steel tower, and observers were stationed in bunkers 10,000 yards away. The explosion vaporized the steel tower, produced a mushroom cloud rising to 40,000 feet, and melted the desert sand into glass for distances up to 800 yards from the tower.

The first operational use of an atom bomb took place only three weeks later, when a uranium bomb was exploded over Hiroshima, Japan, on Aug. 6, 1945. The bomb, cylindrical in shape, 10 feet long with a diameter of 2 feet 4 inches, weighed about 9,000 pounds. Its explosive force was equal to 20,000 tons of TNT, hence the term "20-kiloton bomb." Three days later another atomic bomb, this time of plutonium, was exploded over Nagasaki.

Of course, the Atomic Age did not begin with the explosion of the test bomb at Alamogordo, just as the Space Age did not begin with the orbiting of the first artificial satellite. In both cases these visible feats were just experiments which proved the theory that had been built up patiently over decades.

At the turn of the century, scientists began to wonder whether the atoms of the chemical elements might not be composed of smaller particles. This was actually a contradiction in terms, because the Greek word *atomos,* from which the word *atom* was derived, meant "indivisible." But there were some indications of particles smaller than an atom—the electrons. In 1905, Albert Einstein suggested that matter might just be "condensed energy" and gave the conversion formula E mc^2, in which E represents the energy, m the mass, and c the velocity of light. If this formula was correct, a small piece of matter should represent enormous amounts of energy.

Fission and Fusion

As is now generally known, atomic energy can be released in two ways. One is the *fission* of elements with very heavy atoms, such as uranium and plutonium, which will split when struck by a neutron, a sub-atomic particle. The splitting of the heavy atom releases more neutrons, which are then available to split other atoms—the so-called chain reaction. The other way of obtaining atomic energy is *fusion;* four light atoms (hydrogen) are fused together into the next heavier element (helium). The fusion reaction requires enormous heat and very high pressures. These pressures, coupled with very high temperatures, can most easily be produced by exploding a fission bomb, which is the reason why it is often said that a fission bomb is the trigger for a fusion (hydrogen) bomb.

Interestingly enough, the fusion reaction was discovered first, though only on paper. For the period from, say, 1910 to 1930, most physicists believed that the release of atomic energy, if it could be done, would be of no practical value. They asserted that causing the release would require more energy than could be obtained. Most astronomers, on the other hand, were convinced that atomic energy was released in the sun and the other stars because there was no other way to account for the energy the stars radiated into space. Trying to account for the energy radiated by the stars led to theoretical papers predicting what we now call the fusion reaction. At the time (1930), atomic fission was still unknown; it was discovered first by Enrico Fermi in 1934. But nobody yet knew that the sudden bursts of energy observed in the experiments were due to the fission of the uranium-235 atom. This was established (by way of calculation) by Dr. Lise Meitner. Once it was known what happened, the way to a premeditated release of atomic energy was clear.

But nobody could be quite certain whether the release would take the form of an explosion or whether it would be slow enough to be used to generate power. American scientists proceeded under the assumption that the release would be sudden and violent (and the Alamogordo test proved them right), while Professor Heisenberg in Germany thought the slow release to be more likely, which is the reason why the Germans did not start a large-scale atomic energy project.

Atoms for Peace

The *peaceful* Atomic Age can be said to have been born in 1954, when the original U.S. Atomic Energy Act was amended to release many so-called "secrets" of nuclear energy so that nuclear power plants could be built and radioactive isotopes be used in medicine. The next year, the first International Conference on the Peaceful Uses of the Atom was convened at Geneva, bringing together scientists from all over the world to discuss what hitherto had been considered to be secret.

Actually there was little that was really secret about nuclear energy. When the results of the 1938 experiments were brought to the United States, scientists from different parts of the world openly stated that the possibility of atomic bombs was inherent in the scientific findings.

Once the veil of "secrecy" had been dispelled by revision of the Atomic Energy Act and the Geneva meeting, construction of plants to produce electricity by controlled fission of uranium atoms got under way in the United States and several other industrialized nations. Electric power was first produced as a result of nuclear fission in December 1951 at the National Reactor Testing Station in Idaho. When a reactor was connected to a generator, the nuclear power plant produced enough electricity for about 50 homes.

From that early beginning, the nuclear power industry has grown until, in 1978, 71 nuclear plants were in operation in the United States, supplying about 12% of the nation's electric power. Another 89 power reactors have construction permits from the U.S. Nuclear Regulatory Commission, four have limited work authorizations, and 42 more are on order. If all are built, they will have a total capacity of 200,968 electrical megawatts.

Twenty-one other nations have nuclear power plants in operation and 41 nations have firm commitments to build nuclear plants. Foreign countries have in operation and plan to build nuclear power plants producing 363,000 electrical megawatts.

Both in the United States and other countries, construction of nuclear power plants has been slowed by a combination of public concern over their environmental effects, the possibility of using them as clandestine sources of weapons-grade plutonium, and the general decline in the demand for electric power.

Measures and Weights

Source: Department of Commerce, National Bureau of Standards.

The International System (Metric)

The International System of Units is a modernized version of the metric system, established by international agreement, i.e. provides a logical and interconnected framework for all measurements in science, industry, and commerce. The system is built on a foundation of seven basic units, and all other units are derived from them. (Use of metric weights and measures was legalized in the United States in 1866, and our customary units of weights and measures are defined in terms of the meter and kilogram.)

Length. Meter. The meter is defined as 1,650,763.73 wavelengths in vacuum of the orange-red line of the spectrum of krypton-86.

Time. Second. The second is defined as the duration of 9,192,631,770 cycles of the radiation associated with a specified transition of the cesium 133 atom.

Mass. Kilogram. The standard for the kilogram is a cylinder of platinum-iridium alloy kept by the International Bureau of Weights and Measures at Paris. A duplicate at the National Bureau of Standards serves as the mass standard for the United States. The kilogram is the only base unit still defined by a physical object.

Temperature. Kelvin. The kelvin is defined as the fraction 1/273.16 of the thermodynamic temperature of the triple point of water; that is, the point at which water forms an interface of solid, liquid and vapor. This is defined as 0.01°C on the Centigrade or Celsius scale and 32.02°F on the Fahrenheit scale. The temperature 0°K is called "absolute zero."

Electric Current. Ampere. The ampere is defined as that current that, if maintained in each of two long parallel wires separated by one meter in free space, would produce a force between the two wires (due to their magnetic fields) of 2 x 10^{-7} newton for each meter of length. (A newton is the unit of force which when applied to one kilogram mass would experience an acceleration of one meter per second per second.)

Luminous Intensity. Candela. The candela is defined as the luminous intensity of 1/600,000 of a square meter of a cavity at the temperature of freezing platinum (2,042K).

Amount of Substance. Mole. The mole is the amount of substance of a system that contains as many elementary entities as there are atoms in 0.012 kilograms of carbon-12.

Metric and U.S. Equivalents

1 angstrom[1] (light wave measurement)	0.1 millimicron 0.000 1 micron 0.000 000 1 millimeter 0.000 000 004 inch
1 cable's length	120 fathoms 720 feet 219.456 meters
1 centimeter	0.3937 inch
1 chain (Gunter's or surveyor's)	66 feet 20.1168 meters
1 decimeter	3.937 inches
1 dekameter	32.808 feet
1 fathom	6 feet 1.8288 meters
1 foot	0.3048 meter
1 furlong	10 chains (surveyor's) 660 feet 220 yards 1/8 statute mile 201.168 meters

1 inch	2.54 centimeters
1 kilometer	0.621 mile
1 league (land)	3 statute miles 4.828 kilometers
1 link (Gunter's or surveyor's)	7.92 inches 0.201 168 meter
1 meter	39.37 inches 1.094 yards
1 micron	0.001 millimeter 0.000 039 37 inch
1 mil	0.001 inch 0.025 4 millimeter
1 mile (statute or land)	5,280 feet 1.609 kilometers
1 mile (nautical international)	1.852 kilometers 1.151 statute miles 0.999 U.S. nautical miles
1 millimeter	0.03937 inch
1 millimicron (mμ)	0.001 micron 0.000 000 039 37 inch
1 nanometer	0.001 micrometer or 0.000 000 039 37 inch
1 point (typography)	0.013 837 inch 1/72 inch (approximately) 0.351 millimeter
1 rod, pole, or perch	16 1/2 feet 5.0292 meters
1 yard	0.9144 meter

AREAS OR SURFACES

1 acre	43,560 square feet
	4,840 square yards
	0.405 hectare
1 are	119.599 square yards
	0.025 acre
1 hectare	2.471 acres
1 square centimeter	0.155 square inch
1 square decimeter	15.5 square inches
1 square foot	929.030 square centimeters
1 square inch	6.4516 square centimeters
1 square kilometer	0.386 square mile
	247.105 acres
1 square meter	1.196 square yards
	10.764 square feet
1 square mile	258.999 hectares
1 square millimeter	0.002 square inch
1 square rod, square pole or square perch	25.293 square meters
1 square yard	0.836 square meters

CAPACITIES OR VOLUMES

1 barrel, liquid	31 to 42 gallons[2]
1 barrel, standard for fruits, vegetables, and other dry commodities except cranberries	7,056 cubic inches
	105 dry quarts
	3.281 bushels, struck measure

1 barrel, standard, cranberry	5.286 cubic inches 86 45/64 dry quarts 2.709 bushels, struck measure
1 bushel (U.S.) struck measure	2,150.42 cubic inches 35.238 liters
1 bushel, heaped (U.S.)	2,747.715 cubic inches 1.278 bushels, struck measure[3]
1 cord (firewood)	128 cubic feet
1 cubic centimeter	0.061 cubic inches
1 cubic decimeter	61.024 cubic inches
1 cubic foot	7.481 gallons 28.316 cubic decimeters
1 cubic inch	0.554 fluid ounce 4.433 fluid drams 16.387 cubic centimeters
1 cubic meter	1.308 cubic yards
1 cubic yard	0.765 cubic meter
1 cup, measuring	8 fluid ounces 1/2 liquid pint
1 dram, fluid or liquid (U.S.)	1/8 fluid ounces 0.226 cubic inch 3.697 milliliters 1.041 British fluid drachms
1 dekaliter	2.642 gallons 1.135 pecks
1 gallon (U.S.)	231 cubic inches 3.785 liters 0.833 British gallon 128 U.S. fluid ounces

1 gallon (British Imperial)	277.42 cubic inches
	1.201 U.S. gallons
	4.546 liters
	160 British fluid ounces
1 gill	7.219 cubic inches
	4 fluid ounces
	0.118 liter
1 hectoliter	26.418 gallons
	2.838 bushels
1 liter	1.057 liquid quarts
	0.908 dry quart
	61.024 cubic inches
1 milliliter	0.271 fluid drams
	16.231 minims
	0.061 cubic inch
1 ounce, fluid or liquid (U.S.)	1.805 cubic inch
	29.574 milliliters
	1.041 British fluid ounces
1 peck	8.810 liters
1 pint, dry	33.600 cubic inches
	0.551 liter
1 pint, liquid	28.875 cubic inches
	0.473 liter
1 quart, dry (U.S.)	67.201 cubic inches
	1.101 liters
	0.969 British quart
1 quart, liquid (U.S.)	57.75 cubic inches
	0.946 liter
	0.833 British quart
1 quart (British)	69.354 cubic inches
	1.032 U.S. dry quarts
	1.201 U.S. liquid quarts

1 tablespoon, measuring	3 teaspoons
	4 fluid drams
	1/2 fluid ounce
1 teaspoon, measuring	1/3 tablespoon
	1 1/3 fluid drams
1 assay ton[4]	29.167 grams
1 carat	200 milligrams
	3.086 grains
1 dram, apothecaries	60 grains
	3.888 grams
1 dram, avoirdupois	27 11/32 ($=27.344$) grains
	1.772 grams
1 grain	64.798 91 milligrams
1 gram	15.432 grains
	0.035 ounce, avoirdupois
1 hundredweight, gross or long[5]	112 pounds
	50.802 kilograms
1 hundredweight, net or short	100 pounds
	45.359 kilograms
1 kilogram	2.205 pounds
1 microgram [$\mu\gamma$ (the Greek letter mu in combination with the letter g)]	0.000 001 gram
1 milligram	0.015 grain
1 ounce, avoirdupois	437.5 grains
	0.911 troy or apothecaries ounce
	28.350 grams

1 ounce, troy or apothecaries	480 grains
	1.097 avoirdupois ounces
	31.103 grams
1 pennyweight	1.555 grams
1 point	0.01 carat
	2 milligrams
1 pound, avoirdupois	7,000 grains
	1.215 troy or apothecaries pounds
	453.592 37 grams
1 pound, troy or apothecaries	5,760 grains
	0.823 avoirdupois pound
	373.242 grams
1 ton, gross on long[5]	2,204 pounds
	1.12 net tons
	1.016 metric tons
1 ton, metric	2,204.623 pounds
	0.984 gross ton
	1.102 net tons
1 ton, net or short	2,000 pounds
	0.893 gross ton
	0.907 metric ton

1. The angstrom is basically defined as 10^{10} meter. 2. There is a variety of "barrels" established by law or usage. For example, federal taxes on fermented liquors are based on a barrel of 31 gallons; many state laws fix the "barrel for liquids" at 31 1/2 gallons; one state fixes a 36-gallon barrel for cistern measurement; federal law recognizes a 40-gallon barrel for "proof spirits"; by custom, 42 gallons comprise a barrel of crude oil or petroleum products for statistical purposes, and this equivalent is recognized "for liquids" by four states. 3. Frequently recognized as 1 $^1/_4$ bushels, struck measure. 4. Used in assaying. The assay ton bears the same relation to the milligram that a ton of 2,000 pounds avoirdupois bears to the ounce troy; hence the weight in milligrams of precious metal obtained from one assay ton of ore gives directly the number of troy ounces to the net ton. 5. The gross or long ton and hundredweight are used commercially in the United States to only a limited extent, usually in restricted industrial fields. These units are the same as the British "ton" and "hundredweight."

Miscellaneous Units of Measure

Acre: An area of 43,560 square feet. Originally, the area a yoke of oxen could plow in one day.

Agate: Originally a measurement of type size (5 1/2 points). Now equal to 1/14 inch. Used in printing for measuring column length.

Ampere: Unit of electric current. A potential difference of one volt across a resistance of one ohm produces a current of one ampere.

Astronomical Unit (A.U.): 93,000,000 miles, the average distance of the earth from the sun. Used in astronomy.

Bale: A large bundle of goods. In the U.S., the approximate weight of a bale of cotton is 500 pounds. The weight varies in other countries.

Board Foot (fbm): 144 cubic inches (12 in. x 12 in. x 1 in.). Used for lumber.

Bolt: 40 yards. Used for measuring cloth.

BTU: British thermal unit. Amount of heat needed to increase the temperature of one pound of water by one degree Fahrenheit (252 calories).

Carat (c): 200 milligrams or 3.086 grains troy. Originally the weight of a seed of the carob tree in the Mediterranean region. Used for weighing precious stones. *See also* Karat.

Chain (ch): a chain 66 feet or one-tenth of a furlong in length, divided into 100 parts called links. One mile is equal to 80 chains. Used in surveying and sometimes called Gunter's or surveyor's chain.

Cubit: 18 inches or 45.72 cm. Derived from distance between elbow and tip of middle finger.

Decibel: Unit of relative loudness. One decibel is the smallest amount of change detectable by the human ear.

Ell, English: 1 1/4 yards or 1/32 bolt. Used for measuring cloth.

Freight Ton (also called Measurement Ton): 40 cubic feet of merchandise. Used for cargo freight.

Great Gross: 12 gross or 1728.

Gross: 12 dozen or 144.

Hand: 4 inches or 10.16 cm. Derived from the width of the hand. Used for measuring the height of horses at withers.

Hertz: Modern unit for measurement of electromagnetic wave frequencies (equivalent to "cycles per second").

Hogshead: (hhd): 2 liquid barrels or 14,653 cubic inches.

Horsepower: The power needed to lift 33,000 pounds a distance of one foot in one minute (about 1 1/2 times the power an average horse can exert). Used for measuring power of steam engines, etc.

Karat (kt): A measure of the purity of gold, indicating how many parts out of 24 are pure. For example, 18 karat gold is 3/4 pure. Sometimes spelled *carat*.

Knot: Not a distance, but the rate of speed of one nautical mile per hour. Used for measuring speed of ships.

League: Rather indefinite and varying measure, but usually estimated at 3 miles in English-speaking countries.

Light-Year: 5,880,000,000,000 miles, the distance light travels in a year at the rate of 186,281.7 miles per second. (If an astronomical unit were represented by one inch, a light-year would be represented by about one mile.) Used for measurements in interstellar space.

Magnum: Two-quart bottle. Used for measuring wine, etc.

Ohm: Unit of electrical resistance. A circuit in which a potential difference of one volt produces a current of one ampere has a resistance of one ohm.

Parsec: Approximately 3.26 light-years of 19.2 trillion miles. Term is combination of first syllables of *par*allax and *sec*ond, and distance is that of imaginary star when lines drawn from it to both earth and sun form a maximum angle or parallax of one second (1/3600 degree). Used for measuring interstellar distances.

Pi (π): 3.14159265+. The ratio of the circumference of a circle to its diameter. For practical purposes, the value is used to four decimal places: 3.1416.

Pica: 1/6 inch or 12 points. Used in printing for measuring column width, etc.

Pipe: 2 hogsheads. Used for measuring wine and other liquids.

Point: .013837 (approximately 1/72) inch or 1/12 pica. Used in printing for measuring type size.

Quintal: 100,000 grams or 220.46 pounds avoirdupois.

Quire: Used for measuring paper. Sometimes 24 sheets but more often 25. There are 20 quires in a ream.

Ream: Used for measuring paper. Sometimes 480 sheets, but more often 500 sheets.

Roentgen: Dosage unit of radiation exposure produced by X-rays.

Score: 20 units.

Sound, Speed of: Usually placed at 1,088 ft per second at 32°F at sea level. It varies at other temperatures and in different media.

Span: 9 inches or 22.86 cm. Derived from the distance between the end of the thumb and the end of the little finger when both are outstretched.

Square: 100 square feet. Used in building.

Stone: Legally 14 pounds avoirdupois in Great Britain.

Therm: 100,000 BTU's.

Township: U. S. land measurement of almost 36 square miles. The south border is 6 miles long. The east and west borders, also 6 miles long, follow the meridians, making the north border slightly less than 6 miles long. Used in surveying.

Tun: 252 gallons, but often larger. Used for measuring wine and other liquids.

Watt: Unit of power. The power used by a current of one ampere across a potential difference of one volt equals one watt.

Common Formulas
Circumference
Circle: $C = \pi d$, in which π is 3.1416 and d the diameter.

Area
Triangle: $A = \dfrac{ab}{2}$, in which a is the base and b the height.

Square: $A = a^2$, in which a is one of the sides.

Rectangle: $A = ab$, in which a is the base and b the height.

Trapezoid: $A = \dfrac{h(a+b)}{2}$, in which h is the height, a the longer parallel side, and b the shorter.

Regular pentagon: $A = 1.720a^2$, in which a is one of the sides.

Regular hexagon: $A = 2.598a^2$, in which a is one of the sides.

Regular octagon: $A = 4.828a^2$, in which a is one of the sides.

Circle: $A = \pi r^2$, in which π is 3.1416 and r the radius.

Volume

Cube: $V = a^3$, in which a is one of the edges.

Rectangular prism: $V = abc$, in which a is the length, b the width, and c the depth.

Pyramid: $V = \dfrac{Ah}{3}$, in which A is the area of the base and h the height.

Cylinder: $V = \pi r^2 h$, in which π is 3.1416, r the radius of the base, and h the height.

Cone: $V = \dfrac{\pi r^2 h}{3}$, in which π is 3.1416, r the radius of the base, and h the height.

Sphere: $V = \dfrac{4\pi r^3}{3}$, in which π is 3.1416 and r the radius.

Miscellaneous

Speed per second acquired by falling body: $v = 32t$, in which t is the time in seconds.

Distance in feet traveled by falling body: $d = 16t^2$, in which t is the time in seconds.

Speed of sound in feet per second through any given temperature of air: $V = \dfrac{1087\sqrt{273+t}}{16.52}$, in which t is the temperature Centigrade.

Cost in cents of operation of electrical device: $C = \dfrac{Wtc}{1000}$, in which W is the number of watts, t the time in hours, and c the cost in cents per kilowatt-hour.

Conversion of matter into energy (Einstein's Theorem): $E = mc^2$, in which E is the energy in ergs, m the mass of the matter in grams, and c the speed of light in centimeters per second. ($c^2 = 9 \cdot 10^{20}$).

Conversion Factors

To change	To	Multiply by
acres	hectares	.4047
acres	square feet	43,560
acres	square miles	.001562
atmospheres	cms. of mercury	76
BTU	horsepower-hour	.0003931
BTU	kilowatt-hour	.0002928
BTU/hour	watts	.2931
bushels	cubic inches	2150.4
bushels (U.S.)	hectoliters	.3524
centimeters	inches	.3937
centimeters	feet	.03281
circumference	radians	6.283
cubic feet	cubic meters	.0283
cubic meters	cubic feet	35.3145
cubic meters	cubic yards	1.3079
cubic yards	cubic meters	.7646
degrees	radians	.01745
dynes	grams	.00102
fathoms	feet	6.0
feet	meters	.3048
feet	miles (nautical)	.0001645
feet	miles (statute)	.0001894
feet/second	miles/hour	.6818
furlongs	feet	660.0
furlongs	miles	.125
gallons (U.S.)	liters	3.7853
grains	grams	.0648
grams	grains	15.4324
grams	ounces avdp	.0353
grams	pounds	.002205
hectares	acres	2.4710
hectoliters	bushels (U.S.)	2.8378
horsepower	watts	745.7
hours	days	.04167
inches	millimeters	25.4000
inches	centimeters	2.5400
kilograms	pounds avdp or t	2.2046
kilometers	miles	.6214
kilowatts	horsepower	1.341
knots	nautical miles/hour	1.0
knots	statute miles/hour	1.151
liters	gallons (U.S.)	.2642
liters	pecks	.1135
liters	pints (dry)	1.8162
liters	pints (liquid)	2.1134
liters	quarts (dry)	.9081
liters	quarts (liquid)	1.0567
meters	feet	3.2808

To change	To	Multi-ply by
meters	miles	.0006214
meters	yards	1.0936
metric tons	tons (long)	.9842
metric tons	tons (short)	1.1023
miles	kilometers	1.6093
miles	feet	5280
miles (nautical)	miles (statute)	1.1516
miles (statute)	miles (nautical)	.8684
miles/hour	feet/minute	88
millimeters	inches	.0394
ounces avdp.	grams	28.3495
ounces	pounds	.0625
ounces (troy)	ounces (avdp)	1.09714
pecks	liters	8.8096
pints (dry)	liters	.5506
pints (liquid)	liters	.4732
pounds ap or t	kilograms	.3782
pounds avdp	kilograms	.4536
pounds	ounces	16
quarts (dry)	liters	1.1012
quarts (liquid)	liters	.9463
radians	degrees	57.30
rods	meters	5.029
rods	feet	16.5
square feet	square meters	.0929
square kilometers	square miles	.3861
square meters	square feet	10.7639
square meters	square yards	1.1960
square miles	square kilometers	2.5900
square yards	square meters	.8361
tons (long)	metric tons	1.1060
tons (short)	metric tons	.9072
tons (long)	pounds	2240
tons (short)	pounds	2000
watts	BTU/hour	3.4129
watts	horsepower	.001341
yards	meters	.9144
yards	miles	.0005682

178

Temperature Conversion Table

° Centigrade	° Fahrenheit	° Centigrade	° Fahrenheit
−273.1	−459.6	30	86
−250	−418	35	95
−200	−328	40	104
−150	−238	45	113
−100	−148	50	122
−50	−58	55	131
−40	−40	60	140
−30	−22	65	149
−20	−4	70	158
−10	14	75	167
0	32	80	176
5	41	85	185
10	50	90	194
15	59	95	203
20	68	100	212
25	77		

Cooking Measurement Equivalents

16 tablespoons = 1 cup
12 tablespoons = 3/4 cup
10 tablespoons + 2 teaspoons = 2/3 cup
8 tablespoons = 1/2 cup
6 tablespoons = 3/8 cup
5 tablespoons + 1 teaspoon = 1/3 cup
4 tablespoons = 1/4 cup
2 tablespoons = 1/8 cup
2 tablespoons + 2 teaspoons = 1/6 cup
1 tablespoon = 1/16 cup
2 cups = 1 pint
2 pints = 1 quart
3 teaspoons = 1 tablespoon
48 teaspoons = 1 cup

SPORTS

AUTO RACING

The first automobiles on the road were erratic, and driving them—or even riding in them—was considered somewhat risky, hence it became the sporting thing to do. Experimental excursions in crude cars gave rise to rivalry in speed over the rough roads of the Gay Nineties, which eventually led to formal contests. The first such contest was a road race from Paris to Rouen in 1894, with 26 cars showing up at the starting line. Formal competition in the United States started with a road race in the Chicago district on Thanksgiving Day, 1895, and the winner, J. F. Duryea, covered the road distance of 54.36 miles at the then astonishing average speed of 7.5 miles per hour!

Around 1900, Paris became the hub of European road racing, and each year there were raucous, dusty, and dangerous races from Paris to Berlin, Vienna, Madrid, and other cities on the Continent. Accidents to drivers and spectators were so numerous that after a gory group of mishaps in the forepart of the Paris-Madrid race of 1903 public authorities halted the contest at Bordeaux and brought all road racing under control.

Not all early auto racing was of the cross-country type. Some contests, including 24-hour races for stock models, were held on circular or oval tracks originally built for horse racing. Finally came the special racing strips for autos, including such famous autodromes as Brooklands in England and the Indianapolis Speedway in the United States.

As a test of engine and chassis under severe conditions and great strain, auto racing rendered invaluable assistance in the development of the motor car of today.

THE ONE-MILE SPEED MARK

The first recorded effort for one mile was made on Jan. 12, 1904, by Henry Ford, driving a Ford "999." He established a record of 39.40 sec or 91.370 mph. All prior records were established over the flying kilometer. The first man to travel better than 100 mph was Rigolly, on July 2, 1904, at 103.56 mph. The first over 200 mph was Major H.O.D. Segrave, who drove a Sunbeam at 203.79 mph on March 29, 1927, at Daytona, Fla.

In 1947, John Cobb of London became the first person to travel more than 400 mph on land. The Englishman accomplished the feat on Sept. 16 at Bonneville, Utah, and raised the world mile record to 394.2 mph and the world kilometer mark to 393.8 mph. His car was a Railton-Mobil Special. Cobb's average speed was 9.1325 seconds per mile.

The record held by Cobb was surpassed by Britain's Donald Campbell at Lake Eyre in Australia on July 17, 1964. He drove his 30-foot, 4,250-horsepower Bluebird to two runs of 403.1 mph each. This record was beaten by Bob Summers of Ontario, Calif., who drove his 32-foot, four-engined Goldenrod to a speed of 409.227 mph at Bonneville on Nov. 12, 1965.

Craig Breedlove of Los Angeles, driving "Spirit of America," a three-wheeled, jet-powered car, at Bonneville on Aug. 5, 1963, attained a speed of 8.8355 seconds per mile, or 407.45 mph. The U.S. Auto Club created a new category for the record—jet unlimited class. The record was broken a number of times in 1964, Breedlove lifting it above 500 mph to 526.277 on Oct. 15. Again, in 1965, the mark was topped frequently—Breedlove and Art Arfons of Akron, Ohio, beating one another's records; finally, on Nov. 15, Breedlove surpassed 600 mph, achieving a standard of 600.601 at Bonneville. Gary Gabelich, driving the Blue Flame, raised the record to 622.407 mph on Oct. 23, 1970, at Bonneville. The rocket car, powered by a mixture of peroxide and natural gas, hit 617.602 on the first run and 627.287 on the second.

BASEBALL

The popular tradition that baseball was invented by Abner Doubleday at Cooperstown, N.Y., in 1839 has been enshrined in the Hall of Fame and National Museum of Baseball erected in that town, but research has proved that a game called "Base Ball" was played in this country and England before 1839. The first team baseball as we know it was played at the Elysian Fields, Hoboken, N.J., on June 19, 1846, between the Knickerbockers and the New York Nine. The next fifty years saw a gradual growth of baseball and an improvement of equipment and playing skill.

Historians have it that the first pitcher to throw a curve was William A. (Candy) Cummings in 1867. The Cincinnati Red Stockings were the first all-professional team, and in 1869 they played 64 games without a loss. The standard ball of the same size and weight, still the rule, was adopted in 1872. The first catcher's mask was worn in 1875. The National League was organized in 1876. The first chest protector was worn in 1885. The three-strike rule was put on the books in 1887, and the four-ball ticket to first base was instituted in 1889. The pitching distance was lengthened to 60 feet 6 inches in 1893, and the rules have been modified only slightly since that time.

The American League, under the vigorous leadership of B. B. Johnson, became a major league in 1901. Judge Kenesaw Mountain Landis, by action of the two major leagues, became Commissioner of Baseball in 1921, and upon his death (1944), Albert B. Chandler, former United States Senator from Kentucky, was elected to that office (1945). Chandler failed to obtain a new contract and was succeeded by Ford C. Frick (1951), the National League president. Frick retired after the 1965 season, and William D. Eckert, a retired Air Force lieutenant general, was named to succeed him. Eckert resigned under pressure in December, 1968. Bowie Kuhn, a New York attorney, became interim commissioner for one year in February. His appointment was made permanent with two seven-year contracts until August 1983.

LONGEST GAMES IN THE MAJORS

A 26-inning tie between the Brooklyn Dodgers and the Boston Braves on May 1, 1920, was the longest game in major league history. Played at Braves Field, Boston, the game was called because of darkness with the score 1–1. Both starting pitchers, Leon Cadore of Brooklyn and Joe Oeschger, were still in the game at the end, 3 hours and 50 minutes after it had begun. The longest game in terms of time, 7 hours and 23 minutes, was played by the New York Mets and the San Francisco Giants on May 31, 1964, in New York. The Giants won in 23 innings, 8–6. In the longest night game, the St. Louis Cards defeated the Mets at New York, 4–3, in 25 innings, Sept. 11, 1974. This game was played in 7 hours, 4 minutes.

MAJOR LEAGUE INDIVIDUAL ALL-TIME RECORDS

Highest Batting Average—.438, Hugh Duffy, Boston N.L., 1894 (Since 1900—.424, Rogers Hornsby, St. Louis N.L., 1924.)

Most Times at Bat—12,364, Henry Aaron, Milwaukee N.L., 1954–65; Atlanta N.L., 1966–74; Milwaukee A.L., 1975–76.

Most Years Batted .300 or Better—23, Ty Cobb, Detroit A.L., 1906–26, Philadelphia A.L., 1927–28.

Most hits—4,191, Ty Cobb, Detroit A.L., 1905–26, Philadelphia A.L., 1927–28.

Most Hits, Season—257, George Sisler, St. Louis A.L., 1920.

Most Hits, Game (9 innings)—7, Wilbert Robinson, Baltimore N.L., 6 singles, 1 double, 1892. Rennie Stennett, Pittsburgh N.L., 4 singles, 2 doubles, 1 triple, 1975.

Most Hits, Game (extra innings)—9, John Burnett, Cleveland A.L., 18 innings, 7 singles, 2 doubles, 1932.

Most Hits in Succession—12, Mike Higgins, Boston A.L., in four games, 1938; Walt Dropo, Detroit A.L., in three games, 1952.

Most Consecutive Games Batted Safely—56, Joe DiMaggio, New York A.L., 1941.

Most Runs—2,244, Ty Cobb, Detroit A.L., 1905–26, Philadelphia A.L., 1927–28.

Most Runs, Season—196, William Hamilton, Philadelphia N.L., 1894. (Since 1900—177, Babe Ruth, New York A.L., 1921.)

Most Runs, Game—7, Guy Hecker, Louisville A.A., 1886. (Since 1900—6, by Mel Ott, New York N.L., 1934, 1944; Johnny Pesky, Boston A.L., 1946; Frank Torre, Milwaukee N.L., 1957.)

Most Runs Batted In—2,297, Henry Aaron, Milwaukee N.L., 1954–1965; Atlanta N.L., 1966–74; Milwaukee A.L., 1975–76.

Most Runs Batted in, Season—190, Hack Wilson, Chicago N.L., 1930.

Most Runs Batted In, Game—12, Jim Bottomley, St. Louis N.L., 1924.

Most Home Runs—755, Henry Aaron, Milwaukee N.L., 1954–1965; Atlanta N.L., 1966–74; Milwaukee A.L., 1975–76.

Most Home Runs, Season—61, Roger Maris, New York A.L., 1961 (162-game season); 60, Babe Ruth, New York A.L., 1927 (154-game season)

Most Home Runs, Game—4 (see table on page 968).

Most Home Runs with Bases Filled—23, Lou Gehrig, New York A.L., 1927–39.

Most 2-Base Hits—793, Tris Speaker, Boston A.L., 1907–15, Cleveland A.L., 1916–26, Washington A.L., 1927, Philadelphia A.L., 1928.

Most 2-Base Hits, Season—67, Earl Webb, Boston A.L., 1931.

Most 2-base Hits, Game—4, by many.

Most 3-Base Hits—312, Sam Crawford, Cincinnati N.L., 1899–1902, Detroit A.L., 1903–17.

Most 3-Base Hits, Season—36, Owen Wilson, Pittsburgh N.L., 1912.
Most 3-Base Hits, Game—4, George Strief, Philadelphia A.A., 1885; William Joyce, New York N.L., 1897. (Since 1900—3, by many.)
Most Games Played—3,218. Henry Aaron, Milwaukee N.L., 1954–1965; Atlanta, N.L., 1966–74; Milwaukee A.L., 1975–76.
Most Consecutive Games Played—2,130, Lou Gehrig, New York A.L., 1925–39.
Most Bases on Balls—2,056, Babe Ruth, Boston A.L., 1914–19; New York A.L., 1920–34, Boston N.L., 1935.
Most Bases on Balls, Season—170, Babe Ruth, New York A.L., 1923.
Most Bases on Balls, Game—6, Walter Wilmot, Chicago N.L., 1891; Jimmy Foxx, Boston A.L., 1938.
Most Strikeouts—1,710, Mickey Mantle, New York A.L., 1951–68.
Most Strikeouts, Season—189, Bobby Bonds, San Francisco N.L., 1970.
Most Strikeouts, Game (9 innings)—5, by many.
Most Strikeouts, Game (extra innings)—6, Carl Weilman, St. Louis A.L., 15 innings, 1913; Don Hoak, Chicago N.L., 17 innings, 1956; Fred Reichardt, California A.L., 17, innings, 1966; Billy Cowan, California A.L., 20, 1971; Cecil Cooper, Boston A.L., 15, 1974.
Most pinch-hits, lifetime—144, Forrest Burgess, Chi.-Mil.-Cin.-Pitts., N.L., 1949, 1951–64; Chi., A.L., 1964–67.
Most Pinch-hits, season—25, Jose Morales, Montreal N.L., 1976.
Most consecutive pinch-hits—9, Dave Philley, Phil., N.L., 1958 (8), 1959 (1).
Most pinch-hit home runs, lifetime—18, Gerald Lynch, Pitt.-Cin. N.L., 1957–66.
Most pinch-hit home runs, season—6, Johnny Frederick, Brooklyn, N.L., 1932.
Most stolen bases, lifetime (since 1900)—917, Lou Brock, Chicago N.L. 1961–64; St. Louis, N.L. 1964–78.
Most stolen bases; season—156, Harry Stovey, Philadelphia, American Assn., 1888. Since 1900: 96, Ty Cobb, Detroit A.L. (156 games 1915); 118, Lou Brock, St. Louis, N.L. (162 games, 1974).
Most stolen bases, game—7, George Gore, Chicago N.L. 1881; William Hamilton, Philadelphia N.L. 1894. (Since 1900—6, Eddie Collins, Philadelphia A.L., 1912.)
Most times stealing home, lifetime—35, Ty Cobb, Detroit-Phil. A.L., 1905–28.

MAJOR LEAGUE ALL-TIME PITCHING RECORDS

Most Games Won—511, Cy Young, Cleveland N.L., 1890–98, St. Louis N.L., 1899–1900, Boston A.L., 1901–08, Cleveland A.L., 1909–11, Boston N.L., 1911.
Most Games Won, Season—60, Hoss Radbourne, Providence N.L., 1884. (Since 1900—41, Jack Chesbro, New York A.L., 1904.)
Most Consecutive Games Won—24, Carl Hubbell, New York N.L., 1936 (16) and 1937 (8).
Most Consecutive Games Won, Season—19, Tim Keefe, New York N.L., 1888; Rube Marquard, New York N.L., 1912.
Most Years Won 20 or More Games—16, Cy Young, Cleveland N.L., 1891–98, St. Louis N.L., 1899–1900, Boston A.L., 1901–04, 1907–08.
Most Shutouts—113, Walter Johnson, Wash. A.L., 1907–27.
Most Shutouts, Season—16, Grover Alexander, Philadelphia N.L., 1916.
Most Consecutive Shutouts—6, Don Drysdale, Los Angeles, N.L., 1968.
Most Consecutive Scoreless Innings—58, Don Drysdale, Los Angeles, N.L., 1968.
Most Strikeouts—3,508, Walter Johnson, Washington A.L. 1907–27.
Most Strikeouts, Season—505, Matthew Kilroy, Baltimore A.A., 1886. (Since 1900—383, Nolan Ryan, California, A.L., 1973.)
Most Strikeouts, Game—21, Tom Cheney, Washington A.L. 1962, 16 innings. Nine innings: 19, Charles McSweeney, Providence N.L., 1884; Hugh Dailey, Chicago

U.A., 1884. (Since 1900—19, Steve Carlton, St. Louis N.L. vs. New York, Sept. 15, 1969; Tom Seaver, New York N.L. vs. San Diego, April 22, 1970; Nolan Ryan, California A.L. vs. Boston, Aug. 12, 1974.)

Most Consecutive Strikeouts—10, Tom Seaver, New York N.L. vs. San Diego, April 22, 1970.

Most Games, Season—106, Mike Marshall, Los Angeles, N.L., 1974.

Most Complete Games, Season—74, William White, Cincinnati N.L., 1879. (Since 1900—48, Jack Chesbro, New York A.L., 1904.)

BASEBALL'S PERFECTLY PITCHED GAMES[1]
(no opposing runner reached base)

John Richmond—Worcester vs. Cleveland (NL) June 12, 1880 1–0

John M. Ward—Providence vs. Buffalo (NL) June 17, 1880 5–0

Cy Young—Boston vs. Philadelphia (AL) May 5, 1904 3–0

Addie Joss—Cleveland vs. Chicago (AL) Oct. 2, 1908 1–0

Ernest Shore[2]—Boston vs. Washington (AL) June 23, 1917 4–0

Charles Robertson—Chicago vs. Detroit (AL) April 30, 1922 2–0

Don Larsen[3]—New York (AL) vs. Brooklyn (NL) Oct. 8, 1956 2–0

Jim Bunning—Philadelphia vs. New York (NL) June 21, 1964 6–0

Sandy Koufax—Los Angeles vs. Chicago (NL) Sept. 9, 1965 1–0

Jim Hunter—Oakland vs. Minnesota (AL) May 8, 1968 4–0

1. Harvey Haddix, of Pittsburgh, pitched 12 perfect innings against Milwaukee (NL), May 26, 1959 but lost game in 13th on error and hit. 2. Shore, relief pitcher for Babe Ruth who walked first batter before being ejected by umpire, retired 26 batters who faced him and baserunner was out stealing. 3. World Series.

LARSEN'S PERFECT GAME IN 1956 WORLD SERIES

Don Larsen of the New York Yankees pitched the only no-run no-hit game in World Series history in 1956 and hurled a perfect game in so doing. Facing the Brooklyn Dodgers at the Yankee Stadium in the fifth game before 64,519 on Oct. 8, Larsen retired 27 batters in a row. The Yankees won, 2 to 0.

CONSECUTIVE NO-HITTERS BY VANDER MEER

Johnny Vander Meer, a 23-year-old lefthander with the Cincinnati Reds, pitched consecutive no-hitters in June 1938, setting a mark of 18 innings of no-hit hurling. On June 11, in Cincinnati, he set down Boston without a hit as the Reds won, 3–0. Four days later, June 15, in the first night game in Brooklyn, he again held the opposition hitless as the Reds triumphed, 6–0. He was nicknamed Johnny (Double No-Hitter) Vander Meer.

BASKETBALL

Basketball may be the one sport whose exact origin is definitely known. In the winter of 1891–92, Dr. James Naismith, an instructor in the Y.M.C.A. Training College (now Springfield College) at Springfield, Mass., deliberately invented the game of basketball in order to provide indoor exercise and competition for the students between the closing of the football season and the opening of the baseball season. He affixed peach baskets overhead on the walls at opposite ends of the gymnasium and organized teams to play his new game in which the purpose was to toss an association (soccer) ball into one basket and prevent the opponents from tossing the ball into the other basket. The game is fundamentally the same today, though there have been improvements in equipment and some changes in rules.

Because Dr. Naismith had eighteen available players when he invented the game, the first rule was: "There shall be nine players on each side." Later the number of players became optional, depending upon the size of the available court, but the five-player standard was adopted when the game spread over the country. United States soldiers brought basketball to Europe in World War I, and it soon became a world-wide sport.

BOXING

Whether it be called pugilism, prize fighting or boxing, there is no tracing "the Sweet Science" to any definite source. Tales of rivals exchanging blows for fun, fame or money go back to earliest recorded history and classical legend. There was a mixture of boxing and wrestling called the "pancratium" in the ancient Olympic Games and in such contests the rivals belabored one another with hands fortified with heavy leather wrappings that were sometimes studded with metal. More than one Olympic competitor lost his life at this brutal exercise.

There was little law or order in pugilism until Jack Broughton, one of the early champions of England, drew up a set of rules for the game in 1743. Broughton, called "the father of English boxing," also is credited with having invented boxing gloves. However, these gloves—or "mufflers" as they were called—were used only in teaching "the manly art of self-defense" or in training bouts. All professional championship fights were contested with "bare knuckles" until 1892, when John L. Sullivan lost the heavyweight championship of the world to James J. Corbett in New Orleans in a bout in which both contestants wore regulation gloves.

The Broughton rules were superseded by the London Prize Ring Rules of 1838. The 8th Marquis of Queensberry, with the help of John G. Chambers, put foreward the "Queensberry Rules" in 1866, a code that called for gloved contests. Amateurs took quickly to the Queensberry Rules, the professionals slowly.

FOOTBALL

The pastime of kicking around a ball goes back beyond the limits of recorded history. Ancient savage tribes played football of a primitive kind. There was a ball-kicking game played by Athenians, Spartans, and Corinthians 2500 years ago, which the Greeks called *Episkuros*. The Romans had a somewhat similar game called *Harpastum* and are supposed to have carried the game with them when they invaded the British Isles in the First Century, B.C.

Undoubtedly the game known in the United Stated as Football traces directly to the English game of Rugby, though the modifications have been many. Informal football was played on college lawns well over a century ago, and an annual Freshman-Sophomore series of "scrimmages" began at Yale in 1840. The first formal intercollegiate football game was the Princeton-Rutgers contest at New Brunswick, N.J., on Nov. 6, 1869, with Rutgers winning by 6 goals to 4.

In those days, games were played with 25, 20, 15, or 11 men on a side. In 1880, there was a convention at which Walter Camp of Yale persuaded the delegates to agree to a rule calling for 11 players on a side. The game grew so rough that it was attacked as brutal, and some colleges abandoned the sport. Conditions were so bad in 1906 that President Theodore Roosevelt called a meeting of Yale, Harvard, and Princeton representatives at the White House in the hope of reforming and improving the game. The outcome was that the game, with the forward pass introduced and some other modifications of the rules inserted, became faster and cleaner.

The first professional game was played in 1895 at Latrobe, Pa. The National Football League was founded in
1921. The All-American Conference went into action in
1946. At the end of the 1949 season the two circuits
merged, retaining the name of the older league. In 1960,
the American Football League, began operations. In 1970,
the leagues merged.

GOLF

It may be that golf originated in Holland—historians believe it did—but certainly Scotland fostered the game and
is famous for it. In fact, in 1457 the Scottish Parliament,
disturbed because football and golf had lured young Scots
from the more soldierly exercise of archery, passed an ordi-
nance that "futeball and golf be utterly cryit doun and
nocht usit." James I and Charles I of the royal line of Stuarts
were golf enthusiasts, whereby the game came to be
known as "the royal and ancient game of golf."

The golf balls used in the early games were leather-
covered and stuffed with feathers. Clubs of all kinds were
fashioned by hand to suit individual players. The great step
in spreading the game came with the change from the
feather ball to the guttapercha ball about 1850. In 1860,
formal competition began with the establishment of an
annual tournament for the British Open championship.
There are records of "golf clubs" in the United States as far
back as colonial days but no proof of actual play before John
Reid and some friends laid out six holes on the Reid lawn
in Yonkers, N.Y., in 1888 and played there with golf balls
and clubs brought over from Scotland by Robert Lockhart.
This group then formed the St. Andrews Golf Club of
Yonkers, and golf was established in this country.

However, it remained a rather sedate and almost aristo-
cratic pastime until a 20-year-old ex-caddy, Francis Ouimet of Boston, defeated two great British professionals,
Harry Vardon and Ted Ray, in the United States Open
championship at Brookline, Mass., in 1913. This feat put
the game and Francis Ouimet on the front pages of the
newspapers and stirred a wave of enthusiasm for the sport.
The greatest feat so far in golf history is that of Robert Tyre
Jones, Jr., of Atlanta, who won the British Open, the British
Amateur, the U.S. Open, and the U.S. Amateur titles in one
year, 1930.

HARNESS RACING

Oliver Wendell Holmes, the famous Autocrat of the Breakfast Table, wrote that the running horse was a gambling toy but the trotting horse was useful and, furthermore, "horse-racing is not a republican institution; horse-trotting is." Oliver Wendell Holmes was a born-and-bred New Englander, and New England was the nursery of the harness racing sport in America. Pacers and trotters were matters of local pride and prejudice in Colonial New England, and, shortly after the Revolution, the Messenger and Justin Morgan strains produced many winners in harness racing "matches" along the turnpikes of New York, Connecticut, Rhode Island, Massachusetts, Vermont, and New Hampshire.

There was English thoroughbred blood in Messenger and Justin Morgan, and, many years later, it was blended in Rysdyk's Hambletonian, foaled in 1849. Hambletonian was not particularly fast under harness but his descendants have had almost a monopoly of prizes, titles, and records in the harness racing game. Hambletonian was purchased as a foal with its dam for a total of $124 by William Rysdyk of Goshen, N.Y., and made a modest fortune for the purchaser.

Trotters and pacers often were raced under saddle in the old days, and, in fact, the custom still survives in some places in Europe. Dexter, the great trotter that lowered the mile record from 2:19¾ to 2:17¼ in 1867, was said to handle just as well under saddle as when pulling a sulky. But as sulkies were lightened in weight and improved in design, trotting under saddle became less common and finally faded out in this country.

HOCKEY

Ice hockey, by birth and upbringing a Canadian game, is an offshoot of field hockey. Some historians say that the first ice hockey game was played in Montreal in December 1879 between two teams composed almost exclusively of McGill University students, but others assert that earlier hockey games took place in Kingston, Ontario, or Halifax, Nova Scotia. In the Montreal game of 1879, there were fifteen players on a side, who used an assortment of crude sticks to keep the puck in motion. Early rules allowed nine men on a side, but the number was reduced to seven in 1886 and later to six.

The first governing body of the sport was the Amateur Hockey Association of Canada, organized in 1887. In the winter of 1894–95, a group of college students from the United States visited Canada and saw hockey played. They became enthused over the game and introduced it as a winter sport when they returned home. The first professional league was the International Hockey League, which operated in northern Michigan in 1904–06.

Until 1910, professionals and amateurs were allowed to play together on "mixed teams," but this arrangement ended with the formation of the first "big league," the National Hockey Association, in eastern Canada in 1910. The Pacific Coast League was organized in 1911 for western Canadian hockey. The league included Seattle and later other American cities. The National Hockey League replaced the National Hockey Association in 1917. Boston, in 1924, was the first American city to join that circuit. The league expanded to include western cities in 1967. The Stanley Cup was competed for by "mixed teams" from 1894 to 1910, thereafter by professionals. It was awarded to the winner of the N.H.L. playoffs from 1926–67 and now to the league champion. The World Hockey Association was organized in October 1972 in opposition to the N.H.L.

HORSE RACING

Ancient drawings on stone and bone prove that horse racing is at least 3000 years old, but Thoroughbred Racing is a modern development. Practically every thoroughbred in training today traces its registered ancestry back to one or more of three sires that arrived in England about 1728 from the Near East and became known, from the names of their owners, as the Byerly Turk, the Darley Arabian, and the Godolphin Arabian. The Jockey Club (English) was founded at Newmarket in 1750 or 1751 and became the custodian of the Stud Book as well as the court of last resort in deciding turf affairs.

Horse racing took place in this country before the Revolution, but the great lift to the breeding industry came with the importation in 1798, by Col. John Hoomes of Virginia, of Diomed, winner of the Epsom Derby of 1780. Diomed's lineal descendants included such famous stars of the American turf as American Eclipse and Lexington. From 1800 to the time of the Civil War there were race courses and breeding establishments plentifully scattered through Virginia, North Carolina, South Carolina, Tennessee, Kentucky, and Louisiana.

The oldest stake event in North America is the Queen's Plate, a Canadian fixture that was first run in the Province of Quebec in 1836. The oldest stake event in the United States is The Travers, which was first run at Saratoga in 1864. The gambling that goes with horse racing and trickery by jockeys, trainers, owners, and track officials caused attacks on the sport by reformers and a demand among horse racing enthusiasts for an honest and effective control of some kind, but nothing of lasting value to racing came of this until the formation in 1894 of The Jockey Club.

"TRIPLE CROWN" WINNERS
IN THE UNITED STATES

(Kentucky Derby, Preakness and Belmont Stakes)

Year	Horse	Owner
1919	Sir Barton	J. K. L. Ross
1930	Gallant Fox	William Woodward
1935	Omaha	William Woodward
1937	War Admiral	Samuel D. Riddle
1941	Whirlaway	Warren Wright
1943	Count Fleet	Mrs. John Hertz
1946	Assault	Robert J. Kleberg
1948	Citation	Warren Wright
1973	Secretariat	Meadow Stable
1977	Seattle Slew	Karen Taylor
1978	Affirmed	Louis Wolfson

ANNUAL TURF LEADERS

Year	HORSES (Money Winners) Horse, age	Starts	1st	Earnings	JOCKEYS (No. of Winners) Jockey	Mts.	1st	TRAINERS (Winners Saddled) Trainer	1st	Earnings
1951	Counterpoint, 3	15	7	$250,525	Charley Burr	1,319	310	R. H. McDaniel	164	$539,204
1952	Crafty Admiral, 4	16	9	277,225	Tony DeSpirito	1,482	390	R. H. McDaniel	168	573,837
1953	Native Dancer, 3	10	9	513,425	Wm. Shoemaker	1,683	485	R. H. McDaniel	211	751,957
1954	Determine, 3	15	10	328,700	Wm. Shoemaker	1,251	380	F. H. Merrill, Jr.	206	834,390
1955	Nashua, 3	12	10	752,550	Bill Hartack	1,702	417	V. R. Wright	154	298,794
1956	Needles, 3	8	4	440,850	Bill Hartack	1,387	347	V. R. Wright	177	532,344
1957	Round Table, 3	22	15	600,383	Bill Hartack	1,238	341	V. R. Wright	192	527,271
1958	Round Table,	20	14	662,780	Wm. Shoemaker	1,133	300	F. H. Merrill, Jr.	171	320,827
1959	Sword Dancer, 3	13	8	537,004	Wm. Shoemaker	1,285	347	V. R. Wright	172	534,319
1960	Bally Ache, 3	15	10	455,045	Bill Hartack	1,402	307	F. H. Merrill, Jr.	143	344,459
1961	Carry Back, 3	16	9	565,349	John Sellers	1,394	328	V. R. Wright	178	442,650
1962	Never Bend, 2	10	7	402,969	Ronald Ferraro	1,755	352	W. H. Bishop	162	544,261
1963	Candy Spots, 3	12	7	604,481	Walter Blum	1,704	360	Howard Jacobson	140	730,418
1964	Gun Bow, 4	16	8	580,100	Walter Blum	1,577	324	Howard Jacobson	169	801,869
1965	Buckpasser, 2	11	9	568,096	Jesse Davidson	1,582	319	Howard Jacobson	200	863,721
1966	Buckpasser, 3	14	13	669,078	Avelino Gomez	996	318	Louis Cavalaris, Jr.	175	763,201
1967	Damascus, 3	16	12	817,941	Jorge Velasquez	1,939	438	Everett Hammond	200	325,905
1968	Forward Pass, 3	13	7	546,674	Angel Cordero	1,662	345	Jack Van Berg	256	776,330
1969	Arts and Letters, 3	14	8	555,604	Larry Snyder	1,645	352	Jack Van Berg	239	952,207
1970	Personality, 3	18	8	444,049	Sandy Hawley	1,908	452	Jack Van Berg	282	974,818
1971	Riva Ridge, 2	9	7	503,263	Laffit Pincay, Jr.	1,627	380	Jack Van Berg	245	290,553
1972	Droll Role, 4	19	7	471,633	Sandy Hawley	1,381	367	Dale Baird	286	1,381,067
1973	Secretariat, 3	12	9	860,404	Sandy Hawley	1,925	515	Dale Baird	305	416,592
1974	Chris Evert, 3	8	5	551,063	Chris McCarron	2,199	546	Jack Van Berg	329	1,567,418
1975	Foolish Pleasure, 3	11	5	716,278	Chris McCarron	2,194	468	Dick Dutrow	352	1,840,041
1976	Forego, 6	8	6	491,701	Sandy Hawley	1,637	413	Jack Van Berg	494	2,972,218
1977	Seattle Slew, 3	7	6	641,370	Steve Cauthen	2,075	487	King Leatherbury	322	1,762,062

TENNIS

Lawn tennis is a comparatively modern modification of the ancient game of court tennis. Major Walter Clopton Wingfield thought that something like court tennis might be played outdoors on lawns, and in December, 1873, at Nantclwyd, Wales, he introduced his new game under the name of *Sphairistike* at a lawn party. The game was a success and spread rapidly, but the name was a total failure and almost immediately disappeared when all the players and spectators began to refer to the new game as "lawn tennis." In the early part of 1874, a young lady named Mary Ewing Outerbridge returned from Bermuda to New York, bringing with her the implements and necessary equipment of the new game, which she had obtained from a British Army supply store in Bermuda. Miss Outerbridge and friends played the first game of lawn tennis in the United States on the grounds of the Staten Island Cricket and Baseball Club in the spring of 1874.

For a few years, the new game went along in haphazard fashion until about 1880, when standard measurements for the court and standard equipment within definite limits became the rule. In 1881, the U.S. Lawn Tennis Association (whose name was changed in 1975 to U.S. Tennis Association) was formed and conducted the first national championship at Newport, R.I. The international matches for the Davis Cup began with a series between the British and United States players on the courts of the Longwood Cricket Club, Chestnut Hill, Mass., in 1900, with the home players winning.

Professional tennis, which got its start in 1926 when the French star Suzanne Lenglen was paid $50,000 for a tour, received full recognition in 1968. Staid old Wimbledon, the London home of what are considered the world championships, let the pros compete. This decision ended a long controversy over open tennis and changed the format of the competition. The United States championships at Forest Hills switched, too. Pro tours for men and women became worldwide in play that continued throughout the year.

Only four players, two men and two women, have won the Grand Slam of Tennis by winning the Australian, French, Wimbledon, and United States singles championships. Rod Laver of Australia did it twice, in 1962 and again in 1969 when the tourneys were opens. Don Budge, an American, was the first to complete the slam in 1938. Maureen Connolly of California in 1953 was the first woman to take the four titles. Margaret Smith Court of Australia won them all in 1970.

YACHTING

Jason sailed in search of the Golden Fleece. Cleopatra (according to Shakespeare) had a royal barge with purple sails. Columbus had three sailing ships when he crossed the Atlantic westward in 1492. But who the first sailor was and where he launched his primitive craft nobody ever will know. The word "yacht" is of Dutch origin and the first "yacht race" of record in the English language was a sailing contest from Greenwich to Gravesend and return in 1662 between a Dutch yacht and an English yacht designed and, at some part of the race, sailed by Charles II of England. The royal yacht won.

The first yacht club was organized at Cork, Ireland, in 1720 under the name of the Cork Harbour Water Club, later changed to the Royal Cork Yacht Club. The Royal Yacht Squadron was organized at Cowes in 1812 and the name changed to the Royal Yacht Club in 1820. The New York Yacht Club was organized aboard the Stevens schooner "Gimcrack" on July 30, 1844, and a clubhouse erected at Elysian Fields, Hoboken, N.J., the following year.

From that time until the Civil War, races were held over courses starting from the water off the yacht club promontory.

In 1850 the celebrated "America" was built by a group of New York yachtsmen and sent abroad to compete at Cowes. In a race around the Isle of Wight, with a special cup as a prize, the "America" defeated fourteen English boats and brought back the trophy that has been raced for as "The America's Cup" in many international yacht races since that time.

HISTORY OF THE RECORD FOR THE MILE RUN

Time	Athlete	Country	Year	Location
4:36.5	Richard Webster	England	1865	England
4:29.0	William Chinnery	England	1868	England
4:28.8	Walter Gibbs	England	1868	England
4:26.0	Walter Slade	England	1874	England
4:24.5	Walter Slade	England	1875	London
4:23.2	Walter George	England	1880	London
4:21.4	Walter George	England	1882	London
4:18.4	Walter George	England	1884	Birmingham, England
4:18.2	Fred Bacon	Scotland	1894	Edinburgh
4:17.0	Fred Bacon	Scotland	1895	London
4:15.6	Thomas Conneff	United States	1895	Travers Island, N.Y.
4:15.4	John Paul Jones	United States	1911	Cambridge, Mass.
4:14.4	John Paul Jones	United States	1913	Cambridge, Mass.
4:12.6	Norman Taber	United States	1915	Cambridge, Mass.
4:10.4	Paavo Nurmi	Finland	1923	Stockholm
4:09.2	Jules Ladoumegue	France	1931	Paris
4:07.6	Jack Lovelock	New Zealand	1933	Princeton, N.J.
4:06.8	Glenn Cunningham	United States	1934	Princeton, N.J.
4:06.4	Sydney Wooderson	England	1937	London
4:06.2	Gundar Hägg	Sweden	1942	Göteborg, Sweden
4:06.2	Arne Andersson	Sweden	1942	Stockholm
4:04.6	Gunder Hägg	Sweden	1942	Stockholm
4:02.6	Arne Andersson	Sweden	1943	Göteborg, Sweden
4:01.6	Arne Andersson	Sweden	1944	Malmö, Sweden
4:01.4	Gunder Hägg	Sweden	1945	Malmö, Sweden
3:59.4	Roger Bannister	England	1954	Oxford, England
3:58.0	John Landy	Australia	1954	Turku, Finland
3:57.2	Derek Ibbotson	England	1957	London
3:54.5	Herb Elliott	Australia	1958	Dublin
3:54.4	Peter Snell	New Zealand	1962	Wanganui, N.Z.
3:54.1	Peter Snell	New Zealand	1964	Auckland, N.Z.
3:53.6	Michel Jarzy	France	1965	Rennes, France
3:51.3	Jim Ryun	United States	1966	Berkeley, Calif.
3:51.1	Jim Ryun	United States	1967	Bakersfield, Calif.
3:51.0	Filbert Bayi	Tanzania	1975	Kingston, Jamaica
3:49.4	John Walker	New Zealand	1975	Göteborg, Sweden

STANDARD MEASUREMENTS IN SPORTS

BASEBALL

Home plate to pitcher's box: 60 feet 6 inches.

Plate to second base: 127 feet 3⅜ inches.

Distance from base to base (home plate included): 90 feet.

Size of bases: 15 inches by 15 inches.

Pitcher's plate: 24 inches by 6 inches.

Batter's box: 3 feet by 4 feet.

Home plate: 17 inches by 17 inches, cut to a point at rear.

Home plate to backstop: Not less than 60 feet (recommended).

Weight of ball: Not less than 5 ounces nor more than 5¼ ounces.

Circumference of ball: Not less than 9 inches nor more than 9¼ inches.

Bat: Must be round, not over 2¾ inches in diameter at thickest part, nor more than 42 inches in length, and of solid wood in one piece or laminated.

FOOTBALL

Length of field: 120 yards. (including 10 yards of end zone at each end).

Width of field: 53⅓ yards (160 feet).

Height of goal posts: At least 20 feet.

Height of crossbar: 10 feet.

Width of goal posts (above crossbar): 23 feet 4 inches, inside to inside, and not more than 24 feet, outside to outside.

Length of ball: 11 to 11.25 inches (long axis).

Circumference of ball: 21.25 to 21.50 inches (middle); 28 to 28.5 inches (long axis).

LAWN TENNIS

Size of court: Rectangle 78 feet long and 27 feet wide (singles); 78 feet long and 36 feet wide (doubles).

Height of net: 3 feet in center, gradually rising to reach 3-foot 6-inch posts at a point 3 feet outside each side of court.

Ball: Shall be more than $2\frac{1}{2}$ inches and less than $2\frac{5}{8}$ inches in diameter and weight more than 2 ounces and less than $2\frac{1}{16}$ ounces.

Service line: 21 feet from net.

HOCKEY

Size of rink: 200 feet long by 85 feet wide surrounded by a wooden wall not less than 40 inches and not more than 48 inches above level of ice.

Size of goal: 6 feet wide by 4 feet in height.

Puck: 1 inch thick and 3 inches in diameter; made of vulcanized rubber; weight $5\frac{1}{2}$ to 6 ounces.

Length of stick: Not more than 55 inches from heel to end of shaft nor $12\frac{1}{2}$ inches from heel to end of blade. Blade should not be more than 3 inches in width but not less than 2 inches, except goalkeeper's stick, which shall not exceed $3\frac{1}{2}$ inches in width except at the heel, where it must not exceed $4\frac{1}{2}$ inches.

BOWLING

Lane dimensions: Overall length 62 feet $10\frac{3}{16}$ inches, measuring from foul line to pit (not including tail plank), with $\frac{1}{2}$ inch tolerance permitted. Foul line to center of No. 1 pinspot 60 feet, with $\frac{1}{2}$ inch tolerance permitted. Lane width, $41\frac{1}{2}$ inches with a tolerance of $\frac{1}{2}$ inch permitted. Approach, not less than 15 feet. Gutters, $9\frac{5}{16}$ inches wide with $\frac{3}{16}$ plus or $\frac{5}{16}$ minus tolerances permitted.

Ball: Circumference, not more than 27 inches. Weight, 16 pounds maximum.

GOLF

Weight of ball: Not greater than 1.620 ounces avoirdupois.

Size of ball: Not less than 1.680 inches in diameter.

Velocity of ball: Not greater than 250 feet per second when tested on U.S.G.A. apparatus, with 2 percent tolerance.

Hole: 4¼ inches in diamater and at least 4 inches deep.

Clubs: 14 is the maximum number permitted.

BASKETBALL

(National Collegiate A. A. Rules)

Playing court: College: 94 feet long by 50 feet wide. High School: 84 feet long by 50 feet wide (maximum inside dimensions).

Baskets: Rings 18 inches in inside diameter, with white cord 12-mesh nets, 15 to 18 inches in length. Each ring is made of metal, is not more than ⅝ of an inch in diameter and is bright orange in color.

Height of basket ring: 10 feet (upper edge).

Weight of ball: Not less than 20 ounces nor more than 22.

Circumference of ball: No greater than 30 inches and not less than 29½.

Free-throw line: 15 feet from the face of the backboard.

BOXING

Ring: Professional matches take place in an area not less than 18 nor more than 24 feet square including apron. It is enclosed by four covered ropes, each not less than one inch in diameter. The floor has a 2-inch padding of Ensolite (or equivalent) underneath ring cover that extends at least 6 inches beyond the roped area in the case of elevated rings. For A.A.U. boxing, not less than 16 nor more than 25 feet square within the ropes. The floor must extend beyond the ring ropes not less than 2 feet. The ring posts shall not be nearer to the ring ropes than 18 inches and must be properly padded.

Gloves: In professional fights, not less than 8-ounce gloves generally are used. A.A.U., not less than 10 ounces for all divisions.

THE OLYMPIC GAMES

(W)—Site of Winter Games. (S)—Site of Summer Games

1896	Athens		1948	London (S)
1900	Paris		1952	Oslo (W)
1904	St. Louis		1952	Helsinki (S)
1906	Athens		1956	Cortina d'Ampezzo,
1908	London			Italy (W)
1912	Stockholm		1956	Melbourne (S)
1920	Antwerp		1960	Squaw Valley, Calif. (W)
1924	Chamonix (W)		1960	Rome (S)
1924	Paris (S)		1964	Innsbruck, Austria (W)
1928	St. Moritz (W)		1964	Tokyo (S)
1928	Amsterdam (S)		1968	Grenoble, France (W)
1932	Lake Placid (W)		1968	Mexico City (S)
1932	Los Angeles (S)		1972	Sapporo, Japan (W)
1936	Garmisch-		1972	Munich (S)
	Partenkirchen (W)		1976	Innsbruck, Austria (W)
1936	Berlin (S)		1976	Montreal (S)
1948	St. Moritz (W)		1980	Lake Placid (W)
			1980	Moscow (S)

The first Olympic Games of which there is record occurred in 776 B.C. and consisted of one event, a great foot race of about 200 yards held on a plain by the River Alpheus (now the Ruphia) just outside the little town of Olympia in Greece. It was from that date that the Greeks began to keep their calendar by "Olympiads," the four-year spans between the celebrations of the famous games.

The modern Olympic Games, which started in Athens in 1896, are the result of the devotion of a French educator, Baron Pierre de Coubertin, to the idea that, since young people and athletics have gone together down the ages, education and athletics might well go hand-in-hand toward a better international understanding.

At the top of the organization responsible for the Olympic movement and the staging of the Games every four years is the International Olympic Committee (IOC). Other important roles are played by National Olympic Committees in each participating country, international sports federations, and the Organizing Committee of the host city.

In 1978, the IOC consisted of 89 members, elected by the IOC itself. Its headquarters are in Lausanne, Switzerland. The president of the IOC is Lord Killanin of Ireland.

The Olympic motto is "Citius, Altius, Fortius"—"Faster, Higher, Stronger." The Olympic symbol is five interlocking circles colored blue, yellow, black, green, and red, on a white background, representing the five continents. At least one of these colors appears in the national flag of every country.

Summer Games

TRACK AND FIELD—MEN

100-Meter Dash

1896	Thomas Burke, United States	12s
1900	F. W. Jarvis, United States	10.8s
1904	Archie Hahn, United States	11s
1906	Archie Hahn, United States	11.2s
1908	Reginald Walker, South Africa	10.8s
1912	Ralph Craig, United States	10.8s
1920	Charles Paddock, United States	10.8s
1924	Harold Abrahams, Great Britain	10.6s
1928	Percy Williams, Canada	10.8s
1932	Eddie Tolan, United States	10.3s
1936	Jesse Owens, United States	10.3s
1948	Harrison Dillard, United States	10.3s
1952	Lindy Remigino, United States	10.4s
1956	Bobby Morrow, United States	10.5s
1960	Armin Hary, Germany	10.2s
1964	Robert Hayes, United States	10s
1968	James Hines, United States	9.9s
1972	Valery Borzov, U.S.S.R.	10.14s
1976	Hasely Crawford, Trinidad and Tebago	10.06s

200-Meter Dash

1900	John Tewksbury, United States	22.2s
1904	Archie Hahn, United States	21.6s
1908	Robert Kerr, Canada	22.6s
1912	Ralph Craig, United States	21.7s
1920	Allan Woodring, United States	22s
1924	Jackson Scholz, United States	21.6s
1928	Percy Williams, Canada	21.8s
1932	Eddie Tolan, United States	21.2s
1936	Jesse Owens, United States	20.7s
1948	Melvin E. Patton, United States	21.1s
1952	Andrew Stanfield, United States	20.7s
1956	Bobby Morrow, United States	20.6s
1960	Livio Berruti, Italy	20.5s
1964	Henry Carr, United States	20.3s
1968	Tommie Smith, United States	19.8s
1972	Valery Borzov, U.S.S.R.	20s
1976	Don Quarrie, Jamaica	20.23s

400-Meter Dash

1896	Thomas Burke, United States	54.2s
1900	Maxey Long, United States	49.4s
1904	Harry Hillman, United States	49.2s
1906	Paul Pilgrim, United States	53.2s
1908	Wyndham Halswelle, Great Britain (walkover)	50s
1912	Charles Reidpath, United States	48.2s
1920	Bevil Rudd, South Africa	49.6s
1924	Eric Liddell, Great Britain	47.6s
1928	Ray Barbuti, United States	47.8s
1932	William Carr, United States	46.2s
1936	Archie Williams, United States	46.5s
1948	Arthur Wint, Jamaica, B.W.I.	46.2s
1952	George Rhoden, Jamaica, B.W.I.	45.9s
1956	Charles Jenkins, United States	46.7s
1960	Otis Davis, United States	44.9s
1964	Mike Larrabee, United States	45.1s
1968	Lee Evans, United States	43.8s
1972	Vincent Matthews, United States	44.66s
1976	Alberto Juantorena, Cuba	44.26s

800-Meter Run

1896	Edwin Flack, Australia	2m11s
1900	Alfred Tysoe, Great Britain	2m1.4s
1904	James Lightbody, United States	1m56s
1906	Paul Pilgrim, United States	2m1.2s
1908	Mel Sheppard, United States	1m52.8s
1912	Ted Meredith, United States	1m51.9s
1920	Albert Hill, Great Britain	1m53.4s
1924	Douglas Lowe, Great Britain	1m52.4s
1928	Douglas Lowe, Great Britain	1m51.8s
1932	Thomas Hampson, Great Britain	1m49.8s
1936	John Woodruff, United States	1m52.9s
1948	Malvin Whitfield, United States	1m49.2s
1952	Malvin Whitfield, United States	1m49.2s
1956	Tom Courtney, United States	1m47.7s
1960	Peter Snell, New Zealand	1m46.3s
1964	Peter Snell, New Zealand	1m45.1s
1968	Ralph Doubell, Australia	1m44.3s
1972	David Wottle, United States	1m45.9s
1976	Alberto Juantorena, Cuba	1m43.5s

1,500-Meter Run

1896	Edwin Flack, Australia	4m33.2s
1900	Charles Bennett, Great Britain	4m6s
1904	James Lightbody, United States	4m5.4s
1906	James Lightbody, United States	4m12s
1908	Mel Sheppard, United States	4m3.4s
1912	Arnold Jackson, Great Britain	3m56.8s
1920	Albert Hill, Great Britain	4m1.8s
1924	Paavo Nurmi, Finland	3m53.6s
1928	Harry Larva, Finland	3m53.2s
1932	Luigi Beccali, Italy	3m51.2s

1936	Jack Lovelock, New Zealand	3m47.8s
1948	Henri Eriksson, Sweden	3m49.8s
1952	Joseph Barthel, Luxembourg	3m45.2s
1956	Ron Delany, Ireland	3m41.2s
1960	Herb Elliott, Australia	3m35.6s
1964	Peter Snell, New Zealand	3m38.1s
1968	Kipchoge Keino, Kenya	3m34.9s
1972	Pekka Vasala, Finland	3m36.3s
1976	John Walker, New Zealand	3m39.17s

5,000-Meter Run

1912	Hannes Kolehmainen, Finland	14m36.6s
1920	Joseph Guillemot, France	14m55.6s
1924	Paavo Nurmi, Finland	14m31.2s
1928	Willie Ritola, Finland	14m38s
1932	Lauri Lehtinen, Finland	14m30s
1936	Gunnar Hockert, Finland	14m22.2s
1948	Gaston Reiff, Belgium	14m17.6s
1952	Emil Zatopek, Czechoslovakia	14m6.6s
1956	Vladimir Kuts, U.S.S.R.	13m39.6s
1960	Murray Halberg, New Zealand	13m43.4s
1964	Bob Schul, United States	13m48.8s
1968	Mohamed Gammoudi, Tunisia	14m.05s
1972	Lasse Viren, Finland	13m26.4s
1976	Lasse Viren, Finland	13m24.76s

5-Mile Run

| 1906 | H. Hawtrey, Great Britain | 26m26.2s |
| 1908 | Emil Voigt, Great Britain | 25m11.2s |

10,000-Meter Run

1912	Hannes Kolehmainen, Finland	31m20.8s
1920	Paavo Nurmi, Finland	31m45.8s
1924	Willie Ritola, Finland	30m23.2s
1928	Paavo Nurmi, Finland	30m18.8s
1932	Janusz Kusocinski, Poland	30m11.4s
1936	Ilmari Salminen, Finland	30m15.4s
1948	Emil Zatopek, Czechoslovakia	29m59.6s
1952	Emil Zatopek, Czechoslovakia	29m17s
1956	Vladimir Kuts, U.S.S.R.	28m45.6s
1960	Peter Bolotnikov, U.S.S.R.	28m32.2s
1964	Billy Mills, United States	28m24.4s
1968	Naftali Temu, Kenya	29m27.4s
1972	Lasse Viren, Finland	27m38.4s
1976	Lasse Viren, Finland	27m40.38s

Marathon

1896	Spiridon Loues, Greece	2h58m50s
1900	Michel Teato, France	2h59m45s
1904	Thomas Hicks, United States	3h28m53s
1906	W. J. Sherring, Canada	2h51m23.65s
1908	John J. Hayes, United States	2h55m18.4s

1912	Kenneth McArthur, South Africa	2h36m54.8s
1920	Hannes Kolehmainen, Finland	2h32m35.8s
1924	Albin Stenroos, Finland	2h41m22.6s
1928	A. B. El Ouafi, France	2h32m57s
1932	Juan Zabala, Argentina	2h31m36s
1936	Kitei Son, Japan	2h29m19.2s
1948	Delfo Cabrera, Argentina	2h34m51.6s
1952	Emil Zatopek, Czechoslovakia	2h23m3.2s
1956	Alain Mimoun, France	2h25m
1960	Abebe Bikila, Ethiopia	2h15m16.2s
1964	Abebe Bikila, Ethiopia	2h12m11.2s
1968	Mamo Wold, Ethiopia	2h20m26.4s
1972	Frank Shorter, United States	2h12m19.8s
1976	Walter Cierpinski, East Germany	2h09m55s

110-Meter Hurdles

1896	Thomas Curtis, United States	17.6s
1900	Alvin Kraenzlein, United States	15.4s
1904	Frederick Schule, United States	16s
1906	R. G. Leavitt, United States	16.2s
1908	Forrest Smithson, United States	15s
1912	Frederick Kelly, United States	15.1s
1920	Earl Thomson, Canada	14.8s
1924	Daniel Kinsey, United States	15s
1928	Sydney Atkinson, South Africa	14.8s
1932	George Saling, United States	14.6s
1936	Forrest Towns, United States	14.2s
1948	William Porter, United States	13.9s
1952	Harrison Dillard, United States	13.7s
1956	Lee Calhoun, United States	13.5s
1960	Lee Calhoun, United States	13.8s
1964	Hayes Jones, United States	13.6s
1968	Willie Davenport, United States	13.3s
1972	Rodney Milburn, United States	13.24s
1976	Guy Drut, France	13.30s

200-Meter Hurdles

1900	Alvin Kraenzlein, United States	25.4s
1904	Harry Hillman, United States	24.6s

400-Meter Hurdles

1900	John Tewksbury, United States	57.6s
1904	Harry Hillman, United States	53s
1908	Charles Bacon, United States	55s
1920	Frank Loomis, United States	54s
1924	F. Morgan Taylor, United States	52.6s
1928	Lord David Burghley, Great Britain	53.4s
1932	Robert Tisdall, Ireland	51.8s[1]
1936	Glenn Hardin, United States	52.4s
1948	Roy Cochran, United States	51.1s
1952	Charles Moore, United States	50.8s
1956	Glenn Davis, United States	50.1s
1960	Glenn Davis, United States	49.3s

1964	Rex Cawley, United States	49.6s
1968	David Hemery, Great Britain	48.1s
1972	John Akii-Bua, Uganda	47.8s
1976	Edwin Moses, United States	47.64

1. Record not allowed.

2,500-Meter Steeplechase

| 1900 | George Orton, United States | 7m34s |
| 1904 | James Lightbody, United States | 7m39.6s |

3,000-Meter Steeplechase

1920	Percy Hodge, Great Britain	10m0.4s
1924	Willie Ritola, Finland	9m33.6s
1928	Toivo Loukola, Finland	9m21.8s
1932	Volmari Iso-Hollo, Finland	10m33.4s[1]
1936	Volmari Iso-Hollo, Finland	9m3.8s
1948	Thure Sjoestrand, Sweden	9m4.6s
1952	Horace Ashenfelter, United States	8m45.4s
1956	Chris Brasher, Great Britain	8m41.2s
1960	Zdzislaw Krzyskowiak, Poland	8m34.2s
1964	Gaston Roelants, Belgium	8m30.8s
1968	Amos Biwott, Kenya	8m51s
1972	Kipchoge Keino, Kenya	8m23.6s
1976	Anders Gardervd, Sweden	8m08.02s

1. About 3,450 meters—extra lap by error.

Cross-Country

1912	Hannes Kolehmainen, Finland (8,000 meters)	45m11.6s
1920	Paavo Nurmi, Finland (10,000 meters)	27m15s
1924	Paavo Nurmi, Finland (10,000 meters)	32m54.8s

Cross-Country Team Races

		Pts.
1912	Sweden (8,000 meters)	10
1920	Finland (10,000 meters)	10
1924	Finland (10,000 meters)	11

1,500-Meter Walk

| 1906 | George V. Bonhag, United States | 7m12.6s |

3,000-Meter Walk

| 1920 | Ugo Frigerio, Italy | 13m14.2s |

10,000-Meter Walk

1912	George Goulding, Canada	46m28.4s
1920	Ugo Frigerio, Italy	48m6.2s
1924	Ugo Frigerio, Italy	47m49s
1948	John Mikaelsson, Sweden	45m13.2s
1952	John Mikaelsson, Sweden	45m2.8s

20,000-Meter Walk

1956	Leonid Spirin, U.S.S.R.	1h31m27.4s
1960	Vladimir Golubnichy, U.S.S.R.	1h34m7.2s
1964	Ken Mathews, Great Britain	1h29m34s
1968	Vladimir Golubnichy, U.S.S.R.	1h33m58.4s
1972	Peter Frenkel, East Germany	1h26m42.4s
1976	Daniel Bautista, Mexico	1h24m40.6s

50,000-Meter Walk

1932	Thomas W. Green, Great Britain	4h50m10s
1936	Harold Whitlock, Great Britain	4h30m41.1s
1948	John Ljunggren, Sweden	4h41m52s
1952	Giuseppe Dordoni, Italy	4h28m7.8s
1956	Norman Read, New Zealand	4h30m42.8s
1960	Donald Thompson, Great Britain	4h25m30s
1964	Abdon Pamich, Italy	4h11m12.4s
1968	Christoph Hohne, East Germany	4h20m13.6s
1972	Bern Kannernberg, West Germany	3h56m11.6s

400-Meter Relay (4 x 100)

1912	Great Britain	42.4s
1920	United States	42.2s
1924	United States	41s
1928	United States	41s
1932	United States	40s
1936	United States	39.8s
1948	United States	40.6s
1952	United States	40.1s
1956	United States	39.5s
1960	Germany	39.5s
1964	United States	39s
1968	United States	38.2s
1972	United States	38.19s
1976	United States	38.33s

1,600-Meter Relay (200–200–400–800)

| 1908 | United States | 3m29.4s |

1,600-Meter Relay (4 x 400)

1912	United States	3m16.6s
1920	Great Britain	3m22.2s
1924	United States	3m16s
1928	United States	3m14.2s
1932	United States	3m8.2s
1936	Great Britain	3m9s
1948	United States	3m10.4s
1952	Jamaica, B.W.I.	3m3.9s
1956	United States	3m4.8s
1960	United States	3m2.2s
1964	United States	3m0.7s
1968	United States	2m56.1s
1972	Kenya	2m59.8s
1976	United States	2m58.65s

Team Race

		Pts.
1900	Great Britain (5,000 meters)	26
1904	United States (4 miles)	27
1908	Great Britain (3 miles)	6
1912	United States (3,000 meters)	9
1920	United States (3,000 meters)	10
1924	Finland (3,000 meters)	9

Standing High Jump

1900	Ray Ewry, United States	5 ft 5 in.
1904	Ray Ewry, United States	4 ft 11 in.
1906	Ray Ewry, United States	5 ft 1⅝ in.
1908	Ray Ewry, United States	5 ft 2 in.
1912	Platt Adams, United States	5 ft 4⅛ in.

Running High Jump

1896	Ellery Clark, United States	5 ft 11¼ in.
1900	Irving Baxter, United States	6 ft 2¾ in.
1904	Samuel Jones, United States	5 ft 11 in.
1906	Con Leahy, Ireland	5 ft 9⅞ in.
1908	Harry Porter, United States	6 ft 3 in.
1912	Alma Richards, United States	6 ft 4 in.
1920	Richmond Landon, United States	6 ft 4¼ in.
1924	Harold Osborn, United States	6 ft 5¹⁵/₁₆ in.
1928	Robert W. King, United States	6 ft 4⅜ in.
1932	Duncan McNaughton, Canada	6 ft 5⅝ in.
1936	Cornelius Johnson, United States	6 ft 7¹⁵/₁₆ in.
1948	John Winter, Australia	6 ft 6 in.
1952	Walter Davis, United States	6 ft 8⁵/₁₆ in.
1956	Charles Dumas, United States	6 ft 11¼ in.
1960	Robert Shavlakadze, U.S.S.R.	7 ft 1 in.
1964	Valeri Brumel, U.S.S.R.	7 ft 1¾ in.
1968	Dick Fosbury, United States	7 ft 4¼ in.
1972	Yuri Tarmak, U.S.S.R.	7 ft 3¾ in.
1976	Jacek Wszola, Poland	(2.25) 7 ft 4½ in.

Standing Long Jump

1900	Ray Ewry, United States	10 ft 6²/₅ in.
1904	Ray Ewry, United States	11 ft 4⅞ in.
1906	Ray Ewry, United States	10 ft 10 in.
1908	Ray Ewry, United States	10 ft 11¼ in.
1912	Constantin Tsicilitiras, Greece	11 ft ¼ in.

Long Jump

1896	Ellery Clark, United States	20 ft 9¾ in.
1900	Alvin Kraenzlein, United States	23 ft 6⅞ in.
1904	Myer Prinstein, United States	24 ft 1 in.
1906	Myer Prinstein, United States	23 ft 7½ in.
1908	Frank Irons, United States	24 ft 6½ in.
1912	Albert Gutterson, United States	24 ft 11¼ in.

1920	Wm. Pettersson, Sweden	23 ft 5½ in.
1924	DeHart Hubbard, United States	24 ft 5⅛ in.
1928	Edward B. Hamm, United States	25 ft 4¾ in.
1932	Edward Gordon, United States	25 ft ¾ in.
1936	Jesse Owens, United States	26 ft 5⁵/₁₆ in.
1948	Willie Steele, United States	25 ft 8 in.
1952	Jerome Biffle, United States	24 ft 10 in.
1956	Gregory Bell, United States	25 ft 8¼ in.
1960	Ralph Boston, United States	26 ft 7¾ in.
1964	Lynn Davies, Great Britain	26 ft 5¾ in.
1968	Bob Beamon, United States	29 ft 2½ in.
1972	Randy Williams, United States	27 ft ½ in.
1976	Arnie Robinson, United States	(8.35) 24 ft 7¾ in.

Standing Triple Jump

| 1900 | Ray Ewry, United States | 34 ft 8½ in. |
| 1904 | Ray Ewry, United States | 34 ft 7¼ in. |

Triple Jump

1896	James B. Connolly, United States	45 ft
1900	Myer Prinstein, United States	47 ft 4¼ in.
1904	Myer Prinstein, United States	47 ft
1906	P. G. O'Connor, Ireland	46 ft 2 in.
1908	Timothy Ahearne, Great Britain	48 ft 11¼ in.
1912	Gustaf Lindblom, Sweden	48 ft 5⅛ in.
1920	Vilho Tuulos, Finland	47 ft 6⅞ in.
1924	Archie Winter, Australia	50 ft 11⅛ in.
1928	Mikio Oda, Japan	49 ft 10¹³/₁₆ in.
1932	Chuhei Nambu, Japan	51 ft 7 in.
1936	Naoto Tajima, Japan	52 ft 5⅞ in.
1948	Arne Ahman, Sweden	50 ft 6¼ in.
1952	Adhemar da Silva, Brazil	53 ft 2½ in.
1956	Adhemar da Silva, Brazil	53 ft 7½ in.
1960	Jozef Schmidt, Poland	55 ft 1¾ in.
1964	Jozef Schmidt, Poland	55 ft 3¼ in.
1968	Viktor Saneyev, U.S.S.R.	57 ft ¾ in.
1972	Viktor Saneyev, U.S.S.R.	56 ft 11 in.
1976	Viktor Saneyev, U.S.S.R.	(17.29) 56 ft 8¾ in.

Pole Vault

1896	William Hoyt, United States	10 ft 9¾ in.
1900	Irving Baxter, United States	10 ft 9⅞ in.
1904	Charles Dvorak, United States	11 ft 6 in.
1906	Fernand Gouder, France	11 ft 6 in.
1908	A. C. Gilbert, United States, and	
	Edward Cook, United States (tie)	12 ft 2 in.
1912	Harry Babcock, United States	12 ft 11½ in.
1920	Frank Foss, United States	13 ft 5⁹/₁₆ in.
1924	Lee Barnes, United States	12 ft 11½ in.
1928	Sabin W. Carr, United States	13 ft 9⅜ in.
1932	William Miller, United States	14 ft 1⅞ in.
1936	Earle Meadows, United States	14 ft 3¼ in.
1948	Guinn Smith, United States	14 ft 1¼ in.

1952	Robert Richards, United States	14 ft 11⅛ in.
1956	Robert Richards, United States	14 ft 11½ in.
1960	Don Bragg, United States	15 ft 5⅛ in.
1964	Fred Hansen, United States	16 ft 8¾ in.
1968	Bob Seagren, United States	17 ft 8½ in.
1972	Wolfgang Nordwig, East Germany	18 ft ½ in.
1976	Tadeusz Slusarski, Poland	(5.50) 18 ft ½ in.

16-lb Shot-Put

1896	Robert Garrett, United States	36 ft 9¾ in.
1900	Richard Sheldon, United States	46 ft 3⅛ in.
1904	Ralph Rose, United States	48 ft 7 in.
1906	Martin Sheridan, United States	40 ft 4⅘ in.
1908	Ralph Rose, United States	46 ft 7½ in.
1912	Pat McDonald, United States	50 ft 4 in.
1920	Ville Porhola, Finland	48 ft 7⅛ in.
1924	Clarence Houser, United States	49 ft 2½ in.
1928	John Kuck, United States	52 ft 11¹¹⁄₁₆ in.
1932	Leo Sexton, United States	52 ft 6³⁄₁₆ in.
1936	Hans Woellke, Germany	53 ft 1¾ in.
1948	Wilbur Thompson, United States	56 ft 2 in.
1952	Parry O'Brien, United States	57 ft 1½ in.
1956	Parry O'Brien, United States	60 ft 11 in.
1960	Bill Nieder, United States	64 ft 6¾ in.
1964	Dallas Long, United States	66 ft 8¼ in.
1968	Randy Matson, United States	67 ft 4¾ in.
1972	Wladyslaw Konar, Poland	69 ft 6 in.
1976	Udo Beyer, East Germany	(21.05) 69 ft ¾ in.

16-lb Shot-Put (Both Hands)

1912	Ralph Rose, United States	90 ft 5⅜ in.

Discus Throw

1896	Robert Garrett, United States	95 ft 7½ in.
1900	Rudolf Bauer, Hungary	118 ft 2⅞ in.
1904	Martin Sheridan, United States	128 ft 10½ in.
1906	Martin Sheridan, United States	136 ft ⅓ in.
1908	Martin Sheridan, United States	134 ft 2 in.
1912	Armas Taipale, Finland	145 ft ⁹⁄₁₆ in.
1920	Elmer Niklander, Finland	146 ft 7 in.
1924	Clarence Houser, United States	151 ft 5¼ in.
1928	Clarence Houser, United States	155 ft 2⅘ in.
1932	John Anderson, United States	162 ft 4⅞ in.
1936	Ken Carpenter, United States	165 ft 7⅜ in.
1948	Adolfo Consolini, Italy	173 ft 2 in.
1952	Simeon Iness, United States	180 ft 6½ in.
1956	Al Oerter, United States	184 ft 10½ in.
1960	Al Oerter, United States	194 ft 2 in.
1964	Al Oerter, United States	200 ft 1½ in.
1968	Al Oerter, United States	212 ft 6 in.
1972	Ludvik Danek, Czechoslovakia	211 ft 3 in.
1976	Mac Wilkins, United States	(67.5) 221 ft 5 in.

Discus Throw—Greek Style

| 1906 | Werner Jaervinen, Finland | 115 ft 4 in. |
| 1908 | Martin Sheridan, United States | 124 ft 8 in. |

Discus Throw (Both Hands)

| 1912 | Armas Taipale, Finland | 271 ft 10⅛ in. |

Javelin Throw

1906	Eric Lemming, Sweden	175 ft 6 in.
1908	Eric Lemming, Sweden	179 ft 10½ in.
1912	Eric Lemming, Sweden	198 ft 11¼ in.
1920	Jonni Myyra, Finland	215 ft 9¾ in.
1924	Jonni Myyra, Finland	206 ft 6¾ in.
1928	Eric Lundquist, Sweden	218 ft 6⅛ in.
1932	Matti Jarvinen, Finland	238 ft 7 in.
1936	Gerhard Stoeck, Germany	235 ft 8⁵⁄₁₆ in.
1948	Kaj Rautavaara, Finland	228 ft 10½ in.
1952	Cy Young, United States	242 ft ¾ in.
1956	Egil Danielsen, Norway	281 ft 2¼ in.
1960	Viktor Tsibulenko, U.S.S.R.	277 ft 8⅜ in.
1964	Pauli Nevala, Finland	271 ft 2¼ in.
1968	Janis Lusis, U.S.S.R.	295 ft 7 in.
1972	Klaus Wolfermann, West Germany	296 ft 10 in.
1976	Miklos Nemeth, Hungary	(94.58) 310 ft 4 in.

Javelin Throw—Free Style

| 1908 | Eric Lemming, Sweden | 178 ft 7½ in. |

Javelin Throw (Both Hands)

| 1912 | Julius Saaristo, Finland | 358 ft 11½ in. |

16-lb Hammer Throw

1900	John Flanagan, United States	167 ft 4 in.
1904	John Flanagan, United States	168 ft 1 in.
1908	John Flanagan, United States	170 ft 4¼ in.
1912	Matt McGrath, United States	179 ft 7⅛ in.
1920	Pat Ryan, United States	173 ft 5⅝ in.
1924	Fred Tootell, United States	174 ft 10¼ in.
1928	Patrick O'Callaghan, Ireland	168 ft 7½ in.
1932	Patrick O'Callaghan, Ireland	176 ft 11⅛ in.
1936	Karl Hein, Germany	185 ft 4 in.
1948	Imre Nemeth, Hungary	183 ft 11½ in.
1952	Jozsef Csermak, Hungary	197 ft 11⁹⁄₁₆ in.
1956	Harold Connolly, United States	207 ft 2¾ in.
1960	Vasily Rudenkov, U.S.S.R.	220 ft 1⅝ in.
1964	Romuald Klim, U.S.S.R.	228 ft 9½ in.
1968	Gyula Zsivotzky, Hungary	240 ft 8 in.
1972	Anatoly Bondarchuk, U.S.S.R.	247 ft 8½ in.
1976	Yuri Sedyh, U.S.S.R.	(77.52) 254 ft 4 in.

Throwing the Stone (14 lbs.)

| 1906 | Nicolas Georgantas, Greece | 65 ft 4⅕ in. |

56-lb Weight Throw

| 1904 | Etienne Desmarteau, Canada | 34 ft 4 in. |
| 1920 | Pat McDonald, United States | 36 ft 11⅝ in. |

All-Around

| 1904 | Thomas Kiely, Great Britain | 6,036 pts. |

Pentathlon

1906	H. Mellander, Sweden	24 pts.
1912	Ferdinand Bie, Norway	21 pts.
1920	Eero Lehtonen, Finland	14 pts.
1924	Eero Lehtonen, Finland	16 pts.

Decathlon

1912	Hugo Wieslander, Sweden	7,724.495 pts.
1920	Helge Lovland, Norway	6,804.35 pts.
1924	Harold Osborn, United States	7,710.775 pts.
1928	Paavo Yrjola, Finland	8,053.29 pts.
1932	James Bausch, United States	8,462.23 pts.
1936	Glenn Morris, United States	7,900 pts.[1]
1948	Robert B. Mathias, United States	7,139 pts.
1952	Robert B. Mathias, United States	7,887 pts.
1956	Milton Campbell, United States	7,937 pts.
1960	Rafer Johnson, United States	8,392 pts.
1964	Willi Holdorf, Germany	7,887 pts.[1]
1968	Bill Toomey, United States	8,193 pts.
1972	Nikolai Avilov, U.S.S.R.	8,454 pts.
1976	Bruce Jenner, United States	8,618 pts.

1. Point system revised.

Tug of War

1904	United States	1912	Sweden
1906	Germany	1920	Great Britain
1908	Great Britain		

TRACK AND FIELD—WOMEN

100-Meter Dash

1928	Elizabeth Robinson, United States	12.2s
1932	Stella Walsh, Poland	11.9s
1936	Helen Stephens, United States	11.5s
1948	Fanny Blankers-Koen, Netherlands	11.9s
1952	Marjorie Jackson, Australia	11.5s
1956	Betty Cuthbert, Australia	11.5s
1960	Wilma Rudolph, United States	11s
1964	Wyomia Tyus, United States	11.4s
1968	Wyomia Tyus, United States	11s

| 1972 | Renate Stecher, East Germany | 11.07s |
| 1976 | Annegret Richter, West Germany | 11.08s |

200-Meter Dash

1948	Fanny Blankers-Koen, Netherlands	24.4s
1952	Marjorie Jackson, Australia	23.7s
1956	Betty Cuthbert, Australia	23.4s
1960	Wilma Rudolph, United States	24s
1964	Edith McGuire, United States	23s
1968	Irena Szewinska, Poland	22.5s
1972	Renate Stecher, East Germany	22.4s
1976	Baerbel Eckert, East Germany	22.37s

400-Meter Dash

1964	Betty Cuthbert, Australia	52s
1968	Colette Besson, France	52s
1972	Monika Zehrt, East Germany	51.08s
1976	Irena Szewinska, Poland	49.29s

800-Meter Run

1928	Lina Radke, Germany	2m16.8s
1960	Ljudmila Shevcova, U.S.S.R.	2m4.3s
1964	Ann Packer, Great Britain	2m1.1s
1968	Madeline Manning, United States	2m0.9s
1972	Hildegard Falck, West Germany	1m58.6s
1976	Tatiana Kazankina, U.S.S.R.	1m54.94s

1,500-Meter Run

| 1972 | Ludmila Bragina, U.S.S.R. | 4m01.4s |
| 1976 | Tatiana Kazankina, U.S.S.R. | 4m05.48s |

80-Meter Hurdles

1932	Mildred Didrikson, United States	11.7s
1936	Trebisonda Valla, Italy	11.7s
1948	Fanny Blankers-Koen, Netherlands	11.2s
1952	Shirley S. de la Hunty, Australia	10.9s
1956	Shirley S. de la Hunty, Australia	10.7s
1960	Irina Press, U.S.S.R.	10.8s
1964	Karin Balzer, Germany	10.5s[1]
1968	Maureen Caird, Australia	10.3s

1. Wind assisted.

100-Meter Hurdles

| 1972 | Annelie Ehrhardt, East Garmany | 12.59s |
| 1976 | Johanna Schaller, East Germany | 12.77s |

400-Meter Relay

| 1928 | Canada | 48.4s |
| 1932 | United States | 47s |

1936	United States	46.9s
1948	Netherlands	47.5s
1952	United States	45.9s
1956	Australia	44.5s
1960	United States	44.5s
1964	Poland	43.6s
1968	United States	42.8s
1972	West Germany	42.81s
1976	East Germany	42.55s

1,600-Meter Relay

| 1972 | East Germany | 3m23s |
| 1976 | East Germany | 3m19.23s |

Running High Jump

1928	Ethel Catherwood, Canada	5 ft 3 in.
1932	Jean Shiley, United States	5 ft 5¼ in.
1936	Ibolya Csak, Hungary	5 ft 3 in.
1948	Alice Coachman, United States	5 ft 6⅛ in.
1952	Ester Brand, South Africa	5 ft 5¾ in.
1956	Mildred McDaniel, United States	5 ft 9¼ in.
1960	Iolanda Balas, Romania	6 ft ¾ in.
1964	Iolanda Balas, U.S.S.R.	6 ft 2¾ in.
1968	Miloslava Rezkova, Czechoslovakia	5 ft 11¾ in.
1972	Ulrike Meyfarth, West Germany	6 ft 3⅝ in.
1976	Rosemarie Ackerman, East Germany	(1.93) 6 ft 4 in.

Long Jump

1948	Olga Gyarmati, Hungary	18 ft 8¼ in.
1952	Yvette Williams, New Zealand	20 ft 5¾ in.
1956	Elzbieta Krzesinska, Poland	20 ft 9¾ in.
1960	Vera Krepkina, U.S.S.R.	20 ft 10¾ in.
1964	Mary Rand, Great Britain	22 ft 2 in.
1968	Viorica Ciscopoleanu, Romania	22 ft 4½ in.
1972	Heidemarie Rosendahl, West Germany	22 ft 3 in.
1976	Angela Voigt, East Germany	(6.72) 22 ft ½ in.

Shot-Put

1948	Micheline Ostermeyer, France	45 ft 1½ in.
1952	Galina Zybina, U.S.S.R.	50 ft 1½ in.
1956	Tamara Tishkyevich, U.S.S.R.	54 ft 5 in.
1960	Tamara Press, U.S.S.R.	56 ft 9⅞ in.
1964	Tamara Press, U.S.S.R.	59 ft 6 in.
1968	Margita Gummel, East Germany	64 ft 4 in.
1972	Nadezhda Chizhova, U.S.S.R.	69 ft
1976	Ivanka Christova, Bulgaria	(21.16) 69 ft 5 in.

Discus Throw

1928	Helena Konopacka, Poland	129 ft 11⅞ in.
1932	Lillian Copeland, United States	133 ft 2 in.
1936	Gisela Mauermayer, Germany	156 ft 3³⁄₁₆ in.

1948	Micheline Ostermeyer, France	137 ft 6½ in.
1952	Nina Romaschkova, U.S.S.R.	168 ft 8⁷/₁₆ in.
1956	Olga Fikotova, Czechoslovakia	176 ft 1½ in.
1960	Nina Ponomareva, U.S.S.R.	180 ft 8¼ in.
1964	Tamara Press, U.S.S.R.	187 ft 10¾ in.
1968	Lia Manoliu, Romania	191 ft 2½ in.
1972	Faina Melnik, U.S.S.R.	218 ft 7 in.
1976	Evelin Schlaak, East Germany	(69.0) 226 ft 4 in.

Javelin Throw

1932	Mildred Didrikson, United States	143 ft 4 in.
1936	Tilly Fleischer, Germany	148 ft 2¾ in.
1948	Herma Bauma, Austria	149 ft 6 in.
1952	Dana Zatopek, Czechoslovakia	165 ft 7 in.
1956	Inessa Janzeme, U.S.S.R.	176 ft 8 in.
1960	Elvira Ozolina, U.S.S.R.	183 ft 8 in.
1964	Mihaela Penes, Romania	198 ft 7½ in.
1968	Angela Nemeth, Hungary	198 ft 0 in.
1972	Ruth Fuchs, East Germany	209 ft 7 in.
1976	Ruth Fuchs, East Germany	(65.94) 216 ft 4 in.

Pentathlon

1964	Irina Press, U.S.S.R.	5,246 pts.
1968	Ingrid Becker, West Germany	5,098 pts.
1972	Mary Peters, Britain	4,801 pts.
1976	Siegrun Siegl, East Germany	4,745 pts.

SWIMMING—MEN

50 Yards Freestyle

| 1904 | Zoltan de Halmay, Hungary | 28s |

100 Meters Freestyle

1896	Alfred Hajos, Hungary	1m22.2s
1904	Zoltan de Halmay, Hungary	1m2.8s[1]
1906	Charles Daniels, United States	1m13s
1908	Charles Daniels, United States	1m5.6s
1912	Duke P. Kahanamoku, United States	1m3.4s
1920	Duke P. Kahanamoku, United States	1m1.4s
1924	John Weissmuller, United States	59s
1928	John Weissmuller, United States	58.6s
1932	Yasuji Miyazaki, Japan	58.2s
1936	Ferenc Csik, Hungary	57.6s
1948	Walter Ris, United States	57.3s
1952	Clarke Scholes, United States	57.4s
1956	Jon Henricks, Australia	55.4s
1960	John Devitt, Australia	55.2s
1964	Don Schollander, United States	53.4s
1968	Michael Wenden, Australia	52.2s
1972	Mark Spitz, United States	51.22s
1976	Jim Montgomery, United States	49.99s

1. 100 yards.

200 Meters Freestyle

1900	Frederick Lane, Australia	2m25.2s
1904	Charles Daniels, United States	2m44.2s[1]
1968	Michael Wenden, Australia	1m55.2s
1972	Mark Spitz, United States	1m52.78s
1976	Bruce Furniss, United States	1m50.29s

1. 220 yards.

400 Meters Freestyle

1896	Paul Neumann, Austria	8m12.6s[1]
1904	Charles Daniels, United States	6m16.2s[2]
1906	Otto Sheff, Austria	6m23.8s
1908	Henry Taylor, Great Britain	5m36.8s
1912	George Hodgson, Canada	5m24.4s
1920	Norman Ross, United States	5m26.8s
1924	John Weissmuller, United States	5m4.2s
1928	Albert Zorilla, Argentina	5m1.6s
1932	Clarence Crabbe, United States	4m48.4s
1936	Jack Medica, United States	4m44.5s
1948	William Smith, United States	4m41s
1952	Jean Boiteux, France	4m30.7s
1956	Murray Rose, Australia	4m27.3s
1960	Murray Rose, Australia	4m18.3s
1964	Don Schollander, United States	4m12.2s
1968	Mike Burton, United States	4m9s
1972	Bradford Cooper, Australia[3]	4m00.27s
1976	Brian Goodell, United States	3m51.93s

1. 500 meters. 2. 440 yards. 3. Rick DeMont, United States, won but was disqualified following day for medical reasons.

1,200 Meters Freestyle

1896	Alfred Hajos, Hungary	18m22.2s

1,500 Meters Freestyle

1904	Emil Rausch, Germany	27m18.2s[1]
1906	Henry Taylor, Great Britain	28m28s[2]
1908	Henry Taylor, Great Britain	22m48.4s
1912	George Hodgson, Canada	22m
1920	Norman Ross, United States	22m23.2s
1924	Andrew Charlton, Australia	20m6.6s
1928	Arne Borg, Sweden	19m51.8s
1932	Kusuo Kitamura, Japan	19m12.4s
1936	Noboru Terada, Japan	19m13.7s
1948	James McLane, United States	19m18.5s
1952	Ford Konno, United States	18m30s
1956	Murray Rose, Australia	17m58.9s
1960	Jon Konrads, Australia	17m19.6s
1964	Robert Windle, Australia	17m1.7s
1968	Michael Burton, United States	16m38.9s
1972	Mike Burton, United States	15m52.58s
1976	Brian Goodell, United States	15m02.4s

1. One mile. 2. 1,600 meters.

214

4,000 Meters Freestyle

| 1900 | John Jarvis, Great Britain | 58m24s |

100-Meter Backstroke

1904	Walter Brack, Germany	1m16.8s[1]
1908	Arno Bieberstein, Germany	1m24.6s
1912	Harry Hebner, United States	1m21.2s
1920	Warren Kealoha, United States	1m15.2s
1924	Warren Kealoha, United States	1m13.2s
1928	George Kojac, United States	1m8.2s
1932	Masaji Kiyokawa, Japan	1m8.6s
1936	Adolph Kiefer, United States	1m5.9s
1948	Allen Stack, United States	1m6.4s
1952	Yoshinobu Oyakawa, United States	1m5.4s
1956	David Thiele, Australia	1m2.2s
1960	David Thiele, Australia	1m1.9s
1968	Roland Matthes, East Germany	58.7s
1972	Roland Matthes, East Germany	56.58s
1976	John Naber, United States	55.49s

1. 100 yards

200-Meter Backstroke

1900	Ernst Hoppenberg, Germany	2m47s
1964	Jed Graef, United States	2m10.3s
1968	Roland Matthes, East Germany	2m9.6s
1972	Roland Matthes, East Germany	2m2.82s
1976	John Naber, United States	1m59.19s

100-Meter Breaststroke

1968	Donald McKenzie, United States	1m7.7s
1972	Nobutaka Taguchi, Japan	1m4.94s
1976	John Hencken, United States	1m03.11s

200-Meter Breaststroke

1908	Frederick Holman, Great Britain	3m9.2s
1912	Walter Bathe, Germany	3m1.8s
1920	Haken Malmroth, Sweden	3m4.4s
1924	Robert Skelton, United States	2m56.6s
1928	Yoshiyuki Tsuruta, Japan	2m48.8s
1932	Yoshiyuki Tsuruta, Japan	2m45.4s
1936	Tetsuo Hamuro, Japan	2m41.5s
1948	Joseph Verdeur, United States	2m39.3s
1952	John Davies, Australia	2m34.4s
1956	Masura Furukawa, Japan	2m34.7s
1960	Bill Mulliken, United States	2m37.4s
1964	Ian O'Brien, Australia	2m27.8s
1968	Felipe Munoz, Mexico	2m28.7s
1972	John Hencken, United States	2m21.55s
1976	David Willkie, Britain	2m15.11s

400-Meter Breaststroke

1904	Georg Zacharias, Germany	7m23.6s[1]
1912	Walter Bathe, Germany	6m29.6s
1920	Haken Malmroth, Sweden	6m31.8s

1. 440 yards

100-Meter Butterfly

1968	Douglas Russell, United States	55.9s
1972	Mark Spitz, United States	54.27s
1976	Matt Vogel, United States	54.35s

200-Meter Butterfly

1956	Bill Yorzyk, United States	2m19.3s
1960	Mike Troy, United States	2m12.8s
1964	Kevin Berry, Australia	2m6.6s
1968	Carl Robie, United States	2m8.7s
1972	Mark Spitz, United States	2m00.7s
1976	Mike Bruner, United States	1m59.23s

200-Meter Individual Medley

1968	Charles Hickcox, United States	2m12s
1972	Gunnar Larsson, Sweden	2m7.17s

400-Meter Individual Medley

1964	Dick Roth, United States	4m45.4s
1968	Charles Hickcox, United States	4m48.4s
1972	Gunnar Larsson, Sweden	4m31.98s
1976	Rod Strachan, United States	4m23.68s

60-Meter Underwater

1900	de Vaudeville, France	1m53.4s

200-Meter Obstacle

1900	Frederick Lane, Australia	2m38.4s

Relays

1900	Germany (200 meters, 5 men)	32 pts.
1904	United States (200 yards)	2m4.6s
1906	Hungary (1,000 meters)	16m52.4s

400-Meter Freestyle Relay

1964	United States	3m32.2s
1968	United States	3m31.7s
1972	United States	3m26.42s

800-Meter Freestyle Relay

1908	Great Britain	10m55.6s
1912	Australia	10m11.2s
1920	United States	10m4.4s
1924	United States	9m53.4s
1928	United States	9m36.2s
1932	Japan	8m58.4s
1936	Japan	8m51.5s
1948	United States	8m46s
1952	United States	8m31.1s
1956	Australia	8m23.6s
1960	United States	8m10.2s
1964	United States	7m52.1s
1968	United States	7m52.3s
1972	United States	7m35.78s
1976	United States	7m23.22s

400-Meter Medley Relay

1960	United States	4m5.4s
1964	United States	3m58.4s
1968	United States	3m54.9s
1972	United States	3m48.16s
1976	United States	3m42.22s

Springboard Dive

		Points
1908	Albert Zuerner, Germany	85.5
1912	Paul Guenther, Germany	79.23
1920	Louis Kuehn, United States	675
1924	Albert White, United States	696.4
1928	Pete Desjardins, United States	185.04
1932	Michael Galitzen, United States	161.38
1936	Richard Degener, United States	163.57
1948	Bruce Harlan, United States	163.64
1952	David Browning, United States	205.59
1956	Robert Clotworthy, United States	159.56
1960	Gary Tobian, United States	170.00
1964	Ken Sitzberger, United States	159.90
1968	Bernard Wrightson, United States	170.15
1972	Vladimir Vasin, U.S.S.R.	594.09
1976	Phil Boggs, United States	619.05

Platform Dive

		Points
1904	G. E. Sheldon, United States	12.75
1906	Gottlob Walz, Germany	156
1908	Hialmar Johansson, Sweden	83.75
1912	Erik Adlerz, Sweden	73.94
1920	Clarence Pinkston, United States	100.67
1924	Albert White, United States	487.3
1928	Pete Desjardins, United States	98.74
1932	Harold Smith, United States	124.80
1936	Marshall Wayne, United States	113.58
1948	Samuel Lee, United States	130.05
1952	Samuel Lee, United States	156.28
1956	Joaquin Capilla, Mexico	152.44
1960	Bob Webster, United States	165.56
1964	Bob Webster, United States	148.58
1968	Klaus Dibiasi, Italy	164.18
1972	Klaus Dibiasi, Italy	504.12
1976	Klaus Dibiasi, Italy	600.51

Plain High Dive

		Points
1912	Erik Adlerz, Sweden	40
1920	Arvid Wallman, Sweden	7
1924	Richard Eve, Australia	160

Plunge for Distance

1904	W. E. Dickey, United States	62 ft 6 in.

SWIMMING—WOMEN

100 Meters Freestyle

1912	Fanny Durack, Australia	1m22.2s
1920	Ethelda Bleibtrey, United States	1m13.6s
1924	Ethel Lackie, United States	1m12.4s
1928	Albina Osipowich, United States	1m11s
1932	Helene Madison, United States	1m6.8s
1936	Hendrika Mastenbroek, Netherlands	1m5.9s
1948	Greta Andersen, Denmark	1m6.3s
1952	Katalin Szoke, Hungary	1m6.8s
1956	Dawn Fraser, Australia	1m2s
1960	Dawn Fraser, Australia	1m1.2s
1964	Dawn Fraser, Australia	59.5s
1968	Marge Jan Henne, United States	1m
1972	Sandra Neilson, United States	58.59s
1976	Kornelia Ender, East Germany	55.65s

200 Meters Freestyle

1968	Debbie Meyer, United States	2m10.5s
1972	Shane Gould, Australia	2m3.56s
1976	Kornelia Ender, East Germany	1m59.26s

400 Meters Freestyle

1920	Ethelda Bleibtrey, United States	4m34s[1]
1924	Martha Norelius, United States	6m2.2s
1928	Martha Norelius, United States	5m42.8s
1932	Helene Madison, United States	5m28.5s
1936	Hendrika Mastenbroek, Netherlands	5m26.4s
1948	Ann Curtis, United States	5m17.8s
1952	Valerie Gyenge, Hungary	5m12.1s
1956	Lorraine Crapp, Australia	4m54.6s
1960	Chris von Saltza, United States	4m50.6s
1964	Ginny Duenkel, United States	4m43.3s
1968	Debbie Meyer, United States	4m31.8s
1972	Shane Gould, Australia	4m19.04s
1976	Petra Thumer, East Germany	4m09.89s

1. 300 meters.

800 Meters Freestyle

1968	Debbie Meyer, United States	9m24s
1972	Keena Rothhammer, United States	8m53.68s
1976	Petra Thumer, East Germany	8m37.14s

100-Meter Backstroke

1924	Sybil Bauer, United States	1m23.2s
1928	Marie Braun, Netherlands	1m22s
1932	Eleanor Holm, United States	1m19.4s
1936	Dina Senff, Netherlands	1m18.9s
1948	Karen Harup, Denmark	1m14.4s
1952	Joan Harrison, South Africa	1m14.3s
1956	Judy Grinham, Great Britain	1m12.9s
1960	Lynn Burke, United States	1m9.3s
1964	Cathy Ferguson, United States	1m7.7s
1968	Kaye Hall, United States	1m6.2s
1972	Melissa Belote, United States	1m5.78s
1976	Ulrike Richter, East Germany	1m01.83s

200-Meter Backstroke

1968	Pokey Watson, United States	2m24.8s
1972	Melissa Belote, United States	2m19.19s
1976	Ulrike Richter, East Germany	2m13.43s

100-Meter Breaststroke

1968	Djurdjica Bjedov, Yugoslavia	1m15.8s
1972	Catherine Carr, United States	1m13.58s
1976	Hannelore Anke, East Germany	1m11.16s

200-Meter Breaststroke

1924	Lucy Morton, Great Britain	3m33.2s
1928	Hilde Schrader, Germany	3m12.6s
1932	Clare Dennis, Australia	3m6.3s
1936	Hideko Maehata, Japan	3m3.6s
1948	Nel van Vliet, Netherlands	2m57.2s
1952	Eva Szekely, Hungary	2m51.7s
1956	Ursala Happe, Germany	2m53.1s
1960	Anita Lonsbrough, Great Britain	2m49.5s
1964	Galina Prozumenschikova, U.S.S.R.	2m46.4s
1968	Sharon Wichman, United States	2m44.4s
1972	Beverly Whitfield, Australia	2m41.71s
1976	Marina Koshevaia, U.S.S.R.	2m33.35s

100-Meter Butterfly

1956	Shelley Mann, United States	1m11s
1960	Carolyn Schuler, United States	1m9.5s
1964	Sharon Stouder, United States	1m4.7s
1968	Lynn McClements, Australia	1m5.5s
1972	Mayumi Aoki, Japan	1m3.34s
1976	Kornelia Ender, East Germany	1m00.13s

200-Meter Butterfly

1968	Ada Kok, Netherlands	2m24.7s
1972	Karen Moe, United States	2m15.57s
1976	Andrea Pollack, East Germany	2m11.41s

200-Meter Individual Medley

1968	Claudia Kolb, United States	2m24.7s
1972	Shane Gould, Australia	2m23.07s

400-Meter Individual Medley

1964	Donna de Varona, United States	5m18.7s
1968	Claudia Kolb, United States	5m8.5s
1972	Gail Neall, Australia	5m2.97s
1976	Ulrike Tauber, East Germany	4m42.77s

400-Meter Freestyle Relay

1912	Great Britain	5m52.8s
1920	United States	5m11.6s
1924	United States	4m58.8s
1928	United States	4m47.6s
1932	United States	4m38s
1936	Netherlands	4m36s
1948	United States	4m29.2s
1952	Hungary	4m24.4s
1956	Australia	4m17.1s
1960	United States	4m8.9s
1964	United States	4m3.8s
1968	United States	4m2.5s
1972	United States	3m55.19s
1976	United States	3m44.82s

400-Meter Medley Relay

1960	United States	4m41.1s
1964	United States	4m33.9s
1968	United States	4m28.3s
1972	United States	4m20.75s
1976	East Germany	4m07.95s

Springboard Dive

		Points
1920	Aileen Riggin, United States	539.90
1924	Elizabeth Becker, United States	474.5
1928	Helen Meany, United States	78.62
1932	Georgia Coleman, United States	87.52
1936	Marjorie Gestring, United States	89.27
1948	Victoria M. Draves, United States	108.74
1952	Patricia McCormick, United States	147.30
1956	Patricia McCormick, United States	142.36
1960	Ingrid Kramer, Germany	155.81
1964	Ingrid Kramer Engel, Germany	145.00
1968	Sue Gossick, United States	150.77
1972	Micki King, United States	450.03
1976	Jennifer Chandler, United States	506.19

Platform Dive

		Points
1912	Greta Johansson, Sweden	39.9
1920	Stefani Fryland, Denmark	34.60
1924	Caroline Smith, United States	166
1928	Elizabeth B. Pinkston, United States	31.60
1932	Dorothy Poynton, United States	40.26
1936	Dorothy Poynton Hill, United States	33.92
1948	Victoria M. Draves, United States	68.87
1952	Patricia McCormick, United States	79.37
1956	Patricia McCormick, United States	84.85
1960	Ingrid Kramer, Germany	91.28
1964	Lesley Bush, United States	99.80
1968	Milena Duchkova, Czechoslovakia	109.59
1972	Ulrika Knape, Sweden	390.00
1976	Elena Vaytsekhovskaia, U.S.S.R.	406.59

BOXING
(U.S. winners only)

Flyweight—112 Pounds (51 kilograms)

1904	George V. Finnegan	1952	Nate Brooks
1920	Frank De Genaro	1976	Leo Randolph
1924	Fidel La Barba		

Bantamweight—119 pounds (54 kg)

1904   O.L. Kirk

Featherweight—126 pounds (57 kg)

| 1904 | O.L. Kirk | 1924 | Jackie Fields |

Lightweight—132 Pounds (60 kg)

| 1904 | H.J. Spanger | 1968 | Ronnie Harris |
| 1920 | Samuel Mosberg | 1976 | Howard Davis |

Light Welterweight—140 Pounds (63.5 kg)

| 1952 | Charles Adkins | 1976 | Ray Leonard |
| 1972 | Ray Seales | | |

Welterweight—148 Pounds (67 kg)

| 1904 | Al Young | 1932 | Edward Flynn |

Light Middleweight—157 Pounds (71 kg)

| 1960 | Wilbert McClure |

Middleweight—165 Pounds (75 kg)

1904	Charles Mayer	1960	Eddie Crook
1932	Carmen Barth	1976	Mike Spinks
1952	Floyd Patterson		

Light Heavyweight—179 Pounds (81 kg)

1920	Edward Eagan	1960	Cassius Clay
1952	Norvel Lee	1976	Leon Spinks
1956	James Boyd		

Heavyweight (unlimited)

1904	Sam Berger	1964	Joe Frazier
1952	Edward Sanders	1968	George Foreman
1956	Pete Rademacher		

BASKETBALL—MEN

1904	United States	1960	United States
1936	United States	1964	United States
1948	United States	1968	United States
1952	United States	1972	U.S.S.R.
1956	United States	1976	United States

BASKETBALL—WOMEN

| 1976 | U.S.S.R. |

Winter Games

FIGURE SKATING—MEN

1908	Ulrich Salchow, Sweden
1920	Gillis Grafstrom, Sweden
1924	Gillis Grafstrom, Sweden
1928	Gillis Grafstrom, Sweden
1932	Karl Schaefer, Austria
1936	Karl Schaefer, Austria
1948	Richard Button, United States
1952	Richard Button, United States
1956	Hayes Alan Jenkins, United States
1960	David Jenkins, United States
1964	Manfred Schnelldorfer, Germany
1968	Wolfgang Schwartz, Austria
1972	Ondrej Nepela, Czechoslovakia
1976	John Curry, Britain

FIGURE SKATING—WOMEN

1908	Madge Syers, Britain
1920	Magda Mauroy, Sweden
1924	Herma Szabo-Planck, Austria
1928	Sonja Henie, Norway
1932	Sonja Henie, Norway
1936	Sonja Henie, Norway
1948	Barbara Ann Scott, Canada
1952	Jeannette Altwegg, Britain
1956	Tenley Albright, United States
1960	Carol Heiss, United States
1964	Sjoukje Dijkstra, Netherlands
1968	Peggy Fleming, United States
1972	Beatrix Schuba, Austria
1976	Dorothy Hamill, United States

SPEED SKATING—MEN
(U.S. winners only)

500 Meters

1924	Charles Jewfraw
1932	John A. Shea
1952	Kenneth Henry
1964	Terrence McDermott

1,000 Meters

1976	Peter Mueller

1,500 Meters

1932	John A. Shea

5,000 Meters

1932	Irving Jaffee

10,000 Meters

1932 · Irving Jaffee

SPEED
SKATING—WOMEN
500 Meters

1972 Anne Henning
1976 Sheila Young

1,500 Meters

1972 Dianne Holum

SKIING, ALPINE—MEN

Downhill

1948	Henry Oreiller, France	2m55.0s
1952	Zeno Colo, Italy	2m30.8s
1956	Anton Sailer, Austria	2m52.2s
1960	Jean Vuarnet, France	2m06.2s
1964	Egon Zimmermann, Austria	2m18.16s
1968	Jean-Claude Killy, France	1m59.85s
1972	Bernhard Russi, Switzerland	1m51.43s
1976	Franz Klammer, Austria	1m45.72s

Slalom

1948	Edi Reinalter, Switzerland	2m10.3s
1952	Othmar Schneider, Austria	2m00.0s
1956	Anton Sailer, Austria	194.7 pts.
1960	Ernst Hinterseer, Austria	2m08.9s
1968	Jean-Claude Killy, France	1m39.73s
1972	Francisco Fernandez Ochoa, Spain	1m49.27s
1976	Piero Gros, Italy	2m03.29s

Giant Slalom

1952	Stein Eriksen, Norway	2m25.0s
1956	Anton Sailer, Austria	3m00.1s
1960	Roger Staub, Switzerland	1m48.3s
1964	Francois Bonlieu, France	1m46.71s
1968	Jean-Claude Killy, France	3m29.28s
1972	Gustavo Thoeni, Italy	3m09.52s
1976	Heini Hemmi, Switzerland	3m26.97s

SKIING, ALPINE—WOMEN

Downhill

1948	Hedi Schlunegger, Switzerland	2m28.3s
1952	Trude Jochum-Beiser, Austria	1m47.1s
1956	Madeleine Berthod, Switzerland	1m40.1s
1960	Heidi Biebl, Germany	1m37.6s
1964	Christl Haas, Austria	1m55.39s

1968	Olga Pall, Austria	1m40.87s
1972	Marie-Therese Nadig, Switzerland	1m36.68s
1976	Rosi Mittermeier, West Germany	1m46.16s

Slalom

1948	Gretchen Fraser, United States	1m57.2s
1952	Andrea M. Lawrence, United States	2m10.6s
1956	Renee Colliard, Switzerland	112.3 pts.
1960	Anne Heggtveigt, Canada	1m49.6s
1964	Christine Goitschel, France	1m29.86s
1968	Marielle Goitschel, France	1m25.86s
1972	Barbara Cochran, United States	1m31.24s
1976	Rosi Mittermeier, West Germany	1m30.54s

Giant Slalom

1952	Andrea M. Lawrence, United States	2m06.8s
1956	Ossi Reichert, Germany	1m56.5s
1960	Yvonne Ruegg, Switzerland	1m39.9s
1964	Marielle Goitschel, France	1m52.24s
1968	Nancy Greene, Canada	1m51.97s
1972	Marie-Therese Nadig, Switzerland	1m29.90s
1976	Kathy Kreiner, Canada	1m29.13s

ICE HOCKEY

1920	Canada	1948	Canada	1964	U.S.S.R.
1924	Canada	1952	Canada	1968	U.S.S.R.
1928	Canada	1956	U.S.S.R.	1972	U.S.S.R.
1932	Canada	1960	United States	1976	U.S.S.R.
1936	Britain				

SKIING, NORDIC, JUMPING

90-Meter Hill

1924	Jacob T. Thams, Norway	227.5
1928	Alfred Andersen, Norway	230.5
1932	Birger Ruud, Norway	228.0
1936	Birger Ruud, Norway	232.0
1948	Peter Hugsted, Norway	228.1
1952	A. Bergmann, Norway	226.0
1956	Antti Hyvarinen, Finland	227.0
1960	Helmut Recknagel, Germany	227.2
1964	Toralf Engan, Norway	230.7
1968	Vladimir Beloussov, U.S.S.R.	231.3
1972	Wojciech Fortuna, Poland	219.9
1976	Karl Schnabl, Austria	234.8

Small Hill (70 meters)

1964	Veikko Kankkonen, Finland	229.9
1968	Jiri Raska, Czechoslovakia	216.5
1972	Yukio Kasaya, Japan	244.2
1976	Hans-Georg Aschenbach, East Germany	252.0

DISTRIBUTION OF MEDALS
1976 SUMMER GAMES

	Gold	Silver	Bronze	Total
Soviet Union	47	43	35	125
East Germany	40	25	25	90
United States	34	35	25	94
West Germany	10	12	17	39
Japan	9	6	10	25
Poland	8	6	11	25
Bulgaria	7	8	9	24
Cuba	6	4	3	13
Romania	4	9	14	27
Hungary	4	5	12	21
Finland	4	2	0	6
Sweden	4	1	0	5
Britain	3	5	5	13
Italy	2	7	4	13
France	2	2	5	9
Yugoslavia	2	3	3	8
Czechoslovakia	2	2	4	8
New Zealand	2	1	1	4
South Korea	1	1	4	6
Switzerland	1	1	2	4
Jamaica	1	1	0	2
North Korea	1	1	0	2
Norway	1	1	0	2
Denmark	1	0	2	3
Mexico	1	0	1	2
Trinidad and Tobago	1	0	0	1
Canada	0	5	6	11
Belgium	0	3	3	6
Netherlands	0	2	3	5
Portugal	0	2	0	2
Spain	0	2	0	2
Austalia	0	1	4	5
Iran	0	1	1	2
Mongolia	0	1	0	1
Venezuela	0	1	0	1
Brazil	0	0	2	2
Austria	0	0	1	1
Bermuda	0	0	1	1
Pakistan	0	0	1	1
Puerto Rico	0	0	1	1
Thailand	0	0	1	1

(all weight-lifting medals included)

Other 1976 Olympic Games Champions

SUMMER

Archery

Men—Darrell Pace, United States
Women—Luann Ryon, United States

Boxing

Light flyweight—Jorge Hernandez, Cuba
Bantamweight—Yong Jo Gu, North Korea
Featherweight—Angel Herrera, Cuba
Welterweight—Jochen Bachfield, E. Ger.
Light middleweight—Jerzy Rybicki, Poland
Heavyweight—Teofilo Stevenson, Cuba

Canadian Canoeing

500 m—Aleksandr Rogov, U.S.S.R.
1,000 m—Matija Ljubek, Yugoslavia
500-m pairs—Sergei Petrenko–Aleksandr Vinogradov, U.S.S.R.
1,000-m pairs—Sergei Petrenko–Aleksandr Vinogradov, U.S.S.R.

Kayak—Men

500 m—Vasile Diba, Romania
1,000 m—Rudiger Helm, E. Ger.
500-m pairs—Joachim Mattern–Bernd Olbricht, E. Ger.
1,000-m pairs—Sergei Nagorny—Vladimir Romanovsky, U.S.S.R.
1,000-m fours—U.S.S.R.

Kayak—Women

500 m—Carola Zirzow, E. Ger.
500-m pairs—Nina Gopova–Galina Kreft, U.S.S.R.

Cycling

1,000 m—Klaus–Jurgen Grunke, E. Ger.
Spring—Anton Tkac, Czechoslovakia
Pursuit—Gregor Braun, W. Ger.
Team pursuit—W. Ger.
Road race—Bernt Johansson, Sweden
Team road race—U.S.S.R.

Equestrian

Dressage—Christine Stueckelberger, Switzerland
Dressage team—W. Ger.
Jumping—Alwin Schockemoehle, W. Ger.
Team jumping—France
3-Day event—Tad Coffin, Strafford, Vt.
Team 3-day event—United States (Tad Coffin, Mike Plumb, Mary Ann Tauskey, Bruce Davidson)

Fencing

Foil—Fabio Dal Zotto, Italy
Team foil—W. Ger.
Epee—Alexander Pusch, W. Ger.
Team epee—Sweden
Saber—Victor Kropovskov, U.S.S.R.
Team saber—U.S.S.R.
Women's foil—Ildiko Schwarczenberger, Hungary
Women's team foil—U.S.S.R.

Gymnastics—Men

All around—Nikolai Andrianov, U.S.S.R.
Floor exercises—Nikolai Andrianov, U.S.S.R.
Horizontal bar—Mitsuo Tsukahara, Japan
Long horse—Nikolai Andrianov, U.S.S.R.
Parallel bars—Sawao Kato, Japan
Rings—Nikolai Andrianov, U.S.S.R.
Side horse—Zoltan Magyar, Hungary
Team all-around—Japan

Gymnastics—Women

All-around—Nadia Comaneci, Romania
Balance beam—Nadia Comaneci, Romania
Floor exercises—Nelli Kim, U.S.S.R.
Uneven bars—Nadia Comaneci, Romania
Vault—Nelli Kim, U.S.S.R.
Team all-around—U.S.S.R.

Judo

Light middleweight—Vladimir Nevzorov, U.S.S.R.
Middleweight—Isamu Sonada, Japan
Light heavyweight—Kazuhir Ninomiya, Japan
Heavyweight—Sergi Novikov, U.S.S.R.
Open—Haruki Uemura, Japan
Lightweight—Hector Rodriguez, Cuba

Modern Pentathlon

Individual—Janucz Pyciak–Peciak, Poland
Team—Britain

Rowing—Men

Singles—Pertti Karppinen, Finland
Doubles—Frank and Alf Hansen, Norway
Pairs—Jorg and Bernd Landvoigt, E. Ger.
Pairs with coxswain—Harald Jahrling–Friedrich Ulrich–Georg Spohr, E. Ger.
Fours—E. Ger.
Fours with coxswains—U.S.S.R.
Quadruple sculls—E. Ger.
Eights—E. Ger.

Rowing—Women

Singles—Christine Scheiblich, E. Ger.
Doubles—Svetia Otzetova–Zdravka Yoradanova, Bulgaria
Pairs—Siika Kelbetcheva–Stoyanka Grouitcheva, Bulgaria
Fours with coxswains—E. Ger.
Quadruple sculls—E. Ger.

Shooting

Free pistol—Uwe Potteck, E. Ger.
Rapid fire pistol—Norbert Klaar, E. Ger.
Small-bore rifle, prone—Karlheinz Smieszek, W. Ger.
Small-bore rifle, 3 positions—Lanny Bassham, Bedford, Tex.
Rifle, running game target—Aleksandr Gazov, U.S.S.R.
Trap—Don Haldeman, Souderton, Pa.
Skeet—Josef Panacek, Czechoslovakia

Weight Lifting

Feather—Nikolai Kolesnikov, U.S.S.R.
Fly—Aleksandr Voronin, U.S.S.R.
Bantam—Norair Nurikin, Bulgaria
Light—Zhigniev Kaesmarek, Poland
Middle—Yordan Mitkov, Bulgaria
Light heavy—Valery Shary, U.S.S.R.
Middle heavy—David Rigert, U.S.S.R.
Heavy—Valentin Khristov, Bulgaria
Super heavy—Vasily Alexyev, U.S.S.R.

Wrestling—Freestyle

Paper—Khassan Issaev, Bulgaria
Fly—Yuji Takata, Japan
Bantam—Vladimir Umin, U.S.S.R.
Feather—Jung–Mo Jang, South Korea
Light—Pavel Pinigin, U.S.S.R.
Welter—Date Jiichiro, Japan
Middle—John Peterson, Comstock, Wis.
Light heavy—Levan Tediashvili, U.S.S.R.
Heavy—Ivan Yarygin, U.S.S.R.
Unlimited—Soslan Andiev, U.S.S.R.

Wrestling—Greco-Roman

Paper—Alexei Schumakov, U.S.S.R.
Fly—Vitaly Konstantinov, U.S.S.R.
Bantam—Pertti Ukkola, Finland
Feather—Kazimier Lipien, Poland
Light—Suren Nalbandy, U.S.S.R.
Welter—Anatoly Bykov, U.S.S.R.
Middle—Momir Petkovic, Yugoslavia
Light heavy—Valery Kezantsev, U.S.S.R.
Heavy—Nikolai Bolboshin, U.S.S.R.
Super heavy—Aleksandr Kolchinski, U.S.S.R.

Yachting

Finn—Jocken Schumann, E. Ger.
Flying Dutchman—Joerg Diesch, W. Ger.
470 Class—Frank Huebner, W. Ger.
Soling—Paul Jensen, Denmark
Tempest—John Albrechtson, Sweden
Tornado—Reginald White, Britain

Team Champions

Field hockey—New Zealand
Handball (team), Men—U.S.S.R.
Handball (team), Women—U.S.S.R.
Soccer—East Germany
Volleyball, men—Poland
Volleyball, women—Japan
Water polo—Hungary

WINTER

Biathlon

Individual—Nikolai Kruglov, U.S.S.R.
Relay—U.S.S.R.

Bobsledding

2-man—Meinhard Nehmer–Bernard Germeshausen, East Germany
4-man—East Germany

Figure Skating

Men—John Curry, Britain
Women—Dorothy Hamill, Riverside, Conn.
Pairs—Irina Rodnina–Aleksandr Zaitsev, U.S.S.R.
Dance—Ludmilla Pakhomova–Aleksandr Gorschkov, U.S.S.R.

Speed Skating—Men

500 m—Evgeni Kulikov, U.S.S.R.
1,000 m—Peter Mueller, Mequon, Wis.
1,500 m—Jan Egil Storhold, Norway
5,000 m—Sten Stensen, Norway
10,000 m—Piet Kleine, Netherlands

Speed Skating—Women

500 m—Sheila Young, Detroit
1,000 m—Tatiana Averina, U.S.S.R.
1,500 m—Galina Stepanskaya, U.S.S.R.
3,000 m—Tatiana Averina, U.S.S.R.

Hockey

Team—U.S.S.R.

Luge

Men—Detlef Guenther, East Germany
Doubles—Hans Rinn–Norbert Hahn, East Germany
Women—Margit Schumann, East Germany

Skiing, Nordic—Men

Combined—Ulrich Wehling, East Germany

Cross-Country Skiing—Men

15 km—Nikola Bajukov, U.S.S.R.
30 km—Sergei Saveliev, U.S.S.R.
50 km—Ivar Formo, Norway
40-km relay—Finland

Cross-Country Skiing—Women

5 km—Helena Takalo, Finland
10 km—Raisa Smetanina, U.S.S.R.

STRUCTURES

The Seven Wonders of the World

(Not all classical writers list the same items as the Seven Wonders, but most of them agree on the following.)

The Pyramids of Egypt. A group of three pyramids, *Khufu, Khafra,* and *Menkaura* at Giza, outside modern Cairo, is often called the first wonder of the world. The largest pyramid, built by Khufu (Cheops), a king of the fourth Dynasty, had an original estimated height of 482 ft (now approximately 450 ft). The base has sides 755 ft long. It contains 2,300,000 blocks; the average weight of each is 2.5 tons. Estimated date of construction is 2800 B.C. Of all the Seven Wonders, the pyramids alone survive.

Hanging Gardens of Babylon. Often listed as the second wonder, these gardens were supposedly built by Nebuchadnezzar about 600 B.C. to please his queen, Amuhia. They are also associated with the mythical Assyrian Queen, Semiramis. Archeologists surmise that the gardens were laid out atop a vaulted building, with provisions for raising water. The terraces were said to rise from 75 to 300 ft.

The Walls of Babylon, also built by Nebuchadnezzar, are sometimes referred to as the second (or the seventh) wonder instead of the Hanging Gardens.

Statue of Zeus (Jupiter) at Olympia. The work of Phidias (5th century B.C.), this colossal figure in gold and ivory was reputedly 40 ft high. All trace of it is lost, except for reproductions on coins.

Temple of Artemis (Diana) at Ephesus. A beautiful structure, begun about 350 B.C. in honor of a non-Hellenic goddess who later became identified with the Greek goddess of the same name. The temple, with Ionic columns 60 ft high, was destroyed by invading Goths in A.D. 262.

Mausoleum at Halicarnassus. This famous monument was erected by Queen Artemisia in memory of her husband, King Mausolus of Caria in Asia Minor, who died in 353 B.C. Some remains of the structure are in the British Museum. This shrine is the source of the modern word "mausoleum."

Colossus at Rhodes. This bronze statue of Helios (Apollo), about 105 ft high, was the work of the sculptor Chares, who reputedly labored for 12 years before completing it in 280 B.C. It was destroyed during an earthquake in 224 B.C.

Pharos of Alexandria. The seventh wonder was the Pharos (lighthouse) of Alexandria, built by Sostratus of Cnidus during the 3rd century B.C. on the island of Pharos off the coast of Egypt. It was destroyed by an earthquake in the 13th century.

Famous Structures

Ancient

The *Great Sphinx of Egypt,* one of the wonders of ancient Egyptian architecture, adjoins the pyramids of Giza and has a length of 240 ft. It was built in the 4th dynasty.

Other Egyptian buildings of note include the *Temples of Karnak* and *Edfu* and the *Tombs at Beni Hassan.*

The *Parthenon of Greece,* built on the Acropolis in Athens, was the chief temple to the goddess Athena. It was believed to have been completed by 438 B.C. The present temple remained intact until the 5th century A.D. Today, though the Parthenon is in ruins, its majestic proportions are still discernible.

Other great structures of ancient Greece were the *Temples at Paestum* (about 540 and 420 B.C.); the *Temple of Poseidon* (about 460 B.C.); the *Temple of Apollo* at Corinth (about 540 B.C.); the *Temple of Apollo* at Bassae (about 450–420 B.C.); the famous *Erechtheum* atop the Acropolis (about 421–405 B.C.); the *Temple of Athena Niké* at Athens (about 426 B.C.); the *Olympieum* at Athens (174 B.C.–A.D. 131); the *Athenian Treasury* at Delphi (about 515 B.C.); the *Propylaea* of the Acropolis at Athens (437–432 B.C.); the *Theater of Dionysus* at Athens (about 350–325 B.C.); the *House of Cleopatra* at Delos (138 B.C.) and the *Theater* at Epidaurus (about 325 B.C.).

The *Colosseum (Flavian Amphitheater) of Rome,* the largest and most famous of the Roman amphitheaters, was opened for use A.D. 80. Elliptical in shape, it consisted of three stories and an upper gallery, rebuilt in stone in its present form in the third century A.D. Its seats rise in tiers, which in turn are buttressed by concrete vaults and stone piers. It could seat between 40,000 and 50,000 spectators. It was principally used for gladiatorial combat.

The *Pantheon* at Rome, begun by Agrippa in 27 B.C. as a temple, was rebuilt in its present circular form by Hadrian (A.D. 110–25). Literally the Pantheon was intended as a temple of "all the gods." It is remarkable for its perfect preservation today, and it has served continuously for 20 centuries as a place of worship.

Famous Roman arches include the *Arch of Constantine* (about A.D. 315) and the *Arch of Titus* (about A.D. 80).

Later European

St. Mark's Cathedral in Venice (1063–67), one of the great examples of Byzantine architecture, was begun in the 9th century. Partly destroyed by fire in 976, it was later rebuilt as a Byzantine edifice.

Other famous Byzantine examples of architecture are *St. Sophia* in Istanbul (A.D. 532–37); *San Vitale* in Ravenna (542); *St. Paul's Outside the Walls,* Rome (5th century); the *Kremlin* baptism and marriage church, Moscow (begun in 1397); and *St. Lorenzo Outside the Walls,* Rome, begun in 588.

The *Cathedral Group* at Pisa (1067–1173), one of the most celebrated groups of structures built in Romanesque style, consists of the cathedral, the cathedral's baptistery, and the *Leaning Tower.* This trio forms a group by itself in the northwest corner of the city. The cathedral and baptistery are built in varicolored marble. The campanile *(Leaning Tower)* is 179 ft. high and leans more than 16 ft out of the perpendicular. There is little reason to believe that the architects intended to have the tower lean.

Other examples of Romanesque architecture include the *Vézelay Abbey* in France (1130); the *Church of Notre-Dame-du-Port* at Clermont-Ferrand in France (1100); the *Church of San Zeno* (begun in 1138) at Verona; and *Durham Cathedral* in England.

The *Alhambra* (1248–1354), located in Granada, Spain, is universally esteemed as one of the greatest masterpieces of Moslem architecture. Designed as a palace and fortress for the Moorish monarchs of Granada, it is surrounded by a heavily fortified wall more than a mile in perimeter. The location of the Alhambra in the Sierra Nevada provides a magnificent setting for this jewel of Moorish Spain.

The *Tower of London* is a group of buildings and towers covering 13 acres along the north bank of the Thames. The central *White Tower,* begun in 1078 during the reign of William the Conqueror, was originally a fortress and royal residence, but was later used as a prison. The *Bloody Tower* is associated with Anne Boleyn and other notables.

Westminster Abbey, in London, was begun in 1045 and completed in 1065. It was rebuilt and enlarged in 1245–50.

Notre-Dame de Paris (begun in 1163), one of the great examples of Gothic architecture, is a twin-towered church with a steeple over the crossing and immense flying buttresses supporting the masonry at the rear of the church.

Other famous Gothic structures are *Chartres Cathedral* (12th century); *Sainte Chapelle,* Paris (1246–48); *Laon Cathedral,* France (1160–1205); *Reims Cathedral* (about 1210–50; rebuilt after its almost complete destruction in World War I); *Rouen Cathedral* (13th–16th centuries); *Amiens Cathedral* (1218–69); *Beauvais Cathedral* (begun 1247); *Salisbury Cathedral* (1220–60); *York Minster* or the *Cathedral of St. Peter* (begun in the 7th century); *Milan Cathedral* (begun 1386); and *Cologne Cathedral* (13th–19th centuries; badly damaged in World War II.

The Duomo (cathedral) in Florence was founded in 1298, completed by Brunelleschi and consecrated in 1436. The oval-shaped dome dominates the entire structure.

The *Vatican* is a group of buildings in Rome comprising the official residence of the Pope. The *Basilica of St. Peter,* the largest church in the Christian world, was begun in 1450. The *Sistine Chapel,* begun in 1473, is noted for the art masterpieces of Michelangelo, Botticelli, and others. The *Basilica of the Savior* (known as *St. John Lateran*) is the first-ranking Catholic Church in the world, for it is the cathedral of the Pope.

Other examples of Renaissance architecture are the *Palazzo Riccardi,* the *Palazzo Pitti* and the *Palazzo Strozzi* in Florence; the *Farnese Palace* in Rome; *Palazzo Grimani* (completed about 1550) in Venice; the *Escorial* (1563–93) near Madrid; the *Town Hall* of Seville (1527–32); the *Louvre,* Paris; the *Château* at Blois, France; *St. Paul's Cathedral,* London (1675–1710; badly damaged in World

War II); the *École Militaire,* Paris (1752); the *Pazzi Chapel,* Florence, designed by Brunelleschi (1429); the Palace of *Fontainebleau* and the *Château de Chambord* in France.

The *Palace of Versailles,* containing the famous Hall of Mirros, was built during the reign of Louis XIV and served as the royal palace until 1793.

Outstanding European buildings of the 18th and 19th centuries are the *Superga* at Turin, the *Hôtel-Dieu* in Lyons, the *Belvedere Palace* at Vienna, the *Royal Palace* of Stockholm, the *Opera House* of Paris (1863–75); the *Bank of England,* the *British Museum,* the *University of London,* and the *Houses of Parliament,* all in London; the *Panthéon,* the *Church of the Madeleine,* the *Bourse,* and the *Palais de Justice* in Paris.

The *Eiffel Tower,* in Paris, was built for the Exposition of 1889 by Alexandre Eiffel. It is 984 ft high.[1]

Asiatic and African

The *Taj Mahal* (1632–50), at Agra, India, built by Shah Jahan as a tomb for his wife, is considered by some as the most perfect example of the Mogul style and by others as the most beautiful building in the world. Four slim white minarets flank the building, which is topped by a white dome; the entire structure is of marble.

Other examples of Indian architecture are the temples at Benares and Tanjore.

Among famed Moslem edifices are the *Dome of the Rock* or *Mosque of Omar,* Jerusalem (A.D. 691); the *Citadel* (1166), and the *Tombs of the Mamelukes* (15th century), in Cairo; the *Tomb of Humayun* in Delhi; the *Blue Mosque* (1468) at Tabriz, and the *Tamerlane Mausoleum* at Samarkand.

Angkor Wat, outside the city of Angkor Thom, Cambodia, is one of the most beautiful examples of Cambodian or Khmer architecture. The sanctuary was built during the 12th century.

Great Wall of China (228 B.C.?), designed specifically as a defense against nomadic tribes, has numerous large watch towers which could be called buildings. It was erected by Emperor Ch'in Shih Huang Ti and is 1,400 miles long. Built mainly of earth and stone, it varies in height between 18 and 30 ft.

Typical of Chinese architecture are the pagodas or temple towers. Among some of the better-known pagodas are

1. 1,056 ft, including the television tower.

the *Great Pagoda of the Wild Geese* at Sian (founded in 652); *Nan t'a* (11th century) at Fang Shan; the *Pagoda of Sung Yueh Ssu* (A.D. 523) at Sung Shan, Honan.

Other well-known Chinese buildings are the *Drum Tower* (1273), the *Three Great Halls* in the Purple Forbidden City (1627), *Buddha's Perfume Tower* (19th century), the *Porcelain Pagoda,* and the *Summer Palace,* all at Peking.

United States

Rockefeller Center, in New York City, extends from 5th Ave. to the Avenue of the Americas between 48th and 52nd Sts. (and halfway to 7th Ave. between 47th and 51st Sts.). It occupies more than 22 acres and has 19 buildings.

The Cathedral Church of St. John the Divine, at 112th St. and Amsterdam Ave. in New York City, was begun in 1892 and is now in the final stages of completion. When completed, it will be the largest cathedral in the world: 601 ft long, 146 ft wide at the nave, 320 ft wide at the transept. The east end is designed in Romanesque-Byzantine style, and the nave and west end are Gothic.

St. Patrick's Cathedral, at Fifth Ave. and 50th St. in New York City, has a seating capacity of 2,500. The nave was opened in 1877, and the cathedral was dedicated in 1879.

Louisiana Superdome, in New Orleans, is the largest arena in the history of mankind. The main area can accommodate up to 95,000 people. It is the world's largest steel-constructed room. Unobstructed by posts, it covers 13 ac. and reaches 27 stories at its peak.

World Trade Center, in New York City, was dedicated in 1973. Its twin towers are 110 stories high (1,353 ft), and the complex contains over 9 million sq ft of office space. The world's highest observation deck is at the top of the South Tower. A restaurant is located on the top floor of the North Tower.

Ten Longest Bridges

Suspension

Name	Location	Length of main span, ft	Year completed
Humber	Hull, Britain	4,626	UC
Verrazano-Narrows	Lower New York Bay	4,260	1964
Golden Gate	San Francisco Bay	4,200	1937
Mackinac Straits	Michigan	3,800	1957
Bosporus	Istanbul	3,524	1973
George Washington	Hudson River at New York City	3,500	1931
Ponte 25 de Abril	Tagus River at Lisbon	3,323	1966
Forth Road	Queensferry, Scotland	3,300	1964
Severn	Severn River at Beachley, England	3,240	1966
Tacoma Narrows	Puget Sound at Tacoma, Wash.	2,800	1950

Source: Encyclopaedia Britannica and American Society of Civil Engineers

Famous Tunnels

Railroad, excluding subways

Name	Location	Length mi.	Year completed
Seikan	Tsugara Straits, Japan	33.1	UC
Simplon (I and II)	Alps, Switzerland-Italy	12.3	1906 & 1922
Kammon Straits	Honshu to Kyoshu Islands, Japan	11.6	UC
Apennine	Genoa, Italy	11.5	1934
St. Gotthard	Swiss Alps	9.3	1881

Vehicular

Name	Location	Length mi.	Year completed
St. Gotthard	Alps, Switzerland	10.2	UC
Mt. Blanc	Alps, France-Italy	7.5	1965
Mt. Ena	Japan Alps, Japan	5.3	1976[1]
Great St. Bernard	Alps, Switzerland-Italy	3.4	1964
Mount Royal	Montreal, Canada	3.2	1918

1. Parallel tunnel begun in 1976. NOTE: UC = under construction. *Source:* American Society of Civil Engineers.

America's Ten Tallest Buildings

City	Building	Height Stories	ft
Chicago	Sears Tower	110	1,454
New York	World Trade Center	110	1,369
New York	Empire State	102	1,250
Chicago	Standard Oil (Indiana)	80	1,136
Chicago	John Hancock Center	100	1,127
New York	Chrysler	77	1,046
New York	American International	66	952
New York	Citicorp Center	59	915
New York	40 Wall Tower	71	900
Chicago	Water Tower Place	74	859

NOTE: Does not include buildings under construction and not completed in 1978. Height does not include TV towers and antennas. *Source: Information Please* questionnaires to buildings.

World's Ten Highest Dams

Name	River	Maximum height feet	Reservoir capacity in millions of cubic meters	Year completed
Rogunsky	Vakhsh, U.S.S.R.	1,066	11,700	UC
Nurek	Vakhsh, U.S.S.R.	1,040	10,400	UC
Grand Dixence	Dixence, Switzerland	935	401	1962
Inguri	Inguri, U.S.S.R.	892	1,100	UC
Vaiont	Vaiont, Italy	858	169	1961
Chicoasen	Grijalva, Mexico	820	1,660	UC
Mica	Columbia, Canada	794	24,670	1974
Sayanskaya	Yenesei, U.S.S.R.	794	31,300	UC
Chivor	Bata, Colombia	778	815	1975
Mauvoisin	Drance de Bagnes, Switzerland	777	182	1957

NOTE: UC= under construction in 1977. *Source:* Department of the Interior, Bureau of Reclamation.

UNITED STATES

GEOGRAPHY
Number of states: 50
Land area (1970): 3,615,122 sq mi. Share of world land area (1969): 6.9%
Northermost point: Point Barrow, Alaska
Easternmost point: West Quoddy Head, Me.
Southernmost point: Ka Lae (South Cape), Hawaii
Westernmost point: Cape Wrangell, Alaska
Geographic center: In Butte County, S.D. (44°58′ N.lat., 103°46′ W. long)

POPULATION
Total (est. July 1, 1979): 220,232,000
Center of population (1970): 5 miles east-southeast of Mascoutah, Illinois
Males (est. 1979): 107,309,000
Females (est. 1979): 112,923,000
White persons (est. 1979): 190,194,000
Black and other persons (est. 1979): 30,038,000
Breakdown by age groups (est. 1979):
  Under 5 years: 15,617,000
  5–14 years: 34,555,000
  15–24 years: 41,656,000
  25–64 years: 103,972,000
  65 and over: 24,432,000
Median age (est. 1979): 30.0
Rural population (est. 1978): 61,180,500
Metropolitan population (est. 1978): 157,321,500
Families (est. 1978): 56,958,000
Average family size (est. 1978): 3.33
Married couples (est. 1978): 50,000,000
Unmarried persons (14 years and over) (est. 1978): 45,000,000
Widowers (est.): 2,500,000
Widows (est.): 10,750,000
Divorced persons (est.): 7,250,000

VITAL STATISTICS

Births (1977): 3,313,000
Deaths (1977): 1,898,000
Marriages (1977): 2,176,000
Divorces (1977): 1,097,000

CIVILIAN LABOR FORCE

Males (July 1978): 56,629,000 (95.3% employed).
Females (1978): 33,543,000 (92%
employed)
Teenagers 16–19 (July 1978): 8,881,000 (84.4%
employed)

INCOME

Gross national product (est. 1978):
$2,100,000,000,000
Personal income per capita (1977): $7,057
Family income, median (1977): $16,740
Personal savings accounts (est.): $90,000,000,000
Individual shareholders (est.): 25,270,000
Home ownership (est.): 70,000,000
Number of millionaires (net worth): 200,000
Number below poverty level (1977): white, 16,416,000;
black and other minorities 8,304,000

EDUCATION

Elementary and secondary schools (1976): 85,496
Elementary and secondary pupils (est. 1979):
47,224,000
Elementary and secondary teachers (est. 1979):
2,429,000
High school graduates (1979): 3,080,000
Money spent on elementary and secondary education (est.
1979–80): $74,800,000,000
Institutions of higher learning (est. 1976): 2,765 College
graduates (1979): 1,005,000

CONVENIENCES

TV sets (1978): 138,200,000
Radios (1978): 444,000,000
TV stations (1978): 986. Radio stations (standard and
FM, 1978): 8,527
Automobiles (est. 1977): 109,676,000

Telephones (1977): 155,173,000
Newspaper circulation (morning and evening, 1977):
61,495,140

TRAVEL

Road mileage (all vehicles) (est. 1978):
1,500,000,000,000
Railroad passenger-miles (excluding commuter) (est.
1978): 10,750,000,000
Airline passenger-miles (est. 1978): 180,000,000,000

States of the Union

ALABAMA

Capital: Montgomery
Organized as territory: March 3, 1817
Entered Union & (rank): Dec. 14, 1819 (22)
Present constitution adopted: 1901
Motto: *Audemus jura nostra defendere* (We dare defend our rights)
State flower: Camellia (1959)
State bird: Yellowhammer (1927)
State song: "Alabama" (1931)
State tree: Southern pine (longleaf) (1949)
Nickname: Yellowhammer State
Origin of name: May come from Choctaw meaning "thicket-clearers" or
"vegetation-gatherers"
1970 population & (rank): 3,444,165 (21)
1977 est. population & (rank): 3,690,000 (21)
1970 land area & (rank): 50,708 sq mi. (131,334 sq km) (28)
Geographic center: In Chilton Co., 12 mi. SW of Clanton
Number of counties: 67
Largest cities (1975 est.): Birmingham (276,273); Mobile (196,441);
Montgomery (153,343); Huntsville (136,419); Tuscaloosa (69,425)
State forests: 8 (14,248.58 ac.)
State parks: 39 (41,959.35 ac.)

ALASKA

Capital: Juneau
Organized as territory: 1912
Entered Union & (rank): Jan. 3, 1959 (49)
Constitution ratified: April 24, 1956
Motto: North to the Future
State flower: Forget-me-not
State tree: Sitka spruce
State bird: Willow ptarmigan
State fish: King salmon
State song: "Alaska's Flag"
Nickname: The state is commonly called "The Last Frontier" or "Land of the Midnight Sun"
Origin of name: Corruption of Aleut word meaning "great land" or "that which the sea breaks against"
1970 population & (rank): 302,173 (50)
1977 est. population & (rank): 407,000 (49)
1970 land area & (rank): 566,432 sq mi. (1,467,059 sq km) (1)
Geographic center: 60 mi. NW of Mt. McKinley
Number of boroughs: 12
Largest cities (1975 est.): Anchorage, city and borough (161,018); Fairbanks (29,920); Juneau, city and borough (16,749); Ketchikan (7,527); Sitka, city and borough (6,073)
State forests: None
State parks: 4; 59 waysides and areas (1.5 million ac.)

ARIZONA

Capital: Phoenix
Organized as territory: Feb. 24, 1863
Entered Union & (rank): Feb. 14, 1912 (48)
Present constitution adopted: 1911
Motto: *Ditat Deus* (God enriches)
State flower: Flower of saguaro cactus (1931)
State bird: Cactus wren (1931)
State colors: Blue and old gold (1915)
State song: "Arizona," a march song (1919)
State tree: Paloverde (1957)
Nickname: Grand Canyon State
Origin of name: From the Indian "Arizonac," meaning "little spring"
1970 population & (rank): 1,772,482 (33)
1977 est. population & (rank): 2,296,000 (32)
1970 land area & (rank): 113,417 sq mi. (293,750 sq km) (6)
Geographic center: In Yavapai Co., 55 mi. ESE of Prescott
Number of counties: 14
Largest cities (1975 est.): Phoenix (664,721); Tucson (296,457); Mesa (99,043); Tempe (84,072); Scottsdale (77,529); Glendale (65,671); Flagstaff (31,127)
State forests: None
State parks: 10

ARKANSAS

Capital: Little Rock
Organized as territory: March 2, 1819
Entered Union & (rank): June 15, 1836 (25)
Present constitution adopted: 1874
Motto: *Regnat populus* (The people rule)
State flower: Apple Blossom (1901)
State tree: Pine (1939)
State bird: Mockingbird (1929)
State insect: Honeybee
State song: "Arkansas" (1963)
Nickname: Land of Opportunity
Origin of name: From the Quapaw Indians
1970 population & (rank): 1,923,295 (32)
1977 est. population & (rank): 2,144,000 (33)
1970 land area & (rank): 51,945 sq mi. (134,538 sq km) (27)
Geographic center: In Pulaski Co., 12 mi. NW of Little Rock
Number of counties: 75
Largest cities (1975 est.): Little Rock (141,143); Fort Smith (64,734); North Little Rock (61,768); Pine Bluff (54,631); Hot Springs (38,207)
State forests: None
State parks: 36

CALIFORNIA

Capital: Sacramento
Entered Union & (rank): Sept. 9, 1850 (31)
Present constitution adopted: 1879
Motto: *Eureka* (I have found it)
State flower: Golden poppy (1903)
State tree: California redwoods *(Sequoia sempervirens & Sequoia gigantea)* (1937 & 1953)
State bird: California valley quail (1931)
State animal: California grizzly bear (1953)
State fish: California golden trout (1947)
State insect: California dog-face butterfly (unofficial)
State colors: Blue and gold (1951)
State song: "I Love You, California" (1951)
Nickname: Golden State
Origin of name: From a book, *Las Sergas de Esplandián,* by Garcia Ordóñez de Montalvo, c. 1500
1970 population & (rank): 19,953,134 (1)
1977 est. population & (rank): 21,896,000 (1)
1970 land area & (rank): 156,361 sq mi. (404,975 sq km) (3)
Geographic center: In Madera Co., 35 mi. NE of Madera
Number of counties: 58
Largest cities (1975 est.): Los Angeles (2,727,399); San Diego (773,996); San Francisco (664,520); San Jose (555,707); Long Beach (335,602)
State forests: 8 (70,283 ac.)
State parks and beaches: 180 (723,000 ac.)

COLORADO

Capital: Denver
Organized as territory: Feb. 28, 1861
Entered Union & (rank): Aug. 1, 1876 (38)
Present constitution adopted: 1876
Motto: *Nil sine Numine* (Nothing without Providence)
State flower: Rocky Mountain columbine (1899)
State tree: Colorado blue spruce (1939)
State bird: Lark bunting (1931)
State animal: Rocky Mountain bighorn sheep
State colors: Blue and white (1911)
State gemstone: Aquamarine (1971)
State song: "Where the Columbines Grow" (1915)
Nickname: Centennial State
Origin of name: From the Spanish, meaning "ruddy" or "red"
1970 population & (rank): 2,207,259 (30)
1977 est. population & (rank): 2,619,000 (28)
1970 land area & (rank): 103,766 sq mi. (268,754 sq km) (8)
Geographic center: In Park Co., 30 mi. NW of Pikes Peak
Number of counties: 63
Largest cities (1975 est.): Denver (484,531); Colorado Springs (179,584); Lakewood (120,350); Aurora (118,060); Pueblo (105,312); Boulder (78,560)
State forests: 1 (71,000 ac.)

CONNECTICUT

Capital: Hartford
Entered Union & (rank): Jan. 9, 1788 (5)
Present constitution adopted: Dec. 30, 1965
Motto: *Qui transtulit sustinet* (He who transplanted still sustains)
State flower: Mountain laurel (1907)
State tree: White Oak (1947)
State animal: Sperm whale (1975)
State bird: American robin (1943)
State insect: Praying mantis (1977)
State mineral: Garnet (1977)
State song: "Yankee Doodle" (1978)
Official designation: *Constitution State* (1959)
Nickname: Nutmeg State
Origin of name: From an Indian word (Quinnehtukqut) meaning "beside the long tidal river"
1970 population & (rank): 3,032,217 (24)
1977 est. population & (rank): 3,108,000 (24)
1970 land area & (rank): 4,862 sq mi. (12,593 sq km) (48)
Geographic center: In Hartford Co., at East Berlin
Number of counties: 8
Largest cities (1975 est.): Bridgeport (142,960); Hartford (138,152); New Haven (126,845); Waterbury (107,065); Stamford (105,151); New Britain (78,556)
State forests: 30 (134,461 ac.)
State parks: 88 (30,316 ac.)

DELAWARE

Capital: Dover
Entered Union & (rank): Dec. 7, 1787 (1)
Present constitution adopted: 1897
Motto: Liberty and independence
State colors: Colonial blue and buff
State flower: Peach blossom
State tree: American holly
State bird: Blue Hen chicken
State insect: Ladybug
State song: "Our Delaware"
Nicknames: Diamond State; First State
Origin of name: From Delaware River and Bay; named in turn for Sir Thomas West, Lord De La Warr
1970 population & (rank): 548,104 (46)
1977 est. population & (rank): 582,000 (47)
1970 land area & (rank): 1,982 sq mi. (5,133 sq km) (49)
Geographic center: In Kent Co., 11 mi. S of Dover
Number of counties: 3
Largest cities (1975 est.): Wilmington (76,152); Newark (26,645); Dover (22,480); Elsmere (8,809); Seaford (5,587); Milford (5,411)
State forests: 2 (6,200 ac.)
State parks: 9

DISTRICT OF COLUMBIA (WASHINGTON, D.C.)

Land ceded to Congress: 1788 by Maryland; 1789 by Virginia (retroceded to Virginia Sept. 7, 1846)
Seat of government transferred to D. C.: Dec. 1, 1800
Created municipal corporation: Feb. 21, 1871
Motto: *Justitia omnibus* (Justice to all)
Flower: American beauty rose
Tree: Scarlet oak
Origin of name: In honor of Columbus
1970 population & (rank): 756,668 (9)
1976 est. population & (rank): 702,000 (13)
1970–75 population change: —7.3%
1970 land area: 68 sq mi.
Geographic center: Near corner of Fourth and L Sts., NW
Altitude: Highest, 420 ft; lowest, sea level
Location: Between Virginia and Maryland, on Potomac River
Churches: Protestant, 446; Roman Catholic, 23; Jewish, 10; others, 23
City parks: 753 (7,725 ac.)

FLORIDA

Capital: Tallahassee
Organized as territory: March 30, 1822
Entered Union & (rank): March 3, 1845 (27)
Present constitution adopted: 1969
Motto: In God we trust (1868)
State flower: Orange blossom (1909)
State bird: Mockingbird (1927)
State song: "Suwannee River" (1935)
Nickname: Sunshine State (1970)
Origin of name: From the Spanish, meaning "feast of flowers" (Easter)
1970 population & (rank): 6,789,443 (9)
1977 est. population & (rank): 8,452,000 (8)
1970 land area & (rank): 54,090 sq mi. (140,093 sq km) (26)
Geographic center: In Hernando Co., 12 mi. NNW of Brooksville
Number of counties: 67
Largest cities (1975 est.): Jacksonville (535,030); Miami (365,082); Tampa (280,340); St. Petersburg (234,389); Fort Lauderdale (152,959); Hollywood (119,002)
State forests: 4 (306,881 ac.)
State parks: 68 (187,763 ac.)
State tax receipts (1976–77): $3,587,643,747

GEORGIA

Capital: Atlanta
Entered Union & (rank): Jan. 2, 1788 (4)
Present constitution adopted: 1977
Motto: Wisdom, justice, and moderation
State flower: Cherokee rose (1916)
State tree: Live oak (1937)
State bird: Brown thrasher (1935)
State song: "Georgia" (1922)
Nicknames: Peach State, Empire State of the South
Origin of name: In honor of George II of England
1970 population & (rank): 4,589,575 (15)
1977 est. population & (rank): 5,048,000 (14)
1970 land area & (rank): 58,073 sq mi. (150,409 sq km) (21)
Geographic center: In Twiggs Co., 18 mi. SE of Macon
Number of counties: 159
Largest cities (1975 est.): Atlanta (436,057); Columbus (159,352); Macon (121,157); Savannah (110,348); Albany (73,373); Augusta (54,019)
State forests: 25,258,000 ac. (67% of total state area)
State parks: 53 (42,600 ac.)

HAWAII

Capital: Honolulu (on Oahu)
Organized as territory: 1900
Entered Union & (rank): Aug. 21, 1959 (50)
Motto: *Ua Mau Ke Ea O Ka Aina I Ka Pono* (The life of the land is perpetuated in righteousness)
State flower: Hibiscus
State song: "Hawaii Ponoi"
State bird: Nene (Hawaiian goose)
Nickname: Aloha State
Origin of name: Uncertain. The islands may have been named by Hawaii Loa, their traditional discoverer. Or they may have been named after Hawaii or Hawaiki, the traditional home of the Polynesians.
1970 population & (rank): 769,913 (40)
1977 est. population & (rank): 895,000 (40)
1970 land area & (rank): 6,425 sq mi. (16,641 sq km) (47)
Geographic center: In Hawaii Co., off Maui Island
Number of counties: 4
Largest cities (1975 est.): Honolulu (705,381); **(1970):** Hilo (26,353)[1]
State parks and historic sites: 47

1. Honolulu and Hilo have legally established limits and are therefore treated as incorporated places. All other places are unincorporated.

IDAHO

Capital: Boise
Organized as territory: March 3, 1863
Entered Union & (rank): July 3, 1890 (43)
Present constitution adopted: 1890
Motto: *Esto perpetua* (May you last forever)
State flower: Syringa (1931)
State tree: White pine (1935)
State bird: Mountain bluebird (1931)
State horse: Appaloosa (1975)
State gem: Star garnet (1967)
State song: "Here We Have Idaho"
Nicknames: Gem State; Spud State; Panhandle State
Origin of name: Means "Gem of the Mountains"
1970 population & (rank): 713,008 (42)
1977 est. population & (rank): 857,000 (41)
1970 land area & (rank): 82,677 sq mi. (214,133 sq km) (11)
Geographic center: In Custer Co., at Custer, SW of Challis
Number of counties: 44, plus small part of Yellowstone National Park
Largest cities (1975 est.): Boise (99,771); Pocatello (40,980); Idaho Falls (37,042); Lewiston (26,547); Nampa (23,940); Twin Falls (23,709)
State forests: 981,200 ac.
State parks: 18 (21,838 ac.)

ILLINOIS

Capital: Springfield
Organized as territory: Feb. 3, 1809
Entered Union & (rank): Dec. 3, 1818 (21)
Present constitution adopted: 1970
Motto: State sovereignty, national union
State flower: Violet (1908)
State tree: White oak (1973)
State bird: Cardinal (1929)
State insect: Monarch butterfly
State song: "Illinois" (1925)
State slogan: Land of Lincoln
State mineral: Fluorite (1965)
Nickname: Prairie State
Origin of name: From an Indian word and French suffix meaning "tribe of superior men"
1950 population & (rank): 8,712,176 (4)
1977 est. population & (rank): 11,245,000 (5)
1970 land area & (rank): 56,400 sq mi. (146,076 sq km) (23)
Geographic center: In St. Clair County near Mascoutah
Number of counties: 102
Largest cities (1975 est.): Chicago (3,099,391); Rockford (145,459); Peoria (125,983); Decatur (89,604); Springfield (87,418); Aurora (76,955); Joliet (74,401)
Public use areas: 187 (275,000 ac.), incl. state parks, memorials, forests and conservation areas

INDIANA

Capital: Indianapolis
Organized as territory: May 7, 1800
Entered Union & (rank): Dec. 11, 1816 (19)
Present constitution adopted: 1851
Motto: The Crossroads of America
State flower: Peony (1957)
State tree: Tulip tree (1931)
State bird: Cardinal (1933)
State song: "On the Banks of the Wabash, Far Away" (1913)
Nickname: Hoosier State
Origin of name: Meaning "land of Indians"
1970 population & (rank): 5,193,669 (11)
1977 est. population & (rank): 5,330,000 (12)
1970 land area & (rank): 36,097 sq mi. (93,491 sq km) (38)
Geographic center: In Boone Co., 14 mi. NNW of Indianapolis
Number of Counties: 92
Largest cities (1975 est.): Indianapolis (714,878); Fort Wayne (185,299); Gary (167,546); Evansville (133,566); South Bend (117,478); Hammond (104,892)
State parks: 22 (66,186 ac.)
State memorials: 19 (931 ac.)

IOWA

Capital: Des Moines
Organized as territory: June 12, 1838
Entered Union & (rank): Dec. 28, 1846 (29)
Present constitution adopted: 1857
Motto: Our liberties we prize and our rights we will maintain
State flower: Wild rose (1897)
State bird: Eastern goldfinch (1933)
State colors: Red, white, and blue (in state flag)
State song: "Song of Iowa"
Nickname: Hawkeye State
Origin of name: Probably from an Indian word meaning "I-o-w-a, this is the place," or "The Beautiful Land"
1970 population & (rank): 2,825,041 (25)
1977 est. population & (rank): 2,879,000 (25)
1970 land area & (rank): 55,491 sq mi. (144,887 sq km) (24)
Geographic center: In Story Co., 5 mi. NE of Ames
Number of counties: 99
Largest cities (1975 est.): Des Moines (194,168); Cedar Rapids (108,998); Davenport (99,941); Sioux City (85,719); Waterloo (77,681); Dubuque (61,754); Council Bluffs (58,660)
State forests: 5 (28,000 ac.)
State parks: 95 (49,237)

KANSAS

Capital: Topeka
Organized as territory: May 30, 1854
Entered Union & (rank): Jan. 29, 1861 (34)
Present constitution adopted: 1859
Motto: *Ad astra per aspera* (To the stars through difficulties)
State flower: Sunflower (1903)
State tree: Cottonwood (1937)
State bird: Western meadow lark (1937)
State animal: Buffalo (1955)
State song: "Home on the Range" (1947)
State march: "The Kansas March" (1935)
Nicknames: Sunflower State; Jayhawk State
Origin of name: From a Siouan word meaning "people of the south wind"
1970 population & (rank): 2,249,071 (28)
1977 est. population & (rank): 2,326,000 (31)
1970 land area & (rank): 81,787 sq mi. (211,828 sq km) (13)
Geographic center: In Barton Co., 15 mi. NE of Great Bend
Number of counties: 105
Largest cities (1975 est.): Wichita (264,901); Kansas City (168,153); Topeka (119,203); Overland Park (81,013); Lawrence (50,887); Hutchinson (40,925); Salina (38,960)
State parks: 22 (14,394 ac.)

KENTUCKY

Capital: Frankfort
Entered Union & (rank): June 1, 1792 (15)
Present constitution adopted: 1891
Motto: United we stand, divided we fall
State tree: Coffeetree
State flower: Goldenrod
State bird: Kentucky cardinal
State song: "My Old Kentucky Home"
Nickname: Bluegrass State
Origin of name: From an Iroquoian word "Ken-tah-ten" meaning "land of tomorrow"
1970 population & (rank): 3,219,311 (23)
1977 est. population & (rank): 3,458,000 (23)
1970 land area & (rank): 39,650 sq mi. (102,694 sq km) (37)
Geographic center: In Marion Co., 3 mi. NNW of Lebanon
Number of counties: 120
Largest cities (1975 est.): Louisville (335,954); Lexington-Fayette (186,048); Owensboro (50,788); Covington (44,467); Bowling Green (36,082)
State forests: 9 (44,173 ac.)
State parks: 43 (40,574 ac.)

LOUISIANA

Capital: Baton Rouge
Organized as territory: March 26, 1804
Entered Union & (rank): April 30, 1812 (18)
Present constitution adopted: 1974
Motto: Union, justice, and confidence
State flower: Magnolia (1900)
State tree: Bald cypress
State bird: Pelican
State song: "Give Me Louisiana," and "You Are My Sunshine"
Nicknames: Pelican State; Sportsman's Paradise; Creole State; Sugar State
Origin of name: In honor of Louis XIV of France
1970 population & (rank): 3,643,180 (20)
1977 est. population & (rank): 3,921,000 (20)
1970 land area & (rank): 44,930 sq mi. (116,369 sq km) (33)
Geographic center: In Avoyelles Parish, 3 mi. SE of Marksville
Number of parishes (counties): 64
Largest cities (1975 est.): New Orleans (559,770); Metropolitan Baton Rouge (294,394); Shreveport (185,711); Lake Charles (76,087); Lafayette (75,430)
State forests: 1 (8,000 ac.)
State parks: 31 (14,360 ac.)

MAINE

Capital: Augusta
Entered Union & (rank): March 15, 1820 (23)
Present constitution adopted: 1820
Motto: *Dirigo* (I direct)
State flower: White pine cone and tassel (1895)
State tree: White pine tree (1945)
State bird: Chickadee (1927)
State fish: Landlocked salmon (1969)
State mineral: Tourmaline (1971)
State song: "State of Maine Song" (1937)
Nickname: Pine Tree State
Origin of name: First used to distinguish the mainland from the offshore islands. It has been considered a compliment to Henrietta Maria, Queen of Charles I of England. She was said to have owned the province of Mayne in France.
1970 population & (rank): 993,663 (38)
1977 est. population & (rank): 1,085,000 (38)
1970 land area & (rank): 30,920 sq mi. (80,083 sq km) (39)
Geographic center: In Piscataquis Co., 18 mi. N of Dover-Foxcroft
Number of counties: 16
Largest cities (est. 1975): Portland (59,857); Lewiston (41,045); Bangor (32,262); Auburn (23,304); South Porland (22,677)
State forests: 1 (21,000 ac.)
State parks: 26 (247,627 ac.)
State historic sites: 18 (403 ac.)

MARYLAND

Capital: Annapolis
Entered Union & (rank): April 28, 1788 (7)
Present constitution adopted: 1867
Motto: *Fatti maschii, parole femine* (Manly deeds, womanly words)
State flower: Black-eyed susan (1918)
State tree: White oak (1941)
State bird: Baltimore oriole (1947)
State dog: Chesapeake Bay retriever (1964)
State fish: Rockfish (1965)
State insect: Baltimore checkerspot butterfly (1973)
State sport: Jousting (1962)
State song: "Maryland! My Maryland!" (1939)
Nicknames: Free State; Old Line State
Origin of name: In honor of Henrietta Maria (Queen of Charles I of England)
1970 population & (rank): 3,922,399 (18)
1977 est. population & (rank): 4,139,000 (18)
1970 land area & (rank): 9,891 sq mi. (25,618 sq km) (42)
Geographic center: In Prince Georges Co., 4½ mi. NW of Davidsonville
Number of counties: 23, and 1 independent city
Largest cities (1975 est.): Baltimore (851,698); Rockville (44,299); Bowie (37,323); Hagerstown (37,233); Annapolis (32,458); College Park (27,709)
State forests: 9 (116,213 ac.)
State parks: 42 (65,559 ac.)

MASSACHUSETTS

Capital: Boston
Entered Union & (rank): Feb. 6, 1788 (6)
Motto: *Ense petit placidam sub libertate quietem* (By the sword we seek peace, but peace only under liberty)
State flower: Mayflower (1918)
State tree: American elm (1941)
State bird: Chickadee (1941)
State colors: Blue and gold
State song: "All Hail to Massachusetts" (1966)
State beverage: Cranberry juice (1970)
State horse: Morgan horse (1970)
State insect: Lady bug (1974)
Nicknames: Bay State; Old Colony State
Origin of name: From two Indian words meaning "Great mountain place"
1970 population & (rank): 5,689,170 (10)
1977 est. population & (rank): 5,782,000 (10)
1970 land area & (rank): 7,826 sq mi. (20,269 sq km) (45)
Geographic center: In Worcester Co., in S part of city of Worcester
Number of counties: 14
Largest cities (1975 est.): Boston (636,725); Worcester (171,566); Springfield (170,790); Cambridge (102,420); Fall River (100,430); New Bedford (100,133)
State forests and parks: 123 (270,000 ac.)[1]

1. The Metropolitan District Commission, an agency of the Commonwealth serving municipalities in the Boston area, has about 14,000 acres of parkways and reservations under its jurisdiction.

MICHIGAN

Capital: Lansing
Organized as territory: Jan. 11, 1805
Entered Union & (rank): Jan. 26, 1837 (26)
Present constitution adopted: April 1, 1963, (effective Jan. 1, 1964)
Motto: *Si quaeris peninsulam amoenam circumspice* (If you seek a pleasant peninsula, look around you)
State flower: Apple blossom (1897)
State bird: Robin
State fish: Brook trout (1965)
State gem: Isle Royal Greenstone (Chlorastrolite) (1972)
State stone: Petoskey stone (1965)
Nickname: Wolverine State
Origin of name: From two Indian words meaning "great lake"
1970 population & (rank): 8,875,083 (7)
1977 est. population & (rank): 9,129,000 (7)
1970 land area & (rank): 56,817 sq mi. (147,156 sq km) (22)
Geographic center: In Wexford Co., 5 mi. NNW of Cadillac
Number of counties: 83
Largest cities (1975 est.): Detroit (1,335,085); Grand Rapids (187,946); Flint (174,218); Warren (172,755); Lansing (126,805); Livonia (114,881)
State forests: 33 (3,762,184 ac.)
State parks and recreation areas: 92 (216,857 ac.)

MINNESOTA

Capital: St. Paul
Organized as territory: March 3, 1849
Entered Union & (rank): May 11, 1858 (32)
Present constitution adopted: 1858
Motto: L'Etoile du Nord (The North Star)
State flower: Showy lady slipper (1902)
State tree: Red (or Norway) pine
State bird: Common loon (also called Great Northern Diver)
State song: "Hail Minnesota"
Nicknames: North Star State; Gopher State; Land of 10,000 Lakes
Origin of name: From a Dakota Indian word meaning "sky-tinted water"
1970 population & (rank): 3,805,069 (19)
1977 est. population & (rank): 3,975,000 (19)
1970 land area & (rank): 79,289 sq mi. (205,359 sq km) (14)
Geographic center: In Crow Wing Co., 10 mi. SW of Brainerd
Number of counties: 87
Largest cities (1975 est.): Minneapolis (378,112); St. Paul (279,535); Duluth (93,971); Bloomington (79,210); Rochester (56,211); Edina (47,989)
State forests: 55 (2,984,000 ac.)
State parks: 92 (202,205 ac.)

MISSISSIPPI

Capital: Jackson
Organized as Territory: April 7, 1798
Entered Union & (rank): Dec. 10, 1817 (20)
Present constitution adopted: 1890
Motto: *Virtute es armis* (By valor and arms)
State flower: Flower or bloom of the magnolia or evergreen magnolia (1952)
State tree: Magnolia (1938)
State bird: Mockingbird (1944)
State song: "Go, Mississippi" (1962)
Nickname: Magnolia State
Origin of name: From an Indian word meaning "Father of Waters"
1970 population & (rank): 2,216,912 (29)
1977 est. population & (rank): 2,389,000 (29)
1970 land area & (rank): 47,296 sq mi. (122,497 sq km) (31)
Geographic center: In Leake Co., 9 mi. WNW of Carthage
Number of counties: 82
Largest cities (1975 est.): Jackson (166,512); Biloxi (46,407); Meridian (46,256); Gulfport (43,126); Greenville (42,499); Hattiesburg (38,490); Pascagoula (30,403)
State forests: 1 (1,760 ac.)
State parks: 15 (16,220 ac.)

MISSOURI

Capital: Jefferson City
Organized as territory: June 4, 1812
Entered Union & (rank): Aug. 10, 1821 (24)
Present constitution adopted: 1945
Motto: *Salus populi suprema lex esto* (The welfare of the people shall be the supreme law)
State flower: Hawthorn (1923)
State bird: Bluebird (1927)
State colors: Red, white, and blue (1913)
State song: "Missouri Waltz" (1949)
State rock: Mozarkite (1967)
State mineral: Galena (1967)
Nickname: Show-me State
Origin of name: Named after a tribe called Missouri Indians. "Missouri" means "town of the large canoes."
1970 population & (rank): 4,677,399 (13)
1977 est. population & (rank): 4,801,000 (15)
1970 land area & (rank): 68,995 sq mi. (178,697 sq km) (18)
Geographic center: In Miller Co., 20 mi. SW of Jefferson City
Number of counties: 114, plus 1 independent city
Largest cities (1975 est.): St. Louis (524,964); Kansas City (472,529); Springfield (131,557); Independence (111,481); St. Joseph (77,679); Florissant (70,465)
State forests and Tower sites: 125 (210,000 ac.)
State parks: 57 (79,059 ac.)[1]

1. Includes 19 historic sites and 1 archaeological site.

MONTANA

Capital: Helena
Organized as territory: May 26, 1864
Entered Union & (rank): Nov. 8, 1889 (41)
Present constitution adopted: 1972
Motto: *Oro y plata* (Gold and silver)
State flower: Bitterroot (1895)
State tree: Ponderosa pine (1949)
State stones: Sapphire and agate (1969)
State bird: Western meadow lark (1931)
State song: "Montana" (1945)
Nickname: Treasure State
Origin of name: Chosen from Latin dictionary by J. M. Ashley. It is a Latinized Spanish word.
1970 population & (rank): 694,409 (43)
1977 est. population & (rank): 761,000 (43)
1970 land area & (rank): 145,587 sq mi. (377,070 sq km) (4)
Geographic center: In Fergus Co., 12 mi. W of Lewistown
Number of counties: 56, plus small part of Yellowstone National Park
Largest cities (1975 est.): Billings (68,987); Great Falls (60,868); Missoula (29,569); Helena (26,251); Butte (23,476); Bozeman (19,847)
State forests: 7 (214,000 ac.)
State parks and recreation areas: 68 (18,273 ac.)

NEBRASKA

Capital: Lincoln
Organized as territory: May 30, 1854
Entered Union & (rank): March 1, 1867 (37)
Present constitution adopted: Nov. 1, 1875 (extensively amended 1919–20)
Motto: Equality before the law
State flower: Goldenrod (1895)
State tree: Cottonwood (1972)
State bird: Western meadow lark (1929)
State insect: Honeybee
State gem stone: Blue agate (1967)
State rock: Prairie agate (1967)
State fossil: Mammoth (1967)
State song: "Beautiful Nebraska" (1967)
Nicknames: Cornhusker State; Beef State; Tree Planters State
Origin of name: From an Oto Indian word meaning "flat water"
1970 population & (rank): 1,483,791 (35)
1977 est. population & (rank): 1,561,000 (35)
1970 land area & (rank): 76,483 sq mi. (198,091 sq km) (15)
Geographic center: In Custer Co., 10 mi. NW of Broken Bow
Number of counties: 93
Largest cities (1975 est.): Omaha (371,455); Lincoln (163,112); Grand Island (33,304); Fremont (23,953); Hastings (22,633); Kearney (19,333)
State forests: None
State parks: 93 areas, 4 categories, 5 major areas

NEVADA

Capital: Carson City
Organized as territory: March 2, 1861
Entered Union & (rank): Oct. 31, 1864 (36)
Present constitution adopted: 1864
Motto: All for Our Country
State flower: Sagebrush (1967)
State tree: Single-leaf pinon (1953)
State bird: Mountain bluebird (1967)
State animal: Desert bighorn sheep (1973)
State colors: Silver and blue (unofficial)
State song: "Home Means Nevada" (1933)
Nicknames: Sagebrush State; Silver State; Battle-born State
Origin of name: Spanish: "snowcapped"
1970 population & (rank): 488,738 (47)
1977 est. population & (rank): 633,000 (46)
1970 land area & (rank): 109,889 sq mi. (284,613 sq km) (7)
Geographic center: In Lander Co., 26 mi. SE of Austin
Number of counties: 16, plus 1 independent city
Largest cities (1975 est.): Las Vegas (146,030); Reno (78,097); North Las Vegas (37,476); Sparks (31,639); Carson City (24,928)
State forests: None
State parks: 13 (104,255 ac., including leased lands)

NEW HAMPSHIRE

Capital: Concord
Entered Union & (rank): June 21, 1788 (9)
Present constitution adopted: 1784
Motto: Live free or die
State flower: Purple lilac (1919)
State tree: White birch (1947)
State bird: Purple finch (1957)
State songs: "Old New Hampshire" (1949) and "New Hampshire, My New Hampshire" (1963)
Nickname: Granite State
Origin of name: From the English county of Hampshire
1970 population & (rank): 737,681 (41)
1977 est. population & (rank): 849,000 (42)
1970 land area & (rank): 9,027 sq mi. (23,380 sq km) (44)
Geographic center: In Belknap Co., 3 mi. E of Ashland
Number of counties: 10
Largest cities (1975 est.): Manchester (83,417); Nashua (61,002); Concord (29,321); Portsmouth (24,780); Dover (21,431); Keene (21,107)
State forests & parks: 175 (96,975 ac.)

NEW JERSEY

Capital: Trenton
Entered Union & (rank): Dec. 18, 1787 (3)
Present constitution adopted: 1947
Motto: Liberty and prosperity
State flower: Purple violet (1913)
State bird: Eastern goldfinch (1935)
State insect: Honeybee
State tree: Red oak (1950)
State animal: Horse (1977)
State colors: Buff and blue (1965)
State song: None
Nickname: Garden State
Origin of name: From the Channel Isle of Jersey
1970 population & (rank): 7,168,164 (8)
1977 est. population & (rank): 7,329,000 (9)
1970 land area & (rank): 7,521 sq mi. (19,479 sq km) (46)
Geographic center: In Mercer Co., 5 mi. SE of Trenton
Number of counties: 21
Largest cities (1975 est.): Newark (339,568); Jersey City (243,756); Paterson (136,098); Elizabeth (104,405); Trenton (101,365); Camden (89,214)
State forests: 11
State parks: 40 (73,483 ac.)

NEW MEXICO

Capital: Santa Fe
Organized as territory: Sept. 9, 1850
Entered Union & (rank): Jan. 6, 1912 (47)
Present constitution adopted: 1911
Motto: *Crescit eundo* (It grows as it goes)
State flower: Yucca (1927)
State tree: Pinon (1949)
State animal: Black bear (1963)
State bird: Roadrunner (1949)
State fish: Cutthroat trout (1955)
State vegetables: Chile and frijol (1965)
State gem: Turquoise (1967)
State colors: Red and yellow of old Spain (1925)
State song: "O Fair New Mexico" (1917)
Spanish language state song: "Asi Es Nuevo Mejico" (1971)
Nicknames: Land of Enchantment; Sunshine State
Origin of name: From the country of Mexico
1970 population & (rank): 1,016,000 (37)
1977 est. population & (rank): 1,190,000 (37)
1970 land area & (rank): 121,412 sq mi. (314,457 sq km) (5)
Geographic center: In Torrance Co., 12 mi. SSW of Willard
Number of counties: 32
Largest cities (1975 est.): Albuquerque (279,401); Santa Fe (44,937); Las Cruces (40,336); Roswell (37,980); Clovis (31,734); Farmington (27,802)
State-owned forested land: 933,000 ac.
State parks: 29 (105,012 ac.)

NEW YORK

Capital: Albany
Entered Union & (rank): July 26, 1788 (11)
Present constitution adopted: 1777 (last revised 1938)
Motto: *Excelsior* (Ever upward)
State animal: Beaver (1975)
State fish: Brook trout (1975)
State gem: Garnet (1969)
State flower: Rose (1955)
State tree: Sugar maple (1956)
State bird: Bluebird
State song: None
Nickname: Empire State
Origin of name: In honor of the English Duke of York
1970 population & (rank): 18,241,266 (2)
1977 est. population & (rank): 17,924,000 (2)
1970 land area & (rank): 47,931 sq mi. (123,882 sq km) (30)
Geographic center: In Madison Co., 12 mi. S of Oneida and 26 mi. SW of Utica
Number of counties: 62
Largest cities (1975 est.): New York (7,481,613); Buffalo (407,160); Rochester (267,173); Yonkers (192,509); Syracuse (182,543); Albany, (110,311)
State forest preserves: Adirondacks, 2,500,000 ac., Catskills, 250,000 ac.
State parks: 145 (more than 220,000 ac.)

NORTH CAROLINA

Capital: Raleigh
Entered Union & (rank): Nov. 21, 1789 (12)
Present constitution adopted: 1971
Motto: *Esse quam videri* (To be rather than to seem)
State flower: Dogwood (1941)
State tree: Pine (1963)
State bird: Cardinal (1943)
State mammal: Gray Squirrel (1969)
State insect: Honeybee (1973)
State gem stone: Emerald (1973)
State shell: Scotch bonnet (1965)
State song: "The Old North State" (1927)
State colors: Red and blue (1945)
Nickname: Tar Heel State
Origin of name: In honor of Charles I of England
1970 population & (rank): 5,082,059 (12)
1977 est. population & (rank): 5,525,000 (11)
1970 land area & (rank): 48,798 sq mi. (126,387 sq km) (29)
Geographic center: In Chatham Co., 10 mi. NW of Sanford
Number of counties: 100
Largest cities (1975 est.): Charolotte (281,417); Greensboro (155,848); Winston-Salem (141,018); Raleigh (134,231); Durham (101,224); Fayetteville (65,915)
State forests: 1
State parks: 26 (115,051 ac.)

NORTH DAKOTA

Capital: Bismarck
Organized as territory: March 2, 1861
Entered Union & (rank): Nov. 2, 1889 (39)
Present constitution adopted: 1889
Motto: Liberty and union, now and forever: one and inseparable
State tree: American Elm (1947)
State bird: Western meadow lark (1947)
State song: "North Dakota Hymn" (1947)
Nickname: Sioux State; Flickertail State
Origin of name: From the Dakotah tribe, meaning "allies"
1970 population & (rank): 617,761 (45)
1977 est. population & (rank): 653,000 (45)
1970 land area & (rank): 69,273 sq mi (179,417 sq km) (17)
Geographic center: In Sheridan Co., 5 mi. SW of McClusky
Number of counties: 53
Largest cities (1975 est.): Fargo (56,058); Grand Forks (41,909); Bismarck (38,378); Minot (32,790); Jamestown (15,330); Mandan (12,560)
State forests: None
State parks: 5 (2,981 ac.)

OHIO

Capital: Columbus
Entered Union & (rank): March 1, 1807 (17)
Present constitution adopted: 1851
Motto: With God, all things are possible
State flower: Scarlet carnation (1904)
State tree: Buckeye (1953)
State bird: Cardinal (1933)
State insect: Ladybug (1975)
State gem stone: Flint (1965)
State song: "Beautiful Ohio"
State drink: Tomato juice (1965)
Nickname: Buckeye State
Origin of name: From an Iroquoian word meaning "great river"
1970 population & (rank): 10,652,017 (6)
1977 est. population & (rank): 10,701,000 (6)
1970 land area & (rank): 40,975 sq mi. (106,125 sq km) (35)
Geographic center: In Delaware Co., 25 mi. NNE of Columbus
Number of counties: 88
Largest cities (1975 est.): Cleveland (638,793); Columbus (535,610); Cincinnati (412,564); Toledo (367,650); Akron (251,747); Dayton (205,986)
State forests: 18 (163,972 ac.)
State parks: 64 (199,351 ac.)

OKLAHOMA

Capital: Oklahoma City
Organized as territory: May 2, 1890
Entered Union & (rank): Nov. 16, 1907 (46)
Present constitution adopted: 1907
Motto: *Labor omnia vinci* (Labor conquers all things)
State flower: Mistletoe (1893)
State tree: Redbud (1937)
State bird: Scissor-tailed flycatcher (1951)
State animal: Bison (1972)
State reptile: Mountain boomer lizard (1969)
State stone: Rose Rock (barite rose) (1968)
State colors: Green and white (1915)
State song: "Oklahoma" (1953)
Nickname: Sooner State
Origin of name: From two Choctaw Indian words meaning "red people"
1970 population & (rank): 2,559,253 (27)
1977 est. population & (rank): 2,811,000 (27)
1970 land area & (rank): 68,782 sq mi. (178,145 sq km) (19)
Geographic center: In Oklahoma Co., 8 mi. N of Oklahoma City
Number of counties: 77
Largest cities (1975 est.): Oklahoma City (365,916); Tulsa (331,726); Lawton (76,421); Norman (59,948); Midwest City (50,105); Enid (48,030)
State forests: None
State parks: 28 (88,959 ac.)

OREGON

Capital: Salem
Organized as territory: Aug. 14, 1848
Entered Union & (rank): Feb. 14, 1859 (33)
Present constitution adopted: 1859
Motto: The Union (1957)
State flower: Oregon grape (1899)
State tree: Douglas fir (1939)
State animal: Beaver (1969)
State bird: Western meadow lark (1927)
State fish: Chinook salmon (1961)
State rock: Thunderegg (1965)
State colors: Navy blue and gold (1959)
State song: "Oregon, My Oregon" (1927)
Nickname: Beaver State
Origin of name: Unknown. However, it is generally accepted that the name, first used by Jonathan Carver in 1778, was taken from the writings of Maj. Robert Rogers, an English army officer.
1970 population & (rank): 2,091,385 (31)
1977 est. population & (rank): 2,376,000 (30)
1970 land area & (rank): 96,184 sq mi. (249,117 sq km) (10)
Geographic center: In Crook Co., 25 mi. SSE of Princeville
Number of counties: 36
Largest cities (1975 est.): Portland (356,732); Eugene (92,451); Salem (78,168); Corvallis (38,502); Springfield (33,432); Medford (32,577); Gresham (23,249)
State forests: 785,062 ac.
State parks: 237 (95,800 ac.)

PENNSYLVANIA

Capital: Harrisburg
Entered Union & (rank): Dec. 12, 1787 (2)
Present constitution adopted: 1874
Motto: Virtue, liberty, and independence
State flower: Mountain laurel (1933)
State tree: Hemlock (1931)
State bird: Ruffed grouse (1931)
State insect: Firefly
State dog: Great Dane (1965)
State colors: Blue and gold
State song: None
Nickname: Keystone State
Origin of name: In honor of Adm. Sir. William Penn, father of William Penn. It means "Penn's Woodland."
1970 population & (rank): 11,793,909 (3)
1977 est. population & (rank): 11,785,000 (4)
1970 land area & (rank): 44,966 sq mi. (116,462 sq km) (32)
Geographic center: In Centre Co., 2½ mi. SW of Bellefonte
Number of counties: 67
Largest cities (1975 est.): Philadelphia (1,815,808); Pittsburgh (458,651); Erie (127,895); Allentown (106,624); Scranton (95,884); Reading (81,592)
State forests: 1,930,108 ac.
State parks: 120 (297,438 ac.)

RHODE ISLAND

Capital: Providence
Entered Union & (rank): May 29, 1790 (13)
Present constitution adopted: 1843
Motto: Hope
State flower: Violet (unofficial)
State tree: Red maple (official)
State bird: Rhode Island Red (official)
State colors: Blue, white, and gold (in state flag)
State song: "Rhode Island" (1946)
Nickname: The Ocean State
Origin of name: From the Greek island of Rhodes
1970 population & (rank): 949,723 (39)
1977 est. population & (rank): 935,000 (39)
1970 land area & (rank): 1,049 sq mi. (2,717 sq km) (50)
Geographic center: In Kent Co., 1 mi. SSW of Crompton
Number of counties: 5
Largest cities (1975 est.): Providence (167,724); Warwick (85,875); Cranston (74,381); Pawtucket (72,024); East Providence (49,636); Woonsocket (46,888)
State forests: 11 (20,900 ac.)
State parks: 17 (8,200 ac.)

SOUTH CAROLINA

Capital: Columbia
Entered Union & (rank): May 23, 1788 (8)
Present constitution adopted: 1895
Mottoes: *Animis opibusque parati* (Prepared in mind and resources) and *Dum spiro spero* (While I breathe, I hope)
State flower: Carolina yellow jessamine (1924)
State tree: Palmetto tree (1939)
State bird: Carolina wren (1948)
State song: "Carolina" (1911)
Nickname: Palmetto State
Origin of name: In honor of Charles I of England
1977 est. population & (rank): 2,876,000 (26)
1970 land area & (rank): 30,225 sq mi. (78,283 sq km) (40)
Geographic center: In Richland Co., 13 mi. SE of Columbia
Number of counties: 46
Largest cities (1975 est.): Columbia (111,616); North Charleston (58,544); Greenville (58,518); Charleston (57,470); Spartanburg (46,929); Rock Hill (35,346)
State forests: 4 (124,052 ac.)
State parks: 50 (61,726 ac.)

SOUTH DAKOTA

Capital: Pierre
Organized as territory: March 2, 1861
Entered Union & (rank): Nov. 2, 1889 (40)
Present constitution adopted: 1889
Motto: Under God the people rule
State flower: American pasqueflower (1903)
State grass: Western wheat grass (1970)
State tree: Black Hills spruce (1947)
State bird: Ring-necked pheasant (1943)
State insect: Honeybee (1978)
State animal: Coyote (1949)
State mineral stone: Rose quartz (1966)
State gem stone: Fairburn agate (1966)
State colors: Blue and gold (in state flag)
State song: "Hail! South Dakota" (1943)
Nicknames: Sunshine State; Coyote State
Origin of name: Same as for North Dakota
1970 population & (rank): 666,257 (44)
1977 est. population & (rank): 689,000 (44)
1970 land area & (rank): 75,955 sq mi. (196,723 sq km) (16)
Geographic center: In Hughes Co., 8 mi. NE of Pierre
Number of counties: 67 (64 county governments)
Largest cities (1975 est.): Sioux Falls (73,925); Rapid City (48,156); Aberdeen (26,628); Watertown (14,402); Brookings (13,860); Mitchell (13,696)
State forests: None[1]
State parks: 12 plus 31 recreational areas (87,269 ac.)[2]

1. No designated state forests; about 13,000 ac. of state land is forest land. 2. Acreage includes 31 recreation areas and 80 roadside parks, in addition to 12 state parks.

TENNESSEE

Capital: Nashville
Entered Union & (rank): June 1, 1796 (16)
Present constitution adopted: 1870; amended 1953, 1960, 1965 and 1973
Motto: "Tennessee—America at its best" (1965)
State flower: Iris (1933)
State tree: Tulip poplar (1947)
State bird: Mockingbird (1933)
State horse: Tennessee walking horse
State animal: Raccoon
State wild flower: Passion flower
State song: "Tennessee Waltz" (1965)
Nickname: Volunteer State
Origin of name: Of Cherokee origin; the exact meaning is unknown
1970 population & (rank): 3,924,164 (17)
1977 est. population & (rank): 4,299,000 (17)
1970 land area & (rank): 41,328 sq mi. (107,040 sq km) (34)
Geographic center: In Rutherford Co., 5 mi. NE of Murfreesboro
Number of counties: 95
Largest cities (1975 est.): Memphis (661,319); Nashville-Davidson (423,426); Knoxville (183,383); Chattanooga (161,978); Clarksville (51,910); Jackson (43,357)
State forests: 14 (155,752 ac.)
State parks: 21 (130,000 ac.)

TEXAS

Capital: Austin
Entered Union & (rank): Dec. 29, 1845 (28)
Present constitution adopted: 1876
Motto: Friendship
State flower: Bluebonnet (1901)
State tree: Pecan (1919)
State bird: Mockingbird (1927)
State song: "Texas, Our Texas" (1930)
Nickname: Lone Star State
Origin of name: From an Indian word meaning "friends"
1970 population & (rank): 11,196,730 (4)
1977 est. population & (rank): 12,830,000 (3)
1970 land area & (rank): 262,134 sq mi. (678,927 sq km) (2)
Geographic center: In McCulloch Co., 15 mi. NE of Brady
Number of counties: 254
Largest cities (1975 est.): Houston (1,357,394); Dallas (812,797); San Antonio (773,248); El Paso (385,691); Fort Worth (358,364); Austin (301,147)
State forests: 4 (6,306 ac.)
State parks: 83 (64 developed)

UTAH

Capital: Salt Lake City
Organized as territory: Sept. 9, 1850
Entered Union & (rank): Jan. 4, 1896 (45)
Present constitution adopted: 1896
Motto: Industry
State flower: Sego lily (1911)
State tree: Blue spruce (1933)
State bird: Seagull (1955)
State emblem: Beehive
State song: "Utah, We Love Thee"
Nickname: Beehive State
Origin of name: From the Ute tribe, meaning "people of the mountains"
1970 population & (rank): 1,059,273 (36)
1977 est. population & (rank): 1,268,000 (36)
1970 land area & (rank): 82,096 sq mi. (212,629 sq km) (12)
Geographic center: In Sanpete Co., 3 mi. N. of Manti
Number of counties: 29
Largest cities (1975 est.): Salt Lake City (169,917); Ogden (68,978); Provo (55,593); Orem (35,584); Bountiful (30,358); Logan (23,810)
State forests: None
State parks: 35 (64,097 ac.)

VERMONT

Capital: Montpelier
Entered Union & (rank): March 4, 1791 (14)
Present constitution adopted: 1793
Motto: Vermont, Freedom, and Unity
State flower: Red clover (1894)
State tree: Sugar maple (1949)
State bird: Hermit thrush (1941)
State animal: Morgan horse (1961)
State insect: Honeybee (1978)
State song: "Hail, Vermont!" (1938)
Nickname: Green Mountain State
Origin of name: From the French "vert mont," meaning "green mountain"
1970 population & (rank): 444,732 (48)
1977 est. population & (rank): 483,000 (48)
1970 land area & (rank): 9,276 sq mi. (24,025 sq km) (43)
Geographic center: In Washington Co., 3 mi. E of Roxbury
Number of counties: 14
Largest cities (1975 est.): Burlington (37,133); Rutland (19,010); South Burlington (11,090); Barre (9,805); Montpelier (8,217); St. Albans (7,413)
State forests: 34 (113,953 ac.)
State parks: 45 (31,325 ac.)

VIRGINIA

Capital: Richmond
Entered Union & (rank): June 25, 1788 (10)
Present constitution adopted: 1970
Motto: *Sic semper tyrannis* (Thus always to tyrants)
State flower: American dogwood (1918)
State bird: Cardinal (1950)
State dog: American foxhound (1966)
State shell: Oyster shell
State song: "Carry Me Back to Old Virginia" (1940)
Nicknames: The Old Dominion; Mother of Presidents
Origin of name: In honor of Elizabeth "Virgin Queen" of England
1970 population & (rank): 4,648,494 (14)
1977 est. population & (rank): 5,135,000 (13)
1970 land area & (rank): 39,780 sq mi. (103,030 sq km) (36)
Geographic center: In Buckingham Co., 5 mi. SW of Buckingham
Number of counties: 95, plus 41 independent cities
Largest cities (1975 est.): Norfolk (286,694); Richmond (232,652); Virginia Beach (213,954); Newport News (138,760); Hampton (125,013)
State forests: 8 (49,566 ac.)
State parks and recreational parks: 19, plus 7 in process of acquisition and/or development (42,722 ac.)[1]

1. Does not include portion of Breaks Interstate Park (Va.-Ky., 1,200 ac.) which lies in Virginia.

WASHINGTON

Capital: Olympia
Organized as territory: March 2, 1853
Entered Union & (rank): Nov. 11, 1889 (42)
Present constitution adopted: 1889
Motto: *Al-Ki* (Indian word meaning "by and by")
State flower: Rhododrendron (1949)
State tree: Western hemlock (1947)
State bird: Willow goldfinch (1951)
State gem: Petrified wood (1975)
State colors: Green and gold (1925)
State song: "Washington, My Home" (1959)
Nicknames: Evergreen State; Chinook State
Origin of name: In honor of George Washington
1970 population & (rank): 3,409,169 (22)
1977 est. population & (rank): 3,658,000 (22)
1970 land area & (rank): 66,570 sq mi (172,416 sq km) (20)
Geographic center: In Chelan Co., 10 mi. WSW of Wenatchee
Number of counties: 39
Largest cities (1975 est.): Seattle (487,091); Spokane (173,698); Tacoma (151,267); Bellevue (65,365); Everett (48,371); Vancouver (47,742)
State forest lands: 1,843,020 ac.
State parks: 173 (79,212 ac.)

WEST VIRGINIA

Capital: Charleston
Entered Union & (rank): June 20, 1863 (35)
Present constitution adopted: 1872
Motto: *Montani semper liberi* (Mountaineers are always free)
State flower: Rhododendron (1903)
State tree: Sugar maple (1949)
State bird: Cardinal (1949)
State animal: Black bear
State colors: Blue and gold (unofficial)
State songs: "West Virginia, My Home Sweet Home," "The West Virginia Hills," and "This Is My West Virginia" (adopted by Legislature in 1947, 1961 and 1963 as official state songs)
Nickname: Mountain State
Origin of name: Same as for Virginia
1970 population & (rank): 1,744,237 (34)
1977 est. population & (rank): 1,859,000 (34)
1970 land area & (rank): 24,070 sq mi. (62,341 sq km) (41)
Geographic center: In Braxton Co., 4 mi. E of Sutton
Number of counties: 55
Largest cities (1975 est.): Huntington (68,811); Charleston (67,348); Wheeling (44,369); Parkersburg (38,882); Morgantown (30,318); Fairmont (26,000)
State forests: 9 (77,000 ac.)
State parks: 34 (65,861 ac.)

WISCONSIN

Capital: Madison
Organized as territory: July 4, 1836
Entered Union & (rank): May 29, 1848 (30)
Present constitution adopted: 1848
Motto: Forward
State flower: Wood violet
State tree: Sugar maple
State bird: Robin
State animal: Badger; "wild life" animal: white-tailed deer; "domestic" animal; dairy cow
State insect: Honeybee (1977)
State fish: Musky (Muskellunge)
State song: "On Wisconsin"
State mineral: Galena (1971)
State rock: Red Granite (1971)
Nickname: Badger State
Origin of name: French corruption of an Indian word meaning "gathering of waters"
1970 population & (rank): 4,417,933 (16)
1977 est. population & (rank): 4,651,000 (16)
1970 land area & (rank): 54,464 sq mi. (141,062 sq km) (25)
Geographic center: In Wood Co., 9 mi. SE of Marshfield
Number of counties: 72
Largest cities (1975 est.): Milwaukee (665,796); Madison (168,196); Racine (94,744); Green Bay (91,189); Kenosha (80,727); West Allis (69,084)
State forests: 8 (449,486 ac.)
State parks & scenic trails: 55 parks, 8 trails (61,340 ac.)

WYOMING

Capital: Cheyenne
Organized as territory: May 19, 1869
Entered Union & (rank): July 10, 1890 (44)
Present constitution adopted: 1890
Motto: Equal rights (1955)
State flower: Indian paintbrush (1917)
State tree: Cottonwood (1947)
State bird: Meadow lark (1927)
State gemstone: Jade (1967)
State insignia: Bucking horse (unofficial)
State song: "Wyoming" (1955)
Nickname: Equality State
Origin of name: From the Indian, meaning "mountains and valleys alternating"; named after the Wyoming Valley in Pennsylvania
1970 population & (rank): 332,416 (49)
1977 est. population & (rank): 406,000 (50)
1970 land area & (rank): 97,203 sq mi. (251,756 sq km) (9)
Geographic center: In Fremont Co., 58 mi. ENE of Lander
Number of counties: 23, plus Yellowstone National Park
Largest cities (1975 est.): Cheyenne (46,677); Casper (41,192); Laramie (23,421); Rock Springs (17,773); Sheridan (11,617); Rawlins (9,592)
State parks: 9 (44,732 ac.)

Firsts in America

This selection is based on our editorial judgment. Other sources may list different firsts.

Admiral in U.S. Navy: David Glasgow Farragut, 1866.

Air-mail route, first transcontinental: Between New York City and San Francisco, 1920.

Assembly, representative: House of Burgesses, founded in Virginia, 1619.

Bank established: Bank of North America, Philadelphia, 1781.

Birth in America to English parents: Virginia Dare, born Roanoke Island, N.C., 1587.

Botanic garden: Established by John Bartram in Philadelphia, 1728. (Oldest still existing was established in Cambridge, Mass., in 1807.)

Cartoon, colored: "The Yellow Kid," by Richard Outcault, in *New York World,* 1895.

College: Harvard, founded 1636.

College to confer degrees on women: Oberlin (Ohio) College, 1841.

College to establish coeducation: Oberlin (Ohio) College, 1833.

Electrocution of a criminal: William Kemmler in Auburn Prison, Auburn, N.Y., Aug. 6, 1890.

Five and Ten Cents Store: Founded by Frank Woolworth, Utica, N.Y., 1879 (moved to Lancaster, Pa., same year).

Fraternity: Phi Beta Kappa; founded Dec. 5, 1776, at College of William and Mary.

Law to be declared unconstitutional by U.S. Supreme Court: Judiciary Act of 1789. Case: *Marbury* v. *Madison*, 1803.

Library, circulating: Philadelphia, 1731.

Newspaper, illustrated daily: *New York Daily Graphic,* 1873.

Newspaper published daily: *Pennsylvania Packet and General Advertiser,* Philadelphia, Sept., 1784.

Newspaper published over a continuous period: *The Boston News-Letter,* April, 1704.

Newsreel: Pathé Frères of Paris, in 1910, circulated a weekly issue of their *Pathé Journal.*

Oil well, commercial: Titusville, Pa., 1859.

Panel quiz show on radio: *Information Please,* May 17, 1938.

Postage stamps issued: 1847.

Railroad, transcontinental: Central Pacific and Union Pacific railroads, joined at Promontory, Utah, May 10, 1869.

Savings bank: The Provident Institute for Savings, Boston, 1816.

Science museum: Founded by Charleston (S.C.) Library Society, 1773.

Skyscraper: Home Insurance Co., Chicago, 1885 (10 floors, 2 added later).

Slaves brought into America: At Jamestown, Va., 1619, from a Dutch ship.

Sorority: Kappa Alpha Theta, at De Pauw University, 1870.

State to abolish capital punishment: Michigan, 1847.

State to enter Union after original 13: Vermont, 1791.

Steam-heated building: Eastern Hotel, Boston, 1845.

Steam railroad (carried passengers and freight): Baltimore & Ohio, 1830.

Strike on record by union: Journeymen Printers, New York City, 1776.

Subway: Opened in Boston, 1897.

"Tabloid" picture newspaper: *The Illustrated Daily News* (now *The Daily News*), New York City, 1919.

Vaudeville theater: Gaiety Museum, Boston, 1883.

Woman cabinet member: Frances Perkins, Secretary of Labor, 1933.

Woman candidate for President: Victoria Claflin Woodhull, nominated by National Woman's Suffrage Assn. on ticket of Nation Radical Reformers, 1872.

Woman doctor of medicine: Elizabeth Blackwell; M.D. from Geneva Medical College of Western New York, 1849.

Woman elected governor of a state: Mrs. Nellie Tayloe Ross, Wyoming, 1925.

Woman elected to U.S. Senate: Mrs. Hattie Caraway, Arkansas; elected Nov., 1932.

Woman graduate of law school: Mrs. Ada H. Kepley, Union College of Law, Chicago, 1870.

Woman member of U.S. House of Representatives: Jeannette Rankin; elected Nov., 1916.

Woman member of U.S. Senate: Mrs. Rebecca Latimer Felton of Georgia; appointed Oct. 3, 1922.

Woman suffrage granted: Wyoming Territory, 1869.

Written constitution: *Fundamental Orders of Connecticut,* 1639.

Biographies of the Presidents

GEORGE WASHINGTON was born Feb. 22, 1732 (Feb. 11, 1731/2, old style) in Westmoreland County, Va. He early trained as a surveyor; but in 1752 he was appointed adjutant in the Virginia militia, and for the next three years he took an active part in the wars against the French and Indians, serving as General Braddock's aide in the disastrous campaign against Fort Duquesne. In 1759 he resigned from the militia, married Martha Dandridge Custis, a widow, and settled down as a gentleman farmer at Mount Vernon.

As a militiaman, he had been exposed to the arrogance of the British officers, and his experience as a planter with British commercial restrictions increased his anti-British sentiment. He opposed the Stamp Act of 1765 and after 1770 became increasingly prominent in organizing resistance. A delegate to the Continental Congress, Washington was selected as commander in chief of the Continental Army and took command at Cambridge, Mass., on July 3, 1775.

Inadequately supported and sometimes covertly sabotaged by the Congress, in charge of troops who were inexperienced, badly equipped, and impatient of discipline, Washington conducted the war on the policy of avoiding major engagements with the British and wearing them down by harassing tactics. His able generalship, along with the French alliance and the growing weariness within Britain, brought the war to a conclusion with the surrender of Cornwallis at Yorktown on Oct. 19, 1781.

The chaotic years under the Articles of Confederation led Washington to return to public life in the hope of promoting the formation of a strong central government. He presided over the Constitutional Convention and yielded to the universal demand that he serve as first President. In office, he sought to unite the nation in the service of establishing the authority of the new government at home and abroad. Greatly distressed by the emergence of the Hamilton-Jefferson rivalry, he worked to maintain neutrality but actually sympathized more with Hamilton. Following his unanimous re-election in 1792, his second term was dominated by the Federalists. His Farewell Address rebuked party spirit and warned against foreign entanglements.

He died at Mt. Vernon on Dec. 14, 1799. Tall, dignified and impressive, Washington gave a public impression of austerity, though he was capable of gaiety in private. His life was characterized by a strict sense of duty to his people.

JOHN ADAMS was born on Oct. 30 (Oct. 19, old style), 1735, at Braintree (now Quincy), Mass. A Harvard graduate, he considered teaching and the ministry but finally turned to law and was admitted to the bar in 1758. He opposed the Stamp Act, served as lawyer for patriots indicted by the British and, by the time of the Continental Congresses, was in the vanguard of the movement for independence. In 1778 he went to France as commissioner. Subsequently he helped negotiate the peace treaty with Britain, and in 1785 became the U. S. envoy to London. Resigning in 1788, he was elected Vice President under Washington and was re-elected in 1792.

Though a Federalist, Adams did not get along with Hamilton, who sought to prevent his election to the presidency in 1796 and thereafter intrigued against his administration. Adams was chosen with 71 electoral votes to 68 for his closest competitor, Thomas Jefferson, who became Vice President. In 1798 Adams's independent policy averted a war with France but completed the break with Hamilton and the right-wing Federalists while, at the same time, the enactment of the Alien and Sedition Acts, directed against foreigners and against critics of the government, exasperated the Jeffersonian opposition. The split between Adams and Hamilton elected Jefferson in 1800. Adams retired to his home in Quincy. He later corresponded with Jefferson and they died on the same day, July 4, 1826.

Stout, somewhat vain and irascible, Adams was honest, fearless, and essentially fair-minded. His *Defence of the Constitutions of Government of the United States* (1787) contains original and striking if conservative political ideas. He married Abigail Smith in 1764 and their life together was long and happy.

THOMAS JEFFERSON was born on April 13 (April 2, old style), 1743, at Shadwell in Goochland (now Albemarle) County, Va. A William and Mary graduate, he studied law but from the start showed an interest in science and philosophy. His literary skill and political clarity brought him to the forefront of the revolutionary movement in

Virginia. As delegate to the Continental Congress, he drafted the Declaration of Independence. In 1776 he entered the Virginia House of Delegates and initiated a comprehensive reform program for the abolition of feudal survivals in land tenure and the separation of church and state.

In 1779 he became governor, but constitutional limitations on his power combined with his own lack of executive energy caused an unsatisfactory administration, culminating in Jefferson's virtual abdication when the British invaded Virginia in 1781. He now retired to his beautiful home at Monticello, to his wife, Martha Wayles Skelton, whom he had married in 1772 and who died in 1782, and to his children.

Jefferson's *Notes on Virginia* (1784–85) illustrate his many-faceted interests, his limitless intellectual curiosity, his deep faith in agrarian democracy. Sent to Congress in 1783, he helped lay down the decimal system and drafted basic reports on the organization of the western lands. In 1785 he was appointed minister to France, where the Anglo-Saxon liberalism he had drawn from Locke was stimulated by contact with the thought that would soon ferment in the French Revolution. In 1789 Washington appointed him Secretary of State. While favoring the Constitution and a strengthened central government, Jefferson came to believe that Hamilton contemplated the establishment of a monarchy. Growing differences resulted in Jefferson's resignation on Dec. 31, 1793.

Elected vice president in 1796, Jefferson continued to serve as spiritual leader of the opposition to Federalism, particularly to the repressive Alien and Sedition Acts. He was elected President in 1801 by the House of Representatives as a result of Hamilton's decision to throw the Federalist votes to him rather than to Aaron Burr, who had tied him in electoral votes. The purchase of Louisiana from France in 1803, though in violation of his earlier constitutional scruples, was the most notable act of his administration. Re-elected in 1804 with 162 electoral votes to 14 for the Federalist Charles C. Pinckney, Jefferson tried desperately during his second term to keep the United States out of the Napoleonic Wars in Europe, employing to this end the unpopular embargo policy.

After his retirement to Monticello in 1809, he developed his interest in education, founding the University of Virginia and watching its development with never-flagging interest. He died at Monticello on July 4, 1826. Tall, loose-jointed, a poor speaker, Jefferson had an enormous variety of interests and skills, ranging from education and science to architecture and music. Economically, his conception of democracy presupposed an essentially rural community of small freeholds; but his deep and abiding faith in the common man provides inspiration for future generations.

JAMES MADISON was born in Port Conway, Va., on March 16, 1751 (March 5, 1750/1, old style). A Princeton graduate, he joined the struggle for independence on his return to Virginia in 1771. In the seventies and eighties he was active both in state politics, where he championed the Jefferson reform program, and in the Continental Congress. He was influential in the Constitutional Convention as leader of the group favoring a strong central government and as recorder of the debates; and he subsequently wrote, in collaboration with Alexander Hamilton and John Jay, the *Federalist* papers to aid the campaign for the adoption of the Constitution.

Serving in the new Congress, Madison soon emerged as the leader in the House of the men who opposed Hamilton's financial program and his pro-British leanings in foreign policy. Retiring from Congress in 1797, he continued active in Virginia and drafted the Virginia Resolution protesting the Alien and Sedition Acts. His intimacy with Jefferson made him the natural choice for Secretary of State in 1801.

In 1809 Madison succeeded Jefferson as President, with 122 electoral votes to 47 for the Federalist Pinckney, and 6 scattering. His attractive wife, Dolley Payne Todd, whom he married in 1794, brought a new social sparkle to the executive mansion. In the meantime, increasing tension with Britain culminated in the War of 1812—a war for which the United States was unprepared and for which Madison lacked the executive talent to clear out incompetence and mobilize the nation's energies. Madison was re-elected in 1812, with 128 electoral votes to 89 for the Federalist De Witt Clinton. In 1814 the British actually captured Washington and forced Madison to flee to Virginia.

Madison's domestic program capitulated to the Hamiltonian policies that he had resisted twenty years before and he now signed bills to establish a United States Bank and a higher tariff.

Following his presidency, he remained in retirement in Virginia until his death on June 28, 1836. Small, wrinkled, unimpressive, Madison had an acute political intelligence but lacked executive force.

JAMES MONROE was born on April 28, 1758, in Westmoreland County, Va. A William and Mary graduate, he served in the army during the first years of the Revolution and was wounded at Trenton. He then entered Virginia politics and later national politics under the sponsorship of Jefferson. In 1786 he married Elizabeth (Eliza) Kortright.

Fearing centralization, Monroe opposed the adoption of the Constitution and, as senator from Virginia, was highly critical of the Hamiltonian program. In 1794 he was appointed minister to France where his ardent sympathies with the Revolution exceeded the wishes of the State Department. A troubled diplomatic career ended with his recall in 1796. From 1799 to 1802 he was governor of Virginia. In 1803 Jefferson sent him to France to help negotiate the Louisiana Purchase and for the next few years he was active in various continental negotiations.

In 1808 Monroe flirted with the radical wing of the Republican party, which opposed Madison's candidacy; but the presidential boom came to naught and, after a brief term as governor of Virginia in 1811, Monroe accepted Madison's offer of the State Department. During the war he vainly sought a field command and served as Secretary of War from September 1814 to March 1815.

Elected President in 1816 with 183 electoral votes to 34 for the Federalist Rufus King, and re-elected without opposition in 1820, Monroe, the last of the Virginia dynasty, pursued the course of systematic tranquilization that won for his administrations the name "the era of good feeling." He continued Madison's surrender to the Hamiltonian domestic program, signed the Missouri Compromise, acquired Florida and, with the able assistance of his Secretary of State, John Quincy Adams, promulgated the Monroe Doctrine in 1823, declaring against foreign colonization or intervention in the Americas. He died in New York City on July 4, 1831.

A sound man of medium abilities, Monroe possessed qualities of judgment rather than of leadership.

JOHN QUINCY ADAMS was born on July 11, 1767, at Braintree (now Quincy), Mass., the son of John Adams. He spent his early years in Europe with his father, graduated from Harvard, and entered law practice. His anti-Jeffersonian newspaper articles won him political attention. In 1794 he became minister to the Netherlands, the first of several diplomatic posts that occupied him until his return to Boston in 1801. In 1797 he married Louisa Catherine Johnson.

In 1803 he was elected to the Senate, nominally as a Federalist, but his repeated displays of independence on such issues as the Louisiana Purchase and the embargo caused his party to compel his resignation and ostracize him socially. In 1809 Madison rewarded him for his support of Jefferson by appointing him minister to St. Petersburg. He helped negotiate the Treaty of Ghent in 1814 and in 1815 became minister to London. In 1817 Monroe appointed him Secretary of State where he served with great distinction, gaining Florida from Spain without hostilities and playing an equal part with Monroe in formulating the Monroe Doctrine.

When no presidential candidate received a majority of electoral votes in 1824, Adams, with the support of Henry Clay, was elected by the House in 1825 over Andrew Jackson, who had the original plurality. Adams had ambitious plans of government activity to foster internal improvements and promote the arts and sciences; but congressional obstructionism combined with his own unwillingness or inability to play the role of a politician meant that little was accomplished. Retiring to Quincy after his defeat in 1828, he was elected to the House of Representatives in 1831 where, though nominally a Whig, he pursued as ever an independent course. He led the fight to force Congress to receive antislavery petitions and fathered the Smithsonian Institution.

Stricken on the floor of the House, he died on Feb. 23, 1848. Tactless, brusque, conscientious, a rough and savage debater, Adams spared neither himself nor his enemies.

ANDREW JACKSON was born on March 15, 1767, in what is now generally agreed to be Waxhaw, S.C. After a turbulent boyhood as an orphan and a British prisoner, he moved west to Tennessee where he soon qualified for law practice but found time for such frontier pleasures as horse racing, cockfighting, and dueling. His marriage to Rachel Donelson Robards in 1791 was complicated by subsequent legal uncertainties about the status of her divorce. During the 1790s Jackson served in the Tennessee constitutional convention, the federal House of Representatives, the federal Senate, and the Tennessee supreme court.

After some years as a country gentleman, living at the Hermitage near Nashville, Jackson in 1812 was given command of Tennessee troops sent against the Creeks. He defeated the Indians at Horseshoe Bend in 1814; subsequently he became a major general and won the Battle of New Orleans over veteran British troops, though after the treaty of peace had been signed at Ghent. In 1818 General Jackson invaded Florida, captured Pensacola, and hanged two Englishmen named Arbuthnot and Ambrister, creating an international incident. A presidential boom began for him in 1821 and in its service he returned to the Senate (1823–25). Though he won a plurality of electoral votes in 1824, he lost in the House when Clay threw his strength to Adams; he won easily in 1828 by an electoral vote of 178 to 83.

As President, Jackson greatly expanded the power and prestige of the presidential office and carried through an unexampled program of domestic reform, vetoing the bill to extend the United States Bank, moving toward a hard-money currency policy, and checking the program of federal internal improvements. He also vindicated federal authority against South Carolina with its doctrine of nullification and against France on the question of debts. The support given his policies by the workingmen of the East as well as by the farmers of the East, West, and South resulted in his triumphant re-election in 1832 over Clay by an electoral vote of 219 to 49, with 18 scattering and 2 not cast.

After watching the inauguration of his hand-picked successor, Martin Van Buren, Jackson retired to the Hermitage, where he maintained a lively interest in national affairs until his death on June 8, 1845. A tall, dignified man with a drawn and wrinkled face, Jackson has been endowed by partisan historians with a violence and irascibility he appears not to have possessed. His great contribution was to adjust the presidential office and the democratic doctrines of Jefferson to the new situation created by the Industrial Revolution.

MARTIN VAN BUREN was born on Dec. 5, 1782, at Kinderhook, N.Y. After graduating from the village school, he became a law clerk, entered practice in 1803, and soon became active in state politics as state senator and attorney general. In 1821 he was elected to the United States Senate. He threw the support of his efficient political organization, known as the Albany Regency, to William H. Crawford in 1824 and to Jackson in 1828. After leading the opposition to Adams's administration in the Senate, he served briefly as governor of New York and resigned to become Jackson's Secretary of State. He soon became on close personal terms with Jackson and played an important part in turning the Jacksonian program from the lines intended by his original Western backers.

In 1832 Van Buren became vice president; in 1836, President, with an electoral vote of 170 against 124 scattered among four opponents. The Panic of 1837 overshadowed his term. He attributed it to the overexpansion of the credit and favored the establishment of an independent treasury as repository for the federal funds. In 1840 he established a ten-hour day on public works. Defeated by Harrison in 1840, he was the leading contender for the Democratic nomination in 1844 until he publicly opposed immediate annexation of Texas and was subsequently beaten by the Southern delegations at the Baltimore convention. This incident increased his growing misgivings about the slave power.

After working behind the scenes among the antislavery Democrats, Van Buren joined in the movement that led to the Free-Soil party and became its candidate for President in 1848. He subsequently returned to the Democratic party while continuing to object to its pro-Southern policy. He died in Kinderhook on July 24, 1862. His *Autobiography* throws valuable sidelights on the political history of the times.

Small, erect, dapper, Van Buren had a reputation for slick politicking that won him such sobriquets as the Little Magician and the Red Fox of Kinderhook; but, as his later career showed, he was capable of taking firm and unpopular stands on public issues. His wife Hannah Hoes, whom he married in 1807, died in 1819.

WILLIAM HENRY HARRISON was born in Charles City County, Va., on Feb. 9, 1773. Joining the army in 1791, he was active in Indian fighting in the Northwest, became secretary of the Northwest Territory in 1798 and governor of Indiana in 1800. He married Anna Symmes in 1795. Growing discontent over white encroachments on Indian lands led to the formation of an Indian alliance under Tecumseh to resist further aggressions. In 1811 Harrison won a nominal victory over the Indians at Tippecanoe and in 1813 a more decisive one at the Battle of the Thames, where Tecumseh was killed.

After resigning from the army in 1814, Harrison had an obscure career in politics and diplomacy, ending up in twenty years as a county recorder in Ohio. Nominated for President in 1835 as a military hero whom the conservative politicians hoped to be able to control, he ran surprisingly well against Van Buren in 1836. Four years later he defeated Van Buren by an electoral vote of 234 to 60, but caught pneumonia and died in Washington a month after his inauguration, April 4, 1841. Harrison's qualities were those of a soldier rather than of a statesman or political leader.

JOHN TYLER was born in Charles City County, Va., on March 29, 1790. A William and Mary graduate, he entered law practice and politics, serving in the House of Representatives (1816–21) and later as governor of Virginia (1825–27), and as senator. A thoroughgoing strict constructionist, he supported Crawford in 1824 and Jackson in 1828, but broke with Jackson over his Bank policy and became a member of the Southern state-rights group that cooperated with the Whigs. In 1836 he resigned from the Senate rather than follow instructions from the Virginia legislature to vote for a resolution expunging censure of Jackson from the Senate record.

Elected vice president on the Whig ticket in 1840, Tyler succeeded to the presidency on Harrison's death. His strict-constructionist views soon caused a split with the Henry Clay wing of the Whig party and a stalemate on domestic questions. Tyler's more considerable achievements were his support of the Webster-Ashburton Treaty with Britain and his success in bringing about the annexation of Texas.

After his presidency he lived in retirement in Virginia

until the outbreak of the Civil War, when he emerged briefly as chairman of a peace convention and then as delegate to the provisional Congress of the Confederacy. He died on Jan. 18, 1862. He was married first to Letitia Christian in March 1813 and, two years after her death in 1842, to Julia Gardiner. Witty, amiable, courteous, Tyler was a Virginia gentleman whose presidency was hamstrung by the basic contradiction between his own ideas and those of the party that put him on the ticket as vice president.

JAMES KNOX POLK was born in Mecklenburg County, N.C., on Nov. 2, 1795. A graduate of the University of North Carolina, he moved west to Tennessee, was admitted to the bar, and soon became prominent in state politics. In 1825 he was elected to the House of Representatives where he opposed Adams and, after 1829, became Jackson's floor leader in the fight against the Bank. In 1835 he became Speaker of the House. In 1839 he was elected governor of Tennessee, but was beaten in tries for re-election in 1841 and 1843.

The supporters of Van Buren for the Democratic nomination in 1844 counted on Polk as his running mate; but, when Van Buren's stand on Texas alienated Southern support, the convention swung to Polk on the ninth ballot. He was elected over Henry Clay, the Whig candidate, by an electoral vote of 170 to 105. Rapidly disillusioning those who thought that he would not run his own administration, Polk proceeded steadily and precisely to achieve four major objectives—the acquisition of California, the settlement of the Oregon question, the reduction of the tariff, and the establishment of the independent treasury. He also enlarged the Monroe Doctrine to exclude all non-American intervention in American affairs, whether forcible or not, and he forced Mexico into a war that he waged to a successful conclusion. His wife Sarah Childress, whom he married in 1824, was a woman of charm and ability. Polk died in Nashville, Tenn., on June 15, 1849.

Serious, hardworking, lacking in color, Polk has long been underrated by historians who mistakenly regarded him as a slaveholders' puppet; in fact, few Presidents have so thoroughly controlled their own administration or have so ably accomplished the purposes they set for themselves. Polk's *Diary* reflects the mood and problems of his presidency.

ZACHARY TAYLOR was born at Montebello, Orange County, Va., on Nov. 24, 1784. Embarking on a military career in 1808, Taylor fought in the War of 1812, the Black Hawk War, and the Seminole War, holding in between garrison jobs on the frontier or desk jobs in Washington. A brigadier general as a result of his victory over the Seminoles at Lake Okeechobee (1837), Taylor held a succession of Southwestern commands and in 1846 established a base on the Rio Grande, where his forces engaged in hostilities that precipitated the war with Mexico. He captured Monterrey in September 1846 and, disregarding Polk's orders to stay on the defensive, defeated Santa Anna at Buena Vista in February 1847, ending the war in the northern provinces.

Though Taylor had never cast a vote for President, his party affiliations were Whiggish and his availability was increased by his difficulties with Polk. He was elected President over the Democrat Lewis Cass by an electoral vote of 163 to 127. During the revival of the slavery controversy, which was to result in the Compromise of 1850, Taylor began to take an increasingly firm stand against appeasing the South; but he died in Washington on July 9, 1850, in the midst of the fight over the Compromise. He married Margaret Mackall Smith in 1810. His bluff and simple soldierly qualities won him the name of Old Rough and Ready.

MILLARD FILLMORE was born at Locke, Cayuga County, N.Y., on Jan. 7, 1800. A lawyer, he entered politics as an Antimason under the sponsorship of Thurlow Weed, editor and party boss, and subsequently followed Weed into the Whig party. He served in the House of Representatives (1833–35 and 1837–43) and played a leading role in writing the tariff of 1842. Defeated for governor of New York in 1844, he became comptroller in 1848, was put on the Whig ticket with Taylor as a concession to the Clay wing of the party, and became President upon Taylor's death in 1850.

As President, Fillmore broke with Weed and William H. Seward and associated himself with the pro-Southern Whigs, supporting the Compromise of 1850. Defeated for the Whig nomination in 1852, he ran for President in 1856 as candidate of the American or Know-Nothing party, which sought to unite the country against foreigners in the alleged hope of diverting it from the explosive slavery issue. Fillmore opposed Lincoln during the Civil War. He died in Buffalo on March 8, 1874. He was married in 1826 to Abigail Powers, who died in 1853, and in 1858 to Caroline Carmichael McIntosh. Urbane, gracious, colorless, and weak, Fillmore was an undistinguished President.

FRANKLIN PIERCE was born at Hillsboro, N.H., on Nov. 23, 1804. A Bowdoin graduate and lawyer, he won rapid political advancement in the Democratic party, in part because of the prestige of his father, Governor Benjamin Pierce. By 1831 he was Speaker of the New Hampshire House of Representatives; from 1833 to 1837 he served in the federal House and from 1837 to 1842 in the Senate. His wife, Jane Means Appleton, whom he had married in 1834, disliked Washington and the somewhat dissipated life led by Pierce; and in 1842 Pierce, resigning from the Senate, took up a successful law practice in Concord, N.H. During the Mexican War he was a brigadier general.

Thereafter Pierce continued to oppose antislavery tendencies within the Democratic party. As a result, he was the Southern choice to break the deadlock at the Democratic convention of 1852 and was nominated on the 49th ballot. Pierce rolled up 254 electoral votes to 42 for Winfield Scott, the Whig candidate.

As President, Pierce followed a course of appeasing the South at home and of playing with schemes of territorial expansion abroad. The failure of both his foreign and domestic policies prevented his renomination; and he died in Concord, N.H., on Oct. 8, 1869, in relative obscurity.

JAMES BUCHANAN was born near Mercersburg, Pa., on April 23, 1791. A Dickinson graduate and a lawyer, he entered Pennsylvania politics as a Federalist. With the disappearance of the Federalist party, he became a Jacksonian Democrat. He served with ability in the House (1821–31), as minister to St. Petersburg (1832–33), and in the Senate (1834–45), and in 1845 became Polk's Secretary of State. Disappointed in the presidential nomination in 1852, Buchanan became minister to Britain in 1853 where he participated with other American diplomats in Europe in drafting the expansionist Ostend Manifesto.

In 1856 Buchanan received the Democratic nomination and won the election, gaining 174 electoral votes to 114 for John C. Frémont, the Republican candidate, and 8 for Millard Fillmore, American party. The growing crisis over slavery presented Buchanan with problems he lacked the will to tackle. His appeasement of the South alienated the Stephen Douglas wing of the Democratic party without reducing Southern militancy on slavery issues. While denying the right of secession, Buchanan also denied that the federal government could do anything about it. He supported the administration during the Civil War and died in Lancaster, Pa., on June 1, 1868.

The only President to remain a bachelor throughout his term, Buchanan used his charming niece, Harriet Lane, as White House hostess.

ABRAHAM LINCOLN was born in Hardin (now Larue) County, Ky., on Feb. 12, 1809. His family moved to Indiana and then to Illinois, and Lincoln gained what education he could along the way. While reading law, he worked in a store, managed a mill, surveyed, and split rails. In 1834 he went to the state legislature as a Whig and became the party's floor leader. For the next twenty years he remained in law practice in Springfield, except for a single term (1847–49) in Congress, where he denounced the Mexican War. In 1855 he was a candidate for senator and in 1856 he joined the new Republican party.

A leading but unsuccessful candidate for the vice-presidential nomination with Frémont, Lincoln gained national attention in 1858 when, as Republican candidate for senator from Illinois, he engaged in a series of debates with Stephen A. Douglas, the Democratic candidate. He lost the senatorial election, but continued to prepare the way for the 1860 Republican convention and was rewarded with the presidential nomination on the third ballot. He polled 180 electoral votes, as against the 123 of his three opponents, but had only a plurality of the popular vote.

From the start, Lincoln made clear that, unlike Buchanan, he believed the national government had the power to crush the rebellion. Not an abolitionist, he held the slavery issue subordinate to that of preserving the Union, but soon perceived that the war could not be brought to a successful conclusion without freeing the slaves. His administration was hampered by the incompetence of many Union generals, the inexperience of the troops, and the harassing political tactics both of the Republican Radicals, who favored a hard policy toward the South, and the Democratic Copperheads, who desired a negotiated peace. The Gettysburg Address of Nov. 19, 1863, marks the high point in the record of American eloquence. His patient search for a winning combination finally brought Generals Ulysses S. Grant and William T. Sherman to the top; and their series of victories in 1864 dispelled the mutterings from both Radicals and Peace Democrats that at one time seemed to threaten Lincoln's re-election. He received 212 electoral votes to 21 for George B. McClellan, the Democratic candidate. His inaugural address urged leniency toward the South: "With malice toward none, with charity for all . . . let us strive on to finish the work we are in; to bind up the nation's wounds . . . " This policy aroused growing opposition on the part of the Republican Radicals, but Lincoln was shot by the actor John Wilkes Booth at Ford's Theater, Washington, on April 14, 1865, before the matter could be put to the test. He died the following day.

Lincoln's marriage to Mary Todd in 1842 was often unhappy and turbulent, in part because of his wife's pronounced instability. By his remarkable literary artistry, his essential patience and devotion, his profound sense of the importance of government by, for, and of the people, by the manner of his life and of his death, Lincoln has won a unique place in the hearts of Americans.

ANDREW JOHNSON was born at Raleigh, N.C., on Dec. 29, 1808. Self-educated, he became a tailor in Greeneville, Tenn., but soon went into politics, where he rose steadily. From 1843 to 1853 he served in the House of Representatives, 1853–57 as governor of Tennessee, and in 1857 was elected Senator. Politically he was a Jacksonian Democrat and his specialty was the fight for a more equitable land policy. Alone among the Southern Senators, he stood by the Union during the Civil War. In 1862 he became war governor of Tennessee and carried out a thankless and difficult job with great courage. Johnson became Lincoln's running mate in 1864 as a result of an attempt to give the ticket a nonpartisan and nonsectional character. Succeeding to the presidency on Lincoln's death, Johnson sought to carry out Lincoln's policy but without Lincoln's political skill. The result was a hopeless conflict with the Radical Republicans who dominated Congress, passed measures over Johnson's vetoes, and attempted to limit the power of the executive concerning appointments and removals. The conflict culminated with Johnson's impeachment for attempting to remove his disloyal Secretary of War in defiance of the Tenure of Office Act which required senatorial concurrence for such dismissals. The opposition failed by one vote to get the two thirds necessary for conviction.

After his presidency, Johnson maintained an interest in politics and in 1875 was elected to the Senate. He died near Carter Station, Tenn., on July 31, 1875. He married Eliza McCardle in 1827. An honest, courageous, and intelligent man, Johnson lacked the tact, patience, and self-control to be an effective President.

ULYSSES SIMPSON GRANT was born (as Hiram Ulysses Grant) at Point Pleasant, Ohio, on April 27, 1822. He finished West Point in 1843 and served without particular distinction in the Mexican War. In 1848 he married Julia Dent. He resigned from the army in 1854, following warnings from his commanding officer about his drinking habits, and for the next six years held a wide variety of jobs in the Middle West. With the outbreak of the Civil War, he sought a command and soon, to his surprise, was made a brigadier general. His continuing successes in the western theaters, culminating in the capture of Vicksburg in 1863, brought him national fame and soon the command of all the Union armies. His dogged, implacable policy of concentrating on dividing and destroying the Confederate armies brought the war to an end in 1865.

Grant's relations with Johnson grew steadily worse; and in 1868, as Republican candidate for President, Grant was elected with 214 electoral votes to 80 for the Democrat, Horatio Seymour. From the start Grant showed his unfitness for the office. His cabinet was weak, his domestic policy was confused, many of his intimate associates were corrupt. The notable achievement in foreign affairs was the settlement of controversies with Great Britain in the Treaty of London (1871), negotiated by his able Secretary of State, Hamilton Fish.

Nominated for a second term, he defeated Horace Greeley, the Democratic and Liberal Republican candidate, 286 votes to 63. The Panic of 1873 created difficulties for his second term.

After retiring from office, Grant toured Europe for two years and returned in time to accede to a third-term boom, but was beaten in the convention of 1880. Illness and bad business judgment darkened his last years, but he worked steadily at the *Personal Memoirs,* which were to be so successful when published after his death at Mount McGregor, near Saratoga, N.Y., on July 23, 1885. Inarticulate, taciturn, loyal to his friends, he was an able general who should never have accepted the presidency.

RUTHERFORD BIRCHARD HAYES was born at Delaware, Ohio, on Oct. 4, 1822. A graduate of Kenyon College and the Harvard Law School, he practiced law in Lower Sandusky (now Fremont) and then in Cincinnati. In 1852 he married Lucy Webb. A Whig, he joined the Republican party in 1855. During the Civil War he rose to the rank of major general. He served in Congress from 1865 to 1867 and then confirmed a reputation for honesty and efficiency in two terms as governor of Ohio. His re-election as governor in 1875 made him the logical candidate for those Republicans who wished to stop James G. Blaine in 1876 and he was successfully nominated.

The result of the election was for some time in doubt and hinged upon disputed returns from South Carolina, Louisiana, Florida, and Oregon. Samuel J. Tilden, the Democratic candidate, had the larger popular vote but was adjudged by the strictly partisan decisions of the Electoral Commission to have one less electoral vote, 185 to 184. The national acceptance of this result was due in part to the general understanding that Hayes would pursue a conciliatory policy toward the South. He withdrew the troops from the South, took a conservative position on financial and labor issues, and urged civil service reform.

Hayes served only one term by his own wish and spent the rest of his life in various humanitarian endeavors. He died in Fremont on Jan. 17, 1893. A hard-working, conscientious, sensible man, Hayes represented the best type of Republican of his day.

JAMES ABRAM GARFIELD, the last President to be born in a log cabin, was born at Cuyahoga County, Ohio, on Nov. 19, 1831. A Williams graduate, he taught school for a time and entered Republican politics in Ohio. In 1858 he married Lucretia Rudolph. During the Civil War he had a promising career, rising to the rank of major general of volunteers; but in 1863 he was elected to the House of

Representatives, where he served until 1880. His oratorical and parliamentary abilities soon made him the leading Republican in the House, though his record was marred by his unorthodox acceptance of a fee in the DeGolyer paving contract case and by suspicions of his complicity in the Crédit Mobilier scandal.

In 1880 Garfield was elected to the Senate, but instead became the presidential candidate on the 36th ballot as a result of a deadlock in the Republican convention. He gained 214 electoral votes to 155 for General Winfield Scott Hancock, the Democratic candidate. Garfield's administration was barely under way when he was shot by Charles J. Guiteau, a disappointed office seeker, in July. He died in Elberon, N.J., on Sept. 19, 1881. An attractive and eloquent man, he was much beloved in his day.

CHESTER ALAN ARTHUR was born at Fairfield, Vt., on Oct. 5, 1830. A graduate of Union College, he became a successful New York lawyer. In 1859 he married Ellen Herndon. During the Civil War he held administrative jobs in the Republican state administration and in 1871 was appointed collector of the Port of New York by Grant. This post gave him control over considerable patronage; and, though not personally corrupt, Arthur managed his power in the interests of the New York machine so openly that President Hayes in 1877 called for an investigation and in 1878 Arthur was suspended from his responsibilities.

In 1880 Arthur was nominated for vice president in the hope of conciliating the followers of Grant and the powerful New York machine. As President on Garfield's assassination, Arthur, stepping out of his familiar role as spoilsman, backed civil service reform, reorganized the cabinet, and prosecuted political associates accused of post office graft. Losing machine support and failing to gain the reformers, he was not renominated. He died in New York City on Nov. 18, 1886.

STEPHEN GROVER CLEVELAND was born at Caldwell, N.J., on March 18, 1837. He was admitted to the bar in Buffalo, N.Y., in 1859 and lived there as a lawyer, with occasional incursions into Democratic politics, for more than twenty years. He did not participate in the Civil War. As mayor of Buffalo in 1881, he carried through a reform program so ably that the Democrats ran him successfully for governor in 1882. In 1884 he won the Democratic nomination for President. The campaign contrasted Cleveland's spotless public career with the uncertain record of James G. Blaine, the Republican candidate, and Cleveland received enough Mugwump (independent Republican) support to win by 219 to 182 electoral votes.

As President, Cleveland pushed civil service reform, opposed the pension grab and attacked the high tariff rates. While in the White House he married Frances Folsom (1886). Renominated in 1888, Cleveland was defeated by Benjamin Harrison, polling more popular but fewer electoral votes. In 1892 he was re-elected over Harrison, 277 to 145, with 22 votes for James B. Weaver, the Populist candidate. When the Panic of 1893 burst upon the country, Cleveland's attempts to solve it by sound-money measures alienated the free-silver wing of the party, while his tariff policy alienated the protectionists. In 1894 he sent troops to break the Pullman strike. In foreign affairs his firmness caused Great Britain to back down in the Venezuela border dispute.

In his last years Cleveland was an active and much respected public figure. He died in Princeton, N.J., on June 24, 1908. An honest, stubborn, high-principled man, Cleveland was an old-fashioned liberal in the nineteenth-century sense who was baffled by the new problems of industrial society.

BENJAMIN HARRISON was born in North Bend, Ohio, on Aug. 20, 1833, the grandson of William Henry Harrison. A graduate of Miami University, he took up the law in Indiana and became active in Republican politics. In 1853 he married Caroline Lavinia Scott. During the Civil War he rose to the rank of brigadier general. A sound-money Republican, he was elected senator from Indiana in 1880 and in 1888 received the Republican nomination for President on the 8th ballot. Though behind on the popular vote, he won over Grover Cleveland in the electoral college by 233 to 168.

As President, Benjamin Harrison failed to please either the bosses or the reform element in the party. In foreign affairs he backed Secretary of State Blaine, whose policy foreshadowed later American imperialism. In 1892 Harrison was renominated, but Cleveland beat him in the election. His wife died in the White House in 1892 and

Harrison married her niece, Mary Scott (Lord) Dimmick, in 1896. After his presidency, he resumed law practice. He died in Indianapolis on March 13, 1901.

WILLIAM McKINLEY was born in Niles, Ohio, on Jan. 29, 1843. He taught school, then served in the Civil War, rising from the ranks to become a major. Subsequently he opened a law office in Canton, Ohio, and in 1871 married Ida Saxton. Elected to Congress in 1876, he served there steadily till 1891, except for 1883–85. His faithful advocacy of business interests culminated in the passage of the highly protective McKinley Tariff of 1890. With the support of Mark Hanna, a shrewd Cleveland businessman interested in safeguarding tariff protection, McKinley became governor of Ohio in 1892 and Republican presidential candidate in 1896. The business community, alarmed by the progressivism of William Jennings Bryan, the Democratic candidate, spent considerable money to assure McKinley's victory, which was by the margin of 271 to 176 in the electoral college.

The chief event of McKinley's administration was the war with Spain, which resulted in our acquisition of the Philippines and other islands. With imperialism as an issue, McKinley defeated Bryan again in the election of 1900 by 292 to 155. On Sept. 6, 1901, he was shot at Buffalo, N.Y., by Leon F. Czolgosz, an anarchist, and he died there on Sept. 14.

THEODORE ROOSEVELT was born in New York City on Oct. 27, 1858. A Harvard graduate, he was early interested in ranching, in politics, and in writing picturesque historical narratives. He was a Republican member of the New York Assembly in 1882–84, an unsuccessful candidate for mayor of New York in 1886, a U. S. Civil Service Commissioner under Harrison, Police Commissioner of New York City in 1895, and Assistant Secretary of the Navy under McKinley in 1897. He resigned in 1898 to help organize a volunteer regiment named the Rough Riders and take a more direct part in the war with Spain. He won the New York gubernatorial nomination in 1898 and the vice presidency in 1900, in spite of lack of enthusiasm on the part of the bosses.

Assuming the presidency of the assassinated McKinley in 1901, Roosevelt embarked on a wide-ranging program of government reform and conservation of natural resources. He ordered antitrust suits against several large corporations, threatened to intervene in the anthracite coal strike of 1902, which prompted the operators to accept arbitration, and, in general, championed the rights of the "little man" and fought the "malefactors of great wealth." He was also responsible for such progressive legislation as the Elkins Act of 1901, which outlawed freight rebates by railroads; the bill establishing the Department of Commerce and Labor; the Hepburn Act, which gave the I.C.C. greater control over the railroads; the Meat Inspection Act; and the Pure Food and Drug Act.

In foreign affairs he pursued a strong policy, permitting the instigation of a revolt in Panama to dispose of Colombian objections to the Panama Canal and helping to maintain the balance of power in the East by bringing the Russo-Japanese war to an end, for which he won the Nobel Peace Prize, the first American to achieve a Nobel prize in any category. In 1904 he decisively defeated Alton B. Parker, his conservative Democratic opponent, by an electoral margin of 336 to 140.

Roosevelt's increasing coldness toward Taft after he left the White House led him to overlook his earlier disclaimer of third-term ambitions and to re-enter politics. Defeated by the machine in the Republican convention of 1912, he organized the Progressive Party and polled more votes than Taft, though the split brought about the election of Wilson. From 1915 on, Roosevelt strongly favored intervention in the European war. He became deeply embittered at Wilson's refusal to allow him to raise a volunteer division. He died in Oyster Bay, N.Y., on Jan. 6, 1919.

An advocate of the strenuous life and a man of spirit and vigor, Roosevelt captured the imagination of the American people.

WILLIAM HOWARD TAFT was born in Cincinnati on Sept. 15, 1857. A Yale graduate, he entered Ohio Republican politics in the eighteen eighties. In 1886 he married Helen Herron. From 1887 to 1890, he served on the Ohio superior court; 1890–92, as solicitor general of the United States; 1892–1900, on the federal circuit court. In 1900 McKinley appointed him president of the Philippine Commission and in 1901 governor general. Taft had great success in pacifying the Filipinos, solving the problem of the church lands, improving economic conditions, and establishing limited self-government. His period as Secretary of War (1904–08) further demonstrated his capacity as administrator and conciliator and he was Roosevelt's hand-picked successor in 1908. In the election he polled 321 electoral votes to 162 for William Jennings Bryan.

As President, though he carried on many of Roosevelt's policies, Taft got into increasing trouble with the progressive wing of the party and displayed mounting irritability and indecision. After his defeat in 1912, he became professor of constitutional law at Yale. In 1921 he was appointed Chief Justice of the United States. He died in Washington, D.C., on March 8, 1930. Enormously large, deliberate, and good-humored, Taft excelled as an administrator and judge, not as a political leader.

THOMAS WOODROW WILSON was born in Staunton, Va., on Dec. 28, 1856. A Princeton graduate, he turned from law practice to post-graduate work in political science at Johns Hopkins University, receiving his Ph.D. in 1886. He taught at Bryn Mawr, Wesleyan, and Princeton, and in 1902 was made president of Princeton. After an unsuccessful attempt to democratize the social life of Princeton, he welcomed an invitation in 1910 to be the Democratic gubernatorial candidate in New Jersey. His success in fighting the machine and putting through a reform program attracted national attention.

In 1912, after a protracted contest at Baltimore, Wilson won the Democratic nomination on the 46th ballot. In the election he received 435 electoral votes to 88 for Roosevelt and 8 for Taft. During his first term Wilson proceeded under the standard of the New Freedom to enact a program of domestic reform, including the Federal Reserve Act, the Clayton Antitrust Act, the establishment of the Federal Trade Commission, and other measures designed to restore competition in the face of the great monopolies. In foreign affairs, while privately sympathetic with the Allies, he strove to maintain neutrality in the European war and warned both sides against encroachments on American interests.

Re-elected in 1916 as a peace candidate, he tried to mediate between the warring nations; but when the Germans resumed unrestricted submarine warfare in 1917 Wilson brought the United States into what he now believed was a war to make the world safe for democracy. He supplied the classic formulations of Allied war aims and the armistice of November 1918 was negotiated on the basis of Wilson's Fourteen Points. In 1919 he strove at Versailles to lay the foundations for enduring peace. He accepted the imperfections of the Versailles Treaty in the expectation that they could be remedied by action within the League of Nations. He probably could have secured ratification of the treaty if he had adopted a more conciliatory attitude toward the mild reservationists; but his insistence on all or nothing eventually caused the diehard isolationists and diehard Wilsonites to unite in rejecting a compromise.

In September 1919 Wilson suffered a paralytic stroke that limited his future activity. After the presidency he lived on in retirement in Washington, D.C., dying Feb. 3, 1924. He was married twice—in 1885 to Ellen Louise Axson, who died in 1914, and in 1915 to Edith Bolling Galt. A man of high principle, inspiring eloquence, and great intellectual ability, Wilson was the first leader to fire the imagination of the masses of the world with the vision of world peace.

WARREN GAMALIEL HARDING was born in Morrow County, Ohio, on Nov. 2, 1865. After attending Ohio Central College, Harding became interested in journalism and in 1884 bought the *Marion* (Ohio) *Star.* In 1891 he married a wealthy widow, Florence Kling De Wolfe. As his paper prospered, he entered Republican politics, serving as state senator (1899–1903) and as lieutenant governor (1904–06). In 1910 he was defeated for governor, but in 1914 was elected to the Senate. His reputation as orator made him keynoter in the 1916 convention.

When the 1920 Republican convention was deadlocked between Leonard Wood and Frank O. Lowden, Harding was made the dark-horse nominee on his solemn affirmation that there was no reason in his past that he should not be. Straddling the League question, Harding was elected easily with 404 electoral votes to 127 for James M. Cox, his Democratic opponent. His Cabinet contained some able men, but also some manifestly unfit for public office. Harding's own intimates were mediocre when they were not corrupt. The impending disclosure of scandals in the Interior and Justice departments and in the Veterans' Bureau, as well as political setbacks, profoundly worried him.

On his return from Alaska in 1923, he died suddenly at San Francisco on Aug. 2. A handsome and genial man, undiscriminating in his associates, lacking in political ideas or fortitude, Harding was totally unfitted for the presidency.

JOHN CALVIN COOLIDGE was born in Plymouth, Vt., on July 4, 1872. An Amherst graduate, he went into law practice at Northampton, Mass., in 1897. He married Grace Anna Goodhue in 1905. He entered Republican state politics, becoming successively mayor of Northampton, state senator, lieutenant governor and, in 1919, governor. His conduct in regard to the Boston police strike in 1919 won him a somewhat undeserved reputation for decisive action and brought him the Republican vice-presidential nomination in 1920. After Harding's death Coolidge handled the Washington scandals with care and finally managed to save the Republican party from public blame for the widespread corruption.

In 1924 Coolidge won re-election without difficulty, getting 382 electoral votes to 136 for the Democrat, John W. Davis, and 13 for Robert M. La Follette running on the Progressive ticket. His second term, like his first, was characterized by a general satisfaction with the existing economic order. He stated that he did not choose to run in 1928.

After his presidency, Coolidge lived quietly in Northampton, writing an unilluminating *Autobiography* and conducting a syndicated column. He died there on Jan. 5, 1933. His dry, Yankee humor and his frugality and glumness made him a paradoxically popular President in the boom period.

HERBERT CLARK HOOVER was born at West Branch, Iowa, on Aug. 10, 1874. A Stanford graduate, he worked from 1895 to 1913 as a mining engineer and consultant in North America, Europe, Asia, Africa, and Australia. In 1899 he married Lou Henry. During the First World War he served with distinction as chairman of the American Relief Committee in London, as chairman of the Commission for Relief in Belgium, and as U.S. Food Administrator. His political affiliations were still sufficiently indeterminate for him to be mentioned as a possibility for both Republican and Democratic nominations in 1920, but after the election he served both Harding and Coolidge as Secretary of

Commerce.

In the election of 1928 Hoover received 444 electoral votes to 87 for Alfred E. Smith, the Democratic candidate. He soon faced the worst depression in the nation's history, but his attacks upon it were hampered by his devotion to the theory that the forces that brought the crisis would soon bring the revival and then by his belief that in too many areas the federal government had no power to act. In a succession of vetoes he struck down measures proposing a national employment system or national relief, he reduced income tax rates, and only at the end of his term did he yield to popular pressure and set up agencies such as the Reconstruction Finance Corporation to make emergency loans to assist business.

After his 1932 defeat, Hoover returned to private business. In 1946 President Truman charged him with various world food missions; and from 1947 to 1949 and again from 1953 to 1955 he was head of the Commission on Organization of the Executive Branch of the Government. He died in New York City on Oct. 20, 1964.

FRANKLIN DELANO ROOSEVELT was born in Hyde Park, N.Y., on Jan. 30, 1882. A Harvard graduate, he attended Columbia Law School and was admitted to the New York bar. In 1910 he was elected to the New York state senate as a Democrat. Re-elected in 1912, he was appointed Assistant Secretary of the Navy by Woodrow Wilson in 1913. In 1920 his radiant personality and his war services resulted in his nomination for vice president as James M. Cox's running mate. After his defeat, he returned to law practice in New York. In August 1921 Roosevelt was stricken with infantile paralysis while at Campobello, New Brunswick. After a long and gallant fight against the disease he recovered partial use of his legs. In 1924 and 1928 he led the fight at the Democratic national conventions for the nomination of Gov. Alfred E. Smith of New York and in 1928 Roosevelt was himself induced to run for governor of New York. He was elected and was re-elected in 1930.

In 1932 Roosevelt received the Democratic nomination for President and immediately launched a campaign which brought new spirit to a weary and discouraged nation. He won the election over Herbert Hoover by a margin of 472 to 59 in the electoral college. His first term was characterized by an unfolding of the New Deal program, with greater benefits for labor, the farmers, and the unemployed, and the progressive estrangement of most of the business community.

At an early stage Roosevelt became aware of the menace to world peace involved in the existence of totalitarian fascism, and from 1937 on he tried to focus public attention on the trend of events in Europe and Asia. As a result he was widely denounced as a warmonger. He was re-elected in 1936 over Alfred M. Landon by the overwhelming electoral margin of 523 to 8 and the gathering international crisis caused him to decide to run again in 1940.

Roosevelt's program to bring maximum aid to Britain and, after June 1941, to Russia was opposed, until the Japanese attack on Pearl Harbor restored national unity. During the war Roosevelt shelved the New Deal in the interests of conciliating the business community, both in order to get full production during the war and to prepare the way for a united acceptance of the peace settlements after the war. A series of conferences with Winston Churchill and Joseph Stalin laid down the bases for the postwar world. In 1944 he was elected to a fourth term, running against Thomas E. Dewey.

On April 12, 1945, Roosevelt died at Warm Springs, Ga., shortly after his return from the Yalta Conference. His wife, Anna Eleanor Roosevelt, whom he married in 1905, was a woman of great ability who made significant contributions to her husband's policies.

HARRY S. TRUMAN was born on a farm near Lamar, Mo., on May 8, 1884. During the First World War he served in France with the 129th Field Artillery. He married Bess Wallace in 1919. After engaging briefly and unsuccessfully in the haberdashery business in Kansas City, Mo., Truman entered local politics. Under the sponsorship of Thomas Pendergast, Democratic boss of Missouri, he held a number of local offices, preserving his personal honesty in the midst of a notoriously corrupt political machine. In 1934 he was elected to the Senate and was re-elected in 1940. During his first term he was a loyal but quiet supporter of the New Deal, but in the course of his second term an appointment as head of a Senate committee to investigate war production brought out his special qualities of honesty, common sense, and hard work, and he won widespread respect.

Elected vice president in 1944, Truman became President upon Roosevelt's sudden death in April 1945 and was immediately faced with the problems of winding down the war against the Axis and preparing the nation for postwar adjustment.

The years 1947–48 were distinguished by civil rights proposals, the Truman Doctrine to contain the spread of Communism, and the Marshall Plan to aid in the economic reconstruction of war-ravaged nations. Truman's general record, highlighted by a vigorous Fair Deal campaign, brought about his unexpected election in 1948 over the heavily favored Thomas E. Dewey.

Truman's second term was primarily concerned with the Cold War with the Soviet Union, the implementing of the North Atlantic Pact, the United Nations police action in Korea, and the vast rearmament program with its accompanying problems of economic stabilization.

On March 29, 1952, Truman announced that he would not run again for the presidency. After leaving the White House, he returned to his home in Independence, Mo., to write his memoirs. He further busied himself with the Harry S. Truman Library there. He died in Kansas City, Mo., on Dec. 26, 1972.

DWIGHT DAVID EISENHOWER was born in Denison, Tex., on Oct. 14, 1890. His ancestors lived in Germany and emigrated to America, settling in Pennsylvania, early in the 18th century. His father, David, had a general store in Hope, Kan., which failed. After a brief time in Texas, the family moved to Abilene, Kan.

After graduating from Abilene High School in 1909, Dwight Eisenhower did odd jobs for almost two years. He won an appointment to the Naval Academy at Annapolis, but it turned out that he was too old for admittance. Then he received an appointment in 1910 to West Point. He was graduated a second lieutenant in 1915.

He did not see service in World War I, having been assigned to the 19th Infantry at Fort Sam Houston, Tex. There he met Mamie Geneva Doud, whom he married in Denver on July 1, 1916, and by whom he had two sons: Doud Dwight (died in infancy) and John Sheldon Doud.

Eisenhower served in the Philippines from 1935 to 1939 with Gen. Douglas MacArthur. Afterwards, Gen. George C. Marshall brought him into the War Department's General Staff and in 1942 put him in command of the invasion of North Africa. In 1944, he was made Supreme Allied Commander for the invasion of Europe.

After the war, Eisenhower served as Army Chief of Staff from November 1945 until February 1948, when he was appointed president of Columbia University.

In December 1950, President Truman recalled Eisenhower to active duty to command the North Atlantic Treaty Organization forces in Europe. He held this post until the end of May 1952.

At the Republican Convention of July 1952 in Chicago, Eisenhower won the presidential nomination on the first ballot in a close race with Senator Robert A. Taft of Ohio. In November he won the election, defeating Gov. Adlai E. Stevenson of Illinois by an electoral vote of 442 to 89.

Through two terms, Eisenhower hewed to moderate domestic policies. He quested for peace through Free World strength in an era of new nationalisms, nuclear rockets, and space exploration. He fostered alliances pledging the United States to resist Red aggression in Europe, Asia, and Latin America. The Eisenhower Doctrine of 1957 extended commitments to the Middle East.

At home, the popular President lacked G.O.P. Congressional majorities after 1954, but he was re-elected in 1956 by 457 electoral votes to 73 for Adlai E. Stevenson.

While retaining most Fair Deal programs, he stressed "fiscal responsibility" in domestic affairs. A moderate in civil rights, he sent troops to Little Rock, Ark., to enforce court-ordered school integration.

With his wartime rank restored by Congress, Eisenhower returned to private life and the role of elder statesman with his vigor hardly impaired by a heart attack, an ileitis operation, and a mild stroke suffered while in office. He died in Washington, D.C., on March 28, 1969.

JOHN FITZGERALD KENNEDY was born in Brookline, Mass., on May 29, 1917. His father, Joseph P. Kennedy, was U. S. Ambassador to Great Britain from 1937 to 1940.

Kennedy was graduated from Harvard University in 1940 and joined the Navy in 1941. He became skipper of a PT boat that was sunk in the Pacific by a Japanese destroyer. Although given up for lost, he swam to a safe island, towing an injured enlisted man.

After recovering from a war-aggravated spinal injury,

Kennedy entered politics in 1946 and was elected to Congress. In 1952 he ran against Senator Henry Cabot Lodge, Jr., of Massachusetts, and won.

Kennedy was married on Sept. 12, 1953, to Jacqueline Lee Bouvier, by whom he had three children: Caroline, John Fitzgerald, Jr., and Patrick Bouvier (died in infancy).

In 1957 Kennedy won the Pulitzer Prize for a book he had written earlier, *Profiles in Courage.*

After strenuous primary battles Kennedy won the Democratic presidential nomination on the first ballot at the 1960 Los Angeles convention. With a plurality of only 118,574 votes, he carried the November election with an electoral vote of 303 to Vice President Richard M. Nixon's 219, becoming the first Roman Catholic President.

Kennedy brought to the White House the dynamic idea of a "New Frontier" approach in dealing with problems at home, abroad, and in the dimensions of space. Out of his leadership in his first few months in office came the 10-year Alliance for Progress to aid Latin America, the Peace Corps, and accelerated programs that brought the first Americans into orbit in the race in space.

Failure of the U. S.-supported Cuban invasion in April 1961 led to the entrenchment of the Communist-backed Castro regime, only 90 miles from United States soil. When it became known that Soviet offensive missiles were being installed in Cuba in 1962, the President ordered a naval "quarantine" of the island and moved troops into position to eliminate this threat to U. S. security. The world seemed on the brink of a nuclear war until Khrushchev ordered the removal of the missiles.

A sudden "thaw," or the appearance of one, in the cold war came with the agreement with the Soviet Union on a limited test-ban treaty signed in Moscow on Aug. 6, 1963.

In his domestic policies Kennedy's proposals for medical care for the aged, expanded area redevelopment, and aid to education were defeated, but on minimum wage, trade legislation, and other measures he won important victories.

Widespread racial disorders and demonstrations led to Kennedy's proposing sweeping civil rights legislation. As his third year in office drew to a close, he also recommended an $11-billion tax cut to bolster the economy. Both measures were pending in Congress when Kennedy, looking forward to a second term, journeyed to Texas for a series of speeches.

While riding in a procession in Dallas on Nov. 22, 1963, he was shot to death by an assassin firing from an upper floor of a building. The alleged assassin, Lee Harvey Oswald, was killed two days later in the Dallas city jail by Jack Ruby, owner of a strip-tease place.

At 46 years of age, Kennedy became the fourth President to be assassinated and the eighth to die in office.

LYNDON BAINES JOHNSON was born in Stonewall, Tex., on Aug. 27, 1908. On both sides of his family he had a political heritage mingled with a Baptist background of preachers and teachers. Both his father and his paternal grandfather served in the Texas House of Representatives.

After having been graduated from Southwest Texas State Teachers College, Johnson taught school for two years. He went to Washington in 1932 as secretary to Rep. Richard M. Kleberg. During this time he married Claudia Alta Taylor, known as "Lady Bird." They had two children: Lynda Bird (Robb) and Luci Baines (Nugent).

In 1935, Johnson became Texas administrator for the National Youth Administration. Two years later he was elected to Congress as an all-out supporter of Franklin D. Roosevelt. He was the first member of Congress to enlist in the armed forces after the attack on Pearl Harbor. He served in the Navy in the Pacific and won a Silver Star.

Johnson lost his first bid for a Senate seat in 1941, but won in 1948 after he had captured the Democratic nomination by only 87 votes. He was 40 years old. He became the Senate Democratic leader in 1953. A heart attack in 1955 threatened the end of his active political career, but he recovered fully and resumed his duties.

At the height of his power as Senate leader, Johnson sought the Democratic nomination for President in 1960. When he lost to John F. Kennedy he surprised even some of his closest associates by accepting second place on the ticket.

Johnson was riding in another car in the motorcade when Kennedy was assassinated in Dallas on Nov. 22, 1963. He took the oath of office in the presidential jet on the Dallas airfield.

With Johnson's insistent backing, Congress finally adopted a far-reaching civil rights bill, a voting rights bill, a Medicare program for the aged, and measures to improve education and conservation. Congress also began what Johnson described as "an all-out war" on poverty.

Reaching a record-breaking majority of nearly 16 million votes, Johnson was elected President in his own right in 1964. His electoral vote was 486 to 52 for his Republican opponent, Barry M. Goldwater.

The double tragedy of a war in Asia and urban riots at home marked Johnson's last two years in office. Faced with disunity in the nation and challenges within his own party, Johnson surprised the country on Mar. 31, 1968, with the announcement that he would not be a candidate for re-election. He died of a heart attack on Jan. 22, 1973.

RICHARD MILHOUS NIXON was born in Yorba Linda, Calif., on Jan. 9, 1913, to Midwestern-bred parents, Francis A. and Hannah Milhous Nixon, who raised their five sons as Quakers.

Nixon was a high school debater and was undergraduate president at Whittier College in California, where he was graduated in 1934. As a scholarship student at Duke University Law School in North Carolina, he graduated third in his class in 1937.

After five years as a lawyer, Nixon joined the Navy in August 1942. He was an air transport officer in the South Pacific and a legal officer stateside before his discharge in 1946 as a lieutenant commander.

Running for Congress as a Republican in 1946, Nixon defeated Rep. Jerry Voorhis (D-Calif.). On the House Un-American Activities Committee, he made a name as an investigator of Alger Hiss, who was later jailed for perjury. In 1950 Nixon defeated Rep. Helen Gahagan Douglas, a Democrat, for a vacant California Senate seat. He was criticized for portraying her as a Communist dupe.

Nixon's anti-Communism, his Western base and his youth figured in his selection in 1952 to run for vice president on the ticket headed by Dwight D. Eisenhower. Demands for Nixon's withdrawal followed disclosure that California businessmen had paid some of his Senate office expenses. He televised rebuttal, known as "the Checkers speech" (named for a cocker spaniel given to the Nixons), brought him support from the public and from Eisenhower. The ticket won easily in 1952 and again in 1956.

Eisenhower gave Nixon substantive assignments, including missions to 56 foreign countries. In Moscow in 1959,

Nixon won acclaim for his defense of U.S. interests in an impromptu "kitchen debate" with Soviet Premier Nikita S. Khrushchev.

Nixon won the 1960 GOP Presidential nomination, but lost the election to Democratic Senator John F. Kennedy by 118,574 votes out of 68,838,219. The electoral vote was 303 to 219.

In 1962 Nixon failed in a bid for California's governorship and seemed to be finished as a national candidate. He became a Wall Street lawyer, but kept his old party ties and developed new ones through constant travels to speak for Republicans.

Nixon won the 1968 GOP presidential nomination after a shrewd primary campaign, then made Maryland Governor Spiro T. Agnew his surprise choice for vice president. In the election, they edged out the Democratic ticket headed by Vice President Hubert H. Humphrey by 510,-314 votes out of 73,212,065. The electoral vote was 301 to 191.

Committed to wind down the U.S. role in the Vietnam war, Nixon pursued "Vietnamization"—training and equipping South Vietnamese to do their own fighting. American ground combat forces in Vietnam fell steadily from 540,000 when Nixon took office to none in 1973 when the military draft was ended. But there was heavy continuing use of U.S. air power.

Nixon improved relations with Moscow and reopened the long-closed door to mainland China with a good-will trip there in February 1972. In May of that year, he visited Moscow and signed agreements on arms limitation and trade expansion and approved plans for a joint U.S.-Soviet space mission in 1975.

Inflation was a campaign issue for Nixon, but he failed to master it as President. On Aug. 15, 1971, with unemployment edging up, Nixon abruptly announced a new economic policy: A 90-day wage-price freeze, stimulative tax cuts, a temporary 10% tariff, spending cuts. A second phase, imposing guidelines on wage, price and rent boosts, was announced October 7.

The economy responded in time for the 1972 campaign, in which Nixon played up his foreign-policy achievements. Played down was the burglary on June 17, 1972, of Democratic national headquarters in the Washington, D.C., Watergate apartment complex. The Nixon-Agnew re-election campaign cost a record $60 million and swamped the Democratic ticket headed by Sen. George S. McGovern of South Dakota with a plurality of 17,999,528 out of 77,718,554 votes. Only Massachusetts, with 14 electoral votes, and the District of Columbia, with 3, went for McGovern.

In January 1973 hints of a cover-up emerged at the trial of six men found guilty of the Watergate burglary. With a Senate investigation under way, Nixon announced on April 30 the resignations of his top aides, H. R. Haldeman and John D. Ehrlichman, and the dismissal of White House counsel John Dean III. Dean was the star witness at televised Senate hearings that exposed both a White House cover-up of Watergate and massive illegalities in GOP fund-raising in 1972.

The hearings also disclosed that Nixon had routinely tape-recorded his office meetings and telephone conversations.

On Oct. 10, 1973, Agnew resigned as vice president, then pleaded no-contest to a negotiated federal charge of evading income taxes on alleged bribes. Two days later Nixon nominated the House minority leader, Rep. Gerald R. Ford of Michigan, as the new vice president. Congress confirmed Ford Dec. 6, 1973.

In June 1974 Nixon visited Israel and four Arab nations. In July he met in Moscow with Soviet leader Leonid I. Brezhnev and reached preliminary nuclear arms limitation agreements.

But, in the month after his return, Watergate ended the Nixon regime. On July 24 the Supreme Court ordered Nixon to surrender subpoenaed tapes. On July 30 the Judiciary Committee referred three impeachment articles to the House. On August 5, Nixon bowed to the Supreme Court and released tapes showing he halted an FBI probe of the Watergate burglary six days after it occurred. It was in effect an admission of obstruction of justice, and impeachment appeared inevitable.

Nixon resigned Aug. 9, 1974, the first President ever to do so. A month later, President Ford issued an unconditional pardon for any offenses Nixon might have committed as President, thus forestalling possible prosecution.

In 1940, Nixon married Thelma Catherine (Pat) Ryan. They had two daughters, Patricia (Tricia) Cox and Julie, who married Dwight David Eisenhower II, grandson of the former President.

GERALD RUDOLPH FORD was born in Omaha, Neb., on July 14, 1913, the only child of Leslie and Dorothy Gardner King. His parents were divorced in 1915. His mother moved to Grand Rapids, Mich., and married Gerald R. Ford. The boy was renamed for his stepfather.

Ford captained his high school football team in Grand Rapids and a football scholarship took him to the University of Michigan, where he starred as varsity center before his graduation in 1935. A job as assistant football coach at Yale gave him an opportunity to attend Yale Law School, where he graduated in the top third of his class in 1941.

He returned to Grand Rapids to practice law, but entered the Navy in April 1942. He saw wartime service in the Pacific on the light aircraft carrier *Monterey* and was a lieutenant commander when he returned to Grand Rapids early in 1946 to resume law practice and dabble in politics.

Ford got to Congress in 1948 by scoring a primary victory over Republican Rep. Bartel J. Jonkman, a conservative isolationist, and then winning the first of 13 elections to the House. He was soon assigned to the influential Appropriations Committee and rose to become the ranking Republican on the subcommittee on Defense Department appropriations and an expert in the field.

As a legislator, Ford described himself as "a moderate on domestic issues, a conservative in fiscal affairs, and a dyed-in-the-wool internationalist." He carried the ball for Pentagon appropriations, was a hawk on Vietnam, and kept a low profile on civil rights issues.

He was also dependable and hard-working and popular with his colleagues. In 1963 he was elected chairman of the House Republican Conference. He served in 1963–64 as a member of the Warren Commission that investigated the assassination of President John F. Kennedy. A revolt by dissatisfied younger Republicans in 1965 made him minority leader.

Ford shelved his hopes for the Speakership on Oct. 12, 1973, when Nixon nominated him to fill the vice presidency left vacant by Agnew's resignation under fire. It was the first use of the procedures for filling vacancies in the vice presidency laid down in the 25th Amendment to the Constitution, which Ford had helped enact.

Congress confirmed Ford as vice president on Dec. 6, 1973. Once in office, he said in speeches he did not believe

Nixon was involved in the Watergate scandals, but criticized the President's stubborn court battle against releasing tape recordings of Watergate-related conversations for use as evidence.

The scandals led to Nixon's unprecedented resignation and Ford was sworn in immediately as the 38th President, the first to enter the White House without winning a national election.

Ford assured the nation when he took office that "our long national nightmare is over" and pledged "openness and candor" in all his actions. He won a warm response from the Democratic 93rd Congress when he said he wanted "a good marriage" rather than a honeymoon with his former colleagues. In December 1974 Congressional majorities backed his choice of former New York Governor Nelson A. Rockefeller as his successor in the again-vacant vice presidency.

The cordiality was chilled by Ford's announcement on Sept. 8, 1974, that he had granted an unconditional pardon to Nixon for any crimes he might have committed as President. Although no formal charges were pending, Ford said he feared "ugly passions" would be aroused if Nixon were brought to trial. The pardon was widely criticized.

To fight inflation, the new President first proposed fiscal restraints and spending curbs and a 5% tax surcharge that got nowhere in Congress. But rising unemployment led him early in 1975 to propose a broad tax-reduction program and energy-conservation measures that were expected to produce a record peacetime budget deficit of at least $60 billion in fiscal year 1976. Congress was slow to respond.

Congress rebuffed Ford in the spring of 1975 when he appealed for emergency military aid to help the governments of South Vietnam and Cambodia resist massive Communist offensives.

In November 1974 Ford visited Japan, South Korea, and the Soviet Union, where he and Soviet leader Leonid I. Brezhnev conferred in Vladivostok and reached a tentative agreement to limit the number of strategic offensive nuclear weapons. It was Ford's first meeting as President with Brezhnev, who planned a return visit to Washington in the fall of 1975.

Politically, Ford's fortunes improved steadily in the first half of 1975. Badly divided Democrats in Congress were unable to muster votes to override his vetoes of spending bills that exceeded his budget. He faced some right-wing opposition in his own party, but moved to pre-empt it with an early announcement—on July 8, 1975—of his intention to be a candidate in 1976.

Early state primaries in 1976 suggested an easy victory for Ford despite Ronald Reagan's bitter attacks on administration foreign policy and defense programs. But later Reagan primary successes threatened the President's lead. At the Kansas City convention in August, Ford was nominated by the narrow margin of 1,187 to 1,070. But Reagan had moved the party to the right and Ford himself was regarded as a caretaker President lacking in strength and vision. He was defeated in the November election by Jimmy Carter.

JAMES EARL CARTER, JR. was born in the village of Plains, Ga., Oct. 1, 1924, and grew up on the family farm at nearby Archery. Both parents were fifth-generation Georgians. His father, James Earl Carter, who died in 1953, was known as a segregationist, yet treated his black and white farm workers equally and was known for his lenient credit policies to the black families who made up most of the customers of his store in Archery. His mother, Lillian Gordy, was a matriarchal presence in the family and community and opposed the then-prevailing code of racial inequality.

In 1942 Carter was graduated from the U.S. Naval Academy at Annapolis and entered the nuclear-submarine program, working for Adm. Hyman G. Rickover. In 1946 he married Rosalynn Smith, daughter of a neighboring family.

In 1954, after his father's death, Carter resigned from the Navy to take over the family business, which became one of the most flourishing agricultural enterprises in Georgia.

Carter's political career began in earnest with his election to the Georgia Senate in 1962. In 1966 he ran for governor and was defeated. In 1970 he ran again, successfully. During his term as governor, state government reorganization sharply reduced the number of state agencies. New social programs, judicial reform, and law-enforcement and highway programs were introduced, with no general tax increase.

In 1972, Carter decided to run for President. In 1974 he became chairman of the Democratic Campaign Committee, working to support congressional and gubernatorial candidates while building a base for himself. He crisscrossed the fifty states, tirelessly calling for revival and reform and gradually building support.

Throughout, he explained his position in a soft Southern drawl and faced down with his electric-blue stare the skeptics who mocked his campaign with gibes about "Jimmy who?" Even while phrasing his positions in a way to win most support with least offense, he pressed them with single-minded fervor. In July 1976 his mother said, "Jimmy always had big ideas. But they were never bigger than his willingness to work for them and make them happen."

Carter is a Southern Baptist, a "born again" Christian in a conservative and evangelical church. Despite the major influence of religion in his life, he has repeatedly stressed his commitment to separation of church and state. He is a serious reader of such innovative theologians as Niebuhr and Kierkegaard.

One campaign problem was Carter's image as the typical Southern white. This was erased when in 1975 he won the support of most of the old Southern civil rights coalition after endorsement by Rep. Andrew Young, a Black Democrat from Atlanta, who was a close aide to the late Dr. Martin Luther King, Jr. At his 1971 inauguration as governor, Carter demanded an end to all racial discrimination and later hung a portrait of Dr. King in the state capitol.

In the spring of 1976 Carter won 19 of the 31 primaries with a broad appeal to conservatives and liberals, black and white, poor and well-to-do.

After a closely fought primary campaign, Carter was nominated at the 3,000-delegate 37th Democratic National Convention at New York's Madison Square Garden, chosen on the first roll-call vote after the convention adopted a platform bearing his imprint. His choice of Sen. Walter F. Mondale of Minnesota as his vice president was endorsed enthusiastically by the convention.

Public-opinion polls reflected a gradual drop in Carter's popularity to the point that the election outcome was viewed as a toss-up. However, Carter won the Bicentennial year election with a bare electoral majority, 297 to 241, and a popular plurality of 1,743,866.

Assassinations and Attempts in U. S. Since 1865

Cermak, Anton J. (Mayor of Chicago): Shot Feb. 15, 1933, in Miami by Giuseppe Zangara, who attempted to assassinate Franklin D. Roosevelt; Cermak died March 6.

Ford, Gerald R. (President of U.S.): Escaped assassination attempt Sept. 5, 1975, in Sacramento, Calif., by Lynette Alice (Squeaky) Fromm, who pointed but did not fire .45-caliber pistol.

Ford, Gerald R. (President of U.S.): Escaped assassination attempt in San Francisco, Calif., Sept. 22, 1975, by Sara Jane Moore, who fired one shot from a .38-caliber pistol that was deflected.

Garfield, James A. (President of U.S.): Shot July 2, 1881, in Washington, D.C., by Charles J. Guiteau; died Sept. 19.

Kennedy, John F. (President of U.S.): Shot Nov. 22, 1963, in Dallas, Tex., allegedly by Lee Harvey Oswald; died same day. Injured was Gov. John B. Connally of Texas. Oswald was shot and killed two days later by Jack Ruby.

Kennedy, Robert F. (U.S. Senator from New York): Shot June 5, 1968, in Los Angeles by Sirhan Bishara Sirhan; died June 6.

King, Martin Luther, Jr. (civil rights leader): Shot April 4, 1968, in Memphis by James Earl Ray; died same day.

Lincoln, Abraham (President of U.S.): Shot April 14, 1865, in Washington, D.C., by John Wilkes Booth; died April 15.

Long, Huey P. (U.S. Senator from Louisiana): Shot Sept. 8, 1935, in Baton Rouge by Dr. Carl A. Weiss; died Sept. 10.

McKinley, William (President of U.S.): Shot Sept. 6, 1901, in Buffalo by Leon Czolgosz; died Sept. 14.

Roosevelt, Franklin D. (President-elect of U.S.): Escaped assassination unhurt Feb. 15, 1933, in Miami. *See* Cermak.

Roosevelt, Theodore (ex-President of U.S.): Escaped assassination (though shot) Oct. 14, 1912, in Milwaukee while campaigning for President.

Seward, William H. (Secretary of State): Escaped assassination (though injured) April 14, 1865, in Washington, D.C., by Lewis Powell (or Paine), accomplice of John Wilkes Booth.

Truman, Harry S. (President of U.S.): Escaped assassination unhurt Nov. 1, 1950, in Washington, D.C., as 2 Puerto Rican nationalists attempted to shoot their way into Blair House.

Wallace, George C. (Governor of Alabama): Shot and critically wounded in assassination attempt May 15, 1972, at Laurel, Md., by Arthur Herman Bremer.

Order of Presidential Succession

1. The Vice President
2. Speaker of the House
3. President pro tempore of the Senate
4. Secretary of State
5. Secretary of the Treasury
6. Secretary of Defense
7. Attorney General
8. Secretary of the Interior
9. Secretary of Agriculture
10. Secretary of Commerce
11. Secretary of Labor
12. Secretary of Health, Education, and Welfare
13. Secretary of Housing and Urban Development
14. Secretary of Transportation
15. Secretary of Energy

NOTE: An official cannot succeed to the Presidency unless he meets the Constitutional requirements.

Facts About Elections

Candidate with highest popular vote: Nixon (1972), 47,169,-911.

Candidate with highest electoral vote: F. D. Roosevelt (1936), 523.

Candidate carrying most states: Nixon (1972), 49.

Candidate running most times: Norman Thomas, 6 (1928, 1932, 1936, 1940, 1944, 1948).

Candidate elected, defeated, then reelected: Cleveland (1884, 1888, 1892).

Unusual Voting Results
Election of 1872

The presidential and vice-presidential candidates of the Liberal Republicans and the northern Democrats in 1872 were Horace Greeley and B. Gratz Brown. Greeley died Nov. 29, 1872, before his 66 electors voted. In the electoral balloting for President, 63 of Greeley's votes were scattered among four other men, including Brown.

Election of 1876

In the election of 1876 Samuel J. Tilden, the Democratic candidate, received a popular majority but lacked one undisputed electoral vote to carry a clear majority of the electoral college. The crux of the problem was in the 22 electoral votes which were in dispute because Florida, Louisiana, South Carolina, and Oregon each sent in two sets of election returns. In the three southern states, Republican election boards threw out enough Democratic votes to certify the Republican candidate, Hayes. In Oregon, the Democratic governor disqualified a Republican elector, replacing him with a Democrat. Since the Senate was Republican and the House of Representatives Democratic, it seemed useless to refer the disputed returns to the two houses for solution. Instead Congress appointed an Electoral Commission with five representatives each from the Senate, the House, and the Supreme Court. All but one Justice was named, giving the Commission seven Republican and seven Democratic members. The naming of the fifth Justice was left to the other four. He was a Republican who first favored Tilden but, under pressure from his party, switched to Hayes, ensuring his election by the Commission voting 8 to 7 on party lines.

Minority Presidents

Fifteen candidates have become President of the United States with a popular vote less than 50% of the total cast. It should be noted, however, that in elections before 1872, presidential electors were not chosen by popular vote in all states. Adams' election in 1824 was by the House of Representatives, which chose him over Jackson, who had a plurality of both electoral and popular votes, but not a majority in the electoral college.

Besides Jackson in 1824, only two other candidates receiving the largest popular vote have failed to gain a majority in the electoral college—Samuel J. Tilden (D) in 1876 and Grover Cleveland (D) in 1888.

The "minority" Presidents follow:

Year	President	Electoral Percent	Popular vote Percent
1824	John Q. Adams	31.8	29.8
1844	James K. Polk (D)	61.8	49.3
1848	Zachary Taylor (W)	56.2	47.3
1856	James Buchanan (D)	58.7	45.3
1860	Abraham Lincoln (R)	59.4	39.9
1876	Rutherford B. Hayes (R)	50.1	47.9
1880	James A. Garfield (R)	57.9	48.3
1884	Grover Cleveland (D)	54.6	48.8
1888	Benjamin Harrison (R)	58.1	47.8
1892	Grover Cleveland (D)	62.4	46.0
1912	Woodrow Wilson (D)	81.9	41.8
1916	Woodrow Wilson (D)	52.1	49.3
1948	Harry S. Truman (D)	57.1	49.5
1960	John F. Kennedy (D)	56.4	49.7
1968	Richard M. Nixon (R)	56.1	43.4

How a Bill Becomes a Law

When a Senator or a Representative introduces a bill, he sends it to the clerk of his house, who gives it a number and title. This is the *first reading,* and the bill is referred to the proper committee.

The committee may decide the bill is unwise or unnecessary and *table* it, thus killing it at once. Or it may decide the bill is worthwhile and hold hearings to listen to facts and opinions presented by experts and other interested persons. After members of the committee have debated the bill and perhaps offered amendments, a vote is taken; and if the vote is favorable, the bill is sent back to the floor of the house.

The clerk reads the bill sentence by sentence to the house, and this is known as the *second reading*. Members may then debate the bill and offer amendments. In the House of Representatives, the time for debate is limited by a *cloture rule*, but there is no such restriction in the Senate for cloture, where 60 votes are required. This makes possible a *filibuster*, in which one or more opponents hold the floor to defeat the bill.

The *third reading* is by title only, and the bill is put to a vote, which may be by voice or roll call, depending on the circumstances and parliamentary rules. Members who must be absent at the time but who wish to record their vote may be paired if each negative vote has a balancing affirmative one.

The bill then goes to the other house of Congress, where it may be defeated, or passed with or without amendments. If the bill is defeated, it dies. If it is passed with amendments, a joint Congressional committee must be appointed by both houses to iron out the differences.

After its final passage by both houses, the bill is sent to the President. If he approves, he signs it, and the bill becomes a law. However, if he disapproves, he *vetoes* the bill by refusing to sign it and sending it back to the house of origin with his reasons for the veto. The objections are read and debated, and a roll-call vote is taken. If the bill receives less than a two-thirds vote, it is defeated and goes no farther. But if it receives a two-thirds vote or greater, it is sent to the other house for a vote. If that house also passes it by a two-thirds vote, the President's veto is *overridden*, and the bill becomes a law.

Should the President desire neither to sign nor to veto the bill, he may retain it for ten days, Sundays excepted, after which time it automatically becomes a law without signature. However, if Congress has adjourned within those ten days, the bill is automatically killed, that process of indirect rejection being known as a *pocket veto*.

History of the Income Tax
in the United States

The nation had few taxes in its early history. From 1791 to 1802, the United States Government was supported by internal taxes on distilled spirits, carriages, refined sugar, tobacco and snuff, property sold at auction, corporate bonds, and slaves. The high cost of the War of 1812 brought about the nation's first sales taxes on gold, silverware, jewelry, and watches. In 1817, however, Congress did away with all internal taxes, relying on tariffs on imported goods to provide sufficient funds for running the Government.

In 1862, in order to support the Civil War effort, Congress enacted the nation's first income tax law. It was a forerunner of our modern income tax in that it was based on the principles of graduated, or progressive, taxation and of withholding income at the source. During the Civil War, a person earning from $600 to $10,000 per year paid tax at the rate of 3%. Those with incomes of more than $10,-000 paid taxes at a higher rate. Additional sales and excise taxes were added, and an "inheritance" tax also made its debut. In 1866, internal revenue collections reached their highest point in the nation's 90-year history—more than $310 million, an amount not reached again until 1911.

The Act of 1862 established the office of Commissioner of Internal Revenue. The Commissioner was given the power to assess, levy, and collect taxes, and the right to enforce the tax laws through seizure of property and income and through prosecution. His powers and authority remain very much the same today.

In 1868, Congress again focused its taxation efforts on tobacco and distilled spirits and eliminated the income tax in 1872. It had a short-lived revival in 1894 and 1895. In the latter year, the U.S. Supreme Court decided that the income tax was unconstitutional because it was not apportioned among the states in conformity with the Constitution.

By 1913, with the 16th Amendment to the Constitution, the income tax had become a permanent fixture of the U.S. tax system. The amendment gave Congress legal authority to tax income and resulted in a revenue law that taxed incomes of both individuals and corporations. In fiscal year

1918, annual internal revenue collections for the first time passed the billion-dollar mark, rising to $5.4 billion by 1920. With the advent of World War II, employment increased, as did tax collections—to $7.3 billion. The withholding tax on wages was introduced in 1943 and was instrumental in increasing the number of taxpayers to 60 million and tax collections to $43 billion by 1945.

Arlington National Cemetery

Arlington National Cemetery occupies 578 acres in Virginia on the Potomac River, directly opposite Washington. This land was part of the estate of John Parke Custis, Martha Washington's son, who built the mansion which later became the home of Robert E. Lee. In 1864, Arlington became a military cemetery. Over 170,000 persons, including many thousands of soldiers as well as hundreds of distinguished Americans, are buried there. Expansion of the cemetery began in fiscal year 1965, using a 180-acre tract of land directly east of the present site.

In 1921, an Unknown American Soldier of World War I was buried in a temporary crypt in the cemetery; the completed Tomb was opened to the public without ceremony in 1932. Two additional Unknowns, one from World War II and one from the Korean War, were buried May 30, 1958. The inscription carved on the side of the Tomb, formerly the Tomb of the Unknown Soldier and now called The Tomb of the Unknown, reads:

HERE RESTS IN
HONORED GLORY
AN AMERICAN
SOLDIER
KNOWN BUT TO GOD

The Statue of Liberty

The Statue of Liberty ("Liberty Enlightening the World") is a 225-ton, steel-reinforced copper female figure, 152 ft in height, facing the ocean from Liberty[1] Island in New York Harbor. The right hand holds aloft a torch, and the left hand carries a tablet upon which is inscribed: "July IV MDCCLXXVI."

The statue was designed by Frédéric Auguste Bartholdi of Alsace as a gift to the United States from the people of France to memorialize the alliance of the two countries in the American Revolution and their abiding friendship. The French people contributed the $250,000 cost.

The 150-foot pedestal was designed by Richard M. Hunt and built by Gen. Charles P. Stone, both Americans. It contains steel underpinnings designed by Alexander Eiffel of France to support the statue. The $270,000 cost was borne by popular subscription in this country. President Grover Cleveland accepted the statue for the United States on Oct. 28, 1886.

On Sept. 26, 1972, President Richard M. Nixon dedicated the American Museum of Immigration, housed in structural additions to the base of the statue. Some 200 exhibits memorialize the flow of immigrants into the United States, including as many as 5,000 a day on nearby Ellis Island.

On a tablet inside the pedestal is engraved the following sonnet, written by Emma Lazarus (1849–1887):

The New Colossus

Not like the brazen giant of Greek fame,
With conquering limbs astride from land to land;
Here at our sea-washed, sunset gates shall stand
A mighty woman with a torch, whose flame
Is the imprisoned lightning, and her name
Mother of Exiles. From her beacon-hand
Glows world-wide welcome; her mild eyes command
The air-bridged harbor that twin cities frame.
"Keep, ancient lands, your storied pomp!" cries she
With silent lips. "Give me your tired, your poor,
Your huddled masses yearning to breathe free,
The wretched refuse of your teeming shore.
Send these, the homeless, tempest-tost to me,
I lift my lamp beside the golden door!"

1. Called Bedloe's Island prior to 1956.

Washington Monument

Construction of this magnificent Washington, D.C., monument, which draws some two million visitors a year, took nearly a century of planning, building, and controversy. Provision for a large equestrian statue of George Washington was made in the original city plan, but the project was soon dropped. After Washington's death it was taken up again, and a number of false starts and changes of design were made. Finally, in 1848, work was begun on the monument that stands today. The design, by architect Robert Mills, then featured an ornate base. In 1854, however, political squabbling and a lack of money brought construction to a halt. Work was resumed in 1880, and the monument was completed in 1884 and opened to the public in 1888. The tapered shaft, faced with white marble and rising from walls 15 feet thick (4.6 m) at the base was modeled after the obelisks of ancient Egypt. The monument, one of the tallest masonry constructions in the world, stands just over 555 feet (169 m). Memorial stones from the 50 States, foreign countries, and organizations line the interior walls. The top, reached only by elevator, commands a panoramic view of the city.

U.S. Capitol

When the French architect and engineer Maj. Pierre L'Enfant first began to lay out the plans for a new Federal city (now Washington, D.C.), he noted that Jenkins' Hill, overlooking the area, seemed to be "a pedestal waiting for a monument." It was here that the U.S. Capitol would be built. The basic structure as we know it today evolved over a period of more than 150 years. In 1792 a competition was held for the design of a capitol building. Dr. William Thornton, a physician and amateur architect, submitted the winning plan, a simple, low-lying structure of classical proportions with a shallow dome. Later, internal modifications were made by Benjamin Henry Latrobe. After the building was burned by the British in 1814, Latrobe and architect Charles Bulfinch were responsible for its reconstruction. Finally, under Thomas Walter, who was Architect of the Capitol from 1851 to 1865, the House and Senate wings and the imposing cast iron dome topped with the Statue of Freedom were added, and the Capitol assumed the form we see today. It was in the old Senate chamber that Daniel Webster cried out, "Liberty and Union, now and forever, one and inseparable!" In Statuary Hall, which used to be the old House chamber, a small disk on the floor marks the spot where John Quincy Adams was fatally stricken after more than 50 years of service to his country. A whisper from one side of this room can be heard across the vast space of the hall. Visitors can see the original Supreme Court chamber a floor below the Rotunda.

In addition to its historical association, the Capitol Building is also a vast artistic treasure house. The works of such famous artists as Gilbert Stuart, Rembrandt Peale, and John Trumbull are displayed on the walls. The Great Rotunda, with its 180-foot- (54.9-m-) high dome, is decorated with a massive fresco by Constantino Brumidi, which extends some 300 feet (90 m) in circumference. Throughout the building are many paintings of events in U.S. history and sculptures of outstanding Americans. The Capitol itself is situated on a 68-acre (27.5-ha) park designed by the 19th-century landscape architect Frederick Law Olmsted. There are free guided tours of the Capitol, which include admission to the House and Senate galleries. Those who wish to visit the visitors' gallery in either wing without taking the tour may obtain passes from their Senators or Congressmen. Visitors may ride on the monorail subway that joins the House and Senate wings of the Capitol with the Congressional office buildings.

The Liberty Bell

The Liberty Bell was cast in England in 1752 for the Pennsylvania Statehouse (now named Independence Hall) in Philadelphia. It was recast in Philadelphia in 1753. It is inscribed with the words, "Proclaim liberty throughout all the land unto all the inhabitants thereof" (Lev. 25:10). The bell was rung on July 8, 1776, for the first public reading of the Declaration of Independence. Hidden in Allentown during the British occupation of Philadelphia, it was replaced in Independence Hall in 1778. The bell cracked on July 8, 1835, while tolling the death of Chief Justice John Marshall. In 1976 the Liberty Bell was moved to a special exhibition building near Independence Hall.

Rivers of the United States
(350 or more miles long)

Alabama (735 mi.; 1,183 km): From junction of Tallapoosa R. and Coosa R. in Alabama to Mobile R.

Altamaha-Ocmulgee (392 mi.; 631 km): From junction of Yellow R. and South R., Newton Co. in Georgia to Atlantic Ocean.

Apalachicola-Chattahoochee (524 mi.; 843 km): From Towns Co. in Georgia to Gulf of Mexico in Florida.

Arkansas (1,459 mi.; 2,348 km): From Lake Co. in Colorado to Mississippi R. in Arkansas.

Brazos (870 mi.; 1,400 km): From junction of Salt Fork and Double Mountain Fork in Texas to Gulf of Mexico.

Canadian (906 mi.; 1,458 km): From Las Animas Co. in Colorado to Arkansas R. in Oklahoma.

Cimarron (600 mi.; 966 km): From Colfax Co. in New Mexico to Arkansas R. in Oklahoma.

Clark Fork-Pend Oreille (505 mi.; 813 km): From Silver Bow Co. in Montana to Columbia R. in British Columbia.

Colorado (1,450 mi.; 2,333 km): From Rocky Mountain National Park in Colorado to Gulf of California in Mexico.

Colorado (840 mi.; 1,352 km): From Borden Co. in Texas to Matagorda Bay.

Columbia (1,243 mi.; 2,000 km): From Columbia Lake in British Columbia to Pacific Ocean (entering between Oregon and Washington).

Colville (350 mi.; 563 km): From Brooks Range in Alaska to Beaufort Sea.

Connecticut (407 mi.; 655 km): From Third Connecticut Lake in New Hampshire to Long Island Sound in Connecticut.

Cumberland (720 mi.; 1,159 km): From junction of Poor and Clover Forks in Harlan Co. in Kentucky to Ohio R.

Delaware (390 mi.; 628 km): From Schoharie County in New York to Liston Point, Delaware Bay.

Gila (630 mi.; 1,014 km): From Catron Co. in New Mexico to Colorado R. in Arizona.

Green (360 mi.; 579 km): From Lincoln Co. in Kentucky to Ohio R. in Kentucky.

Green (730 mi.; 1,175 km): From Sublette Co. in Wyoming to Colorado R. in Utah.

Humboldt (390 mi.; 628 km): From Wells, Nevada, to Humboldt Lake in Nevada.

Illinois (420 mi.; 676 km): From St. Joseph Co. in Indiana to Mississippi R. at Grafton in Illinois.

James (sometimes called *Dakota*) (710 mi.; 1,143 km): From Wells Co. in North Dakota to Missouri R. in South Dakota.

Kanawha-New (352 mi.; 566 km): From junction of North and South Forks of New R. in North Carolina to Ohio R.

Koyukuk (470 mi.; 756 km): From Brooks Range in Alaska to Yukon R.

Kuskokwim (680 mi.; 1,094 km): From Alaska Range in Alaska to Kuskokwim Bay.

Licking (350 mi.; 563 km): From Magoffin Co. in Kentucky to Ohio R. at Cincinnati in Ohio.

Little Missouri (560 mi.; 901 km): From Crook Co. in Wyoming to Missouri R. in North Dakota.

Milk (625 mi.; 1,006 km): From junction of forks in Alberta Province to Missouri R.

Mississippi (2,348 mi.; 3,779 km): From Lake Itasca in Minnesota to mouth of Southwest Pass.

Mississippi-Missouri-Red Rock (3,710 mi.; 5,971 km): From source of Red Rock R. in Montana to mouth of Southwest Pass in Louisiana.

Missouri (2,315 mi.; 3,726 km): From junction of Jefferson R., Gallatin R., and Madison R. in Montana to Mississippi R. near St. Louis.

Missouri-Red Rock (2,533 mi.; 4,076 km): From source of Red Rock R. in Montana to Mississippi R. near St. Louis.

Mobile-Alabama-Coosa (780 mi.; 1,255 km): From junction of Etowah R. and Oostanaula R. in Georgia to Mobile Bay.

Neosho (460 mi.; 740 km): From Morris Co. in Kansas to Arkansas R. in Oklahoma.

Niobrara (431 mi.; 694 km): From Niobrara Co. in Wyoming to Missouri R. in Nebraska.

Noatak (350 mi.; 563 km): From Brooks Range in Alaska to Kotzebue Sound.

North Canadian (760 mi.; 1,223 km): From Union Co. in New Mexico to Canadian R. in Oklahoma.

North Platte (618 mi.; 995 km): From Jackson Co. in Colorado to junction with So. Platte R. in Nebraska to form Platte R.

Ohio (981 mi.; 1,579 km): From junction of Allegheny R. and Monongahela R. at Pittsburgh to Mississippi R. between Illinois and Kentucky.

Ohio-Allegheny (1,306 mi.; 2,102 km): From Potter Co. in Pennsylvania to Mississippi R. at Cairo in Illinois.

Osage (500 mi.; 805 km): From east-central Kansas to Missouri R. near Jefferson City in Missouri.

Ouachita (605 mi.; 974 km): From Polk Co. in Arkansas to Red R. in Louisiana.

Pearl (411 mi.; 661 km): From Neshoba County in Mississippi to Gulf of Mexico (Mississippi-Louisiana).

Pecos (735 mi.; 1,183 km): From Mora Co. in New Mexico to Rio Grande in Texas.

Pee Dee-Yadkin (435 mi.; 700 km): From Watauga Co. in North Carolina to Winyah Bay in South Carolina.

Pend Oreille (490 mi.; 789 km): Near Butte in Montana to Columbia R. on Washington-Canada border.

Porcupine (460 mi.; 740 km): From Yukon Territory, Canada, to Yukon R. in Alaska.

Potomac (383 mi.; 616 km): From Garrett Co. in Maryland to Chesapeake Bay at Point Lookout in Maryland.

Powder (375 mi.; 603 km): From junction of forks in Johnson Co. in Wyoming to Yellowstone R. in Montana.

Red (1,270 mi.; 2,044 km): From junction of forks in Harmon Co. in Oklahoma to Mississippi R. in Louisiana.

Red (officially called *Red River of the North*) (545 mi.; 877 km): From junction of Otter Tail R. and Bois de Sioux R. in Minnesota to Lake Winnipeg in Manitoba.

Republican (445 mi.; 716 km): From junction of North Fork and Arikaree R. in Nebraska to junction with Smoky Hill R. in Kansas to form Kansas R.

Rio Grande (1,885 mi.; 3,034 km): From San Juan Co. in Colorado to Gulf of Mexico.

Roanoke (380 mi.; 612 km): From junction of forks in Montgomery Co. in Virginia to Albemarle Sound in North Carolina.

Sabine (380 mi.; 612 km): From junction of forks in Hunt Co. in Texas to Sabine Lake between Texas and Louisiana.

Sacramento (377 mi.; 607 km): From Siskiyou Co. in California to Suisun Bay.

Saint Francis (425 mi.; 684 km): From Iron Co. in Missouri to Mississippi R. in Arkansas.

Salmon (420 mi.; 676 km): From Custer Co. in Idaho to Snake R.

San Joaquin (350 mi.; 563 km): From junction of forks in Madera Co. in California to Suisun Bay.

San Juan (360 mi.; 579 km): From Archuleta Co. in Colorado to Colorado R. in Utah.

Santee-Wateree-Catawba (538 mi.; 866 km): From McDowell Co. in North Carolina to Atlantic Ocean in South Carolina.

Smoky Hill (540 mi.; 869 km): From Cheyenne Co. in Colorado to junction with Republican R. in Kansas to form Kansas R.

Snake (1,038 mi.; 1,670 km): From Ocean Plateau in Wyoming to Columbia R. in Washington.

South Platte (424 mi.; 682 km): From Park Co. in Colorado to junction with North Platte R. in Nebraska to form Platte R.

Susquehanna (444 mi.; 715 km): From Otsego Lake in New York to Chesapeake Bay in Maryland.

Tanana (620 mi.; 998 km): From Wrangell Mts. in Yukon Territory, Canada, to Yukon R. in Alaska.

Tennessee (652 mi.; 1,049 km): From junction of Holston R. and French Broad R. in Tennessee to Ohio R. in Kentucky.

Tennessee-French Broad (900 mi.; 1,448 km): From Bland Co. in Virginia to Ohio R. at Paducah in Kentucky.

Tombigbee (525 mi.; 845 km): From junction of forks in Itawamba Co. in Mississippi to Mobile R. in Alabama.

Trinity (360 mi.; 579 km): From junction of forks in Dallas Co. in Texas to Galveston Bay.

Wabash (529 mi.; 851 km): From Darke Co. in Ohio to Ohio R. between Illinois and Indiana.

Washita (500 mi.; 805 km): From Hemphill Co. in Texas to Red R. in Oklahoma.

White (720 mi.; 1,159 km): From Madison Co. in Arkansas to Mississippi R.

Wisconsin (430 mi.; 692 km): From Vilas Co. in Wisconsin to Mississippi R.

Yellowstone (671 mi.; 1,080 km): From Park Co. in Wyoming to Missouri R. in North Dakota.

Yukon (1,770 mi.; 2,848 km): From junction of Lewes R. and Pelly R. in Yukon Territory, Canada, to Bering Sea in Alaska.

U.S. Territorial Expansion

Accession	Date	Area[1]
United States	—	3,615,122
Territory in 1790	—	888,685
Louisiana Purchase	1803	827,192
Florida	1819	58,560
By treaty with Spain	1819	13,443
Texas	1845	390,143
Oregon	1846	285,580
Mexican Cession	1848	529,017
Gadsden Purchase	1853	29,640
Alaska	1867	586,412
Hawaii	1898	6,450
Other territory	—	12,944
Philippines	1898	115,600[2]
Puerto Rico	1899	3,435
Guam	1899	212
American Samoa	1900	76
Canal Zone	1904	553
Corn Islands[3]	1914	4
Virgin Islands of U.S.	1917	133
Trust Territory of Pacific Islands	1947	8,489
All other	—	42
Total, 1970	**—**	**3,628,066**

1. Total land and water area in square miles. 2. Became independent in 1946; area not included in total. 3. Leased from Nicaragua for 99 years in 1914, but returned April 25, 1971; area included in total. *Source:* Department of Commerce, Bureau of the Census.

Annual Salaries of Federal Officials

President of the U.S.	$200,000[1]
Vice President of the U.S.	75,000[2]
Cabinet members	66,000
Under secretaries of executive departments	52,500
Deputy Secretaries of State, Defense, Treasury	57,500
Deputy Attorney General	57,500
Under Secretary of Transportation	57,500
Secretaries of the Army, Navy, Air Force	57,500
Senators and Representatives	57,500
President Pro Tempore of Senate	65,000
Speaker of the House	75,000
Majority and Minority Leader of the Senate	65,000
Majority and Minority Leader of the House	65,000
Chief Justice of the United States	75,000
Associate Justices of the Supreme Court	72,000

1. Plus taxable $50,000 for expenses and a nontaxable sum (not to exceed $40,000 a year) for travel expenses. 2. Plus taxable $10,000 for expenses. NOTE: All salaries shown above are taxable.

Government Employment and Payrolls

Year and function	Employees (in thousands)				Monthly payrolls (in millions)			
	Total	Federal[1]	State	Local	Total	Federal[1]	State	Local
1940	4,474	1,128	3,346		$566	$177	$389	
1950	6,402	2,117	1,057	3,228	1,528	613	218	696
1960	8,808	2,421	1,527	4,860	3,333	1,118	524	1,691
1970	13,028	2,881	2,755	7,392	8,334	2,428	1,612	4,294
1977, total	15,406	2,848	3,467	9,091	15,198	3,918	3,200	8,079
National defense and international relations	989	989	(²)	(²)	1,327	1,327	(²)	(²)
Postal service	652	652	(²)	(²)	890	890	(²)	(²)
Education	6,515	22	1,483	5,010	5,782	29	1,237	4,516
Instructional employees	3,642	(²)	444	3,198	5,012	(²)	589	4,423
Highways	592	5	260	327	550	9	275	266
Health and hospitals	1,509	254	638	616	1,391	318	573	498
Police protection	684	56	70	558	785	89	88	607
Local fire protection	301	(²)	(²)	301	292	(²)	(²)	292
Sewerage and sanitation	223	(²)	(²)	223	199	(²)	(²)	199
Local parks and recreation	221	(²)	(²)	221	142	(²)	(²)	142
Natural resources	483	273	176	34	557	372	159	26
Financial administration	415	108	119	189	409	140	123	146
All other	2,822	489	721	1,612	2,874	744	745	1,387

1. Civilians only. 2. Not applicable. *Source:* Department of Commerce, Bureau of the Census.

Population of Cities over 50,000

Asterisk denotes more than one ZIP code for a city and refers to general delivery. To find the ZIP code for a particular address, consult the ZIP code directory available in every post office. NOTE: U = unincorporated area; T = town. For latest population figures of many cities, see listing for individual states in The United States section.

City and major ZIP code	1970 census	1970 rank	% change 1960–70
Abilene, Tex. (79604*)	89,653	181	—0.8
Akron, Ohio (44309*)	275,425	52	—5.1
Alameda, Calif. (94501)	70,968	260	11.1
Albany, Ga. (31706*)	72,263	249	29.9
Albany, N.Y. (12201*)	115,781	127	—10.8
Albuquerque, N.M. (87101*)	243,751	59	21.2
Alexandria, Va. (22313*)	110,927	134	21.9
Alhambra, Calif. (91802*)	62,125	310	13.4
Allentown, Pa. (18105*)	109,871	139	1.4
Altoona, Pa. (16603*)	63,115	305	—9.1
Amarillo, Tex. (79105*)	127,010	116	—7.9
Anaheim, Calif. (92803*)	166,408	82	59.7
Anderson, Ind. (46011*)	70,787	261	44.3
Ann Arbor, Mich. (48106*)	100,035	157	48.5
Appleton, Wis. (54911)	57,143	342	18.0
Arden, Calif. (U)	82,492	209	12.5
Arlington, Tex. (76010*)	90,032	180	101.0
Arlington, Va. (U) (22210*)	174,284	78	6.9
Arlington Heights, Ill. (60004*)	64,884	294	132.7
Asheville, N.C. (28801*)	57,681	336	—4.2
Atlanta, Ga. (30301*)	495,039	27	1.6
Augusta, Ga. (30903*)	59,864	344	—15.2
Aurora, Colo. (80010*)	74,974	237	54.5
Aurora, Ill. (60507*)	74,182	241	16.4
Austin, Tex. (78767*)	251,808	57	35.0
Bakersfield, Calif. (93302*)	69,515	268	22.3
Baltimore, Md. (21233*)	905,787	7	—3.5
Baton Rouge, La. (70821*)	165,921	83	8.9
Bayonne, N.J. (07002)	72,743	245	—2.0
Beaumont, Tex. (77704*)	117,548	125	—1.4
Bellevue, Wash. (98009*)	61,102	317	377.0
Bellflower, Calif. (90706)	51,454	380	12.1
Berkeley, Calif. (94701*)	114,091	128	2.5
Berwyn, Ill. (60402)	52,502	376	—3.2
Bethesda, Md. (U) (20014)	71,621	255	26.7
Bethlehem, Pa. (18015*)	72,686	247	—3.6
Billings, Mont. (59101*)	61,581	314	16.5
Binghamton, N.Y. (13902*)	64,123	297	—15.6
Birmingham, Ala. (35203*)	300,910	48	—11.7
Bloomington, Minn. (55420)	81,970	211	62.3
Boise, Idaho (83701*)	74,990	236	117.5
Boston, Mass. (02109*)	641,071	16	—8.1
Boulder, Colo. (80302*)	66,870	287	77.3
Bridgeport, Conn. (06601*)	156,542	88	—0.1
Bristol, Conn. (06010)	55,487	355	22.0

City and major ZIP code	1970 census	1970 rank	% change 1960–70
Brockton, Mass. (02403)	89,040	184	22.3
Brownsville, Tex. (78520*)	52,522	375	9.3
Buena Park, Calif. (90622*)	63,646	301	37.2
Buffalo, N.Y. (14240*)	462,768	28	−13.1
Burbank, Calif. (91505*)	88,871	185	−1.4
Cambridge, Mass. (02138*)	100,361	155	−6.8
Camden, N.J. (08101*)	102,551	150	−12.5
Canton, Ohio (44711*)	110,053	137	−3.1
Carson, Calif. (90745*)	71,150	259	89.6
Cedar Rapids, Iowa (52401*)	110,642	135	20.2
Champaign, Ill. (61820)	56,532	346	14.0
Charleston, S.C. (29401*)	66,945	284	1.5
Charleston, W. Va. (25301*)	71,505	257	−16.7
Charlotte, N.C. (28202*)	274,640	53	36.2
Chattanooga, Tenn. (37401*)	141,904	97	9.1
Chesapeake, Va. (23320*)	89,580	182	—
Chester, Pa. (19013*)	56,331	348	−11.5
Chicago, Ill. (60607*)	3,369,359	2	−5.1
Chicopee, Mass. (01021*)	66,676	288	8.3
Chula Vista, Calif. (92010*)	67,901	280	61.5
Cicero, Ill. (60650)	67,058	283	−3.0
Cincinnati, Ohio (45202*)	451,410	30	−10.1
Clearwater, Fla. (33515*)	52,074	379	50.3
Cleveland, Ohio (44101*)	750,879	10	−14.3
Cleveland Heights, Ohio (44118)	60,767	318	−1.7
Clifton, N.J. (07015*)	82,437	210	0.4
Colorado Springs, Colo. (80901*)	135,060	107	92.4
Columbia, Mo. (65201)	58,804	330	60.4
Columbia, S.C. (29201*)	113,542	129	16.5
Columbus, Ga. (31908*)	155,028	90	32.7
Columbus, Ohio (43215*)	540,025	21	14.6
Compton, Calif. (90220*)	78,611	223	9.5
Concord, Calif. (94520*)	85,164	205	136.5
Corpus Christi, Tex. (78408*)	204,525	62	22.0
Costa Mesa, Calif. (92626*)	72,660	248	93.5
Council Bluffs, Iowa (51501)	60,348	320	8.5
Covington, Ky. (41011*)	52,535	374	−13.0
Cranston, R.I. (02910)	74,287	240	11.3
Dallas, Tex. (75221*)	844,401	8	24.2
Daly City, Calif. (94015*)	66,922	285	49.4
Danbury, Conn. (06810)	50,781	384	121.5
Davenport, Iowa (52802*)	98,469	160	10.7
Dayton, Ohio (45401*)	242,917	60	−7.4
Dearborn, Mich. (48120*)	104,199	148	−7.0
Dearborn Heights, Mich. (48127)	80,069	215	—
Decatur, Ill. (62521*)	90,397	177	15.9
Denver, Colo (80201*)	514,678	25	4.2
Des Moines, Iowa (50318*)	201,404	64	−3.9
Des Plaines, Ill. (60018*)	57,239	341	64.1
Detroit, Mich. (48226*)	1,514,063	5	−9.4

City and major ZIP code	1970 census	1970 rank	% change 1960–70
Downey, Calif. (90241*)	88,445	187	7.2
Duluth, Minn. (55806*)	100,578	154	−5.9
Dundalk, Md. (U) (21222)	85,377	203	3.6
Durham, N.C. (27701*)	95,438	165	21.9
East Los Angeles, Calif. (U) (90022)	105,033	146	0.7
East Orange, N.J. (07019*)	75,471	234	−2.3
East St. Louis, Ill. (62201*)	69,996	266	−14.3
El Cajon, Calif. (92020*)	52,273	377	39.0
El Monte, Calif. (91734*)	69,852	267	430.7
El Paso, Tex. (79940*)	322,261	45	16.5
Elgin, Ill. (60120)	55,691	353	12.6
Elizabeth, N.J. (07207*)	112,654	131	4.6
Elyria, Ohio (44035*)	53,427	367	22.0
Erie, Pa. (16501*)	129,231	114	−6.7
Euclid, Ohio (44117)	71,552	256	13.6
Eugene, Ore. (97401*)	78,389	224	53.8
Evanston, Ill. (60204*)	79,808	216	0.7
Evansville, Ind. (47708*)	138,764	103	−2.0
Everett, Wash. (98201*)	53,622	365	33.0
Fall River, Mass. (02722*)	96,898	162	−3.0
Fargo, N.D. (58102)	53,365	368	14.4
Fayetteville, N.C. (28302*)	53,510	366	13.6
Flint, Mich. (48502*)	193,317	67	−1.8
Florissant, Mo. (63033*)	65,908	290	72.7
Fort Lauderdale, Fla. (33310*)	139,590	101	66.9
Fort Smith, Ark. (72901*)	62,802	308	18.5
Fort Wayne, Ind. (46802*)	178,021	74	10.0
Fort Worth, Tex. (76101*)	393,476	33	10.4
Framingham, Mass. (T) (01701)	64,048	299	43.8
Fremont, Calif. (94538*)	100,869	153	130.3
Fresno, Calif. (93706*)	165,655	84	23.6
Fullerton, Calif. (92631*)	85,987	199	53.1
Gadsden, Ala. (35901*)	53,928	362	−7.2
Gainesville, Fla. (32601*)	64,510	295	117.2
Galveston, Tex (77553*)	61,809	311	−8.0
Garden Grove, Calif. (92640*)	121,155	121	43.8
Garland, Tex. (75040*)	81,437	213	111.5
Gary, Ind. (46401*)	188,398	69	5.6
Glendale, Calif. (91209*)	132,664	111	11.1
Grand Prairie, Tex. (75051*)	50,904	382	67.5
Grand Rapids, Mich. (49501*)	197,649	65	11.5
Great Falls, Mont. (59401*)	60,091	321	8.8
Green Bay, Wis. (54305*)	87,809	191	39.6
Greensboro, N.C. (27420*)	144,076	96	20.5
Greenville, S.C. (29602*)	61,436	315	−7.2
Hamilton, Ohio (45012*)	67,865	281	−6.2
Hammond, Ind. (46320*)	107,983	143	−3.3
Hampton, Va. (23669*)	120,779	122	35.3
Harrisburg, Pa. (17105*)	68,061	277	−14.6

City and major ZIP code	1970 census	1970 rank	% change 1960–70
Hartford, Conn. (06101*)	158,017	87	−2.6
Hawthorne, Calif. (90250)	53,304	369	61.4
Hayward, Calif. (94544*)	93,058	169	28.0
Hialeah, Fla. (33010*)	102,452	151	52.9
High Point, N.C. (27260*)	63,259	304	4.2
Hollywood, Fla. (33022*)	106,873	144	203.3
Holyoke, Mass. (01040)	50,112	390	−4.9
Honolulu, Hawaii (96820*)	324,871	44	10.4
Houston, Tex. (77052*)	1,233,535	6	31.5
Huntington, W. Va. (25701*)	74,315	239	−11.1
Huntington Beach, Calif. (92647*)	115,960	126	909.0
Huntsville, Ala. (35804*)	139,282	102	90.9
Independence, Mo. (64050*)	111,630	132	79.2
Indianapolis, Ind. (46204*)	742,925	11	55.9
Inglewood, Calif. (90306*)	89,985	179	42.0
Irving, Tex. (75061*)	98,961	159	115.2
Jackson, Miss. (39205*)	162,380	86	12.4
Jacksonville, Fla. (32201*)	528,865	23	163.1
Jersey City, N.J. (07303*)	260,350	55	−5.7
Joliet, Ill. (60431*)	78,887	221	18.0
Kalamazoo, Mich. (49003*)	85,555	202	4.2
Kansas City, Kan. (66110*)	178,561	73	46.4
Kansas City, Mo. (64108*)	507,330	26	6.7
Kenosha, Wis. (53141*)	78,805	222	16.1
Kettering, Ohio (45429)	71,864	252	32.0
Knoxville, Tenn. (37901*)	174,587	77	56.1
La Crosse, Wis. (54601)	51,153	381	7.5
Lafayette, La. (70502*)	68,908	273	70.6
Lake Charles, La. (70601*)	77,998	228	23.0
Lakewood, Calif. (90714*)	82,973	208	23.6
Lakewood, Colo. (80215)	92,743	170	379.8
Lakewood, Ohio (44107)	70,173	264	6.1
Lancaster, Pa. (17604*)	57,690	335	−5.5
Lansing, Mich. (48924*)	131,403	113	21.8
Laredo, Tex. (78040*)	69,024	272	13.8
Las Vegas, Nev. (89114*)	125,787	118	95.3
Lawrence, Mass. (01842*)	66,915	286	−5.7
Lawton, Okla. (73501*)	74,470	238	20.7
Lexington, Ky. (40507*)	108,137	141	72.2
Lima, Ohio (45801*)	53,734	364	5.3
Lincoln, Neb. (68501*)	149,518	92	16.3
Lincoln Park, Mich. (48146)	52,984	372	−1.8
Little Rock, Ark. (72201*)	132,483	112	22.9
Livonia, Mich. (48150*)	110,109	136	65.1
Long Beach, Calif. (90801*)	358,879	40	4.3
Lorain, Ohio (44052*)	78,185	226	13.4
Los Angeles, Calif. (90055*)	2,811,801	3	13.4
Louisville, Ky. (40202*)	361,706	38	−7.4
Lowell, Mass. (01853*)	94,239	168	2.3
Lubbock, Tex. (79408*)	149,101	93	15.9
Lynchburg, Va. (24505*)	54,083	361	−1.3

City and major ZIP code	1970 census	1970 rank	% change 1960–70
Lynn, Mass. (01901*)	90,294	178	−4.4
Macon, Ga. (31201*)	122,423	120	75.5
Madison, Wis. (53714*)	171,809	80	35.6
Malden, Mass. (02148)	56,127	350	−2.7
Manchester, N.H. (03103*)	87,754	192	−0.6
Mansfield, Ohio (44901)	55,047	358	16.3
Medford, Mass. (02155)	64,397	296	−0.9
Memphis, Tenn. (38101*)	623,530	17	25.3
Meriden, Conn. (06450)	55,959	351	7.9
Mesa, Ariz. (85201*)	62,853	307	86.1
Mesquite, Tex. (75149*)	55,131	356	100.3
Metairie, La. (U) (70002*)	136,477	106	—
Miami, Fla. (33101*)	334,859	42	14.8
Miami Beach, Fla. (33139)	87,072	196	37.9
Midland, Tex. (79702*)	59,463	327	−5.0
Milford, Conn. (06460)	50,858	383	22.1
Milwaukee, Wis. (53201*)	717,372	12	−3.2
Minneapolis, Minn. (55440*)	434,400	32	−10.0
Mobile, Ala. (36601*)	190,026	68	−2.5
Modesto, Calif. (95350*)	61,712	312	68.7
Monroe, La. (71201*)	56,374	347	8.0
Monterey Park, Calif. (91754)	49,166	395	30.0
Montgomery, Ala. (36104*)	140,102	99	4.2
Mount Vernon, N.Y. (10551*)	72,778	244	−4.3
Mountain View, Calif. (94042*)	54,206	359	75.5
Muncie, Ind. (47302*)	69,082	271	0.7
Nashua, N.H. (03060)	55,820	352	42.8
Nashville, Tenn. (37202*)	447,877	31	162.1
New Bedford, Mass. (02741*)	101,777	152	−0.7
New Britain, Conn. (06050*)	83,441	207	1.5
New Haven, Conn. (06510*)	137,707	105	−9.4
New Orleans, La. (70140*)	593,471	19	−5.4
New Rochelle, N.Y. (10802*)	75,385	235	−1.9
New York, N.Y.	7,895,563	1	1.1
Bronx borough (10451*)	1,471,701	—	3.3
Brooklyn borough (11201*)	2,602,012	—	−1.0
Manhattan borough (10001*)	1,539,233	—	10.2
Queens borough[1]	1,987,174	—	9.1
Staten Island borough (10314)	295,443	—	33.1
Newark, N.J. (07101*)	381,930	35	−5.7
Newport News, Va. (23607*)	138,177	104	21.6
Newton, Mass. (02158)	91,263	176	−1.2
Niagara Falls, N.Y. (14302*)	85,615	201	−16.4
Norfolk, Va. (23501*)	307,951	47	1.0
Norman, Okla. (73070*)	52,117	378	56.0
North Little Rock, Ark. (72114*)	60,040	322	3.5
Norwalk, Calif. (90650)	91,827	173	3.5
Norwalk, Conn. (06856*)	79,113	217	16.7
Oak Park, Ill. (60303*)	62,511	309	2.3
Oakland, Calif. (94617*)	361,561	39	−1.6

City and major ZIP code	1970 census	1970 rank	% change 1960–70
Odessa, Tex. (79760*)	78,380	225	−2.4
Ogden, Utah (84401*)	69,478	269	−1.0
Oklahoma City, Okla. (73125*)	368,164	37	13.5
Omaha, Neb. (68108*)	354,389	41	17.5
Ontario, Calif. (91761*)	64,118	298	37.5
Orange, Calif. (92667*)	77,365	231	192.6
Orlando, Fla. (32802*)	99,006	158	12.3
Oshkosh, Wis. (54901)	53,221	370	18.0
Overland Park, Kan. (66204)	79,034	219	274.4
Owensboro, Ky. (42301)	50,329	387	18.5
Oxnard, Calif. (93030)	71,225	258	76.9
Palo Alto, Calif. (94302*)	56,181	349	7.4
Parma, Ohio (44129)	100,216	156	21.0
Pasadena, Calif. (91109*)	112,951	130	−2.9
Pasadena, Tex. (77501*)	89,277	183	52.0
Passaic, N.J. (07055*)	55,124	357	2.2
Paterson, N.J. (07510*)	144,824	95	0.8
Pawtucket, R.I. (02860*)	76,984	232	−5.0
Pensacola, Fla. (32502*)	59,507	326	4.9
Peoria, Ill. (61601*)	126,963	117	23.1
Philadelphia, Pa. (19104*)	1,949,996	4	−2.6
Phoenix, Ariz. (85026*)	587,213	20	33.7
Pico Rivera, Calif. (90660)	54,170	360	10.2
Pine Bluff, Ark. (71601*)	57,389	338	30.3
Pittsburgh, Pa. (15230*)	520,089	24	−13.9
Pittsfield, Mass. (01201)	57,020	343	−1.5
Pomona, Calif. (91766*)	87,384	195	30.1
Pontiac, Mich. (48056*)	85,279	204	3.7
Port Arthur, Tex. (77640)	57,371	340	−14.0
Portland, Me (04101*)	65,116	293	−10.3
Portland, Ore. (97208*)	379,967	36	1.9
Portsmouth, Va. (23705*)	110,963	133	−3.3
Providence, R.I. (02940*)	179,116	72	−13.6
Provo, Utah (84601)	53,131	371	47.4
Pueblo, Colo. (81002*)	97,774	160	7.2
Quincy, Mass. (02169)	87,966	190	0.6
Racine, Wis. (53401*)	95,162	167	6.8
Raleigh, N.C. (27611*)	123,793	119	31.7
Reading, Pa. (19603*)	87,643	194	−10.7
Redondo Beach, Calif. (90277*)	57,425	337	22.2
Redwood City, Calif. (94063*)	55,686	354	20.3
Reno, Nev. (89501*)	72,863	242	41.6
Richmond, Calif. (94802*)	79,043	218	10.0
Richmond, Va. (23232*)	249,431	58	13.4
Riverside, Calif. (92502*)	140,089	100	66.1
Roanoke, Va. (24001*)	92,115	171	−5.1
Rochester, Minn. (55901*)	53,766	363	32.2
Rochester, N.Y. (14603*)	295,011	49	−7.4
Rock Island, Ill. (61201)	50,166	388	−3.3
Rockford, Ill. (61125*)	147,370	94	16.3
Rome, N.Y. (13440)	50,148	389	−2.9

City and major ZIP code	1970 census	1970 rank	% change 1960-70
Roseville, Mich. (48066)	60,529	319	20.6
Royal Oak, Mich. (48067*)	86,238	198	7.0
Sacramento, Calif. (95814*)	257,105	56	34.1
Saginaw, Mich. (48605*)	91,849	172	−6.5
St. Clair Shores, Mich. (48083*)	88,093	189	14.9
St. Joseph, Mo. (64501*)	72,691	246	−8.8
St. Louis, Mo. (63166*)	622,236	18	−17.0
St. Paul, Minn. (55101*)	309,866	46	−1.1
St. Petersburg, Fla. (33733*)	216,159	61	19.3
Salem, Ore. (97301*)	68,856	274	40.1
Salinas, Calif. (93901*)	58,896	328	103.4
Salt Lake City, Utah (84101*)	175,885	76	−7.2
San Angelo, Tex. (76902*)	63,884	300	8.6
San Antonio, Tex. (78205*)	707,503	14	20.3
San Bernadino Calif. (92401*)	106,869	145	16.2
San Diego, Calif. (92101*)	697,027	15	21.6
San Francisco, Calif. (94101*)	715,674	13	−3.3
San Jose, Calif. (95113*)	459,913	29	124.7
San Leandro, Calif. (94577*)	68,698	275	4.1
San Mateo, Calif. (94402*)	78,991	220	13.1
Santa Ana, Calif. (92711*)	155,710	89	55.1
Santa Barbara, Calif. (93102*)	70,215	263	19.5
Santa Clara, Calif. (95050)	87,717	193	49.0
Santa Monica, Calif. (90406*)	88,289	188	6.1
Santa Rosa, Calif. (95402*)	50,006	391	61.2
Savannah, Ga. (31402*)	118,349	124	−20.7
Schenectady, N.Y. (12305*)	77,958	229	−4.6
Scottsdale, Ariz. (85251*)	67,823	282	576.5
Scranton, Pa. (18501*)	103,564	149	−7.1
Seattle, Wash. (98101*)	530,831	22	−4.7
Shreveport, La. (71101*)	182,064	70	10.8
Silver Spring, Md. (U) (20907*)	77,496	230	16.8
Simi Valley, Calif. (93065*)	59,832	325	—
Sioux City, Iowa (51101*)	85,925	200	−3.6
Sioux Falls, S.D. (57101*)	72,488	251	10.7
Skokie, Ill. (60076)	68,627	276	15.6
Somerville, Mass. (02143)	88,779	186	−6.2
South Bend, Ind. (46624*)	127,328	115	−3.8
South Gate, Calif. (90280)	56,909	344	5.7
Southfield, Mich. (48037*)	69,285	270	119.9
Spokane, Wash. (90210*)	170,516	81	−6.1
Springfield, Ill. (62708*)	91,753	174	10.2
Springfield, Mass. (01101*)	163,905	85	−6.1
Springfield, Mo. (65801*)	120,096	123	25.3
Springfield, Ohio (45501*)	81,941	212	−1.0
Stamford, Conn. (06904*)	108,798	140	17.3
Sterling Heights, Mich. (48077)	61,365	316	—
Stockton, Calif. (95208*)	109,963	138	27.4
Sunnyvale, Calif. (94088*)	95,976	164	81.4
Syracuse, N.Y. (13201*)	197,297	66	−8.7
Tacoma, Wash. (98402*)	154,407	91	4.3

City and major ZIP code	1970 census	1970 rank	% change 1960–70
Tallahassee, Fla. (32301*)	72,586	250	50.1
Tampa, Fla. (33602*)	277,714	50	1.0
Taylor, Mich. (48180)	70,020	265	—
Tempe, Ariz. (85282*)	63,550	302	155.3
Terre Haute, Ind. (47808*)	70,335	262	−3.1
Toledo, Ohio (43601*)	383,062	34	20.4
Topeka, Kan. (66601*)	132,952	110	11.2
Torrance, Calif. (90510*)	134,968	108	33.3
Towson, Md. (21204)	77,999	227	307.6
Trenton, N.J. (08608*)	104,786	147	−8.2
Troy, N.Y. (12180*)	62,918	306	−6.8
Tucson, Ariz. (85702*)	265,799	54	24.8
Tulsa, Okla. (74101*)	330,350	43	26.2
Tuscaloosa, Ala. (35401*)	65,773	291	3.8
Tyler, Tex. (75702*)	57,770	334	12.8
Union City, N.J. (07087)	58,537	332	12.2
Utica, N.Y. (13503*)	91,611	175	−8.8
Vallejo, Calif. (94590*)	71,710	253	17.8
Ventura, Calif. (93001*)	57,964	333	99.0
Virginia Beach, Va. (23458*)	172,106	78	1,000+
Waco, Tex. (76703*)	95,326	166	−2.5
Waltham, Mass. (02154)	61,582	313	11.1
Warren, Mich. (48089*)	179,260	71	100.9
Warren, Ohio (44482*)	63,494	303	6.4
Warwick, R.I. (02887*)	83,694	206	22.2
Washington, D.C. (20013*)	756,668	9	−1.0
Waterbury, Conn. (06720*)	108,033	142	0.8
Waterloo, Iowa (50701*)	75,533	233	5.3
Waukegan, Ill. (60085*)	65,269	292	17.1
Wauwatosa, Wis. (53213)	58,676	331	3.1
West Allis, Wis. (53214)	71,649	254	5.1
West Covina, Calif. (91793*)	68,034	278	34.3
West Hartford, Conn. (T) (06107)	68,031	279	9.1
West Haven, Conn. (06516)	52,851	373	—
West Palm Beach, Fla. (33401*)	57,375	339	2.1
Westland, Mich. (48185)	86,749	197	—
Westminster, Calif. (92683)	59,874	323	132.5
Wheaton, Md. (U) (20902)	66,247	289	21.3
White Plains, N.Y. (10602*)	50,346	385	−0.3
Whittier, Calif. (90605*)	72,863	243	116.4
Wichita, Kan. (67209*)	276,554	51	8.6
Wichita Falls, Tex. (76307*)	96,265	163	−5.3
Wilkes-Barre, Pa. (18703*)	58,856	329	−7.4
Wilmington, Del. (19899*)	80,386	214	−16.1
Winston-Salem, N.C. (27102*)	133,683	109	21.2
Worcester, Mass. (01613*)	176,572	75	−5.4
Wyoming, Mich. (49509)	56,560	345	23.4
Yonkers, N.Y. (10701*)	204,297	63	7.2
York, Pa. (17405*)	50,335	386	−7.6
Youngstown, Ohio (44501*)	140,909	98	−15.5

1. Queens has four major ZIP codes: 11690*—Far Rockaway; 11352*—Flushing; 11431*—Jamaica; 11101*—Long Island City. Source: Department of Commerce, Bureau of the Census.

Crime Rates for Population Groups and Selected Cities, 1976

(offenses known to the police per 100,000 population)

Group and city	Total all crimes[1]	Violent crime					Property crime			
		Total	Murder	Forcible rape	Robbery	Aggravated assault	Total	Burglary—breaking or entering	Larceny—theft	Motor vehicle theft
59 cities over 250,000	8,263	1,095	19.3	54.2	626	396	7,167	2,287	3,886	994
110 cities, 100,000 to 250,000	7,558	573	10.0	34.9	238	290	6,985	2,000	4,376	610
265 cities, 50,000 to 100,000	6,243	416	6.1	26.0	161	223	5,827	1,606	3,731	490
604 cities, 25,000 to 50,000	5,537	338	5.4	18.9	115	199	5,199	1,328	3,486	386
1,398 cities, 10,000 to 25,000	4,676	254	4.0	13.9	69	167	4,422	1,112	3,029	281
4,925 cities, under 10,000	3,988	216	3.6	11.1	38	163	3,772	929	2,644	199
Total, 7,361 cities	6,366	580	9.9	30.8	276	264	5,786	1,652	3,561	572
Suburbs, 4,022 agencies[2]	4,627	292	5.1	20.0	85	182	4,334	1,253	2,757	325
Rural areas, 1,677 agencies	2,215	174	7.5	13.3	21	133	2,041	826	1,103	112
Total, 9,512 agencies	5,525	488	9.1	27.9	213	238	5,038	1,502	3,064	472
Selected cities:										
New York	8,740	1,781	21.5	45.1	1,144	570	6,958	2,593	3,082	1,284
Chicago	6,829	978	26.0	37.6	561	353	5,852	1,233	3,583	1,036
Los Angeles	8,057	1,167	18.3	74.7	519	554	6,890	2,403	3,341	1,146
Philadelphia	4,018	684	17.6	39.9	406	220	3,334	1,046	1,578	710
Houston	7,196	545	21.7	46.7	374	102	6,651	2,052	3,781	819

Detroit	11,512	2,226	49.7	92.2	1,590	494	9,286	3,347	3,847	2,093
Dallas	10,274	815	25.9	66.5	350	373	9,459	2,581	6,300	578
Baltimore	7,847	1,648	23.2	53.5	901	671	6,199	1,779	3,736	684
San Diego	8,092	532	7.6	30.1	294	201	7,559	2,049	4,706	804
San Antonio	8,172	436	15.8	34.9	168	218	7,736	2,759	4,484	493
Cleveland	8,274	1,323	36.7	78.0	849	359	6,951	2,047	2,940	1,964
Washington, D.C.	7,083	1,481	26.8	72.4	1,003	379	5,602	1,691	3,491	421
Indianapolis	7,877	838	13.7	70.0	478	276	7,040	2,093	4,135	811
San Francisco	11,622	1,618	19.7	93.1	997	508	10,004	3,307	5,165	1,532
Milwaukee	5,671	413	8.7	25.7	248	130	5,259	1,095	3,533	631

CRIME INDEX TRENDS
(percent change, 1976–77)

Cities over 1,000,000 (total population 18,132,000)	−6	−7	−3	+13	−11	−2	−6	−7	−6	−3
All cities over 25,000 (total population 97,154,000)	−5	0	+2	+11	−5	+4	−5	−3	−8	−1
Suburban areas (total population 70,469,000)	−4	+6	−1	+9	+3	+8	−5	−2	−7	+4
Rural areas (total population 25,525,000)	−1	+2	−3	+8	0	+2	−2	0	−4	+11
All areas (total population 196,695)	−4	+1	+1	+10	−4	+5	−5	−2	−7	0

1. Includes manslaughter by negligence, not shown separately. 2. Agencies also included in other city groups. NOTE: Population in 1976 as estimated by FBI. *Source:* Department of Justice, Federal Bureau of Investigation, *Uniform Crime Reports for the United States, 1976.*

Selected Characteristics of Families, 1977

(in thousands)

Characteristics	Number	Percent
TYPE OF RESIDENCE		
Metropolitan areas	37,955	66.9
Nonmetropolitan areas	18,755	33.1
Nonfarm	54,526	96.1
Farm	2,184	3.9
SIZE OF FAMILY		
2 persons	21,530	38.0
3 persons	12,472	22.0
4 persons	11,483	20.2
5 persons	6,209	10.9
6 persons	2,800	4.9
7 persons or more	2,216	3.9
Average number per family	—	3.37
RACE AND ORIGIN		
White	50,083	88.3
Black	5,804	10.2
Other	823	1.5
Spanish origin[1]	2,583	4.6
PRESENCE OF OWN CHILDREN		
None under 18 years	26,565	46.8
Average number per family	—	2.24
1 or more under 18 years	30,145	53.2
Average number per family	—	1.13
TYPE OF RESIDENT		
Homeowners	40,815	72.0
Renters of private housing	14,844	26.2
Renters of public housing	1,050	1.9
EDUCATION OF MEN AND WOMEN MAINTAINING FAMILIES		
Did not complete high school	19,687	34.7
High school graduate, no college	19,614	34.6
1 to 3 years of college	7,924	14.0
4 or more years of college	9,486	16.7
OCCUPATION OF MEN AND WOMEN MAINTAINING FAMILIES		
White collar	19,000	33.5
Blue collar	17,523	30.9
Service	3,486	6.1
Farm related	1,489	2.6
Armed Forces	808	1.4
Unemployed	2,188	3.9
Not in labor force	12,215	21.5
AGE OF FAMILY MEMBERS		
All members	190,844	100.0
Under 18 years	63,885	33.5
18 to 64 years	111,886	58.6
65 years and over	15,073	7.9
Total families	**56,710**	**100.0**

1. Persons of Spanish origin may be of any race. NOTE: There were 5,639,000 and 9,893,000 females living alone in 1977, an increase of 43.1% over 1970. *Source:* Department of Commerce, Bureau of the Census.

Population by Age, Sex, and Race, 1977
(in thousands)

Age	White Male	White Female	Black Male	Black Female	Other races Male	Other races Female	All persons Male	All persons Female
Under 5	6,424	6,111	1,172	1,144	194	190	7,790	7,446
Under 1	1,345	1,276	235	228	40	38	1,620	1,542
1-4	5,079	4,835	937	916	155	152	6,170	5,904
5-9	7,293	6,958	1,278	1,264	190	187	8,760	8,409
10-14	8,200	7,843	1,411	1,394	179	174	9,790	9,411
15-19	9,106	8,787	1,450	1,446	193	185	10,749	10,418
20-24	8,692	8,476	1,216	1,297	197	197	10,104	9,969
25-29	7,725	7,636	929	1,060	173	210	8,827	8,906
30-34	6,750	6,738	729	859	158	181	7,637	7,778
35-39	5,318	5,450	609	736	103	126	6,030	6,311
40-44	4,818	4,956	555	665	92	115	5,466	5,736
45-49	4,977	5,164	546	622	91	111	5,614	5,897
50-54	5,115	5,475	519	599	79	92	5,713	6,166
55-59	4,759	5,181	451	520	60	64	5,269	5,765
60-64	3,979	4,500	357	438	45	43	4,381	4,981
65-69	3,342	4,201	358	476	39	31	3,739	4,708
70-74	2,365	3,259	199	251	33	29	2,597	3,540
75-79	1,448	2,296	113	155	28	28	1,589	2,479
80-84	897	1,633	78	124	15	16	989	1,774
85 and over	583	1,292	60	119	12	13	655	1,424
All ages	91,791	95,957	12,030	13,169	1,878	1,993	105,699	111,119
14 and over	71,651	76,745	8,470	9,663	1,351	1,476	81,471	87,883
18 and over	64,436	69,833	7,279	8,490	1,201	1,332	72,916	79,655
21 and over	58,885	64,439	6,436	7,631	1,080	1,220	66,400	73,290
65 and over	8,635	12,681	808	1,125	126	118	9,569	13,925
Median age	29.0	31.6	22.9	25.2	24.7	26.5	28.2	30.6

NOTE: Figures represent resident population of the 50 states and Armed Forces overseas. *Source:* Department of Commerce, Bureau of the Census.

According to the Office of Management and Budget, the total hours spent by the American people filling out federal forms was 784,862,000 per year (as of March 1978). This is down from the 870,420,000 hours in the year ending the month after President Carter took office.

Live Births and Birth Rates

Year	Births[1]	Rate[2]	Year	Births[1]	Rate[2]
1910	2,777,000	30.1	1950	3,632,000	24.1
1915	2,965,000	29.5	1955	4,104,000	25.0
1920	2,950,000	27.7	1960[3]	4,257,850	23.7
1925	2,909,000	25.1	1965[3]	3,760,358	19.4
1930	2,618,000	21.3	1970	3,731,386	18.4
1935	2,377,000	18.7	1975	3,144,198	14.8
1940	2,559,000	19.4	1977[4]	3,313,000	15.3
1945	2,858,000	20.4			

1. Figures through 1959 include adjustment for underregistration; beginning 1960, figures represent number registered. For comparison, the 1959 registered count was 4,245,000. 2. Rates are per 1,000 population estimated as of July 1 for each year except 1940, 1950, 1960, and 1970, which are as of April 1, the census date; for 1941–46 based on population including armed forces overseas. 3. Based on 50% sample of births. 4. Provisional. NOTE: Alaska is included beginning 1959, Hawaii beginning 1960. Since 1972, based on 100% of births in selected states and on 50% sample in all other states. *Sources:* Department of Commerce, Bureau of the Census; and Department of Health, Education, and Welfare, Center for Health Statistics.

Marriages and Divorces

Year	Marriage Number	Marriage Rate[2]	Divorce[1] Number	Divorce Rate[2]
1900	709,000	9.3	55,751	.7
1910	948,166	10.3	83,045	.9
1920	1,274,476	12.0	170,505	1.6
1930	1,126,856	9.2	195,961	1.6
1940	1,595,879	12.1	264,000	2.0
1950	1,667,231	11.1	385,144	2.6
1960	1,523,000	8.5	393,000	2.2
1970	2,158,802	10.6	708,000	3.5
1977[3]	2,176,000	10.1	1,097,000	5.1

1. Includes annulments. 2. Per 1,000 population. 3. Provisional. NOTE: Marriage and divorce figures for most years include some estimated data. Alaska is included beginning 1959, Hawaii beginning 1960. *Source:* Department of Health, Education, and Welfare, National Center for Health Statistics.

Average of Annual Death Rates for Selected Causes

Cause of death	Death rates per 100,000				
	1977	1950	1940–44	1920–24	1900–04
Typhoid fever	0.0	0.1	0.6	7.3	26.7
Communicable diseases of childhood	0.0	1.3	4.6	33.8	65.2
Measles	0.0	0.3	1.1	7.3	10.0
Scarlet fever	0.0	0.2	0.4	4.0	11.8
Whooping cough	0.0	0.7	2.2	8.9	10.7
Diphtheria	0.0	0.3	1.0	13.7	32.7
Gastritis, duodenitis, enteritis, and colitis	0.7	5.1	9.8	42.8	115.3
Pneumonia and influenza	23.1	31.3	63.7	140.3	184.3
Influenza	0.5	4.4	13.0	34.8	22.8
Pneumonia	22.6	26.9	50.7	105.5	161.5
Tuberculosis	1.4	22.5	43.4	96.7	184.7
Cancer	178.4	139.8	123.1	86.9	67.7
Diabetes melitus	15.5	16.2	26.2	17.1	12.2
Major cardiovascular diseases	443.6	510.8	490.4	369.9	359.5
Diseases of the heart	331.6	356.8	303.2	169.8	153.0
Cerebral hemorrhage	n.a.	104.0	91.7	93.5	106.3
Chronic nephritis	3.8	16.4	72.1	81.5	84.3
Syphilis	0.1	5.0	12.7	17.6	12.9
Appendicitis	n.a.	2.0	7.2	14.0	9.4
Accidents, all forms	46.8	60.6	73.0	70.8	79.2
Motor vehicle accidents	22.3	23.1	22.7	12.9	n.a.
Infant mortality[1]	10.7	29.2	42.4	76.7	n.a.
Neonatal mortality[1]	n.a.	20.5	26.2	39.7	n.a.
Fetal mortality[1]	n.a.	22.9	28.5	39.2[2]	n.a.
Maternal mortality[1]	n.a.	0.8	2.8	6.9	n.a.
All causes	877.5	963.8	1,062.0	1,196.6	1,621.6

1. Rates per 1,000 live births. 2. 1922–24. NOTE: Includes only deaths occurring within the registration areas. Beginning with 1940, area includes the entire United States; beginning with 1960, Alaska and Hawaii were included. Rates per 100,000 population residing in areas, enumerated as of April 1 for 1940 and 1950 and estimated as of July 1 for all other years. Average rates computed from 5-year totals of deaths occurring in area and corresponding population. Due to changes in statistical methods, death rates are not strictly comparable. n.a. = not available. *Source:* Department of Health, Education, and Welfare, National Center for Health Statistics.

U.S. Societies and Associations

Names are listed alphabetically according to key word in title; figure in parentheses is year of founding; other figure is membership.

Abortion Federation, National (1976): 110 E. 59th St., New York, N.Y. 10022. Judith Widdicombe, President.

Aeronautic Association, National (1922): 821 15th St., N.W., Washington, D.C. 20005. 160,000; Vic Powell, Executive Director.

Aeronautics and Astronautics, American Institute of (1932): 1290 Avenue of the Americas, New York, N.Y. 10019. 26,750; James J. Harford, Executive Secretary.

African-American Institute, The (1953): 833 United Nations Plaza, New York, N.Y. 10017. M. Sandra Sennett, Assistant to the President.

Air Pollution Control Association (1907): P.O. Box 2861, Pittsburgh, Pa. 15230. 6,700; Lewis H. Rogers, Executive Vice President.

Alcoholics Anonymous (1935): P.O. Box 459, Grand Central Station, New York, N.Y. 10017. 1,000,000. Address communications to Secretary.

America-Mideast Educational and Training Services, Inc. (1951): 1717 Massachusetts Ave., N.W., Washington, D.C. 20036. 500; Virgil C. Crippin, President.

American Federation of Labor and Congress of Industrial Organizations (AFL-CIO) (1955): 815 16th St., N.W., Washington, D.C. 20006. 13,600,000; Albert J. Zack, Director of Public Relations.

American Friends Service Committee (1917): 1501 Cherry St., Philadelphia, Pa. 19102. Marjorie Seeley, Information Associate.

American Legion (1919): P.O. Box 1055, Indianapolis, Ind. 46206. 2,500,000; Frank C. Momsen, National Adjutant.

American Legion Auxiliary (1919): 777 N. Meridian St., Indianapolis, Ind. 46204. 940,000; Doris Anderson, National Secretary.

Americans for Democratic Action (1947): 1411 K St., N.W., Washington D.C. 20005. 75,000; Leon Shull, National Director.

Animals, American Society for the Prevention of Cruelty to (1866): 441 E. 92nd St., New York, N.Y. 10028. 3,000; Louis F. Bishop, Jr., Chairman.

Anti-Vivisection Society, The American (1883): 1903 Chestnut St., Philadelphia, Pa. 19103. 15,000; Owen B. Hunt, President.

Arbitration Association, American (1926): 140 W. 51st St., New York, N.Y. 10020. 4,310; E. W. Dippold, Corporate Secretary.

Arthritis Foundation (1948): 3400 Peachtree Rd., N.E., Atlanta, Ga. 30326. 73 local chapters; Clifford M. Clarke, President.

Arts and Letters, American Academy and Institute of (1904): 633 W. 155th St., New York, N.Y. 10032. 250; Margaret M. Mills, Executive Director.

Astronomical Society, American (1899): Leander-McCormick Observatory, Box 3818, University Station, Charlottesville, Va. 22903. 3,500; Laurence W. Fredrick, Secretary.

Athletic Union of the U.S., Amateur (1888): 3400 W. 86th St., Indianapolis, Ind. 46268. 372,000 registered athletes; Ollan Cassell, Executive Director.

Audubon Society, National (1905): 950 Third Ave., New York, N.Y. 10022. 365,000; Andrew Bihun, Environmental Information.

Authors League of America (1912): 234 W. 44th St., New York, N.Y. 10036. 7,500.

Automobile Association, American (1902): 8111 Gatehouse Rd., Falls Church, Va. 22042. 19,500,000; J. B. Creal, President.

Bible Society, American (1816): 1865 Broadway, New York, N.Y. 10023. 514,000; Charles W. Baas, John D. Erickson, General Officers.

Big Brothers/Big Sisters of America (1977): 220 Suburban Station Bldg., Philadelphia, Pa. 19103. Caroline Meline, Information Services Coordinator.

Blind, National Federation of the (1940): 212 Dupont Circle Bldg., 1346 Connecticut Ave., N.W., Washington, D.C. 20036. 50,000; Ralph Sanders, President.

Blindness, National Society for the Prevention of (1908): 79 Madison Ave., New York, N.Y. 10016. 327; Virginia Boyce, Executive Director.

Blue Shield Association (1946): 211 E. Chicago Ave., Chicago, Ill. 60611. 70 affiliates; Tom K. Mura, Vice President, Public Relations and Advertising.

B'nai B'rith (1843): 1640 Rhode Island Ave., N.W., Washington, D.C. 20036. 500,000; Hank Siegel, Director of Communications.

B'nai B'rith, Anti-Defamation League of (1913): 315 Lexington Ave., New York, N.Y. 10016.

Boy Scouts of America (1910): North Brunswick, N.J. 08902. 4,884,082.

Boys' Clubs of America (1906): 771 First Ave., New York, N.Y. 10017. 1,000,000; Joan R. Licursi, Director of Communications Services.

Brookings Institution, The (1927): 1775 Massachusetts Ave., N.W., Washington, D.C. 20036. James D. Farrell, Information Editor.

Camp Fire Girls, Inc. (1910): 4601 Madison Ave., Kansas City, Mo. 64112. 750,000; Dr. Hester Turner, National Executive Director.

Camping Association, The American (1910): Bradford Woods, Martinsville, Ind. 46151. 6,000; Armand Ball, Executive Vice President.

Cancer Society, American (1913): 777 Third Ave., New York, N.Y. 10017. 2,300,000; Lane W. Adams, Executive Vice President.

CARE (Cooperative for American Relief Everywhere) (1945): 660 First Ave., New York, N.Y. 10016. 24 agencies; Frank Goffio, Executive Director.

Catholic Bishops, National Conference of (1966): 1312 Massachusetts Ave., N.W., Washington, D.C. 20005. 340; Most Rev. John R. Quinn, President.

Catholic Charities, National Conference of (1910): 1346 Connecticut Ave., N.W., Washington, D.C. 20036. 3,000; Rev. Msgr. Lawrence Corcoran, Executive Director.

Catholic Conference, United States (1966): 1312 Massachusetts Ave., N.W., Washington, D.C. 20005. Bishop Thomas C. Kelly, O.P., General Secretary.

Catholic Daughters of America (1903): 10 W. 71st St., New York, N.Y. 10023. 180,000; Lorraine McMahon, Executive Secretary.

Catholic War Veterans of the U.S.A. (1935): 2 Massachusetts Ave., N.W., Washington, D.C. 20001. 75,000; Henry W. Woyach, National Commander.

Cerebral Palsy Associations, Inc., United (1949): 66 E. 34th St., New York, N.Y. 10016. 250 affiliates; Earl H. Cunerd, Executive Director.

Chamber of Commerce of the U.S. (1912): 1615 H St., N.W., Washington, D.C. 20006. 74,000; Richard L. Lesher, President.

Chemical Society, American (1876): 1155 16th St., N.W., Washington, D.C. 20036. 111,000; Raymond P. Mariella, Executive Director.

Child Study Association of America/Wel Met, Inc. (1900): 50 Madison Ave., New York, N.Y. 10010. Harriet Dronska, Executive Director.

Christians and Jews, National Conference of (1928): 43 W. 57th St., New York, N.Y. 10019. 200,000; David Hyatt, President.

Churches, National Council of (1950): 475 Riverside Drive, New York, N.Y. 10027. 31 Protestant and Orthodox communions; Claire Randall, General Secretary.

Civil Liberties Union, American (1920): 22 E. 40th St., New York, N.Y. 10016. 200,000; Alan Reitman, Associate Director.

Colored Women's Clubs, National Association of (1896): 5808 16th St., N.W., Washington, D.C. 20011. 50,000; Mrs. Inez W. Tinsley, National President.

Common Cause (1970): 2030 M St., N.W., Washington, D.C. 20036. 255,000; Nan Waterman, Chairwoman.

Composers, Authors, and Publishers, American Society of (ASCAP) (1914): One Lincoln Plaza, New York, N.Y. 10023. 23,400; Stanley Adams, President.

Congress of Racial Equality (CORE) (1942): 1916–38 Park Ave., New York, N.Y. 10035. Nationwide network of chapters; Roy Innis, National Director.

Conscientious Objectors, Central Committee for (1948): 2016 Walnut St., Philadelphia, Pa. 19103.

Contract Bridge League, American (1927): 2200 Democrat Rd., Memphis, Tenn. 38116. 200,000; Richard L. Goldberg, Executive Secretary.

Cooperative League of the U.S.A. (1916): 1828 L St., N.W., Washington, D.C. 20036. 30,000,000 families; Glenn M. Anderson, President.

Country Music Association (1958): 7 Music Circle North, Nashville, Tenn. 37203. 5,000; Jo Walker, Executive Director.

Crime and Delinquency, National Council on (1907): Continental Plaza, Hackensack, N.J. 07601. Nationwide membership; Milton G. Rector, President.

Daughters of the American Revolution, National Society (1890): 1776 D St., N.W., Washington, D.C. 20006. 206,000; Mrs. George Upham Baylies, President General.

Daughters of the Confederacy, United (1894): 328 N. Boulevard, Richmond, Va. 23220. 26,000; Mrs. Charlotte P. Crippen, Executive Secretary.

Democratic Club, National (1834): Chemists Club, 52 E. 41st St., New York, N.Y. 10017. 500; James Driscoll, Secretary.

Dental Association, American (1859): 211 E. Chicago Ave., Chicago, Ill. 60611. 131,066; C. Gordon Watson, Executive Director.

Diabetes Association, American (1940): 600 Fifth Ave., New York, N.Y. 10020. John L. Dugan, Jr., Executive Vice President.

Dignity (1969): 3719 Sixth Ave., San Diego, Calif. 92103. 6,000; Carla Kaesbauer, Acting President.

Disabled American Veterans (1922): P.O. Box 14301, Cincinnati, Ohio 45214. 550,000; Richard M. Wilson, Assistant Adjutant for Public Relations.

Eagles, Fraternal Order of (1898): 2401 W. Wisconsin Ave., Milwaukee, Wis. 53233. 850,000; Art Ehrmann, Publications Editor.

Easter Seal Society for Crippled Children and Adults, The National (1921): 2023 W. Ogden Ave., Chicago, Ill. 60612. 52 affiliated state societies; Donald W. Ullman, Acting Executive Director.

Eastern Star, Order of the, General Grand Chapter (1876): 1618 New Hampshire Ave., N.W., Washington, D.C. 20009. 3,000,000; Mabel L. Mackereth, Most Worthy Grand Matron.

Education Association, National (1857): 1201 16th St., N.W., Washington, D.C. 20036. 1,600,000; Terry Herndon, Executive Director.

Electrochemical Society, Inc., The (1902): P.O. Box 2071, Princeton, N.J. 08540. 4,476; V. H. Branneky, Executive Secretary.

Elks of the U.S.A., Benevolent and Protective Order of the (1868): 2750 Lake View Ave., Chicago, Ill. 60614. 1,630,000; Stanley F. Kocur, Grand Secretary.

English-Speaking Union of the United States (1920): 16 E. 69th St., New York, N.Y. 10021. 32,000; Charles P. Dennison, Executive Director.

Exploration Geophysicists, Society of (1930): P.O. Box 3098, Tulsa, Okla. 74101. 11,200; H. R. Breck, Executive Director.

Family Service Association of America (1911): 44 E. 23rd St., New York, N.Y. 10010. 290 member agencies; W. Keith Daugherty, General Director.

Farm Bureau Federation, American (1919): 225 Touhy Ave., Park Ridge, Ill. 60068. 2,800,000 member families; J. Patrick Batts, Director of Information.

Fleet Reserve Association (1924): 1303 New Hampshire Ave., N.W., Washington, D.C. 20036. 140,000; Robert W. Nolan, National Executive Secretary.

Foreign Policy Association (1918): 345 E. 46th St., New York, N.Y. 10017. Thetis Reavis, Director of Public Programs.

Foreign Relations, Inc., Council on (1921): 58 E. 68th St., New York, N.Y. 10021. 1,796; Winston Lord, President.

Foster Parents Plan International (1937): Box 400, Warwick, R.I. 02887. 103,000; George W. Ross, International Executive Director.

4-H Program (early 1900s): SEA-Extension, U.S. Department of Agriculture, Washington, D.C. 20250. 5,500,000; E. Dean Vaughan, Director.

Geographic Society, National (1888): 17th and M Sts., N.W., Washington, D.C. 20036. 10,000,000; Gilbert M. Grosvenor, Editor.

Geriatrics Society, American (1942): 10 Columbus Circle, New York, N.Y. 10019. 9,000; Kathryn S. Henderson, Executive Director.

Gideons International, The (1899): 2900 Lebanon Rd., Nashville, Tenn. 37214. 55,000; M.A. Henderson, Executive Director.

Girl Scouts of the U.S.A., Inc. (1912): 830 Third Ave., New York, N.Y. 10022. 3,140,000; Richard G. Knox, Director of Public Relations.

Girls Clubs of America (1945): 205 Lexington Ave., New York, N.Y. 10016. 215,000; Edith B. Phelps, National Executive Director.

Hadassah, The Women's Zionist Organization of America (1912): 50 W. 58th St., New York, N.Y. 10019. 360,000; Aline Kaplan, Executive Director.

Health, Physical Education and Recreation, American Alliance for (1885): 1201 16th St., N.W., Washington, D.C. 20036. 50,000; George F. Anderson, Executive Director.

Hearing and Speech Action, National Association for (1919): 814 Thayer Ave., Silver Spring, Md. 20910. 153 agencies.

Heart Association, Inc., American (1924): 7320 Greenville Ave., Dallas, Tex. 75231. 115,000; William W. Moore, Executive Vice President.

Hemispheric Affairs, Council on (1975): 1735 New Hampshire Ave., N.W., Washington, D.C. 20009. Laurence R. Birns, Director.

Home Economics Association, American (1909): 2010 Massachusetts Ave., N.W., Washington, D.C. 20036. 52,000; Kinsey Green, Executive Director.

Horticultural Society, American (1922): Mt. Vernon, Va. 22121. 35,000; Thomas W. Richards, Executive Vice President.

Hospital Association, American (1898): 840 N. Lake Shore Dr., Chicago, Ill. 60611. 6,300 institutions; J. Alexander McMahon, President.

Humane Association, American (1877): 5351 S. Roslyn St., Englewood, Colo. 80110. Milton C. Searle, Executive Director.

Imperial Council of Ancient Arabic Order of Nobles of the Mystic Shrine (1872): 323 N. Michigan Ave., Chicago, Ill. 60601. 937,712; Charles Cumpstone, Executive Secretary.

Indian Rights Association (1882): 1505 Race St., Philadelphia, Pa. 19102. 2,400; Sandra L. Cadwalader, Executive Director.

Intercollegiate Athletics, National Association of (1940): 1221 Baltimore St., Kansas City, Mo. 64105. 515; Harry Fritz, Executive Director.

Intercollegiate (Big Ten) Conference (1896): 1111 Plaza Dr., Schaumburg, Ill. 60195. Jeff Elliott, Service Bureau Director.

Interfraternity Conference, National (1909): 3901 W. 86th St., Indianapolis, Ind. 46268. 48; Jack L. Anson, Executive Director.

Jewish Appeal Inc., United (1939): 1290 Avenue of the Americas, New York, N.Y. 10019. Irving Bernstein, Executive Vice Chairman.

Jewish Committee, American (1906): 165 E. 56th St., New York, N.Y. 10022. 40,000; Morton Yarmon, Director of Public Relations.

Jewish Community Centers, World Confederation of (1946): 15 E. 26th St., New York, N.Y. 10010. Herbert Millman, Executive Director.

Jewish War Veterans of the U.S.A. (1896): 1712 New Hampshire Ave., N.W., Washington, D.C. 20009.

Jewish Women, National Council of (1893): 15 E. 26th St., New York, N.Y. 10010.

John Birch Society (1958): 395 Concord Ave., Belmont, Mass. 02178. 100,000; Ellen Sproul, Clerk of Corporation.

Judaism, American Council for (1943): 307 Fifth Ave., New York, N.Y. 10016. 10,000; Clarence L. Coleman, Jr., President.

Junior Achievement, Inc. (1919): 550 Summer St., Stamford, Conn. 06901. 300,000; Glenn V. Gardinier, National Public Relations Director.

Junior Leagues, Inc., Association of (1921): 825 Third Ave., New York, N.Y. 10022. 130,000.

Kennel Club, American (1884): 51 Madison Ave., New York, N.Y. 10010. 406 member clubs; Mark T. Mooty, Secretary.

Kiwanis International (1915): 101 E. Erie, Chicago, Ill. 60611. 293,000; R. P. Merridew, Secretary.

Knights of Columbus (1882): One Columbus Plaza, New Haven, Conn. 06507. 1,280,859; Virgil Dechant, Supreme Knight.

Knights of Pythias, Supreme Lodge (1864): 47 N. Grant St., Stockton, Calif. 95202. 145,326; Jule O. Pritchard, Supreme Secretary.

Knights Templar, Grand Encampment of (1816): 14 E. Jackson Blvd., Suite 1700, Chicago, Ill. 60604. 365,000; Paul C. Rodenhauser, Grand Recorder.

Library Association, American (1876): 50 E. Huron St., Chicago, Ill. 60611. 33,767; Robert Wedgeworth, Executive Director.

Lions Clubs, The International Association of (1917): 300 22nd St., Oak Brook, Ill. 60570. 1,225,000; Roy Schaetzel, Executive Administrator.

Management Associations, American (1923): 135 W. 50th St., New York, N.Y. 10020. 65,000; Joseph P. Keyes, Vice President of Public Relations.

Manufacturers, National Association of (1895): 1776 F St., N.W., Washington, D.C. 20006. 13,000; Edmund W. Haskins, Secretary.

March of Dimes—National Foundation (1938): 1275 Mamaroneck Ave., White Plains, N.Y. 10605. 1,400 chapters; Arthur A. Gallway, Vice President.

Marine Corps League (1923): 933 N. Kenmore St., Arlington, Va. 22201. 20,000; F. B. Starr, National Adjutant Paymaster.

Masons, Ancient and Accepted Scottish Rite, Northern Masonic Jurisdiction, Supreme Council 33° (1867): 33 Marrett Rd., Lexington, Mass. 02173. 511,687; Winthrop L. Hall, Executive Secretary.

Masons, Ancient and Accepted Scottish Rite, Southern Jurisdiction, Supreme Council (1801): 1733 16th St., N.W., Washington, D.C. 20009. 653,000; C. Fred Kleinknecht, Grand Secretary General.

Mayflower Descendants, General Society of (1897): 4 Winslow St., P.O. Box 297, Plymouth, Mass. 02360. 17,-500; Mrs. Lester A. Hall, Historian General.

Medical Association, American (1847): 535 N. Dearborn St., Chicago, Ill. 60610.

Mental Health Association (1909): 1800 N. Kent St., Arlington, Va. 22209. 1,000,000; William Perry, Jr., Director of Communications.

Modern Language Association of America (1883): 62 Fifth Ave., New York, N.Y. 10011. 30,000; Jeffrey Howitt, Promotion and Production Manager.

Moose, Loyal Order of (1888): Mooseheart, Ill. 60539. 1,624,221; Carl A. Weis, Supreme Secretary.

Multiple Sclerosis Society, National (1946): 205 E. 42nd St., New York, N.Y. 10017. Sylvia Lawry, Executive Director.

Museums, American Association of (1906): 1055 Thomas Jefferson St., N.W., Washington, D.C. 20007. 6,406; Lawrence Reger, Director.

National Association for the Advancement of Colored People (1909): 1790 Broadway, New York, N.Y. 10019. 450,000; Benjamin L. Hooks, Executive Director.

National Grange, The (1867): 1616 H St., N.W., Washington, D.C. 20006. 600,000; John Scott, Master.

Negro College Fund, Inc., United (1944): 500 E. 62nd St., New York, N.Y. 10021. 41 colleges; Christopher F. Edley, Executive Director.

Newspaper Publishers Association, American (1887): P.O. Box 17407, Dulles International Airport, Washington, D.C. 20041. 1,291; Jerry W. Friedheim, Executive Vice President and General Manager.

Nurses' Association, American (1896): 2420 Pershing Rd., Kansas City, Mo. 64108. 200,000.

Odd Fellows, Independent Order of (1819): 16 W. Chase St., Baltimore, Md. 21201. 1,200,000; Edward T. Rogers, Sovereign Grand Secretary.

Olympic Committee, United States (1921): 1760 Boulder St., Colorado Springs, Colo. 80909. Bob Paul, Director of Communications.

Organization of American States (1890): 17th Street and Constitution Avenue, N.W., Washington, D.C. 20006. 26 member nations.

Parents and Teachers, National Congress of (1897): 700 N. Rush St., Chicago, Ill. 60611. 6,328,348; Becky Schergens, Executive Director.

Parks and Conservation Association, National (1919): 1701 18th St., N.W., Washington, D.C. 20009. 45,000; Anthony Wayne Smith, President.

Philatelic Society, American (1886): P.O. Box 800, State College, Pa. 16801. 44,000; James DeVoss, Executive Secretary.

Philosophical Society, American (1743): 104 S. 5th St., Philadelphia, Pa. 19106. 600; W. J. Bell, Jr., Executive Officer.

Photographic Society of America (1933): 2005 Walnut St., Philadelphia, Pa. 19103. 18,600; Philip Katcher, Executive Secretary.

Physical Society, American (1899): 335 E. 45th St., New York, N.Y. 10017. 29,000; W. W. Havens, Jr., Executive Secretary.

Planned Parenthood Federation of America (1916): 810 Seventh Ave., New York, N.Y. 10019. 191 affiliates; Robin Elliott, Public Information Director.

Political Science, Academy of (1880): 2852 Broadway, New York, N.Y. 10025. 11,000; Robert H. Connery, President.

Psychiatric Association, American (1844): 1700 18th St., N.W., Washington, D.C. 20009. 22,000; Jules Masserman, M.D., President.

Public Health Association, American (1872): 1015 18th St., N.W., Washington, D.C. 20036. 29,000; William H. McBeath, M.D., Executive Director.

Red Cross, American (1881): 17th and D Sts., N.W., Washington, D.C. 20006. George M. Elsey, President.

Retarded Citizens, National Association for (1950): 2709 Avenue E East, Arlington, Tex. 76011. 1,800 units; Philip Roos, Executive Director.

Retired Federal Employees, National Association of (1914): 1533 New Hampshire Ave., N.W., Washington, D.C. 20036. 285,029; John F. McClelland, President.

Retired Persons, American Association of (1958): 1909 K St., N.W., Washington, D.C. 20049. 12,000,000; Cyril F. Brickfield, Executive Director.

Rifle Association of America, National (1871): 1600 Rhode Island Ave., N.W., Washington, D.C. 20036. 1,100,000; Harlon B. Carter, Executive Vice President.

Rotary International (1905): 1600 Ridge Ave., Evanston, Ill. 60201. 818,000; Harry A. Stewart, General Secretary.

Safety Council, National (1913): 444 N. Michigan Ave., Chicago, Ill. 60611. James C. Shaffer, Director of Public Relations.

Salvation Army (1865): 120 W. 14th St., New York, N.Y. 10011. 380,618; Col. Orval Taylor, National Chief Secretary.

Science, American Association for the Advancement of (1848): 1515 Massachusetts Ave., N.W., Washington, D.C. 20005. 125,000; Carol L. Rogers, Public Information.

Screen Actors Guild (1933): 7750 Sunset Blvd., Hollywood, Calif. 90046. 36,000; Judith Rheiner, Information Director.

Seeing Eye (1929): Morristown, N.J. 07960. 25,000; Stuart Grout, Executive Vice President.

Sierra Club (1892): 530 Bush St., San Francisco, Calif. 94108. 180,000; Michael McCloskey, Executive Director.

Social Welfare, National Conference on (1873): 22 W. Gay St., Columbus, Ohio 43215. 8,500; Margaret E. Berry, Executive Director.

Social Workers, Inc., National Association of (1955): 1425 H St., N.W., Washington, D.C. 20005. 70,000; Chauncey A. Alexander, Executive Director.

Sons of Italy in America, Order (1905): 1520 Locust St., Philadelphia, Pa. 19102. 2,300 lodges; Frank J. Montemuro, Supreme Venerable.

Sons of the American Revolution, National Society of the (1889): 2412 Massachusetts Ave., N.W., Washington, D.C. 20008. 22,000; Dr. Warren S. Woodward, Executive Secretary.

Soroptimist International of the Americas (1921): 1616 Walnut St., Philadelphia, Pa. 19103. 31,000; Valerie F. Levitan, Executive Director.

Southern Christian Leadership Conference (1957): 334 Auburn Ave., N.E., Atlanta, Ga. 30303. 1,000,000; 350

chapters, 260 affiliated organizations; Dr. Joseph E. Lowery, President.

Speech and Hearing Association, American (1925): 10801 Rockville Pike, Rockville, Md. 20852. 27,500; Kenneth Johnson, Executive Secretary.

Sports Car Club of America (1944): P.O. Box 22476, Denver, Colo. 80222. 23,000; Brian VanDercook, Director of Public Relations.

Teachers, American Federation of (1916): 11 Dupont Circle, N.W., Washington, D.C. 20036. 475,000; Albert Shanker, President.

Travel Agents, Inc., American Society of (ASTA) (1931): 711 Fifth Ave., New York, N.Y. 10022. 16,000; Richard P. Ramaglia, Executive Vice President.

Travelers Aid Society of New York (1905): 204 E. 39th St., New York, N.Y. 10016. 3,253; Elizabeth P. Anderson, General Director.

University Women, American Association of (1882): 2401 Virginia Ave., N.W., Washington, D.C. 20037. 190,-000; Helen B. Wolfe, General Director.

Urban League, National (1910): 500 E. 62nd St., New York, N.Y. 10021. 107; James D. Williams, Director of Communications.

Veterans Committee, American (AVC) (1944): 1333 Connecticut Ave., N.W., Washington, D.C. 20036. 25,000; June A. Willenz, Executive Director.

Veterans of Foreign Wars of the U.S. (1899): V.F.W. Bldg., 34th and Broadway, Kansas City, Mo. 64111. V.F.W. and Auxiliary, 2,375,000; Julian Dickenson, Adjutant General.

Veterinary Medical Association, American (1863): 930 N. Meacham Rd., Schaumburg, Ill. 60196. 29,000; Dr. D. A. Price, Executive Vice President.

Women Voters of the U.S., League of (1920): 1730 M St., N.W., Washington, D.C. 20036. 137,000; Peggy Lampl, Executive Director.

Women's American ORT (1927): 1250 Broadway, New York, N.Y. 10001. 135,000; Nathan Gould, National Executive Director.

Women's Clubs, General Federation of (1890): 1734 N St., N.W., Washington, D.C. 20036. 600,000; Mrs. W. Ed Hamilton, Administrative Assistant.

Young Men's Christian Associations, National Council of (1844): 291 Broadway, New York, N.Y. 10007. 8,900,-000; Robert W. Harlan, Executive Director.

Young Women's Christian Association of the U.S.A. (1858 in U.S.A., 1855 in England): 600 Lexington Ave., New York, N.Y. 10022. 2,471,000; Kit Kolchin, Public Relations Consultant.

Youth Hostels, Inc., American (1934): National Campus, Delaplane, Va. 22025. 70,000.

Zionist Organization of America (1897): ZOA House, 4 E. 34th St., New York, N.Y. 10016. 120,000; Leon Ilutovich, National Executive Director.

Authorized 2-Letter State Abbreviations

When the Post Office instituted the ZIP Code for mail in 1963, it also drew up a list of two-letter abbreviations for the states which would gradually replace the traditional ones in use. Following is the official list, including the District of Columbia, Guam, Puerto Rico, and the Virgin Islands (note that only capital letters are used):

Alabama	AL	Montana	MT
Alaska	AK	Nebraska	NE
Arizona	AZ	Nevada	NV
Arkansas	AR	New Hampshire	NH
California	CA	New Jersey	NJ
Colorado	CO	New Mexico	NM
Connecticut	CT	New York	NY
Delaware	DE	North Carolina	NC
Dist. of Columbia	DC	North Dakota	ND
Florida	FL	Ohio	OH
Georgia	GA	Oklahoma	OK
Guam	GU	Oregon	OR
Hawaii	HI	Pennsylvania	PA
Idaho	ID	Puerto Rico	PR
Illinois	IL	Rhode Island	RI
Indiana	IN	South Carolina	SC
Iowa	IA	South Dakota	SD
Kansas	KS	Tennessee	TN
Kentucky	KY	Texas	TX
Louisiana	LA	Utah	UT
Maine	ME	Vermont	VT
Maryland	MD	Virginia	VA
Massachusetts	MA	Virgin Islands	VI
Michigan	MI	Washington	WA
Minnesota	MN	West Virginia	WV
Mississippi	MS	Wisconsin	WI
Missouri	MO	Wyoming	WY

WEATHER

Fahrenheit and Celsius (Centigrade) Scales

Zero on the Fahrenheit scale represents the temperature produced by the mixing of equal weights of snow and common salt.

	F	C
Boiling point of water	212°	100°
Freezing point of water	32°	0°
Absolute zero	−459.6°	−273.1°

Absolute zero is theoretically the lowest possible temperature, the point at which all molecular motion would cease.

To convert Fahrenheit to Celsius (Centigrade), subtract 32 and multiply by 5/9.

To convert Celsius (Centigrade) to Fahrenheit, multiply by 9/5 and add 32.

World and U.S. Extremes of Climate

Highest recorded temperature

	Place	Date	F°	C°
World (Africa)	El Azizia, Libya	Sept. 13, 1922	136	58
North America (U.S.)	Death Valley, Calif.	July 10, 1913	134	57
Asia	Tirat Tsvi, Israel	June 21, 1942	129	54
Australia	Cloncurry, Queensland	Jan. 16, 1889	128	53
Europe	Seville, Spain	Aug. 4, 1881	122	50
South America	Rivadavia, Argentina	Dec. 11, 1905	120	49
Antarctica	Esperanza, Palmer Peninsula	Oct. 20, 1956	58	14

Lowest recorded temperature

	Place	Date	F°	C°
World (Antarctica)	Vostok	Aug. 24, 1960	−127	−88
Asia	Verkhoyansk/Oimekon	Feb. 6, 1933	−90	−68
Greenland	Northice	Jan. 9, 1954	−87	−66
North America (excl. Greenland)	Snag, Yukon, Canada	Feb. 3, 1947	−81	−63
Europe	Ust 'Shchugor, U.S.S.R.	n.a.	−67	−55
South America	Sarmiento, Argentina	Jan. 1, 1907	−27	−33
Africa	Ifrane, Morocco	Feb. 11, 1935	−11	−24
Australia	Charlotte Pass, N.S.W.	July 22, 1947	−8	−22
United States	Prospect Creek, Alaska	Jan. 23, 1971	−80	−62

Greatest rainfalls

	Place	Date	Inches
1 minute (U.S.)	Unionville, Md.	—	1.23
20 minutes (Romania)	Curtea-de-Arges	—	8.1
42 minutes (U.S.)	Holt, Mo.	—	12
12 hours (Indian Ocean)	Belouve, La Réunion	—	53
24 hours (Indian Ocean)	Cilaos, La Réunion	—	74
5 days (Indian Ocean)	Cilaos, La Réunion	—	152
1 month (India)	Cherrapunji	—	366
1 month (U.S.)	Kukui, Maui, Hawaii	—	460
12 months (India)	Cherrapunji	—	1,042

Greatest snowfalls

	Place	Date	Inches
1 month (U.S.)	Tamarack, Calif.	Jan. 1911	390
24 hours (U.S.)	Silver Lake, Colo.	April 14–15, 1921	76
19 hours (France)	Bessans	—	68
1 storm (U.S.)	Mt. Shasta Ski Bowl, Calif.	—	189
1 season (U.S.)	Paradise Ranger Sta., Wash.	—	1,122

NOTE: n.a. = not available. *Source:* National Oceanic and Atmospheric Administration, Environmental Data Service.

Month	Temperature, °F				Precipitation		
	Average maximum	Average minimum	Record high	Record low	Rainfall, inches	Snowfall, inches	Days with precipitation

Dallas-Fort Worth, Texas (Regional Airport): lat. 32° 54′ N, long. 97° 02′ W; elevation: 551 ft

Month	Average maximum	Average minimum	Record high	Record low	Rainfall, inches	Snowfall, inches	Days with precipitation
January	43.8	25.6	67	10	2.39	5.4	11
April	77.5	56.0	89	43	4.31	0.0	10
July	100.1	74.1	108	71	2.20	0.0	6
October	79.6	53.7	98	35	2.96	0.0	6
Annual	77.5	54.8	108	10	27.19	5.4	68

Denver, Colorado (Stapleton International Airport): lat. 39° 45′ N, long. 104° 52′ W; elevation: 5,283 ft

Month	Average maximum	Average minimum	Record high	Record low	Rainfall, inches	Snowfall, inches	Days with precipitation
January	43.9	14.4	60	−4	0.16	2.4	5
April	63.3	38.8	81	25	2.13	4.7	12
July	87.8	60.7	98	51	2.98	0.0	10
October	69.4	37.1	83	25	0.48	3.3	4
Annual	66.6	38.4	98	−4	10.34	27.9	81

Duluth, Minnesota (International Airport): lat. 46° 50′ N, long. 92° 11′ W; elevation: 1,428 ft

Month	Average maximum	Average minimum	Record high	Record low	Rainfall, inches	Snowfall, inches	Days with precipitation
January	8.4	−8.7	29	−35	0.36	8.8	13
April	55.5	33.2	84	15	1.27	0.1	8
July	76.3	55.4	89	47	3.91	0.0	9
October	52.6	35.9	65	27	3.20	1.7	8
Annual	48.1	30.4	89	−35	34.02	59.0	139

Great Falls, Montana (International Airport): lat. 47° 29′ N, long. 111° 22′ W; elevation: 3,662 ft

Month	Average maximum	Average minimum	Record high	Record low	Rainfall, inches	Snowfall, inches	Days with precipitation
January	31.8	11.4	53	−19	1.04	13.9	12
April	61.5	32.7	79	7	0.26	1.0	5
July	82.7	53.3	95	45	1.87	0.0	10
October	59.8	35.8	78	20	0.51	3.2	4
Annual	57.1	33.0	95	−27	14.93	66.5	113

Kansas City, Missouri (International Airport): lat. 39° 17′ N, long. 94° 43′ W; elevation: 1,014 ft

Month	Average maximum	Average minimum	Record high	Record low	Rainfall, inches	Snowfall, inches	Days with precipitation
January	24.4	6.7	42	−13	1.15	14.2	12
April	69.6	49.7	83	31	2.35	0.6	10
July	89.2	70.2	96	57	2.74	0.0	6
October	65.0	46.3	84	34	7.67	0.0	13
Annual	63.6	45.1	97	−13	49.74	16.3	120

	Temperature, °F				Precipitation		
Month	Average maximum	Average minimum	Record high	Record low	Rainfall, inches	Snowfall, inches	Days with precipitation

Los Angeles, California (International Airport): lat. 33° 56′ N, long. 118° 24′ W; elevation: 97 ft

January	65.7	49.4	82	41	3.21	0.0	7
April	68.3	53.8	77	48	T	0.0	0
July	75.4	61.8	87	59	0.00	0.0	0
October	72.9	59.5	83	52	T	0.0	0
Annual	70.8	56.1	91	40	13.68	0.0	32

Miami, Florida (International Airport): lat. 25° 48′ N, long. 80° 16′ W; elevation: 7 ft

January	70.5	51.7	83	31	1.44	0.0	5
April	80.9	68.7	91	59	1.97	0.0	6
July	88.5	78.8	92	73	5.23	0.0	13
October	83.0	70.0	92	58	1.25	0.0	7
Annual	81.6	69.2	92	31	64.95	0.0	118

Nashville, Tennessee (Metropolitan Airport): lat. 36° 07′ N. long. 86° 41′ W; elevation: 590 ft

January	33.7	15.2	52	−5	2.53	18.5	13
April	74.6	51.3	87	31	7.87	T	11
July	92.3	72.1	99	63	1.15	0.0	6
October	68.0	45.9	86	31	4.22	0.0	7
Annual	69.9	48.9	99	−5	50.71	18.6	116

New Orleans, Louisiana (International Airport): lat. 29° 59′ N, long. 90° 15′ W; elevation: 4 ft

January	52.5	34.2	73	19	5.62	T	9
April	80.4	57.5	84	41	6.38	0.0	6
July	93.3	74.4	97	71	2.91	0.0	14
October	77.7	58.7	92	42	4.33	0.0	5
Annual	77.8	59.0	97	19	72.80	T	132

New York, New York (Central Park): lat. 40° 47′ N, long. 73° 58′ W; elevation: 132 ft

January	27.7	16.4	44	−2	2.25	13.0	8
April	63.6	43.8	90	25	3.75	T	7
July	88.2	69.7	104	58	1.60	0.0	7
October	61.0	48.8	70	40	5.03	0.0	11
Annual	61.6	47.0	104	−2	54.73	20.0	114

Month	Temperature, °F				Precipitation		
	Average maximum	Average minimum	Record high	Record low	Rainfall, inches	Snowfall, inches	Days with precipitation

Phoenix, Arizona (Sky Harbor International Airport): lat. 33° 26′ N, long. 112° 01′ W; elevation: 1,112 ft

Month	Average maximum	Average minimum	Record high	Record low	Rainfall, inches	Snowfall, inches	Days with precipitation
January	64.8	42.8	76	31	0.35	0.0	5
April	88.2	58.8	99	40	0.06	0.0	1
July	106.1	83.8	112	78	0.30	0.0	4
October	91.0	66.4	102	56	0.61	0.0	3
Annual	87.6	62.1	114	31	3.16	0.0	28

Salt Lake City, Utah (International Airport): lat. 40° 46′ N, long. 111° 58′ W; elevation: 4,220 ft

Month	Average maximum	Average minimum	Record high	Record low	Rainfall, inches	Snowfall, inches	Days with precipitation
January	35.6	18.0	49	−2	0.76	8.6	4
April	67.4	40.8	85	27	0.59	4.8	3
July	91.7	62.9	100	53	0.61	0.0	6
October	69.4	41.8	80	33	0.83	0.2	5
Annual	65.1	41.2	101	−2	17.67	76.0	96

San Francisco, California (International Airport): lat. 37° 37′ N, long. 122° 23′ W; elevation: 8 ft

Month	Average maximum	Average minimum	Record high	Record low	Rainfall, inches	Snowfall, inches	Days with precipitation
January	53.9	40.1	63	35	2.22	0.0	5
April	64.4	46.6	77	41	T	0.0	0
July	71.6	53.2	97	50	0.35	0.0	1
October	68.6	52.3	82	47	0.15	0.0	3
Annual	64.5	48.9	97	35	12.54	0.0	50

Seattle, Washington (Seattle-Tacoma Airport): lat. 47° 27′ N, long. 122° 18′ W; elevation: 400 ft

Month	Average maximum	Average minimum	Record high	Record low	Rainfall, inches	Snowfall, inches	Days with precipitation
January	44.7	34.1	57	24	1.77	1.0	13
April	63.2	43.9	78	37	0.55	0.0	9
July	75.2	55.0	87	52	0.42	0.0	5
October	59.0	45.4	69	41	2.60	0.0	13
Annual	60.5	45.4	96	21	32.84	5.4	147

Washington, D.C. (National Airport): lat. 38° 51′ N, long. 77° 02′ W; elevation: 10 ft

Month	Average maximum	Average minimum	Record high	Record low	Rainfall, inches	Snowfall, inches	Days with precipitation
January	33.3	17.5	49	2	1.50	9.7	8
April	71.5	48.7	90	30	2.66	T	7
July	90.2	71.5	100	60	4.06	0.0	11
October	67.2	50.8	82	37	5.35	0.0	11
Annual	67.5	49.7	100	2	36.14	10.0	113

Source: Department of Commerce, National Oceanic and Atmospheric Administration, Environmental Data Service.

Wind Chill Factors

Wind speed (mph)	Thermometer reading (degrees Fahrenheit)																
	35	30	25	20	15	10	5	0	-5	-10	-15	-20	-25	-30	-35	-40	-45
5	33	27	21	19	12	7	0	-5	-10	-15	-21	-26	-31	-36	-42	-47	-52
10	22	16	10	3	-3	-9	-15	-22	-27	-34	-40	-46	-52	-58	-64	-71	-77
15	16	9	2	-5	-11	-18	-25	-31	-38	-45	-51	-58	-65	-72	-78	-85	-92
20	12	4	-3	-10	-17	-24	-31	-39	-46	-53	-60	-67	-74	-81	-88	-95	-103
25	8	1	-7	-15	-22	-29	-36	-44	-51	-59	-66	-74	-81	-88	-96	-103	-110
30	6	-2	-10	-18	-25	-33	-41	-49	-56	-64	-71	-79	-86	-93	-101	-109	-116
35	4	-4	-12	-20	-27	-35	-43	-52	-58	-67	-74	-82	-89	-97	-105	-113	-120
40	3	-5	-13	-21	-29	-37	-45	-53	-60	-69	-76	-84	-92	-100	-107	-115	-123
45	2	-6	-14	-22	-30	-38	-46	-54	-62	-70	-78	-85	-93	-102	-109	-117	-125

NOTES: This chart gives equivalent temperatures for combinations of wind speed and temperatures. For example, the combination of a temperature of 10° Fahrenheit and a wind blowing at 10 mph has a cooling power equal to − 9° F. Wind speeds of higher than 45 mph have little additional cooling effect.

Weather Glossary

blizzard: storm characterized by strong winds, low temperatures, and large amounts of snow.

blowing snow: snow lifted from ground surface by wind; restricts visibility.

cold wave warning: indicates that a change to abnormally cold weather is expected; greater than normal protective measures will be required.

cyclone: circulation of winds rotating counterclockwise in the northern hemisphere and clockwise in the southern hemisphere. Hurricanes and tornadoes are both examples of cyclones.

drifting snow: strong winds will blow loose or falling snow into significant drifts.

drizzle: uniform close precipitation of tiny drops with diameter of less than .02 inch.

flash flood: dangerous rapid rise of water levels in streams, rivers, or over land area.

freezing rain or drizzle: rain or drizzle that freezes on contact with the ground or other objects forming a coating of ice on exposed surfaces.

gale warning: winds in the 33–48 knot (38–55 mph) range forecast.

hail: small balls of ice falling separately or in lumps; usually associated with thunderstorms and temperatures that may be well above freezing.

hazardous driving warnings: indicates that drizzle, freezing rain, snow, sleet, or strong winds make driving conditions difficult.

heavy snow warnings: issued when 4 inches or more of snow are expected to fall in a 12-hour period or when 6 inches or more are anticipated in a 24-hour period.

hurricane: devastating cyclonic storm; winds over 74 mph near storm center; usually tropical in origin; called cyclone in Indian Ocean, typhoon in the Pacific.

hurricane warning: winds in excess of 64 knots (74 mph) in connection with hurricane.

livestock warning: alerts farmers and ranchers that livestock will require protection from bad weather conditions.

rain: precipitation of liquid particles with diameters larger than .02 inch.

sleet: translucent or transparent ice pellets; frozen rain; generally a winter phenomenon.

small craft warning: indicates winds as high as 33 knots (38 mph) and sea conditions dangerous to small boats.

snow: precipitation of ice crystals.

snow flurries: snow falling for a short time at intermittent periods; accumulations are usually small.

snow squall: brief, intense falls of snow, usually accompanied by gusty winds.

storm warnings: winds greater than 48 knots (55 mph) are forecast.

temperature-humidity index (THI): measure of personal discomfort based on the combined effects of temperature and humidity. Most people are uncomfortable when the THI is 75. A THI of 80 produces acute discomfort for almost everyone.

tidal waves: series of ocean waves caused by earthquakes; can reach speeds of 600 mph; they grow in height as they reach shore and can crest as high as 100 feet.

thunder: the sound produced by the rapid expansion of air heated by lightning.

tornado: dangerous whirlwind associated with the cumulonimbus clouds of severe thunderstorms; winds up to 300 mph.

tornado warning: tornado has actually been detected by radar or sighted in designated area.

tornado watch: potential exists in the watch area for storms that could contain tornadoes.

travelers' warning: *see* hazardous driving warning.

tsunami: *see* tidal waves.

warning: the designated condition is imminent.

wind-chill factor: combined effect of temperature and wind speed as compared to equivalent temperature in calm air.

WORLD FACTS

COUNTRIES OF THE WORLD

AFGHANISTAN

Democratic Republic of Afghanistan
Area: 249,999 sq mi. (647,497 sq km)
Population (est. 1978): 20,900,000 (Pushtu, 60.5%; Tajik, 30.7%; Uzbek, 5%)
Capital: Kabul
Largest cities (est. 1976): Kabul, 749,000; (est. 1973): Kandahar, 140,000; Baghlan, 110,900; Herat, 108,750
Monetary unit: Afghani
Languages: Pushtu and Dari Persian (both official)
Religion: Islam (Sunni, 90%; Shiah, 10%)
Gross national product (1976): $2.3 billion
National name: Jamhouriat Afghánistán

Geography. Afghanistan, approximately the size of Texas, lies wedged between the U.S.S.R., China, Pakistan, and Iran. The country is split east to west by the Hindu Kush mountain range, rising in the east to heights of 24,000 feet (7,315 m). With the exception of the southwest, most of the country is covered by high snow-capped mountains and is traversed by deep valleys.

ALBANIA

People's Socialist Republic of Albania
Area: 11,100 sq mi. (28,748 sq km)
Population (est. 1978): 2,690,000
Capital and largest city (est. 1975): Tirana, 192,000
Monetary unit: Lek
Language: Albanian
Religions: Historically Islam 70%; Greek Orthodox, 20%; Roman Catholic, 10%
Gross national product: $1.3 billion
National name: Republika Popullore Socialiste e Shqipërisë

Geography. Albania is situated on the eastern shore of the Adriatic Sea, with Yugoslavia to the north and east and Greece to the south. Slightly larger than Maryland, it is a mountainous country, mostly over 3,000 feet above sea level with a narrow, marshy coastal plain crossed by several rivers. The centers of population are contained in the interior mountain plateaus and basins.

ALGERIA

Democratic and Popular Republic of Algeria
Area: 919,595 sq mi. (2,381,741 sq km)
Population (est. 1978): 18,500,000
Capital: Algiers
Largest cities (est. 1978): Algiers, 2,000,000; Oran, 700,000; Constantine, 600,000; Annaba (Bône), 500,000
Monetary unit: Dinar
Languages: Arabic, French, Berber
Religion: Islam
Gross national product (1976): $16.1 billion
National name: République Algérienne Democratiqe et Populaire—El Djemouria El Djazaïrïa Demokratia Echaabia

Geography. Nearly four times the size of Texas, Algeria is bordered on the west by Morocco and on the east by Tunisia and Libya. To the south are Mauritania, Mali, and Niger. Low plains cover small areas near the Mediterranean coast, with 68% of the country a plateau between 2,625 and 5,250 feet (800 and 1,600 m) above sea level. The highest point is Mt. Tahat in the Sahara, which rises 9,850 feet (3,000 m).

ANDORRA

Valleys of Andorra
Area: 175 sq mi. (453 sq km)
Population (est. 1978): 25,000
Capital (est. 1975): Andorra la Vella, 10,900
Monetary units: French franc and Spanish peseta
Languages: Catalán (official); French, Spanish
Religion: Roman Catholic
National names: Les Vallées d'Andorre-Valls d'Andorra

Geography. Andorra lies high in the Pyrenees Mountains on the French-Spanish border. The country is drained by the Valira River.

ANGOLA

People's Republic of Angola
Area: 481,350 sq mi. (1,246,700 sq km)
Population (est. 1976): 6,761,000
Capital and largest city (est. 1970): Luanda, 480,600
Monetary unit: Kwanza
Languages: Bantu, Portuguese (official)
Religions: Animist, 50%; Roman Catholic, 38%; Protestant, 12%
Gross national product (1976): $1.8 billion

Geography. Angola, more than three times the size of California, extends for more than 1,000 miles along the South Atlantic in southwestern Africa. Zaire is to the north and east; Zambia to the east, and South-West Africa (Namibia) to the south. A plateau averaging 6,000 feet (1,829 m) above sea level rises abruptly from the coastal lowlands. Nearly all the land is desert or savanna, with hardwood forests in the northeast.

ARGENTINA

Argentine Republic
Area: 1,068,296 sq mi. (2,766,889 sq km)
Population (est. 1978): 26,400,000
Capital: Buenos Aires
Largest cities (est. 1977): Buenos Aires, 2,980,000; (1970 census for urban agglomeration): Rosario, 810,840; Córdoba, 798,663; La Plata, 506,287; Mendoza, 470,896
Monetary unit: Peso
Language: Spanish
Religion: Predominantly Roman Catholic
Gross national product (1976): $39.9 billion
National name: República Argentina

Geography. With an area slightly less than one third of the United States and second in South America only to its eastern neighbor, Brazil, in size and population, Argentina is a plain, rising from the Atlantic to the Chilean border and the towering Andes peaks. Aconcagua (23,034 ft.; 7,021 m) is the highest peak in the world outside Asia. The northern area is the swampy and partly wooded Gran Chaco, bordering on Bolivia and Paraguay. South of that are the rolling, fertile pampas, rich for agriculture and grazing and supporting most of the population. Next southward is Patagonia, a region of cool, arid steppes with some wooded and fertile sections. The eastern part of Tierra del Fuego, the island southern tip of South America, belongs to Argentina.

The three great rivers that make up the Plata system—the Uruguay, forming Argentina's eastern border with the country of Uruguay, the Paraná, and the Paraguay—are important commercial arteries in northern Argentina. Rosario and Santa Fé, 260 miles (418 km) and 360 miles (579 km), respectively, above Buenos Aires on the Paraná, are accessible to ocean vessels.

AUSTRALIA

Commonwealth of Australia
Area: 2,967,892 sq mi. (7,686,848 sq km)
Population (est. 1978): 14,220,000 (including aborigines)
Capital (1976 census): Canberra, 215,414
Largest cities (1976 census): Sydney, 3,021,299; Melbourne, 2,603,578; Brisbane, 957,710; Adelaide, 900,379; Perth, 805,489; Hobart (on Tasmania), 162,059
Monetary unit: Australian dollar
Language: English
Religions (1971 census): Anglican, 31%; Roman Catholic, 27%; Uniting Church, 17%
Gross national product (1976): $93.2 billion

Geography. The continent of Australia, with the island state of Tasmania, is approximately equal in area to the United States (excluding Alaska and Hawaii), and is more than three fourths the size of Europe.

Mountain ranges run from north to south along the east coast, reaching their highest point in Mt. Kosciusko (7,328 ft; 2,234 m). The western half of the continent is occupied by a desert plateau that rises into barren, rolling hills near the west coast. It includes the Great Victoria Desert to the south and the Great Sandy Desert to the north. The Great Barrier Reef lies along the northeast coast.

The island of Tasmania (26,215 sq mi.; 67,897 sq km) is off the southeastern coast.

Australian External Territories

Norfolk Island (14 sq mi.; 36.3 sq km) was placed under Australian administration in 1914. Population in 1977 was about 1,600.

The Ashmore and Cartier Islands (.8 sq mi.) were placed under Australian administration in 1931. In 1938 the islands, which are uninhabited, were annexed to the Northern Territory.

The Australian Antarctic Territory (2,360,000 sq mi.; 6,112,-400 sq km), comprising all the islands and territories, other than Adélie Land, situated south of lat. 60° S and lying between long. 160° to 45° E, was placed under Australian administration in 1936.

Heard Island and the McDonald Islands (158 sq mi.; 409.2 sq km), lying in the sub-Antarctic, were placed under Australian administration in 1947.

The Cocos (Keeling) Islands (5.5 sq mi.; 14.2 sq. km) placed under Australian administration in 1955. Population in 1977 was 447.

Christmas Island (52 sq mi.; 134.7 sq km) was placed under Australian administration in 1958. Population in 1977 was about 3,300.

Coral Sea Islands (400,000 sq mi.; 1,036,000 sq km, but only a few sq mi. of land) became a territory of Australia in 1969. There is no permanent population on the islands.

AUSTRIA

Republic of Austria
Area: 32,375 sq mi. (83,849 sq km)
Population (est. 1978): 7,500,000
Capital: Vienna
Largest cities (est. 1976): Vienna, 1,592,800; **(1971 census):** Graz, 248,500; Linz, 202,874; Salzburg, 128,845; Innsbruck, 115,197; Klagenfurt, 74,326
Monetary unit: Schilling
Language: German
Religion: Roman Catholic, 90%
Gross national product (1976): $40.6 billion
National name: Republik Österreich

Geography. Slightly smaller than Maine, Austria includes much of the mountainous territory of the eastern Alps (about 75% of the area). The country contains many snow-fields, glaciers, and snow-capped peaks, the highest being the Grossglockner (12,530 ft; 3,819 m). The Danube is the principal river. Forests and woodlands cover about 40% of the land area.

Almost at the heart of Europe, Austria has as its neighbors Italy, Switzerland, West Germany, Czechoslovakia, Hungary, Yugoslavia, and Liechtenstein.

BAHAMAS

Commonwealth of the Bahamas
Area: 5,382 sq mi. (13,935 sq km)
Population (est. 1978): 230,000
Capital and largest city (est. 1976 for urban agglomeration): Nassau, 125,000
Monetary unit: Bahamian dollar
Language: English
Religions: Baptist, 29%; Anglican, 23%; Roman Catholic, 23%; Methodist, 7%
Gross national product (1976): $700 million

Geography. The Bahamas are an archipelago of about 700 islands, east of Florida and north of Cuba, extending from northwest to southeast for about 800 miles. Only 29 of the islands are inhabited; the most important is New Providence (83 sq mi.), on which Nassau is located. Other islands include Grand Bahama, Abaco, Eleuthera, Andros, Cat Island, San Salvador (or Watling's Island), Exuma, Long Island, Crooked Island, Acklins Island, Mayaguana, and Inagua.

The islands are mainly flat, few rising above 200 feet. There are a few streams, one river (on Andros), and one large lake (on Inagua).

BAHRAIN

State of Bahrain
Area: 240 sq mi. (622 sq km)
Population (est. 1978): 280,000
Capital (est. 1976): Manama, 105,400
Monetary unit: Bahrain dinar
Languages: Arabic (official); Persian, English
Religion: Islam
Gross national product (1976): $660 million

Geography. Bahrain is an archipelago in the Persian Gulf off the coast of Saudi Arabia. The islands for the most part are level expanses of sand and rock.

BANGLADESH

People's Republic of Bangladesh
Area: 55,598 sq mi. (143,998 sq km)
Population (est. 1978): 82,500,000
Capital and largest city (est. 1974): Dacca, 1,679,600
Monetary unit: Taka
Principal languages: Bengali (official), English
Religions: Islam, 85%; Hindu, 13%
Gross national product (1976): $8.5 billion

Geography. Bangladesh, on the northern coast of the Bay of Bengal, is surrounded by India, with a small common border with Burma in the southeast. It is approximately the size of Wisconsin. The country is low-lying riverine land traversed by the many branches and tributaries of the Ganges and Brahmaputra rivers. Elevation averages less than 600 feet above sea level. Tropical monsoons and frequent floods and cyclones inflict heavy damage in the delta region.

BARBADOS

Area: 166 sq mi. (431 sq km)
Population (est. 1978): 260,000
Capital and largest city (1970 census): Bridgetown, 8,900
Monetary unit: Barbados dollar
Language: English
Religions: Anglican, 53%; Methodist, 9%; Roman Catholic, 4%
Gross national product (1976): $380 million

Geography. An island in the Atlantic about 300 miles north of Venezuela, Barbados is only 21 miles long and 14 miles across at its widest point. It is circled by fine beaches and narrow coastal plains. The highest point is Mount Hillaby (1,105 ft; 337 m) in the north central area.

BELGIUM

Kingdom of Belgium
Area: 11,781 sq mi. (30,513 sq km)
Population (est. 1978): 9,845,000
Capital: Brussels
Largest cities (est. urban area 1977): Brussels, 1,042,000; **(est. 1974):** Antwerp, 673,000; Liège, 444,000; Ghent, 235,000
Monetary unit: Belgian franc
Languages: Dutch, 56%; French, 32%; bilingual (Brussels), 11%
Religion: Roman Catholic, 97%
Gross national product (1976): $68.5 billion
National name: Royaume de Belgique—Koninkrijk België

Geography. A neighbor of France, West Germany, the Netherlands, and Luxembourg, Belgium has about 40 miles of seacoast on the North Sea at the Strait of Dover. In area, it is approximately the size of Maryland. The northern third of the country is a plain extending eastward from the seacoast. North of the Sambre and Meuse Rivers is a low plateau; to the south lies the heavily wooded Ardennes plateau, attaining an elevation of about 2,300 feet (700 m).

The Schelde River, which rises in France and flows through Belgium, emptying into the Schelde estuaries, enables Antwerp to be an ocean port.

BENIN

People's Republic of Benin
Area: 43,483 sq mi. (112,622 sq km)
Population (est. 1978): 3,380,000

Capital: Porto-Novo
Largest cities (est. 1972): Cotonou, 175,000; Porto-Novo, 100,000; Abomey, 50,000; Ouidah, 30,000
Monetary unit: Franc CFA
Ethnic groups: Fons and Adjas, Boribas, Yorubas, Mahis
Languages: French, African languages
Religions: Animist, Christian, Islam
Gross national product (1976): $430 million
National name: République Populaire du Benin

Geography. This West African nation on the Gulf of Guinea, between Togo on the west and Nigeria on the east, is about the size of Tennessee. The land consists of a narrow coastal strip that rises to a swampy, forested plateau and then to highlands in the north. A hot and humid climate blankets the entire country.

BHUTAN

Kingdom of Bhutan
Area: 18,147 sq mi. (47,000 sq km)
Population (est. 1977): 1,235,000
Capital (est. 1974): Thimphu, 15,000
Monetary unit: Ngultrum and Indian rupee
Language: Dzongkha
Religions: Buddhist, 75%; Hindu, 25%
Gross national product (1976): $90 million
National name: Druk-yul

Geography. Mountainous Bhutan, half the size of Indiana, is situated on the southeast slope of the Himalayas, bordered on the north and east by Tibet and on the south and west by India. The landscape consists of a succession of lofty and rugged mountains running generally from north to south and separated by deep valleys. In the north, towering peaks reach a height of 24,000 feet (7,315 m).

BOLIVIA

Republic of Bolivia
Area: 424,162 sq mi. (1,098,581 sq km)
Population (est. 1978): 6,110,000 (Indian, 53%; mestizo, 32%; white, 15%)
Administrative capital: La Paz
Judicial capital (est. 1976): Sucre, 90,000
Largest cities (est. 1976 by U.N.): La Paz, 654,700; Santa Cruz, 237,100; Cochabamba, 194,150; Oruro, 124,100
Monetary unit: Peso boliviano
Languages: Spanish, Quechua, Aymara

Religion: Roman Catholic, 94%
Gross national product (1976): $2.3 billion
National name: República de Bolivia

Geography. Landlocked Bolivia, equal in size to California and Texas combined, lies to the west of Brazil. It is a low alluvial plain throughout 60% of its area toward the east, drained by the Amazon and Plata river systems. The western part, enclosed by two chains of the Andes, is a great plateau—the Altiplano, with an average altitude of 12,000 feet (3,658 m). More than 80% of the population lives on the plateau, which also contains La Paz, the highest capital city in the world.

Lake Titicaca, half the size of Lake Ontario, is one of the highest large lakes in the world, at an altitude of 12,507 feet (3,812 m). Islands in the lake hold ruins of the ancient Incas.

BOPHUTHATSWANA
See South Africa

BOTSWANA

Republic of Botswana
Area: 231,804 sq mi. (600,372 sq km)
Population (est. 1978): 725,000
Capital and largest city (est. 1976): Gaborone, 36,900
Monetary unit: Pula
Languages: English, Setswana
Religions: Christian, 60%; Animist
Gross national product (1976): $280 million

Geography. Twice the size of Arizona, Botswana is in south central Africa, bounded by South-West Africa, Zambia, Rhodesia, and South Africa. Most of the country is near-desert, with the Kalahari occupying the western part of the country. The eastern part is hilly, with salt lakes in the north.

BRAZIL

Federative Republic of Brazil
Area: 3,286,487 sq mi. (8,511,965 sq km)
Population (est. 1978): 115,450,000 (approx.: white, 60%; mestizo, 26%; black, 11%)

Capital (est. 1977): Brasília, 763,250
Largest cities (est. 1977): São Paulo, 7,198,600; Rio de Janeiro, 4,857,500; Belo Horizonte, 1,557,500; Recife, 1,249,800
Monetary unit: Cruzeiro
Language: Portuguese
Religion: Roman Catholic, 89%
Gross national product (1976): $125.6 billion
National name: Brasil

Geography. Brazil covers about three sevenths of South America, extends 2,965 miles north-south, 2,691 miles east-west, and borders every South American state except Chile and Ecuador. It is the fifth largest country in the world, ranking after the U.S.S.R., China, Canada, and the U.S.

More than a third of Brazil is drained by the Amazon and its more than 200 tributaries. The Amazon is navigable for ocean steamers to Iquitos, Peru, 2,300 miles (3,700 km) upstream. Southern Brazil is drained by the Plata system— the Paraguay, Uruguay, and Paraná rivers. The most important stream entirely within Brazil is the Sao Francisco, navigable for a thousand miles, but broken near its mouth by the 275-foot (84 m) Paulo Afonso Falls.

BULGARIA

People's Republic of Bulgaria
Area: 42,823 sq mi. (110,912 sq km)
Population (est. 1978): 8,840,000
Capital: Sofia
Largest cities (est. 1975): Sofia, 965,700; (est. 1974 by U.N.): Plovdiv, 305,100; Varna, 270,000; Ruse, 171,300; Burgas, 148,200; Stara Zagora, 121,500
Monetary unit: Lev
Language: Bulgarian
Religions: Orthodox, 84%; Islam, 14%
Gross national product (1976): $20.3 billion
National name: Narodna Republika Bŭlgariya

Geography. Two mountain ranges and two great valleys mark the topography of Bulgaria, a country the size of Tennessee. Situated on the Black Sea in the eastern part of the Balkan peninsula, it shares borders with Yugoslavia, Romania, Greece, and Turkey. The Balkan belt crosses the center of the country, almost due east-west, rising to a height of 7,800 feet (2,377 m). The Rhodope range breaks off from the Balkans in the west, curves, and then straightens out to run nearly parallel along the southern border. Between the two ranges, is the valley of the Maritsa, Bulgaria's principal river. Between the Balkan range and the Danube, which forms most of the northern boundary with Romania, is the Danubian tableland.

Southern Dobruja, a fertile region of 2,900 square miles (7,511 sq km), below the Danube delta, is an area of low hills, fens, and sandy steppes.

BURMA

Socialist Republic of the Union of Burma
Area: 261,217 sq mi. (676,552 sq km)
Population (est. 1978): 32,200,000
Capital: Rangoon
Largest cities (est. 1973 for urban agglomeration): Rangoon, 2,056,100; Mandalay, 417,300; Moulmein, 171,800; Bassein, 126,150
Monetary unit: Kyat
Language: Burmese
Religions: Buddhist, 80%; Christian, Islam, Hindu
Gross national product (1976): $3.7 billion
National name: Pyidaungsu Socialist Thammada Myanma Naingngandau

Geography. Burma occupies the northwest portion of the former Indochinese peninsula. India lies to the northwest and China to the northeast. The Bay of Bengal touches the southwestern coast.

Slightly smaller than Texas, the country is divided into three natural regions: the Arakan Yoma, a long, narrow mountain range forming the barrier between Burma and India; the Shan Plateau in the east, extending southward into Tenasserim; and the Central Basin, running down to the flat fertile delta of the Irrawaddy in the south. This delta contains a network of intercommunicating canals and nine principal river mouths.

BURUNDI

Republic of Burundi
Area: 10,747 sq mi. (27,834 sq km)
Population (est. 1978): 4,100,000
Capital and largest city (est. 1970 for urban agglomeration): Bujumbura, 110,000
Monetary unit: Burundi franc
Languages: Kirundi (official), French
Religions: Roman Catholic, 61%; Animist, 35%; Protestant, 4%
Gross national product (1976): $460 million
National name: Republika Y'Uburundi

Geography. Wedged between Tanzania and Zaire in east central Africa, Burundi occupies a high plateau divided by several deep valleys. It is equal in size to Maryland.

CAMBODIA

Democratic Kampuchea
Area: 69,898 sq mi. (181,035 sq km)
Population (est. 1978): 8,890,000
Capital and largest city (est. 1976): Phnom Penh, 40,000–100,000
Monetary unit: Riel
Ethnic groups: Cambodian, 85%; Annamese, 5%; Chinese, 6%
Languages: Khmer (official), French, Vietnamese, Chinese, Cham, English
Religion: Theravada Buddhist

Geography. Situated on the Indochinese peninsula, Cambodia is bordered by Thailand and Laos on the north and Vietnam on the east and south. The Gulf of Siam is off the western coast. The country, the size of Missouri, consists chiefly of a large alluvial plain ringed in by mountains and on the east by the Mekong River. The plain is centered on Lake Tonle Sap, which is a natural storage basin of the Mekong.

CAMEROON

United Republic of Cameroon
Area: 183,569 sq mi. (475,442 sq km)
Population (est. 1978): 6,820,000
Capital: Yaoundé
Largest cities (est. 1975): Douala, 485,800; Yaoundé, 274,400
Monetary unit: Franc CFA
Languages: French and English (both official); Foulbé, Bamiléke, Ewondo, Donala, Mungaka, Bassa
Religions: Animist, Christian, Islam
Gross national product (1976): $2.2 billion
National name: République Unie du Cameroun

Geography. Cameroon is a West African nation on the Gulf of Guinea, bordered by Nigeria, Chad, the Central African Empire, the Congo, Equatorial Guinea, and Gabon. It is nearly twice the size of Oregon.

The interior consists of a high plateau, rising to 4,500 feet (1,372 m), with the land descending to a lower, densely wooded plateau and then to swamps and plains along the coast. Mount Cameroon (13,350 ft.; 4,069 m), near the coast, is the highest elevation in the country. The main rivers are the Benue, Nyong, and Sanaga.

CANADA

See separate Canada section

CAPE VERDE

Republic of Cape Verde
Area: 1,557 sq mi. (4,033 sq km)
Population: (est. 1978): 310,000
Capital (1970 census): Praia, 21,494
Largest city: Mindelo (est. 1970): 28,800
Monetary unit: Cape Verde escudo
Language: Portuguese
Religions: Mainly Roman Catholic, Protestant, and Christian Racionalist
National name: República de Cabo-Verde.

Geography: Cape Verde, only slightly larger than Rhode Island, is an archipelago in the Atlantic 385 miles west of Dakar, Senegal.

The islands are divided into two groups: Barlavento in the north, comprising Santo Antao (291 sq mi.; 754 sq km), Boa Vista (240 sq mi.; 622 sq km), Sao Nicolau (132 sq mi.; 342 sq km), Sao Vicente (88 sq mi.; 246 sq km), Sal Rei (83 sq mi.; 298 sq km), and Santa Luzia (13 sq mi.; 34 sq km); and Sotavento in the south, consisting of Sao Tiago (383 sq mi.; 992 sq km), Fogo (184 sq mi.; 477 sq km), Maio (103 sq mi.; 267 sq km), and Brava (25 sq mi.; 65 sq km). The islands are mostly mountainous, with the land deeply scarred by erosion. There is an active volcano on Fogo.

CENTRAL AFRICAN EMPIRE

Area: 240,535 sq mi. (622,984 sq km)
Population (est. 1978): 2,000,000
Capital and largest city (est. 1976): Bangui, 320,000
Monetary unit: Franc CFA
Ethnic groups: Mandja-Baya, Banda, Mbaka, Azande
Languages: French (official) and Sango
Religions: Animist, 60%; Christian, 35%; Islam, 5%
Gross national product (1976): $420 million
National name: L'Empire Centrafricain

Geography. Situated about 500 miles north of the equator, the Central African Empire is a landlocked nation bordered by Cameroon, Chad, the Sudan, Zaire, and the Congo. Twice the size of New Mexico, it is covered by tropical forests in the south and semidesert land in the east. The Ubangi and Shari are the largest of many rivers.

CHAD

Republic of Chad
Area: 495,752 sq mi. (1,284,000 sq km)
Population (est. 1978): 4,290,000
Capital and largest city (est. 1975): N'djamena, 224,000
Monetary unit: Franc CFA
Ethnic groups: Baguirmiens, Kanembous, Saras, Massas, Arabs, Toubous, Goranes
Languages: French (official), Sara, Kanembou, Ouddai, Massa, Arabic, Gorane
Religions: Islam, 52%; Animist, 43%; Roman Catholic, 5%
Gross national product (1976): $510 million
National name: République de Tchad

Geography. A landlocked country in north central Africa, Chad is about 85% the size of Alaska. Its neighbors are Niger, Libya, the Sudan, the Central African Empire, Cameroon, and Nigeria.

Lake Chad, from which the country gets its name, lies on the western border with Niger and Nigeria. In the north is a desert that runs into the Sahara.

CHILE

Republic of Chile
Area: 292,257 sq mi. (756,945 sq km)
Population (est. 1978): 10,880,000
Capital: Santiago
Largest cities (est. 1975 for urban agglomeration): Santiago, 3,263,000; **(est. 1971 by U.N.):** Valparaiso, 250,400; Viña del Mar, 179,600; Concepción, 161,000; Talcahuano, 148,000; Antofagasta, 125,100
Monetary unit: Peso
Language: Spanish
Religion: Roman Catholic
Gross national product (1976): $11.1 billion
National name: República de Chile

Geography. Situated south of Peru and west of Bolivia and Argentina, Chile fills a narrow 1,800-mile strip between the Andes and the Pacific. Its area is nearly twice that of Montana.

One third of Chile is covered by the towering ranges of the Andes. In the north is the mineral-rich Atacama Desert, between the coast mountains and the Andes. In the center is a 700-mile-long valley, thickly populated, between the Andes and the coastal plateau. In the south, the Andes border on the ocean.

At the southern tip of Chile's mainland is Punta Arenas, the southernmost city in the world, and beyond that lies the Strait of Magellan and Tierra del Fuego, an island divided between Chile and Argentina. The southernmost point of South America is Cape Horn, a 1,390-foot (424-m) rock on Horn Island in the Wollaston group, which belongs to Chile.

The Juan Fernández Islands, in the South Pacific about 400 miles (644 km) west of the mainland, and Easter Island, about 2,000 miles (3,219 km) west, are Chilean possessions.

CHINA

People's Republic of China
Area: 3,705,387 sq mi. (9,596,961 sq km)[1]
Population (est. 1978): 880,000,000
Capital: Peking
Largest cities (est. 1975): Shanghai, 10,888,000; Peking, 8,487,000; (est. 1970): Tientsin, 4,280,000; Wuhan, 4,250,000; Lüta (Port Arthur and Dairen), 4,000,000; Mukden, 3,750,000; Chungking, 3,500,000; Harbin, 2,750,000; Taiyüan, 2,725,000; Canton, 2,300,000; Nanking, 2,000,000
Monetary unit: Yuan
Language: Chinese, (Mandarin, Cantonese, and local dialects)
Religions: Principally Confucianist, Buddhist, and Taoist
Gross national product (1976): $343.1 billion
National name: Chung-Hua Jen-Min Kung-Ho Kuo

Geography. China, which occupies the eastern part of Asia, is slightly larger in area than the U.S. Its coastline is roughly a semicircle, about 2,150 miles long. The greater part of the country is mountainous, and only in the lower reaches of the Yellow and Yangtze rivers are there extensive low plains.

The principal mountain ranges are the Tien Shan, to the northwest; the Kunlun chain, running south of the Takla Makan and Gobi deserts; and the Trans-Himalaya, connecting the Kunlun with the borders of China and Tibet. Manchuria is largely an undulating plain connected with the north China plain by a narrow lowland corridor. Inner Mongolia contains the relatively fertile southern and eastern portions of the Gobi. The large island of Hainan (13,500 sq mi.; 34,965 sq km) lies off the southern coast.

Hydrographically, China proper consists of three great river systems. The northern part of the country is drained by the Yellow River (Hwang Ho), 2,900 miles long (4,667 km) and mostly unnavigable. The central part is drained by the Yangtze Kiang, the fourth longest river in the world

1. Including Manchuria and Tibet.

3,602 miles (5,797 km). The Si Kiang in the south is 1,236 miles long (1,989 km) and navigable for a considerable distance. In addition, the Amur (2,704 mi.; 4,352 km) forms part of the northeastern boundary.

CHINA (TAIWAN)

Republic of China
Area: 13,893 sq mi. (35,566 sq km)[1]
Population (est. 1977): 16,678,000
Capital: Taipei
Largest cities (est. 1978): Taipei, 2,130,800; Kao-hsiung, 1,042,000; T'ai-chung, 570,750; T'ai-nan, 547,000; Chi-lung, 341,700
Monetary unit: New Taiwan dollar
Language: Chinese (Mandarin)
Religions: Confucianist, Buddhist, Christian, Taoist
Gross national product (1976): $17.1 billion

Geography. The Republic of China today consists of the former Taiwan Province, including Taiwan, an island 100 miles off the Asian mainland in the Pacific; two offshore islands, Quemoy and Matsu; and the nearby islets of the Pescadores chain. It is slightly larger than the combined areas of Massachusetts and Connecticut.

The country is divided by a central mountain range that runs from north to south, rising sharply on the east coast and descending gradually to a broad western plain, where cultivation is concentrated.

1. Excluding Quemoy and Matsu.

COLOMBIA

Republic of Colombia
Area: 439,735 sq mi. (1,138,914 sq km)
Population (est. 1978): 25,800,000; (mestizo, 68%; white, 20%; Indian, 7%; black, 5%)
Capital: Bogotá
Largest cities (est. 1977): Bogotá, 3,618,800; **(1973 census):** Medellín, 1,064,741; Cali, 898,253; Barranquilla, 664,533; Cartagena, 356,424; Bucaramanga, 328,328
Monetary unit: Peso
Language: Spanish
Religion: Roman Catholic
Gross national product (1976): $15.4 billion
National name: República de Colombia

Geography. Colombia, in the northwestern part of South America, is the only country on that continent that borders on both the Atlantic and Pacific Oceans. It is nearly equal to the combined areas of California and Texas.

Through the western half of the country, three Andean ranges run north and south, merging into one at the Ecuadorean border. The eastern half is a low, jungle-covered plain, drained by spurs of the Amazon and Orinoco, inhabited mostly by isolated, tropical-forest Indian tribes. The fertile plateau and valley of the eastern range are the most densely populated parts of the country.

COMORO ISLANDS

Area: 838 sq mi. (2,171 sq km)
Population (est. 1978): 370,000
Capital and largest city (est. 1976): Moroni (on Grande Comoro), 18,300
Monetary unit: Franc CFA
Language: French
Religions: Islam and Christian
Gross national product (1976): $60 million
National name: État Comorien

Geography. The Comoro Islands—Grande Comoro, Anjouan, Mohéli, and Mayotte (which retains ties to France)—are an archipelago of volcanic origin in the Indian Ocean between Mozambique and Madagascar.

CONGO

People's Republic of the Congo
Area: 132,046 sq mi. (342,000 sq km)
Population (est. 1978): 1,500,000
Capital and largest city (est. 1974): Brazzaville, 310,500
Monetary unit: Franc CFA
Ethnic groups: Bavilis, Balalis, Batékés, M'Bochis
Languages: French, Lingala, Kokongo
Religions: Animist, 60%; Roman Catholic, 38%
Gross national product (1976): $700 million
National name: République Populaire du Congo

Geography. The Congo is situated in west central Africa astride the Equator. It borders on Gabon, Cameroon, the Central African Empire, Zaire, and the Angola exclave of Cabinda, with a short stretch of coast on the South Atlantic. Its area is nearly three times that of Pennsylvania.

Most of the inland is tropical rain forest, drained by tributaries of the Zaire (Congo) River, which flows south along the eastern border with Zaire to Stanley Pool. The narrow coastal plain rises to highlands separated from the inland plateaus by the 200-mile-wide Niari River Valley, which gives passage to the coast.

COSTA RICA

Republic of Costa Rica
Area: 19,575 sq mi. (50,700 sq km)
Population (est. 1978): 2,120,000 (approx.: white and Mestizo, 97.6%; black, 1.9%; Indian, .4%; Asiatic, .1%)
Capital and largest city (est. 1977): San José, 547,200
Monetary unit: Colón
Language: Spanish
Religion: Roman Catholic
Gross national product (1976): $2.3 billion
National name: República de Costa Rica

Geography. This Central American country lies between Nicaragua to the north and Panama to the south. Its area slightly exceeds that of Vermont and New Hampshire combined.

Most of Costa Rica is tableland, from 3,000 to 6,000 feet (914 to 1,829 m) above sea level. Cocos Island (10 sq mi.), about 300 miles off the Pacific Coast, is under Costa Rican sovereignty; although it is mostly tropical jungle, it is of potential strategic importance in defense of the Panama Canal.

CUBA

Republic of Cuba
Area: 44,218 sq mi. (114,524, sq km)
Population (est. 1977): 9,590,000
Capital: Havana
Largest cities (est. 1975 by U.N.): Havana, 1,861,400; Santiago de Cuba, 315,800; Camagüey, 221,800; Holguín, 151,900; Guantánamo, 148,800; Santa Clara, 146,650
Monetary unit: Peso
Language: Spanish
Religion: Roman Catholic
Gross national product (1976): $8.1 billion
National name: República de Cuba

Geography. The largest island of the West Indies group (equal in area to Pennsylvania), Cuba is also the westernmost—just west of Hispaniola (Haiti and the Dominican Republic), and 90 miles south of Key West, Fla., at the entrance to the Gulf of Mexico.

The island has mountainous areas in the southeast, central area, and the west (Sierra Maestra). The rest of the country is flat or rolling.

CYPRUS

Republic of Cyprus
Area: 3,572 sq mi (9,251 sq km)
Population (est. 1978): 700,000 (Greek, 82%, Turkish, 18%)
Capital and largest city (est. 1977): Nicosia, 120,000
Monetary unit: Cyprus pound
Languages: Greek, Turkish, English
Religions: Greek Orthodox, 77%; Islam, 18%
Gross national product (1976): $789 million
National name: Kypriaki Dimokratia—Kibris Cumhuriyeti

Geography. The third largest island in the Mediterranean (half again larger than Delaware), Cyprus lies off the southern coast of Turkey and the western shore of Syria. Most of the country consists of a wide plain lying between two mountain ranges that cross the island. The highest peak is Mt. Olympus at 6,406 feet (1,953 m).

CZECHOSLOVAKIA

Czechoslovak Socialist Republic
Area: 49,373 sq mi. (127,869 sq km)
Population (est. 1978): 15,150,000 (Czech 68%; Slovak, 32%)
Capital: Prague
Largest cities (est. 1977): 1,179,600; Prague, 1,179,600; **(est. 1974 by U.N.):** Brno, 343,860; Bratislava, 328,765; Ostrava, 292,404; Košice, 166,240; Plzeň, 154,126
Monetary unit: Koruna
Languages: Czech, Slovak, Hungarian
Religions: Roman Catholic, 70%; Czechoslovak Church, 8%; Protestant, 7%; Greek Orthodox, 5%.
Gross national product (1976): $57.3 billion
National name: Ceskoslovenská Socialistická Republika

Geography. Czechoslovakia lies in central Europe, a neighbor of East and West Germany, Poland, the U.S.S.R., Hungary, and Austria. It is equal in size to New York State. The principal rivers—the Elbe, Danube, Oder, and Moldau—are vital commercially to this landlocked country, both for waterborne commerce and agriculture, which flourishes in fertile valleys irrigated by these rivers and their tributaries.

DENMARK

Kingdom of Denmark
Area: 16,629 sq mi. (43,069 sq km)[1]
Population (est. 1978): 5,110,000[1]
Capital: Copenhagen
Largest cities (est. 1974): Copenhagen (including Frederiksberg) 1,380,000;
(est. 1974 by U.N.): Arhus, 245,900; Odense, 168,200; Alborg, 154,600
Monetary unit: Krone
Language: Danish
Religion: Lutheran (established)
Gross national product (1976): $38.2 billion
National name: Kongeriget Danmark

Geography. Smallest of the Scandinavian countries (half
the size of Maine), Denmark occupies the Jutland peninsula, which extends north from Germany between the tips
of Norway and Sweden. To the west is the North Sea and
to the east the Baltic.

The country also consists of several Baltic islands; the
two largest are Sjaelland, the site of Copenhagen, and Fyn.
The narrow waters off the north coast are called the Ska-
gerrak and those off the east, the Kattegat.

1. Excluding Faeroe Islands and Greenland.

Outlying Territories of Denmark

FAEROE ISLANDS

Status: Autonomous part of Denmark
Area: 540 sq mi. (1,399 sq km)
Population (est. 1978): 43,000
Capital (est. 1975): Thorshavn, 11,300
Monetary unit: Faeroese krone

GREENLAND

Status: Integral part of Kingdom of Denmark.
Area: 839,999 sq mi. (incl. 708,069 sq mi. covered by icecap) (2,175,600 sq
km).
Population (est. 1978): 57,500.
Capital (est. 1975): Godthaab, 8,300.
Chief exports: fish, fur skins, cryolite.

DJIBOUTI

Republic of Djibouti
Area: 8,494 sq mi. (22,000 sq km)
Population (est. 1978): 225,000
Capital (est. 1977): Djibouti, 160,000
Monetary unit: Djibouti franc
Languages: Arabic, French, Saho-Afar, Somali
Religions: Islam and Christian

Geography. Djibouti lies in northeastern Africa on the Gulf of Aden at the southern entrance to the Red Sea. It borders on Ethiopia and Somalia. The country, the size of Massachusetts, is mainly a stony desert, with scattered plateaus and highlands.

DOMINICAN REPUBLIC

Area: 18,816 sq mi. (48,734 sq km)
Population (est. 1978): 5,170,000 (approx.: mestizo and mulatto, 73%; white, 16%; black, 11%
Capital: Santo Domingo[1]
Largest cities (est. 1977): Santo Domingo, 1,000,000; **(1970 census):** Santiago de los Caballeros, 155,151
Monetary unit: Peso
Language: Spanish
Religion: Roman Catholic
Gross national product (1976): $3.8 billion
National name: República Dominicana

Geography. The Dominican Republic in the West Indies, occupies the eastern two thirds of the island of Hispaniola, which it shares with Haiti. Its area equals that of Vermont and New Hampshire combined.

Crossed from northwest to southeast by a moutain range with elevations exceeding 10,000 feet (3,048 m), the country has fertile, well-watered land in the northeast, where nearly two thirds of the population lives. The southwest part is arid and has poor soil, except around Santo Domingo.

1. Called Ciudad Trujillo from 1936 to 1961.

ECUADOR

Republic of Ecuador
Area: 109,483 sq mi. (283,561 sq km)
Population (est. 1978): 7,825,000
Capital: Quito
Largest cities (est. 1977): Quito, 977,400; **(1974 census):** Guayaquil, 823,200
Monetary unit: Sucre
Languages: Spanish, Quéchua, Jibaro
Religion: Roman Catholic
Gross national product (1976): $4.8 billion
National name: República del Ecuador

Geography. Ecuador, equal in area to Nevada, is in the northwest part of South America fronting on the Pacific.

To the north is Colombia and to the east and south is Peru. Two high and parallel ranges of the Andes, traversing the country from north to south, are topped by tall volcanic peaks. The highest is Chimborazo at 20,577 feet (6,272 m).

The Galápagos Islands (or Colón Archipelago) (3,029 sq mi.; 7,845 sq km) in the Pacific Ocean about 600 miles (966 km) west of the South American mainland, became part of Ecuador in 1832.

EGYPT

Arab Republic of Egypt
Area: 386,661 sq mi. (1,001,449 sq km)
Population (est. 1978): 39,500,000
Capital: Cairo
Largest cities (est. 1976): Cairo, 6,133,000; (est. 1974 by U.N.): Alexandria, 2,259,000; Giza, 853,700; Suez, 368,000; Subra el Khema, 346,000; Port Said, 342,000; El Mahalla el Kûbra, 287,800
Monetary unit: Egyptian pound
Language: Arabic
Religions: Islam, 93%; Christian (mostly Copt), 7%
Gross national product (1976): $10.5 billion

Geography. Egypt, at the northeast corner of Africa on the Mediterranean Sea, is bordered on the west by Libya, on the south by the Sudan, and on the east by the Red Sea and Israel. It is nearly half again the size of Texas.

The historic Nile flows through the eastern third of the country. On either side of the Nile valley are desert plateaus, spotted with oases. In the north, toward the Mediterranean, plateaus are low, while south of Cairo they rise to a maximum of 1,015 feet (309 m) above sea level. At the head of the Red Sea is the Sinai Peninsula, between the Suez Canal and Israel.

Navigable throughout its course in Egypt, the Nile is used largely as a means of cheap transport for heavy goods. The principal port is Alexandria.

The Nile delta starts 100 miles south of the Mediterranean and fans out to a sea front of 155 miles between the cities of Alexandria and Port Said. From Cairo north, the Nile branches into many streams, the principal ones being the Damietta and the Rosetta.

Except for a narrow belt along the Mediterranean, Egypt lies in an almost rainless area, in which high daytime temperatures fall quickly at night.

EL SALVADOR

Republic of El Salvador
Area: 8,124 sq mi. (21,041 sq km)
Population (est. 1978): 4,340,000
Capital: San Salvador
Largest cities (est. 1976): San Salvador, 500,000; (est. 1969): Santa Ana, 168,000
Monetary unit: Colón
Language: Spanish
Religion: Roman Catholic
Gross national product (1976): $2.2 billion
National name: República de El Salvador

Geography. Situated on the Pacific coast of Central America, El Salvador has Guatemala to the west and Honduras to the north and east. It is the smallest of the Central American countries, its area equal to that of Massachusetts, and the only one without an Atlantic coastline.

Most of the country is a fertile volcanic plateau about 2,000 feet (607 m) high. There are some active volcanoes and many scenic crater lakes.

EQUATORIAL GUINEA

Republic of Equatorial Guinea
Area: 10,830 sq mi. (28,051 sq km)
Population (est. 1978): 325,000
Capital and largest city (est. 1970): Malabo (formerly Santa Isabel), 19,300
Monetary unit: Ekpwele
Languages: Spanish, Fang, Bubi
Religions: Roman Catholic, Protestant, Animist
Gross national product (1976): $110 million
National name: Repúblika de Guinea Ecuatorial

Geography. Equatorial Guinea, formerly Spanish Guinea, consists of Rio Muni (10,045 sq mi.; 26,117 sq km), on the western coast of Africa, and several islands in the Gulf of Guinea, the largest of which is Macias Nguema Biyogo (formerly Fernando Po) (785 sq mi.; 2,033 sq km). The other islands are Pagalu (formerly Annobón), Corisco, Elobey Grande, and Elobey Chico. The total area is twice that of Connecticut.

ETHIOPIA

Area: 471,778 sq mi. (1,221,900 sq km)
Population (est. 1978): 29,700,000 (Amhara, 20%; Gala, 40%; others 40%)
Capital: Addis Ababa

Largest cities (est. 1977): Addis Ababa, 1,327,200; Asmara, 340,200
Monetary unit: Birr
Languages: Amharic (official), Galligna, Tigrigna
Religions: Copt (Christian), Islam
Gross national product (1976): $2.9 billion

Geography. Ethiopia is in east central Africa, bordered on the west by the Sudan, the east by Somalia and Djibouti, the south by Kenya, and the north by the Red Sea. It is nearly three times the size of California.

Over its main plateau land, Ethiopia has several high mountains, the highest of which is Ras Dashan at 15,158 feet (4,620 m). The Blue Nile, or Abbai, rises in the northwest and flows in a great semicircle east, south, and northwest before entering Sudan. Its chief reservoir, Lake Tana, lies in the northwestern part of the plateau.

FIJI

Dominion of Fiji
Area: 7,055 sq mi. (18,272 sq km)
Population (est. 1978): 620,000
Capital (est. 1976): Suva (on Viti Levu), 63,600
Monetary unit: Fijian dollar
Languages: Fijian, Hindustani, English, Chinese
Religions: Christian, Hindu, Islam
Gross national product (1976): $670 million

Geography. Fiji consists of more than 500 islands in the southwestern Pacific Ocean about 1,960 miles from Sydney, Australia. The two largest islands are Viti Levu (4,109 sq mi.; 10,642 sq km) and Vanua Levu (2,242 sq mi.; 5,807 sq km). The island of Rotuma (18 sq mi.; 47 sq km), about 400 miles to the north, is a dependency of Fiji. Overall, Fiji is nearly as large as New Jersey.

The largest islands in the group are mountainous and volcanic, with the tallest peak being Mount Victoria (4,341 ft; 1,323 m) on Viti Levu. The islands in the south have dense forests on the windward side and grasslands on the leeward.

FINLAND

Republic of Finland
Area: 130,119 sq mi. (337,009 sq km)
Population (est. 1978): 4,750,000 (Finnish, 90%; Swedish, 10%)

Capital: Helsinki
Largest cities (est. 1977): Helsinki, 493,300; (est. 1974 by U.N.): Tampere, 165,500; Turku, 162,500
Monetary unit: Markka
Languages: Finnish, Swedish
Religions: Lutheran, 98.6%; Orthodox, 1.3%
Gross national product (1976): $27.7 billion
National name: Suomen Tasavalta—Republiken Finland

Geography. Finland stretches 700 miles (1,127 km) from the Gulf of Finland on the south to Soviet Petsamo, north of the Arctic Circle. The U.S.S.R. extends along the entire eastern frontier. In area, Finland is three times the size of Ohio.

Off the southwest coast are the Aland Islands, controlling the entrance to the Gulf of Bothnia. Finland has more than 60,000 lakes. Of the few rivers, only the Oulu (Ulea) is navigable to any important extent.

The Swedish-populated Aland Islands (581 sq mi.; 1,505 sq km) have an autonomous status under a law passed in 1951.

FRANCE

French Republic
Area: 211,208 sq mi. (547,026 sq km)
Population (est. 1978): 53,250,000
Capital: Paris
Largest cities (1975 census): Paris, 2,317,227; Marseilles, 914,356; Lyons, 462,841; Toulouse, 383,176; Nice, 346,620; Nantes, 263,689; Strasbourg, 257,300; Bordeaux, 226,281
Monetary unit: Franc
Religion (est.): Roman Catholic, 90%; Protestant, Jewish, Islam, and others, 10%
Gross national product (1976): $346.7 billion
National name: République Française

Geography. France (80% the size of Texas) is second in size to Russia among Europe's nations. In the Alps near the Italian and Swiss borders is France's highest point—Mont Blanc (15,781 ft; 4,810 m). The forest-covered Vosges Mountains are in the northeast, and the Pyrenees are along the Spanish border.

Except for extreme Northern France, which is part of the Flanders plain, the country may be described as four river basins and a plateau. Three of the streams flow west—the Seine into the English Channel, the Loire into the

Atlantic, and the Garonne into the Bay of Biscay. The Rhône flows south into the Mediterranean. For about a hundred miles, the Rhine is France's eastern border.

West of the Rhône and northeast of the Garonne lies the Central Plateau, covering about 15% of France's area and rising to a maximum elevation of 6,188 feet (1,886 m). In the Mediterranean, about 115 miles (185 km) east-south-east of Nice, is Corsica (3,367 sq mi.; 8,721 sq km).

Overseas Departments and Territories of France

FRENCH GUIANA (including ININI)

Status: Overseas Department
Area: 35,135 sq mi. (91,000 sq km)
Population (est. 1978): 62,000
Capital (1974 census): Cayenne, 29,404
Agricultural products: bananas, cacao, corn, manioc, rice, sugar cane
Mineral: gold

FRENCH POLYNESIA

Status: Overseas Territory
Area: 1,544 sq mi. (4,000 sq km)
Population (est. 1978): 140,000
Capital (1971): Papeete (on Tahiti), 25,300
Agricultural products: copra, vanilla, coffee
Mineral: phosphates

GUADELOUPE

Status: Overseas Department
Area: 687 sq mi. (1,779 sq km)
Population (est. 1978): 375,000
Capital (1974 census): Basse-Terre, 15,778
Largest city (1974 census): Pointe-à-Pitre-Les Abymes, 77,937
Agricultural products: sugar, bananas, coffee, cacao, vanilla, tobacco
Manufactures: rum, sugar

MARTINIQUE

Status: Overseas Department
Area: 425 sq mi. (1,102 sq km)
Population (est. 1978): 375,000
Capital (1974 census): Fort-de-France 100,576
Agricultural products: sugar, bananas, pineapples, cacao, coffee
Manufactures: rum, sugar

MAYOTTE

Status: Territorial collectivity
Area: 146 sq mi. (378 sq km)
Population (est. 1976): 40,000
Capital: Dzaoudzi, (about 3,200)
Principal products: vanilla, essential oils, copra

NEW CALEDONIA AND DEPENDENCIES

Status: Overseas Territory
Area: 7,358 sq mi. (19,058 sq km)[1]

1. Including dependencies.

Population (est. 1978): 140,000
Capital (1976 census): Nouméa, 56,100
Agricultural products: coffee, copra, corn, cotton, manioc, rice, tobacco
Minerals: nickel, chromite, iron ore
Sea product: mother-of-pearl

NEW HEBRIDES

Status: Anglo-French condominium
Area: 5,700 sq mi. (14,763 sq km)
Population (est. 1978): 100,000
Capital (est. 1976): Vila (metropolitan area), 17,400
Agricultural products: copra, cocoa, coffee
Sea products: trochus and burghaus shell

REUNION (BOURBON)

Status: Overseas Department
Prefect:
Area: 970 sq mi. (2,510 sq km)
Population (est. 1978): 500,000
Capital (1974 census): Saint-Denis, 104,603
Agricultural products: sugar, vanilla, tea, tobacco.

ST. PIERRE AND MIQUELON

Status: Overseas Department
Area: 93 sq mi. (242 sq km)
Population (est. 1976): 6,000
Capital (1974 census): St. Pierre, 5,232
Industries: Fishing and canneries.

SOUTHERN AND ANTARCTIC LANDS

Status: Overseas Territory
Area: 169,614 sq mi. (439,300 sq km)
Population (1972): 189
Capital (1972): Port-au-Français: 93

WALLIS AND FUTUNA ISLANDS

Status: Overseas Territory
Area: 77 sq mi. (200 sq km)
Population (est. 1978): 9,200
Capital: Mata-Utu (on Uvea), (1969): 600
Agricultural products: copra, taro, hams, cassava, bananas

GABON

Gabon Republic
Area: 103,346 sq mi. (267,667 sq km)
Population (est. 1978): 540,000
Capital and largest city (est. 1975 for urban agglomeration): Libreville, 169,200
Monetary unit: Franc CFA
Ethnic groups: Bateke, Obamba, Bakota, Shake, Pongwés, Adumas, Chiras, Punu, and Lumbu
Languages: French (official) and Bantu dialects
Religions: Animist, Christian, Islam

Gross national product (1976): $1.4 billion
National name: République Gabonaise

Geography. This west African land with the Atlantic as its western border is also bounded by Equatorial Guinea, Cameroon, and the Congo. Its area is slightly less than Kentucky's.

From mangrove swamps on the coast, the land becomes divided plateaus in the north and east and mountains in the north. Most of the country is covered by a dense tropical forest.

GAMBIA

Republic of the Gambia
Area: 4,361 sq mi. (11,295 sq km)
Population (est. 1978): 560,000
Capital and largest city (est. 1975): Banjul, 42,400
Monetary unit: Dalasi
Languages: Native tongues, English (official)
Religions: Islam, Christian, Animist
Gross national product (1976): $100 million

Geography. Situated on the Atlantic coast in westernmost Africa and surrounded on three sides by Senegal, Gambia is twice the size of Delaware. The Gambia River flows for 200 miles (322 km) through Gambia on its way to the Atlantic. The country, the smallest on the continent, averages only 20 miles (32 km) in width.

GERMANY, EAST

German Democratic Republic
Area: 41,923 sq mi. (108,178 sq km)[1]
Population (est. 1978): 16,570,000
Capital: Berlin (eastern sector)
Largest cities (est. 1977): East Berlin, 1,106,300; (est. 1976 by U.N.): Leipzig, 565,400; Dresden, 509,250; Karl-Marx Stadt, 305,900; Magdeburg, 278,000; Halle, 235,550; Rostock, 215,000; Erfurt, 204,500
Monetary unit: Mark of the Deutsche Demokratische Republik
Language: German
Religions (est. 1969): Protestant, 80%; Roman Catholic, 10%
Gross national product (1976): $70.9 billion
National name: Deutsche Demokratische Republik

Geography. East Germany lies on the Baltic Sea with Poland to the east and Czechoslovakia to the south. The bor-

1. Including East Berlin (156 square miles), which has been incorporated into the German Democratic Republic.

der with West Germany is roughly a line running south
from Lübeck for about 250 miles. The main river is the
Elbe, which flows from Dresden in the southeast to the
North Sea in the northwest. The Oder and Neisse rivers
form the border with Poland. Most of the country, which
is the size of Tennessee, is situated in the north German
plain.

GERMANY, WEST

Federal Republic of Germany
Area: 95,791 sq mi. (248,577 sq km)[1]
Population (est. 1978): 61,250,000[1]
Capital (est. 1977): Bonn, 285,000
Largest cities (est. 1977): Hamburg, 1,707,400; Munich, 1,311,300; Cologne,
   1,010,400; Essen, 674,000; Düsseldorf, 658,400; Frankfurt, 631,000;
   Dortmund, 627,600; Stuttgart, 594,100; Bremen, 570,700; Hannover,
   549,100
Monetary unit: Deutsche Mark
Language: German
Religions: Protestant, 51%; Roman Catholic, 45%
Gross national product (1976): $446.7 billion
National name: Bundesrepublik Deutschland

1. Excluding West Berlin (184 square miles with 1977 population of 1,966,700).

Geography. The Federal Republic of Germany occupies
the western half of the central European area historically
regarded as German. This was the part of Germany occupied by the U.S., U.K., and France after the German
defeat in World War II, when the eastern half of prewar
Germany was split roughly between a Soviet-occupied
zone, which became the present German Democratic
Republic, and an area annexed by Poland.

The northern plain, the central hill country, and the
southern mountain district constitute the main physical
divisions of West Germany, which is slightly smaller than
Oregon. The Bavarian plateau in the southwest averages
1,600 feet (488 m) above sea level, but it reaches 9,721 feet
(2,963 m) in the Zugspitze, which is the highest point in
Germany.

There are several important navigable rivers. In the
south the Danube, rising in the Black Forest, flows east
across Bavaria into Austria. The other important rivers flow
north. The Rhine, which rises in Switzerland and flows
across the Netherlands in two channels to the North Sea,
is navigable by smaller vessels as far as Cologne. The Rhine

and the Elbe, which also empties into the North Sea, are
navigable within Germany for ships of 400 tons. The Weser, flowing into the North Sea, and the Main and Mosel
(Moselle), both tributaries of the Rhine, are also important.

BERLIN

Status: West Berlin: State of West Germany; East Berlin: capital of East
Germany
Area: 340 square miles (West Berlin, 184; East Berlin, 156
Population (est. 1977): 3,057,000 (West Berlin, 1,950,700; East Berlin,
1,106,300)

GHANA

Republic of Ghana
Area: 92,100 sq mi. (238,537 sq km)
Population (est. 1978): 10,650,000
Capital: Accra
Largest cities (est. 1975): Accra, 716,600; **(est. 1972):** Kumasi, 342,982;
Sekondi-Takoradi, 161,071
Monetary unit: New cedi
Languages: Native tongues (Twi, Fanti, Ga, Ewe, Dagbani); English
Religions: Christian 43%, Islam, 12%, Animist 38%
Gross national product (1976): $5.9 billion

Geography. A West African country bordering on the Gulf
of Guinea, Ghana has the Ivory Coast to the west, Upper
Volta to the north, and Togo to the east. It compares in size
to Oregon.

The coastal belt, extending about 270 miles (435 km), is
sandy, marshy, and generally exposed. Behind it is a gradually widening grass strip. The forested plateau region to
the north is broken by ridges and hills. The largest river is
the Volta.

GREECE

Hellenic Republic
Area: 50,944 sq mi. (131,944 sq km)
Population (est. 1977): 9,300,000
Capital: Athens
Largest cities (1971 census): Athens (metropolitan area), 1,378,586; Salonika,
302,634; Patras, 94,192; Volos, 73,877
Monetary unit: Drachma
Language: Greek
Religion: Greek Orthodox
Gross national product (1976): $22.9 billion
National name: Elliniki Dimokratia

Geography. Greece, on the Mediterranean Sea, is the southernmost country on the Balkan Peninsula in Eastern Europe. It is bordered on the north by Albania, Yugoslavia, and Bulgaria; on the west by the Ionian Sea; and on the east by the Aegean Sea and Turkey. It is slightly smaller than Alabama.

North central Greece, Epirus, and western Macedonia all are mountainous. The main chain of the Pindus Mountains rises to 9,000 feet (2,743 m) in places, separating Epirus from the plains of Thessaly. Greek Thrace is mostly a lowland region separated from European Turkey by the lower Maritsa River.

Among the many islands are the Ionian group off the west coast; the Cyclades group to the southeast; other islands in the eastern Aegean, including Lesbos, Samos, and Chios; and Crete, the fourth largest Mediterranean island.

The Dodecanese, a group of islands in the Aegean Sea near the coast of Asia Minor, were ceded to Greece by the 1947 Italian peace treaty and were formally transferred on March 7, 1948.

GRENADA

State of Grenada
Area: 133 sq mi. (344 sq km)
Population (est. 1978): 110,000 (black, 53%; mixed, 42%)
Capital and largest city (est. 1974): St. George's, 6,600
Monetary unit: East Caribbean dollar
Ethnic groups: Caribs and Indians
Language: English
Religions: Roman Catholic, Anglican, Methodist
Gross national product (1976): $50 million

Geography. Grenada (the first "a" is pronounced as in "gray") is the most southerly of the Windward Islands, about 100 miles from the South American coast. It is a volcanic island traversed by a mountain range, the highest peak of which is Mount St. Catherine (2,756 ft.; 840 m).

GUATEMALA

Republic of Guatemala
Area: 42,042 sq mi. (108,889 sq km)
Population (est. 1978): 6,630,000
Capital and largest city (est. 1978): Guatemala City, 1,227,800
Monetary unit: Quetzal

Languages: Spanish, some Indian dialects
Religion: Roman Catholic
Gross national product (1976): $4.1 billion
National name: República de Guatemala

Geography. The northernmost of the Central American nations, Guatemala is the size of Tennessee. The country consists of two main regions—the cool highlands with the heaviest population and the tropical area along the Pacific and Caribbean coasts. The principal mountain range rises to the highest elevation in Central America and contains many volcanic peaks. Volcanic eruptions are frequent.

GUINEA

Republic of Guinea
Area: 94,925 sq mi. (245,857 sq km)
Population (est. 1978): 4,775,000 (chiefly Fulani, Malinké, and Susu)
Capital and largest city (est. 1977): Conakry, 600,000
Monetary unit: Syli
Languages: French (official), native tongues (Malinké, NomSusu, Fulani)
Religions: Islam and animist
Gross national product (1976): $880 million
National name: République de Guinée

Geography. Guinea, in western Africa on the Atlantic, is also bordered by Guinea-Bissau, Senegal, Mali, the Ivory Coast, Liberia, and Sierra Leone. Slightly smaller than Oregon, the country consists of a coastal plain, a mountainous region, a savanna interior, and a forest area in the Guinea Highlands. The highest peak is Mt. Nimba at about 6,000 feet (1,829 m).

GUINEA-BISSAU

Republic of Guinea-Bissau
Area: 13,948 sq mi. (36,125 sq km)
Population (est. 1978): 545,000
Capital and largest city (est. 1970 for urban agglomeration): Bissau, 71,200
Monetary unit: Guinea-Bissau peso
Language: French (official)
Religions: Animist, Islam, Roman Catholic
Gross national product (1976): $70 million
National name: Guiné Bissau

Geography. A neighbor of Senegal and Guinea in western Africa, on the Atlantic coast, Guinea-Bissau is about half the size of South Carolina.

The country is a low-lying coastal region of swamps, rain forests, and mangrove-covered wetlands, with about 60 islands off the coast. The Bissagos archipelago extends 30 miles out to sea. Internal communications depend mainly on deep estuaries and meandering rivers, since there are no railroads. Bissau, the capital, is the main port.

GUYANA

Republic of Guyana
Area: 83,000 sq mi. (214,969 sq km)
Population (est. 1978): 825,000 (East Indian, 52%; African, 31%; mixed 10%; Amerindian, 5%)
Capital and largest city (est. 1972): Georgetown, 101,000
Monetary unit: Guyanan dollar
Languages: English (official), Hindi, Urdu
Religions: Protestant, Islam, Roman Catholic, Hindu
Gross national product (1976): $430 million

Geography. Guyana is situated on the northern coast of South America to the east of Venezuela and north of Brazil. The country consists of a low coastal area and the Guiana Highlands in the south. There is an extensive north-south network of rivers. Guyana is the size of Idaho.

HAITI

Republic of Haiti
Area: 10,714 sq mi. (27,750 sq km)
Population (est. 1978): 4,830,000
Capital and largest city (est. 1976): Port-au-Prince, 652,900
Monetary unit: Gourde
Languages: French, Creole
Religion: Roman Catholic
Gross national product (1976): $930 million
National name: République d'Haïti

Geography. Haiti, in the West Indies, occupies the western third of the island of Hispaniola, which it shares with the Dominican Republic. About the size of Maryland, Haiti is two thirds mountainous, with the rest of the country marked by great valleys, extensive plateaus, and small plains. The most densely populated region is the Cul-de-Sac plain near Port-au-Prince.

HONDURAS

Republic of Honduras
Area: 43,277 sq mi. (112,088 sq km)
Population (est. 1977): 2,900,000 (90% mestizo)
Capital and largest city (est. 1975): Tegucigalpa, 350,000
Monetary unit: Lempira
Languages: Spanish, some Indian dialects
Religion: Roman Catholic
Gross national product (1976): $1.2 billion
National name: República de Honduras

Geography. Honduras, in the north central part of Central America, has a 400-mile (644-km) Caribbean coastline and a 40-mile (64-km) Pacific frontage. Its neighbors are Guatemala to the west, El Salvador to the south, and Nicaragua to the east. Honduras is slightly larger than Tennessee.

Generally mountainous, the country is marked by fertile plateaus, river valleys, and narrow coastal plains.

HUNGARY

Hungarian People's Republic
Area: 35,919 sq mi. (93,030 sq km)
Population (est. 1978): 10,700,000 (Magyar, German, Slovak)
Capital: Budapest
Largest cities (est. 1977): Budapest, 2,081,700 **(est. 1975 by U.N.):** Miskolc, 198,000; Debrecen, 184,700; Szeged, 168,800; Pécs, 162,350; Györ, 117,500
Monetary unit: Forint
Language: Magyar
Religions: Roman Catholic, 60%; Protestant, atheist
Gross national product: (1976): $24.1 billion
National name: Magyar Népköztársaság

Geography. This central European country the size of Indiana is bordered by Austria to the west, Czechoslovakia to the north, the U.S.S.R. and Romania to the east, and Yugoslavia to the south.

Most of Hungary is a fertile, rolling plain lying east of the Danube River and drained by the Danube and Tisza rivers. In the extreme northwest is the Little Hungarian Plain. South of that area is Lake Balaton (250 sq mi.; 648 sq km).

ICELAND

Republic of Iceland
Area: 39,768 sq mi. (103,000 sq km)

Population (est. 1978): 227,000
Capital and largest city (est. 1976): Reykjavik, 84,500
Monetary unit: Króna
Language: Icelandic
Religion: Evangelical Lutheran
Gross national product (1976): $1.4 billion
National name: Lyoveldio Island

Geography. Iceland, a bleak island about the size of Kentucky, lies in the north Atlantic Ocean east of Greenland and just touches the Arctic Circle. It is one of the most volcanic regions in the world.

Small fresh-water lakes are to be found throughout the island, and there are many natural oddities, including hot springs, geysers, sulfur beds, canyons, waterfalls, and swift rivers. More than 13% of the area is covered by snowfields and glaciers, and most of the people live in the 7% of the island comprising fertile coastlands.

INDIA

Republic of India
Area: 1,269,338 sq mi. (3,287,590 sq km)
Population (est. 1978): 643,000,000
Capital (1971 census): New Delhi, 301,801
Largest cities (1971 census): Calcutta, 7,031,382; Greater Bombay, 5,970,575; Delhi, 3,287,883; Madras, 2,469,449; Bangalore, 1,540,741; Ahmedabad, 1,585,544; Kanpur, 1,154,388
Monetary unit: Rupee
Principal languages; Hindi (official), Bengali, Sindhi, Gujarati, Kannarese, Kashmiri, Malayalam, Marathi, Oriya, Punjabi, Tamil, Telugu, Urdu, English
Religions: Hindu, 83%; Islam, 11%; Christian, 3%; Sikh, 2%
Gross national product (1976): $95.9 billion
National name: Bharat

Geography. One third the area of the United States, the Republic of India occupies most of the subcontinent of India in south Asia. It borders on China in the northeast.

The country contains a large part of the great Indo-Gangetic plain, which extends from the Bay of Bengal on the east to the Afghan frontier on the Arabian Sea on the west. This plain is the richest and most densely settled part of the subcontinent. Another distinct natural region is the Deccan, a plateau of 2,000 to 3,000 feet (610 to 914 m) in elevation, occupying the southern portion of the subcontinent.

Forming a part of the republic are several groups of

islands—the Laccadives (14 islands) in the Arabian Sea and the Andamans (204 islands) and the Nicobars (19 islands) in the Bay of Bengal.

India's three great river systems, all rising in the Himalayas, have extensive deltas. The Ganges flows south and then east for 1,540 miles (2,478 km) across the northern plain to the Bay of Bengal; part of its delta, which begins 220 miles (354 km) from the sea, is within the republic. The Indus, starting in Tibet, flows northwest for several hundred miles in Kashmir before turning southwest toward the Arabian Sea; it is important for irrigation in Pakistan. The Brahmaputra, also rising in Tibet, flows eastward first through India and then south into Bangladesh and the Bay of Bengal.

INDONESIA

Republic of Indonesia
Area: 741,031 sq mi. (1,919,270 sq km)
Population (est. 1978): 147,000,000
Capital: Jakarta
Largest cities (est. 1977): Jakarta, 6,178,500; **(1971 census):** Surabaja, 1,556,255; Bandung, 1,201,730; Semarang, 646,590; Medan, 635,562; Palembang, 582,961
Monetary unit: Rupiah
Languages: Bahasa Indonesia (Malay) (official), Dutch, Javanese, Sundanese, Madurese
Religions: Islam, 89%; Christian, 7%; Hindu, Buddhist
Gross national product (1976): $36.2 billion
National name: Republik Indonesia

Geography. Indonesia is part of the Malay archipelago in Southeast Asia with an area nearly three times that of Texas. It consists of the islands of Sumatra, Java, Madura, central and southern Borneo, the Celebes, and the Moluccas. Its neighbor to the north is Malaysia and to the east Papua and New Guinea.

A backbone of mountain ranges extends throughout the main islands of the archipelago. Earthquakes are frequent, and there are many active volcanoes.

IRAN

Empire of Iran
Area: 636,296 sq mi. (1,648,000 sq km)

Population (est. 1977): 34,200,000 (Iranian, Kurdish, Azerbaijani)
Capital: Teheran
Largest cities (est. 1976): Teheran, 4,002,000; Isfahan, 700,000; Mashed, 600,000; Tabriz, 510,000
Monetary unit: Rial
Languages: Farsi (Persian), Kurdish, Azerbaijani
Religions: Shi'ite Moslem, 93%; Sunni Moslem, 5%
Gross national product (1976): $66.7 billion
National name: Keshvaré Shahanshahiyé Iran

Geography. Iran, a Middle Eastern country south of the Caspian Sea and north of the Persian Gulf, is three times the size of Arizona. It shares borders with Iraq, Turkey, the U.S.S.R., Afghanistan, and Pakistan.

In general, the country is a plateau averaging 4,000 feet (1,219 m) elevation. There are also maritime lowlands along the Persian Gulf and the Caspian Sea. The Elburz Mountains in the north rise to 18,603 feet (5,670 m) at Mt. Damavend. From northwest to southeast, the country is crossed by a desert 800 miles (1,287 km) long.

IRAQ

Republic of Iraq
Area: 167,924 sq mi. (434,924 sq km)
Population (est. 1978): 12,350,000 (Arab, 75%; Kurdish, 15%; Iranian, 3.8%)
Capital: Baghdad
Largest cities (est. 1975): Baghdad, 2,987,000; **(1965 census):** Basra, 310,950, Mosul, 264,146; Kirkuk, 175,303; An Najaf, 134,027
Monetary unit: Iraqi dinar
Languages: Arabic and Kurdish
Religions: Islam, 96%; Christian, 3%
Gross national product (1975): $13.6 billion
National name: Al Jumhouriya Al Iraqia

Geography. Iraq, a triangle of mountains, desert, and fertile river valley, is bounded on the east by Iran, on the north by Turkey, the west by Syria and Jordan, and the south by Saudi Arabia. It is twice the size of Idaho.

The country has arid desertland west of the Euphrates, a broad central valley between the Euphrates and Tigris, and mountains in the northeast. The fertile lower valley is formed by the delta of the two rivers, which join about 120 miles from the head of the Persian Gulf. The gulf coastline is 26 miles (42 km).

IRELAND

Republic of Ireland
Area: 27,136 sq mi. (70,283 sq km)
Population (est. 1978): 3,240,000
Capital: Dublin
Largest cities (1971 census): Dublin, 566,034; Cork, 128,235
Monetary unit: Irish pound
Languages: Irish, English
Religions: Roman Catholic, 95%; Protestant, 5%
Gross national product (1976): $8.1 billion
National name: Saorstát Éireann

Geography. Ireland is situated on the island in the Atlantic Ocean that is the second largest of the British Isles. Half the size of Arkansas, it occupies the entire island except for the six northern counties of Ulster.

Ireland resembles a basin—a central plain rimmed with mountains, except in the Dublin region. The mountains are low, with the highest peak, Carrantuohill in County Kerry, rising to 3,415 feet (1,041 m).

The principal river is the Shannon, which begins in the north central area, flows south and southwest for about 240 miles (386 km), and empties into the Atlantic.

ISRAEL

State of Israel
Area: 8,019 sq mi. (20,770 sq km)[1]
Population (est. 1978): 3,700,000
Capital: Jerusalem
Largest cities (est. 1977): Jerusalem, 366,300[2] (est. 1976): Tel Aviv, 348,500; Haifa, 227,200; Ramat-Gan, 121,000
Monetary unit: Israeli pound
Languages: Hebrew, Arabic, English
Religions: Jewish, 85%; Islam, Christian
Gross national product (1976): $12 billion
National name: Medinat Israel

Geography. Israel, slightly smaller than Massachusetts, lies at the eastern end of the Mediterranean Sea. It is bordered by Egypt on the west, Syria and Jordan on the east, and Lebanon on the north.

Northern Israel is largely a plateau traversed from north to south by mountains and broken by great depressions also running from north to south.

The maritime plain of Israel is remarkably fertile. The

1. Excluding 26,473 sq mi. (68,565 sq km) occupied in 1967 war. 2. Includes East Jerusalem.

southern Negev region, which comprises almost half the total area, is largely a wide desert steppe area. The National Water Project irrigation scheme is now transforming it into fertile land. The Jordan, the only important river, flows from the north through Lake Hule (Waters of Merom) and Lake Kinneret (Sea of Galilee or Sea of Tiberias), finally entering the Dead Sea, 1,290 feet (393 m) below sea level. This "sea," which is actually a salt lake (394 sq mi.; 1,020 sq km), has no outlet, its water balance being maintained by evaporation.

ITALY

Italian Republic
Area: 116,304 sq mi. (301,225 sq km)
Population (est. 1978): 56,675,000
Capital: Rome
Largest cities (est. 1977): Rome, 2,884,000; **(est. 1976):** Milan, 1,700,000; Palermo, 700,000; (est. 1975): Naples, 1,300,000; Turin, 1,200,000; Genoa, 806,400; Bologna, 493,000; Venice, 364,900; (1971 census): Florence, 457,803; Catania, 400,886
Monetary unit: Lira
Language: Italian
Religion: Roman Catholic,
Gross national product (1976): $170.0 billion
National name: Repubblica Italiana

Geography. Italy is a long peninsula shaped like a boot bounded on the west by the Tyrrhenian Sea and on the east by the Adriatic. Slightly larger than Arizona, it has for neighbors France, Switzerland, Austria, and Yugoslavia.

Approximately 600 of Italy's 708 miles (1,139 km) of length are in the long peninsula that projects into the Mediterranean from the fertile basin of the Po River. The Apennines, branching off from the Alps between Nice and Genoa, form the peninsula's backbone, and rise to a maximum height of 9,560 feet at the Gran Sasso d'Italia (Corno). The Alps form Italy's northern boundary.

Several islands form part of Italy. Sicily (9,926 sq mi.; 2,769 sq km) lies off the toe of the boot, across the Strait of Messina, with a steep and rock-bound northern coast and gentler slopes to the sea in the west and south. Mt. Etna, an active volcano, rises to 10,741 feet (3,274 m), and most of Sicily is more than 500 feet (3,274 m) in elevation. Sixty-two miles (100 km) southwest of Sicily lies Pantelleria (45 sq mi.; 117 sq km), and south of that are Lampedusa and Linosa. Sardinia (9,301 sq mi.; 2,409 sq km), which is located just south of Corsica and about 125 miles (200 km) west of the mainland, is mountainous, stony, and unproductive.

Italy has many northern lakes, lying below the snow-covered peaks of the Alps. The largest are Garda (143 sq mi.; 370 sq km), Maggiore (83 sq mi.; 215 sq km), and Como (55 sq mi.; 142 sq km).

The Po, the principal river, flows from the Alps on Italy's western border and crosses the Lombard plain to the Adriatic.

IVORY COAST

Republic of Ivory Coast
Area: 124,502 sq mi. (322,462 sq km)
Population (est. 1978): 6,714,000
Capital and largest city (est. 1975): Abidjan, 685,800
Monetary unit: Franc CFA
Ethnic groups: Agnis, Baoulés, Senoufos, Kroumen, Mandes, Dan-Gouros
Languages: French and African languages
Religions: Animist, 65%; Islam, 23%; Christian, 12%
National name: République de la Côte d'Ivoire
Gross national product (1976): $4.3 billion

Geography. The Ivory Coast, in western Africa on the Gulf of Guinea, is a little larger than New Mexico. Its neighbors are Liberia, Guinea, Mali, Upper Volta, and Ghana.

The country consists of a coastal strip in the south, dense forests in the interior, and savannas in the north. Rainfall is heavy, especially along the coast.

JAMAICA

Area: 4,244 sq mi. (10,991 sq km)
Population (1978): 2,110,000
Capital and largest city (est. 1974): Kingston, 169,800
Monetary unit: Jamaican dollar
Language: English
Religions: Anglican, Baptist, Roman Catholic
Gross national product (1976): $2.9 billion

Geography. Jamaica is an island in the West Indies, 90 miles south of Cuba and west of Haiti. It is a little smaller than Connecticut.

The island is made up of a plateau and the Blue Mountains, a group of volcanic hills, in the east. Blue Mountain (7,402 ft.; 2,256 m) is the tallest peak.

JAPAN

Area: 143,750 sq mi. (372,313 sq km)
Population (est. 1978): 114,850,000
Capital: Tokyo
Largest cities (est. 1977)[1]**:** Tokyo, 8,568,700; **(est. 1975):** Osaka, 2,779,000;
Yokohama, 2,622,000; Nagoya, 2,080,000; Kyoto, 1,461,000; Kobe, 1,361,000;
Sapporo, 1,241,000; Kitakyushu, 1,058,000
Monetary unit: Yen
Language: Japanese
Religions: Shintoist, Buddhist, Christian
Gross national product (1976): $554.4 billion
National name: Nippon

Geography. An archipelago extending more than 1,000 miles from north to south in the Pacific, Japan is separated from the east coast of Asia by the Sea of Japan. It is approximately the size of Montana.

Japan's four main islands are Honshu, Hokkaido, Kyushu, and Shikoku. The Ryukyu chain to the southwest was U.S.-occupied and the Kuriles to the northeast are Russian-occupied. The surface of the main islands consists largely of mountains separated by narrow valleys. There are about 50 more or less active volcanoes, of which the best-known is Mount Fuji.

1. Except for Tokyo, figures refer to *shi,* a minor division that may include some scattered or rural population as well as an urban center.

JORDAN

The Hashemite Kingdom of Jordan
Area: 37,738 sq mi. (97,740 sq km)[1]
Population (est. 1977 by U.N.): 2,080,000
Capital: Amman
Largest cities (est. 1976): Amman, 691,100; **(est. 1973 by U.N.):** Zarka,
220,000; Irbid, 116,000
Monetary unit: Jordanian dinar
Language: Arabic
Religions: Islam, 94%; Christian, 6%
Gross national product (1976): $1.6 billion
National name: Al Mamlaka al Urduniya al Hashemiyah

Geography. The Middle Eastern country of Jordan is bordered on the west by Israel and the Dead Sea, on the north by Syria, on the east by Iraq, and on the south Saudi Arabia. It is comparable in size to Indiana.

Arid hills and mountains make up most of the country. The southern section of the Jordan River flows through the country.

1. Includes territory occupied by Israel in 1967 war.

KAMPUCHEA
See Cambodia

KENYA

Republic of Kenya
Area: 224,960 sq mi. (582,646 sq km)
Population (est. 1978): 14,800,000
Capital: Nairobi
Largest cities (est. 1976 by U.N.): Nairobi, 736,000; Mombasa, 351,000
Monetary unit: Kenyan shilling
Languages: Swahili (official), Bantu, Kikuyu, English
Religions: Protestant, 36%; Roman Catholic, 22%; Islam, 6%; Animist
Gross national product 1976): $3.3 billion

Geography. Kenya lies on the equator in east central Africa on the coast of the Indian Ocean. It is twice the size of Nevada. Kenya's neighbors are Tanzania, Uganda, the Sudan, Ethiopia, and Somalia.

In the north, the land is arid; the southwestern corner is in the fertile Lake Victoria Basin; and a length of the eastern depression of Great Rift Valley separates western highlands from those that rise from the lowland coastal strip. Large game reserves have been developed.

KOREA, NORTH

Democratic People's Republic of Korea
Area: 46,540 sq mi. (120,538 sq km)
Population (est. 1978): 17,000,000
Capital and largest city (est. 1976): Pyongyang, 1,500,000
Monetary unit: Won
Language: Korean
Religions: None
National name: Chosun Minchu-chui Inmin Konghwa-guk
Gross national product (1976): $7.6 billion

Geography. Korea is a 600-mile peninsula jutting from Manchuria and China (and a small portion of the U.S.S.R.) into the Sea of Japan and the Yellow Sea off eastern Asia. North Korea occupies an area slightly smaller than Pennsylvania north of the 38th parallel.

The country is almost completely covered by a series of north-south mountain ranges separated by narrow valleys. The Yalu River forms part of the northern border with Manchuria.

KOREA, SOUTH

Republic of Korea
Area: 38,022 sq mi. (98,484 sq km)
Population (est. 1978): 37,000,000
Capital: Seoul
Largest cities (1975 census): Seoul, 6,899,470; Pusan, 2,454,051; Taegu, 1,311,078; Inchon, 799,982; Kwangju, 607,058; Taujon, 506,703; Chonju, 311,432.
Monetary unit: Won
Language: Korean
Religions: Buddhist, Confucianist, Taoist, Christian
Gross national product (1976): $25.1 billion
National name: Han Kook

Geography. Slightly larger than Indiana, South Korea lies below the 38th parallel on the Korean peninsula. It is mountainous in the east; in the west and south are many harbors on the mainland and offshore islands.

KUWAIT

State of Kuwait
Area: 6,880 sq mi. (17,818 sq km)
Population (est. 1978): 1,190,000
Capital (est. 1975): Al-Kuwait, 78,000
Largest city (est. 1975): Hawalli, 130,300
Monetary unit: Kuwaiti dinar
Languages: Arabic and English
Religions: Islam, 95%; Christian, 5%
Gross national product (1976): $16.5 billion
National name: Dowlat al Kuwait

Geography. Kuwait is situated northeast of Saudi Arabia at the northern end of the Persian Gulf, south of Iraq. It is slightly larger than Hawaii. The low-lying land is mainly sandy and barren.

LAOS

Lao People's Democratic Republic
Area: 91,429 sq mi. (236,800 sq km)
Population (est. 1978): 3,540,000
Capital and largest city (est. 1973): Vientiane, 176,600
Monetary unit: New kip
Languages: Lao (official); French, English
Religion: Buddhist
Gross national product (1976): $310 million

Geography. A landlocked nation in Southeast Asia occupying the northwestern portion of the Indochinese peninsula, Laos is surrounded by China, Vietnam, Cambodia, Thailand, and Burma. It is twice the size of Pennsylvania.

Laos is a mountainous country, especially in the north, where peaks rise above 8,000 feet (2,438 m). Dense forests cover the northern and eastern areas. The Mekong River flows through the country for 300 miles (483 km) of its course.

LEBANON

Republic of Lebanon
Area: 4,015 sq mi. (10,400 sq km)
Population (est. 1978): 3,165,000 (Arabian and Armenian).
Capital: Beirut
Largest cities (est. 1975): Beirut, 1,172,000; (est. 1964): Tripoli, 127,611
Monetary unit: Lebanese pound
Languages: Arabic (official); French, English
Religions: Christian and Islam
National name: Al-Joumhouriya al-Lubnaniya

Geography. Lebanon lies at the eastern end of the Mediterranean Sea north of Israel and west of Syria. It is four fifths the size of Connecticut.

The Lebanon Mountains, which parallel the coast on the west, cover most of the country, while on the eastern border is the Anti-Lebanon range. Between the two lies the El Bika Valley, the principal agricultural area.

LESOTHO

Kingdom of Lesotho
Area: 11,720 sq mi. (30,355 sq km)
Population (est. 1977): 1,090,000
Capital and largest city (est. 1976): Maseru, 14,700
Monetary unit: South African rand
Languages: English and Sesotho (official)
Religions: Roman Catholic (38.7%), Lesotho Evangelical Church (24.3%), Anglican (10.4%), non-Christian (18.2%).
Gross national product (1976): $210 million

Geography. Mountainous Lesotho, the size of Maryland, is surrounded by the Republic of South Africa in the east central part of that country except for short borders on the east and south with two discontinuous units of the Republic of Transkei. The Drakensberg Mountains in the east are Lesotho's principal chain. Elsewhere the region consists of rocky tableland.

LIBERIA

Republic of Liberia
Area: 43,000 sq mi. (11,369 sq km)
Population (est. 1978): 1,850,000
Capital and largest city (est. 1977): Monrovia, 172,100
Monetary unit: Liberian dollar
Languages: English (official) and tribal dialects
Religions: Protestant Christian, Islam, Catholic, Animist
Gross national product (1976): $720 million

Geography. Lying on the Atlantic in the southern part of west Africa, Liberia is bordered by Sierra Leone, Guinea, and the Ivory Coast. It is comparable in size to Tennessee.

Most of the country is a plateau covered by dense tropical forests, which thrive under an annual rainfall of about 160 inches a year.

LIBYA

People's Socialist Libyan Arab Public
Area: 679,362 sq mi. (1,759,540 sq km)
Population (est. 1977): 2,600,000
Capital: Tripoli
Largest cities (1973 census): Tripoli, 551,477; Bengasi, 282,192
Monetary unit: Libyan dinar
Language: Arabic
Religion: Islam
Gross national product (1976): $16.0 billion
National name: Al-Jumhuria al-Arabia al-Libya

Geography. Libya stretches along the northeastern coast of Africa between Tunisia and Algeria on the west and Egypt on the east; to the south are Chad and Niger. It is one sixth larger than Alaska.

A greater part of the country lies within the Sahara. There are many oases along the Mediterranean coast; farther inland is arable plateau land.

LIECHTENSTEIN

Principality of Liechtenstein
Area: 61 sq mi. (157 sq km).
Population (est. 1978): 22,850.
Capital and largest city (est. 1975: Vaduz, 4,500.
Monetary unit: Swiss franc.
Language: German (Alemannish dialect).
Religion: Roman Catholic.

Geography. Tiny Liechtenstein, not quite as large as Washington, D.C., lies on the east bank of the Rhine River south of Lake Constance between Austria and Switzerland. It consists of low valley land and Alpine peaks. Falknis (8,401 ft.; 2,561 m) and Naatkopf (8,432 ft.; 2,570 m) are the tallest.

LUXEMBOURG

Grand Duchy of Luxembourg
Area: 999 sq mi. (2,586 sq km)
Population (est. 1978): 370,000. (Luxembourgian, French, German)
Capital and largest city (est. 1975): Luxembourg, 78,300
Monetary unit: Luxembourg franc
Languages: Letzeburgesch, French, German
Religion: Mainly Roman Catholic
Gross national product (1976): $2.3 billion
National name: Grand-Duché de Luxembourg

Geography. Luxembourg is a neighbor of Belgium on the west, Germany on the east, and France on the south. The Ardennes Mountains extend from Belgium into the northern section of Luxembourg.

MADAGASCAR

Democratic Republic of Madagascar
Area: 226,658 sq mi. (587,041 sq km)
Population (est. 1978): 8,775,000
Capital and largest city (est. 1975): Antananarivo (Tananarive), 438,800
Monetary unit: Malagasy franc
Languages: Malagasy, French
Ethnic groups: Merina (or Hova), Betsimisaraka, Betsileo, Tsimihety, Antaisaka, Sakalava, Antandroy
Religions: Christian, 50%; Animist
Gross national product (1976): $1.9 billion
National name: Repoblika Demokratika Malagasy

Geography. Madagascar lies in the Indian Ocean off the southeast coast of Africa opposite Mozambique. The world's fourth-largest island, it is twice the size of Arizona. The country's low-lying coastal area gives way to a central plateau. The once densely wooded interior has largely been cut down.

MALAWI

Republic of Malawi
Area: 45,747 sq mi. (118,484 sq km)

Population (est. 1977 by U.N.): 5,530,000
Capital (est. 1976): Lilongwe, 75,000
Largest city (est. 1976): Blantyre, 219,000
Monetary unit: Kwacha
Languages: English (official), Chichewa
Religion: Animist
Gross national product (1976): $703 million

Geography. Malawi is a landlocked country the size of Pennsylvania in southeastern Africa, surrounded by Mozambique, Zambia, and Tanzania. Lake Malawi, formerly Lake Nyasa, occupies most of the country's eastern border. The north-south Rift Valley is flanked by mountain ranges and high plateau areas.

MALAYSIA

Federation of Malaysia
Area: 127,316 sq mi. (329,749 sq km)
Population (est. 1978): 12,950,000
Capital: Kuala Lumpur
Largest cities (est. 1975 by U.N.): Kuala Lumpur, 557,000; (1970 census): Pulau Pinang, 270,019; Ipoh, 247,689
Monetary unit: Ringgit
Languages: Malay (official), Chinese, Tamil, English
Religions: Islam, Buddhist, Hindu.
Gross national product (1976): $10.6 billion

Geography. Malaysia is at the southern end of the Malay Peninsula in southeast Asia. The nation also includes Sabah and Sarawak on the island of Borneo to the southeast. Its area slightly exceeds that of New Mexico.

Most of Malaysia is covered by dense jungle and swamps, with a mountain range running the length of the peninsula. Extensive forests provide ebony, sandalwood, teak, and other woods.

MALDIVES

Republic of Maldives
Area: 115 sq mi. (298 sq km)
Population (est. 1978): 145,000
Capital and largest city (est. 1977): Male, 29,500
Monetary unit: Maldivian rupee
Languages: Divehi
Religion: Islam

Geography. The Republic of Maldives is a group of atolls in the Indian Ocean about 500 miles southwest of Sri Lanka. Its 1,087 coral islets stretch over an area of 45,000 square miles (116,550 sq km).

MALI

Republic of Mali
Area: 478,766 sq mi. (1,240,000 sq km)
Population (est. 1978): 6,150,000
Capital and largest city (est. 1976): Bamako, 404,000
Monetary unit: Mali franc
Ethnic groups: Bambara, Peul, Soninke, Malinke, Songhai, Dogon, Senoufo, Minianka, Berbers, and Moors
Languages: French (official), African languages
Religions: Islam, 65%; Animist, 30%; Christian
Gross national product (1976): $590 million
National name: République de Mali

Geography. Most of Mali, in western Africa, lies in the Sahara. A landlocked country four fifths the size of Alaska, it is bordered by Guinea, Senegal, Mauritania, Algeria, Niger, Upper Volta, and the Ivory Coast.

The only fertile area is in the south, where the Niger and Senegal Rivers provide irrigation.

MALTA

Republic of Malta
Area: 122 sq mi. (316 sq km)
Population (est. 1978): 330,000
Capital (est. 1977): Valetta, 14,100
Largest city (est. 1977): Sliema, 20,100
Monetary unit: Maltese pound
Languages: Maltese and English
Religion: Roman Catholic
Gross national product (1976): $522 million
National name: Repubblika Ta Malta

Geography. The five Maltese islands—with a combined land area smaller than Philadelphia—are in the Mediterranean about 60 miles south of the southeastern tip of Sicily.

MAURITANIA

Islamic Republic of Mauritania
Area: 397,955 sq mi. (1,030,700 sq km)[1]

1. Does not include any of Spanish Sahara, reportedly divided between Mauritania and Morocco.

Population (est. 1977): 1,400,000
Capital and largest city (1976 census): Nouakchott, 135,000
Monetary unit: Ouguyia
Ethnic groups: Moors; a black minority (Poulars, Soninkes, and Wolofs)
Languages: Arabic and French
Religion: Islam
Gross national product (1976): $460 million
National name: République Islamique de Mauritanie

Geography. Mauritania, three times the size of Arizona, is situated in northwest Africa with about 350 miles (592 km) of coastline on the Atlantic Ocean. It is bordered by Morocco on the north, Algeria and Mali on the east, and Senegal on the south.

The country is mostly desert, with the exception of the fertile Senegal River valley in the south and grazing land in the north.

MAURITIUS

Area: 790 sq mi. (2,045 sq km)
Population (est. 1978): 890,000 (Indian, 51%; Creole, 33%, Pakistani, 16%)
Capital and largest city (est. 1977): Port Louis, 141,300
Monetary unit: Mauritius rupee
Languages: English (official), French, Creole.
Religions: Hindu, 51%, Christian (mainly Roman Catholic), 30%; Islam, 16%; Buddhist, 3%
Gross national product (1976): $600 million

Geography. Mauritius is a mountainous island in the Indian Ocean east of Madagascar.

MEXICO

United Mexican States
Area: 761,600 sq mi. (1,972,547 sq km)
Population (est. 1978): 66,950,000 (55% mestizo; 29% Indian)
Capital: Mexico City
Largest cities (est 1977): Mexico City, 8,941,900; (est. 1976 by U.N.): Guadalajara, 1,640,900; Monterrey, 1,090,200; Juarez, 544,900
Monetary unit: Peso
Languages: Spanish, Indian languages
Religion: Mainly Roman Catholic
Gross national product (1976): $67.6 billion
National name: Estados Unidos Mexicanos

Geography. The United States' neighbor to the south, Mexico is about one fifth its size. Baja California in the west, an

800-mile (1,287-km) peninsula, forms the Gulf of California. In the east are the Gulf of Mexico and the Bay of Campeche, which is formed by Mexico's other peninsula, the Yucatán.

Mexico is a great, high plateau, open to the north, with mountain chains on east and west and with ocean-front lowlands lying outside of them.

MONACO

Principality of Monaco
Area: 0.73 square mile (465 acres)
Population (est. 1978): 30,000, of whom 5,500 are Monégasque citizens
Largest city (1968 census): Monte Carlo, 9,948
Monetary unit: French franc
Languages: French and Monégasque
Religion: Roman Catholic
National name: Principauté de Monaco

Geography. Monaco is a tiny, hilly wedge driven into the French Mediterranean coast nine miles east of Nice.

MONGOLIA

Mongolian People's Republic
Area: 604,250 sq mi. (1,565,000 sq km)
Population (est. 1978): 1,575,000
Capital and largest city (est. 1976): Ulan Bator, 331,800
Monetary unit: Tugrik
Language: Khalkha Mongolian
Religion: Lamaistic Buddhism
Gross national product (1976): $1.3 billion
National name: Bugd Nayramdakh Mongol Ard Uls

Geography. Mongolia lies in eastern Asia between Soviet Siberia on the north and China on the south. It is slightly larger than Alaska.

The productive regions of Outer Mongolia—a tableland ranging from 3,000 to 5,000 feet (914 to 1,524 m) in elevation—are in the north, which is well drained by numerous rivers, including the Hovd, Onon, Selenga, and Tula.

Much of the Gobi Desert falls within Mongolia. There several mountain ranges, one of which, the Altai Mountains, contains the highest peak in the country—Tabun Bogdo at 15,266 feet (4,653 m).

MOROCCO

Kingdom of Morocco
Area: 172,414 sq mi. (446,550 sq km)
Population (est. 1978): 18,675,000
Capital: Rabat
Largest cities (est. 1975 by U.N.): Casablanca, 1,856,000; (1971 census): Rabat, 435,510; Marrakech, 330,400; Fez, 321,460
Monetary unit: Dirham
Languages: Arabic, French, Spanish
Religions: Chiefly Islam
Gross national product (1976): $8.5 billion
National name: al-Mamlaka al-Maghrebia

Geography. Morocco, about one tenth larger than California, is just south of Spain across the Strait of Gibraltar and looks out on the Atlantic from the northwest shoulder of Africa. Algeria is to the east and Mauritania to the south.

On the Atlantic coast there is a fertile plain. The Mediterranean coast is mountainous. The Atlas Mountains, running northeastward from the south to the Algerian frontier, average 11,000 feet (3,353 m) in elevation.

MOZAMBIQUE

People's Republic of Mozambique
Area: 302,328 sq mi. (783,030 sq km)
Population (est. 1978): 9,950,000
Capital and largest city (est. 1978): Maputo, 500,000
Monetary unit: Mozambique escudo
Languages: Portuguese (official); Bantu languages
Religions: Animist, 70%; Christian, 15%; Islam, 13%
Gross national product (1976): $1.6 billion
National name: República Popular de Moçambique

Geography. Mozambique stretches for 1,535 miles (2,470 km) along Africa's southeast coast. It is nearly twice the size of California. Tanzania is to the north; Malawi, Zambia, and Rhodesia to the west; and South Africa and Swaziland to the south.

The country is generally a low-lying plateau broken up by 25 sizable rivers that flow into the Indian Ocean. The largest is the Zambezi, which provides access to central Africa.

NAMIBIA
See South-West Africa

NAURU

Republic of Nauru
Area: 8.2 sq mi. (21 sq km)
Population (est. 1978): 8,000
Capital: Yaren
Monetary unit: Australian dollar
Languages: Nauruan, English
Religions: Nauruan Protestant and Roman Catholic

Geography. Nauru is an island in the Pacific just south of the equator, about 2,500 miles southwest of Honolulu.

NEPAL

Kingdom of Nepal
Area: 54,362 sq mi. (140,797 sq km)
Population (est. 1978): 13,420,000 (Magar, Gurung, Bhotia, Newar)
Capital and largest city (est. 1976): Katmandu, 171,400
Monetary unit: Nepalese rupee
Languages: Nepali (official), Newari, Bhutia
Religions: Hindu, 89.4%; Buddhist, 7.5%
Gross national product (1976): $1.5 billion

Geography. A landlocked country the size of Arkansas, lying between India and the Tibetan Autonomous Region of China, Nepal contains Mt. Everest (29,028 ft.; 8,848 m), the tallest mountain in the world. Along its southern border, Nepal has a strip of level land that is partly forested, partly cultivated. North of that is the slope of the main section of the Himalayan range, including Everest and many other peaks higher than 20,000 feet (6,096 m).

THE NETHERLANDS

Kingdom of the Netherlands
Area: 15,700 sq mi. (40,844 sq km)
Population (est. 1978): 13,930,000
Capital: Amsterdam; seat of government: The Hague
Largest cities (est. 1977): Rotterdam, 1,022,700; Amsterdam, 975,500; The Hague, 677,500; Utrecht, 467,900
Monetary unit: Guilder
Language: Dutch
Religions: Roman Catholic, 40%; Dutch Reformed, 24%; unaffiliated, 24%
Gross national product (1976): $89.5 billion
National name: Koninkrijk der Nederlanden

Geography. The Netherlands, on the coast of the North Sea, has West Germany to the east and Belgium to the south. It is twice the size of New Jersey.

Part of the great plain of north and west Europe, the Netherlands has maximum dimensions of 190 by 160 miles (360 by 257 km) and is low and flat except in Limburg in the southeast, where some hills rise to 300 feet (92 m). About half the country's area is below sea level, making the famous Dutch dikes a requisite to the use of much land. Reclamation of land from the sea through dikes has continued through recent times.

All drainage reaches the North Sea, and the principal rivers—Rhine, Maas (Meuse), and Schelde—have their sources outside the country. The Rhine is the most heavily used waterway in Europe.

Netherlands Autonomous Country
NETHERLANDS ANTILLES

Status: Part of the Kingdom of the Netherlands
Area: 371 sq mi. (961 sq km)
Population (est. 1978): 250,000.
The Capital (est. 1978): Willemstad, 152,000

Geography. The Netherlands Antilles comprise two groups of Caribbean islands 500 miles apart: one, about 40 miles off the Venezuelan coast, consists of Curaçao (173 sq mi.; 448 sq km), Bonaire (95 sq mi.; 246 sq km), and Aruba (69 sq mi.; 179 sq km); the other, lying to the northeast, consists of three small islands with a total area of 34 square miles (88 sq km). The Dutch acquired the island of Curaçao from Spain in 1643.

NEW ZEALAND

Dominion of New Zealand
Area: 103,736 sq mi. (268,676 sq km) (excluding dependencies)
Population (est. 1978): 3,130,000 (European, 90%; Maori and other Polynesian, 10%)
Capital: Wellington
Largest cities (1976 census): Christchurch, 172,000; Auckland, 150,700; Wellington, 139,600
Monetary unit: New Zealand dollar
Languages: English, Maori
Religions (1971): Church of England (31%); Presbyterian (20%); Roman Catholic (16%)
Gross national product (1976): $12.8 billion

Geography. New Zealand, about 1,250 miles east of Australia, consists of two main islands and a number of smaller, outlying islands so scattered that they range from the tropical to the antarctic. The country is the size of Colorado.

New Zealand's two main components are North Island and South Island, separated by Cook Strait, which varies from 16 to 190 miles (25.7 to 305.8 km) in width. North Island (44,281 sq mi.; 114,688 sq km) is 515 miles (828.8 km) long and volcanic in its south-central part. It contains many hot springs and beautiful geysers. South Island (58,-093 sq mi.; 150,461 sq km) has the Southern Alps along its west coast, with Mt. Cook (12,349 ft; 3,764 m) the highest point.

The largest of the outlying islands are the Auckland Islands (234 sq mi.; 606 sq km), Campbell Island (44 sq mi.; 114 sq km), the Antipodes Islands (24 sq mi.; 62.2 sq km), and the Kermadec Islands (13 sq mi.; 33.7 sq km).

Cook Islands and Overseas Territories

The Cook Islands (93 sq mi.; 241 sq km) were placed under New Zealand administration in 1901. They achieved self-governing status in association with New Zealand in 1965. Population in 1975 was 18,068. The seat of government is on Rarotonga Island.

Chief exports in 1973 were citrus juice (41%), bananas (6%), canned fruit (6%), and pineapple juice (5%). Leading customer in 1970 was New Zealand (98%). Leading suppliers were New Zealand (83%), Japan (5%).

Niue (100 sq mi.; 259 sq km) was formerly administered as part of the Cook Islands. It was placed under separate New Zealand administration in 1901 and achieved self-governing status in association with New Zealand in 1974. The capital is Alofi.

Chief exports in 1973 were passion fruit (23%), copra (15%), plaited ware (10%), and honey (8%). Leading customer in 1975 was New Zealand (73%). Leading supplier was New Zealand (79%).

The Ross Dependency (160,000 sq mi.; 414,400 sq km), an Antarctic region, was placed under New Zealand administration in 1923.

Tokelau (4 sq mi.; 10 sq km) was formerly administered as part of the Gilbert and Ellice Islands colony. It was placed under New Zealand administration in 1925. Its population in 1975 was 1,603.

NICARAGUA

Republic of Nicaragua
Area: 50,193 sq mi. (130,000 sq km)
Population (est. 1978): 2,390,000 (mestizo, 70%; white, 17%; black, 9%; Indian, 4%)
Capital and largest city (est. 1976): Managua, 400,000
Monetary unit: Cordoba
Language: Spanish
Religion: Roman Catholic
Gross national product (1976): $1.8 billion
National name: República de Nicaragua

Geography. Largest but most sparsely populated of the Central American nations, Nicaragua borders on Honduras to the north and Costa Rica to the south. It is slightly larger than New York State.

Nicaragua is mountainous in the west, with fertile valleys. A plateau slopes eastward toward the Caribbean.

Two big lakes—Nicaragua, about 100 miles long (161 km), and Managua, about 38 miles long (61 km)—are connected by the Tipitapa River. The Pacific coast is bald and rocky. The Caribbean coast, swampy and indented, is aptly called the "Mosquito Coast."

NIGER

Republic of Niger
Area: 489,191 sq mi. (1,267,000 sq km)
Population (est. 1978): 5,000,000
Capital and largest city (est. 1975): Niamey, 130,000
Monetary unit: Franc CFA
Ethnic groups: Hausa, 53.7%; Djerma and Songhai, 23.6%; Peul, 10.6%
Languages: French (official); Hausa, Songhai; Arabic
Religions: Islam, Animist, Christian
Gross national product (1976): $740 million
National name: République du Niger

Geography. Niger, in western Africa's Sahara region, is four fifths the size of Alaska. It is surrounded by Mali, Algeria, Libya, Chad, Nigeria, Benin, and Upper Volta.

The Niger River in the southwest flows through the country's only fertile area. Elsewhere the land is semiarid.

NIGERIA

Federal Republic of Nigeria
Area: 356,669 sq mi. (923,768 sq km)

Population (est. 1978): 66,650,000[1]
Capital: Lagos
Largest cities (est. 1975 by U.N.): Lagos, 1,060,850; Ibadan, 847,000; Ogbomosho, 432,000; Kano, 399,000
Monetary unit: Naira
Languages: English (official) and native tongues
Religions: Islam, 47%; Christian, 34%; Animist
Gross national product (1976): $29.3 billion

Geography. Nigeria, one third larger than Texas, is situated on the Gulf of Guinea in West Africa. Its neighbors are Benin, Niger, and Cameroon.

The lower course of the Niger River flows south through the western part of the country into the Gulf of Guinea. Swamps and mangrove forests border the southern coast; inland are hardwood forests.

1. While U.N. and similar sources continue to report this figure, interpretations of election data by demographers suggest that, in reality, the population of Nigeria in 1978 approached 100,000,000.

NORWAY

Kingdom of Norway
Area: 125,182 sq mi. (324,219 sq km)
Population (est. 1978): 4,050,000
Capital: Oslo
Largest cities (est. 1977): Oslo, 462,500; Bergen, 212,750; Trondheim, 135,550
Monetary unit: Krone
Language: Norwegian
Religions: Evangelical Lutheran (state), 94%
Gross national product (1976): $29.9 billion
National name: Kongeriket Norge

Geography. Norway is situated in the western part of the Scandinavian peninsula. It extends about 1,100 miles (1,-770 km) from the North Sea along the Norwegian Sea to more than 300 miles (483 km) above the Arctic Circle, the farthest north of any European country. It is slightly larger than New Mexico. Sweden borders on most of the eastern frontier, with Finland and the U.S.S.R. in the northeast.

Nearly 70% of Norway is uninhabitable and covered by mountains, glaciers, moors, and rivers. The hundreds of deep fiords that cut into the coastline give Norway an overall oceanfront of more than 12,000 miles (19,312 km). Nearly 150,000 islands off the coast form a breakwater and make a safe coastal shipping channel.

415

Dependencies of Norway

Svalbard (23,957 sq mi.; 62,049 sq km), in the Arctic Ocean about 360 miles north of Norway, consists of the Spitsbergen group and several smaller islands, including Bear Island, Hope Island, King Charles Land, and White Island (or Gillis Land). It came under Norwegian administration in 1925. The population in 1975 was 3,500.

Bouvet Island (23 sq mi.; 60 sq km), in the South Atlantic about 1,600 miles south-southwest of the Cape of Good Hope, came under Norwegian administration in 1928.

Jan Mayen Island (144 sq mi.; 273 sq km), in the Arctic Ocean between Norway and Greenland, came under Norwegian administration in 1929. Its population in 1973 was 37.

Peter I Island (96 sq mi.; 249 sq km), lying off Antarctica in the Bellinghausen Sea, came under Norwegian administration in 1931.

Queen Maud Land, a section of Antarctica, came under Norwegian administration in 1939.

OMAN

Sultanate of Oman
Area: 82,030 sq mi. (212,457 sq km)
Population (est. 1978): 850,000[1]
Capital (est. 1973): Muscat, 15,000
Largest city (est. 1973): Matrah, 18,000
Monetary unit: Omani rial
Language: Arabic
Religion: Islam
Gross national product (1976): $2.1 billion
National name: Saltanat Oman

Geography. Oman is a 1,000-mile (1,609-km) long coastal plain at the southeastern tip of the Arabian peninsula lying on the Arabian Sea and the Gulf of Oman. The interior is a plateau. The country is the size of Kansas.

PAKISTAN

Islamic Republic of Pakistan
Area: 310,403 sq mi. (803,943 sq km)[1]

1. Excluding Kashmir and Jammu.

Population (est. 1978): 77,500,000
Capital (1972 census): Islamabad, 77,000
Largest cities (est. 1975): Karachi, 4,465,000; **(1972 census):** Lahore, 2,165,372; Lyallpur, 822,263; Hyderabad, 628,310; Rawalpindi, 615,392
Monetary unit: Pakistan rupee
Principal languages: Urdu (national), English (official), Punjabi, Sindhi, Pashtu, and Baluchi
Religions: Islam, 90%; Hindu, Christian, Buddhist
Gross national product (1976): $13.4 billion

Geography. Pakistan is situated in the western part of the Indian subcontinent, with Afghanistan and Iran on the west, India on the east, and the Arabian Sea on the south.

Nearly twice the size of California, Pakistan consists of towering mountains, including the Hindu Kush in the west; a desert area in the east, the Punjab plains in the north, and an expanse of alluvial plains. The 1,000-mile-long Indus River flows through the country from the Kashmir to the Arabian Sea.

PANAMA

Republic of Panama
Area: 29,208 sq mi. (75,650 sq km)
Population (est. 1978): 1,820,000 (mestizo, 65.34%; black, 13.31%; white, 11.07%; Indian, 9.53%; others, .75%)
Capital and largest city (est. 1977): Panama City, 427,700
Monetary unit: Balboa
Language: Spanish (official)
Religion: Roman Catholic, 90%, Protestant
Gross national product (1976): $2.0 billion
National name: República de Panamá

Geography. The southernmost of the Central American nations, Panama is south of Costa Rica and north of Colombia. The Panama Canal bisects the isthmus at its narrowest and lowest point, allowing passage from the Caribbean Sea to the Pacific Ocean.

Panama is slightly smaller than South Carolina. It is marked by a chain of volcanic mountains in the west, moderate hills in the interior, and a low range on the east coast. There are extensive forests in the fertile Caribbean area.

PAPUA NEW GUINEA

Area: 178,259 sq mi. (461,691 sq km)
Population (est. 1978): 2,980,000

Capital and largest city (1976 census): Port Moresby, 113,449
Monetary unit: Kina
Languages: English, Police Motu, Pidgin English (all official)
Religions: Roman Catholic, Lutheran, Anglican
Gross national product (1976): $1.4 billion

Geography. Papua New Guinea occupies the eastern half
of the island of New Guinea, just north of Australia, and
many outlying islands. The Indonesian province of Irian
Jaya is to the west. To the north and east are the islands of
Manus, New Britain, New Ireland, and Bougainville.

Papua New Guinea is about one tenth larger than California. Its mountainous interior has only recently been ex-
plored. The high-plateau climate is temperate, in contrast
to the tropical climate of the coastal plains. Two major
rivers, the Sepik and the Fly, are navigable for shallow-
draft vessels.

PARAGUAY

Republic of Paraguay
Area: 157,047 sq mi. (406,752 sq km)
Population (est. 1978): 2,870,000 (mestizo, 94.9%; white, 3.0%; Indian, 2.1%)
Capital and largest city (est. 1975 by U.N.): Asunción, 574,000
Monetary unit: Guaraní
Languages: Spanish (official), Guaraní
Religion: Roman Catholic (official)
Gross national product (1976): $1.7 billion
National name: República del Paraguay

Geography. California-size Paraguay is surrounded by Brazil, Bolivia, and Argentina in south central South America.
Eastern Paraguay, between the Paraná and Paraguay Rivers, is upland country with the thickest population settled
on the grassy slope that inclines toward the Paraguay River. The greater part of the Chaco region to the west is
covered with marshes, lagoons, dense forests, and jungles.

PERU

Republic of Peru
Area: 496,222 sq mi. (1,285,216 sq km)
Population (est. 1978): 17,000,000 (white and mestizo, 52%; Indian, 46%;
  Asiatic, black, and other, 2%
Capital: Lima
Largest cities (est. 1975 by U.N. for metropolitan area): Lima, 3,901,000.
  Arequipa, 304,600; Callao, 296,200; Trujillo, 241,900

Monetary unit: Sol
Languages: Spanish, Quéchua
Religion: Roman Catholic
Gross national product (1976): $13.2 billion
National name: República del Perú

Geography. Peru, in western South America, extends for nearly 1,500 miles (2,414 km) along the Pacific Ocean. Colombia and Ecuador are to the north, Brazil and Bolivia to the east, and Chile to the south.

Five sixths the size of Alaska, Peru is divided by the Andes Mountains into three sharply differentiated zones. To the west is the coastline, much of it arid, extending 50 to 100 miles inland. The mountain area, with peaks over 20,000 feet (6,096 m), lofty plateaus, and deep valleys, lies centrally. Beyond the mountains to the east is the heavily forested slope leading to the Amazonian plains.

THE PHILIPPINES

Republic of the Philippines
Area: 115,831 sq mi. (300,000 sq km)
Population (est. 1978): 46,400,000
Capital: Manila
Largest cities (est. 1976 for urban agglomeration): Manila, 7,800,000; (est. 1975 by U.N.): Quezon City, 994,700; Davao, 515,500; Cebu, 418,500
Monetary unit: Peso
Languages: Filipino, English, Tagalog, Visayan, Spanish, Ilocano, Bicol
Religions: Roman Catholic, 85%; Islam, 4%; Aglipayan (Independent Philippine Christian), 4%; Protestant, 3%
Gross national product (1976): $17.7 billion
National name: República de Filipinas—Republike ñg Pilipinas

Geography. The Philippine Islands are an archipelago of over 7,000 islands lying about 500 miles (805 km) off the southeast coast of Asia. The overall land area is comparable to that of Arizona. The northernmost island, Y'Ami, is 65 miles (105 km) from Taiwan, while the southernmost, Saluag, is 40 miles (48 km) east of Borneo.

Only about 7% of the islands are larger than one square mile, and only one third have names. The largest are Luzon in the north (40,420 sq mi.; 104,687 sq km), Mindanao in the south (36,537 sq mi.; 94,631 sq km), Samar (5,124 sq mi.; 13,271 sq km), Negros (4,903 sq mi.; 12,699 sq km), and Palawan (4,550 sq km).

The islands are of volcanic origin, with the larger ones

crossed by mountain ranges. The highest peak is Mt. Apo
(9,690 ft.; 2,954 m) on Mindanao.

POLAND

Polish People's Republic
Area: 120,725 sq mi. (312,677 sq km)
Population (est. 1978): 35,050,000
Capital: Warsaw
Largest cities (est. 1976 by U.N.): Warsaw, 1,448,900; Lódz, 804,300; Kraków,
   693,800; Wroclaw, 579,600; Poznan, 521,600; Gdansk, 426,800; Szczecin,
   372,900
Monetary unit: Zloty
Language: Polish (more than 90%)
Religions: Roman Catholic, Greek Orthodox, Protestant, Jewish
Gross national product (1976): $98.1 billion
National name: Polska Rzeczpospolita Ludowa

Geography. Poland, a country the size of New Mexico in
north Central Europe, borders on East Germany to the
west, Czechoslovakia to the south, and the U.S.S.R. to the
east. In the north is the Baltic Sea.

   Most of the country is a plain with no natural boundaries
except the Carpathian Mountains in the south and the
Oder and Neisse Rivers in the east. Other major rivers,
which are important to commerce, are the Warta, Bug, and
Vistula.

PORTUGAL

Republic of Portugal
Area: 35,553 sq mi. (92,082 sq km)
Population (est. 1977): 10,000,000
Capital: Lisbon
Largest cities (est. 1976): Lisbon, 847,300; (est. 1974 by U.N.): Oporto,
   311,800
Monetary unit: Escudo
Language: Portuguese
Religion: Roman Catholic
Gross national product (1976): $16.5 billion
National name: República Portuguesa

Geography. Portugal occupies the western part of the
Iberian Peninsula, bordering on the Atlantic Ocean to the
west and Spain to the north and east. It is slightly smaller
than Indiana.

   The country is crossed by many small rivers, and also by
three large ones that rise in Spain, flow into the Atlantic,

and divide the country into three geographic areas. The Minho (Miño in Spain) River, part of the northern boundary, cuts through a mountainous area that extends south to the vicinity of the Douro (Duero) River. South of the Douro, the mountains slope to the plains about the Tagus (Tejo) River. The remaining division is the southern one of Alentejo.

The Azores, stretching over 340 miles (547 km) in the Atlantic, consist of nine islands divided into three groups, with a total area of 924 square miles (2,393 sq km). The nearest continental land is Cape da Roca, Portugal, about 900 miles (1,448 km) to the east. The Azores are an important station on Atlantic air routes, and both the U.K. and U.S. established air bases there during World War II.

Madeira, consisting of two inhabited islands, Madeira and Porto Santo, and two groups of uninhabited islands, lies in the Atlantic about 535 (861 km) southwest of Lisbon.

Portuguese Overseas Territory

MACAO

Status: Territory
Area: 6 sq mi. (15.5 sq km)
Population (est. 1978): 280,000
Capital (1970 census): Macao, 241,413

Macao comprises the peninsula of Macao and the two small islands of Taipa and Colôane on the South China coast, about 35 miles from Hong Kong.

QATAR

State of Qatar
Area: 4,274 sq mi. (11,000 sq km)
Population (est. 1978): 200,000
Capital (est. 1977): Doha, 150,000
Monetary unit: Qatari riyal
Language: Arabic
Religion: Islam
Gross national product (1976): $2.4 billion

Geography. Qatar occupies a small peninsula that extends into the Persian Gulf from the east side of the Arabian Peninsula. Saudi Arabia is to the west and the United Arab Emirates to the south. The country is mainly barren.

RHODESIA

Area: 150,803 sq mi. (390,580 sq km)
Population (est. 1978): 6,950,000 (black, 96%; white, 4%)
Capital: Salisbury
Largest cities (est. 1977 for urban agglomeration): Salisbury, 561,000; Bulawayo, 339,000
Monetary unit: Rhodesian dollar
Languages: English (official), Sindebele, Shona
Religions: Christian, 20%; Animist
Gross national product (1976): $3.6 billion

Geography. Rhodesia, a landlocked country in south central Africa, is slightly smaller than California. It is bordered by Botswana on the west, Zambia on the north, Mozambique on the east, and South Africa on the south.

A high veld up to 6,000 feet (1,829 m) crosses the country from northeast to southwest. This is flanked by a somewhat lower veld that contains ranching country. Tropical forests that yield hardwoods lie in the southeast.

In the north, on the border with Zambia, is the 175-mile-long (128-m) Kariba Lake, formed by the Kariba Dam across the Zambezi River. It is the site of one of the world's largest hydroelectric projects.

ROMANIA

Socialist Republic of Romania
Area: 91,700 sq mi. (237,500 sq km)
Population (est. 1978): 21,630,000 (Romanian, 88%; Hungarian, 8%)
Capital: Bucharest
Largest cities (est. 1977): Bucharest, 1,807,000; Timisoara, 268,800; Iasi, 265,000; Cluj-Napoca, 262,400; Brasov, 257,100; Constanta, 256,900; Galati, 239,300; Craiova, 222,400
Monetary unit: Leu
Languages: Romanian, Hungarian, Serbian, German, Turkish
Religions: Romanian Orthodox, 85%; Catholic and Protestant, 15%
Gross national product (1976): $31.1 billion
National name: Republica Socialista România

Geography. A country in southeastern Europe slightly smaller than Oregon, Romania is bordered on the west by Hungary and Yugoslavia, on the north and east by the U.S.S.R., on the east by the Black Sea, and on the south by Bulgaria.

The Carpathian Mountains divide Romania's upper half from north to south and connect near the center of the country with the Transylvanian Alps, running east and west.

North and west of these ranges lies the Transylvanian plateau, and to the south and east are the plains of Moldavia and Walachia. In its last 190 miles (306 km), the Danube River flows through Romania only. It enters the Black Sea in northern Dobruja, just south of the border with the Soviet Union.

RWANDA

Republic of Rwanda
Area: 10,169 sq mi. (26,338 sq km)
Population (est. 1978): 4,600,000
Capital and largest city (est. 1977): Kigali, 90,000
Monetary unit: Rwanda franc
Languages: Kinyarwanda and French
Religions: Roman Catholic, 50%; Protestant, 40%; Islam, 5%; Animist
Gross national products (1976): $480 million

Geography. Rwanda, in east central Africa, is surrounded by Zaire, Uganda, Tanzania, and Burundi. It is slightly smaller than Maryland.

Steep mountains and deep valleys cover most of the country. Lake Kivu in the northwest, at an altitude of 4,829 feet (1,472 m) is the highest lake in Africa. From it, extending south, are the Virunga Mountains, which include Volcan Karisimbi (14,187 ft.; 4,324 m), Rwanda's highest point.

SAN MARINO

Republic of San Marino
Area: 23.6 sq mi. (62 sq km)
Population (est. 1978): 20,500 (mostly Italian)
Capital and largest city (est. 1976 for metropolitan area): San Marino, 4,600
Monetary unit: Italian lira
Language: Italian
Religion: Roman Catholic
National name: Repubblica di San Marino

Geography: One tenth the size of New York City, San Marino is surrounded by Italy. It is situated in the Apennines, a little inland from the Adriatic Sea near Rimini.

SÃO TOMÉ AND PRÍNCIPE

Democratic Republic of São Tomé and Príncipe
Area: 372 sq mi. (964 sq km)
Population (est. 1978): 85,500

Capital and largest city (est. 1977): São Tomé, 20,000
Monetary unit: São Tomé and Príncipe escudo
Language: Portuguese
Religion: Roman Catholic
Gross national product (1976): $40 million

Geography. The tiny volcanic islands of São Tomé and Príncipe lie in the Gulf of Guinea about 150 miles off West Africa. São Tomé (about 330 sq mi.; 855 sq km) is covered by a dense mountainous jungle, out of which have been carved large plantations. Príncipe (about 40 sq mi.; 104 sq km) consists of jagged mountains. Other islands in the republic are Pedras Tinhosas and Rolas.

SAUDI ARABIA

Kingdom of Saudi Arabia
Area: 829,995 sq mi. (2,149,690 sq km)
Population (est. 1978): 9,800,000
Capital: Riyadh
Largest cities (1974 census): Riyadh, 666,840; Jiddah, 561,104; Mecca, 366,801
Monetary unit: Riyal
Language: Arabic
Religion: Islam
Gross national product (1976): $41.2 billion
National name: Al-Mamlaka al-'Arabiya as-Sa'udiya

Geography. The Middle East oil country of Saudi Arabia occupies most of the Arabian Peninsula, with the Red Sea and the Gulf of Aqaba on the west and the Persian Gulf on the east. Neighbors are Jordan, Iraq, and Kuwait in the north, and, along the perimeter from southwest to east, the two Yemens, Oman, and the United Arab Emirates. The country is more than three times the size of Texas.

Saudi Arabia's oil region lies along the Persian Gulf. The country is mostly desert. The Asir Mountains inland rise to a height of 9,000 feet (2,743 m).

SENEGAL

Republic of Senegal
Area: 75,750 sq mi. (196,192 sq km)
Population (est. 1976 by U.N.): 5,090,000
Capital and largest city (est. 1976): Dakar, 798,800
Monetary unit: Franc CFA
Ethnic groups: Wolofs, Sereres, Peuls, Tukulers, and others
Language: French (official); Wolof, Serer, other tribal dialects

Religion: Islam, 80%; Christian, 10%
Gross national product (1976): $2 billion
National name: République du Sénégal

Geography. The capital of Senegal, Dakar, is the western-most point in Africa. The country, slightly smaller than South Dakota, surrounds Gambia on three sides and is bordered on the north by Mauritania, on the east by Mali, and on the south by Guinea and Guinea-Bissau.

Senegal is mainly a low-lying country, with a semidesert area in the north and northeast and forests in the southwest. The largest rivers include the Senegal in the north and the Gambia in the central region.

SEYCHELLES

Republic of Seychelles
Area: 108 sq mi. (280 sq km)
Population (est. 1978): 65,000
Capital (est. 1976): Victoria, 14,500
Monetary unit: Seychelles rupee
Languages: English, French (both official), Creole patois
Religions: Roman Catholic, 91%; Anglican, 8%

Geography. Seychelles consists of an archipelago of 89 islands in the Indian Ocean northeast of Madagascar. The principal islands are Mahé (55 sq mi.; 142 sq km), Praslin (15 sq mi.; 38 sq km), and La Digue (4 sq mi.; 10 sq km). The Aldabra, Farquhar, and Desroches groups are included in the territory of the republic.

SIERRA LEONE

Republic of Sierra Leone
Area: 27,699 sq mi. (71,740 sq km)
Population (U.N. est. 1977): 3,470,000
Capital and largest city (est. 1974): Freetown, 314,340
Monetary unit: Leone
Languages: English (official), Mende, Temne, Creole
Religions: Animist, 66%; Islam, 28%; Christian, 6%
Gross national product (1976): $542 million

Geography. Sierra Leone, on the Atlantic Ocean in West Africa, is half the size of Illinois. Guinea, in the north and east, and Liberia, in the south, are its neighbors.

Mangrove swamps lie along the coast, with wooded hills and a plateau in the interior. The eastern region is mountainous.

SINGAPORE

Republic of Singapore
Area: 226 sq mi. (581 sq km)
Population (est. 1978): 2,340,000 (Chinese, 76%; Malay, 15%; Indian, 7%)
Capital (est. 1975 by U.N.): Singapore, 2,249,900
Monetary unit: Singapore dollar
Languages: Malay, Chinese (Mandarin), Tamil, English
Religions: Islam, Christian, Buddhist, Hindu, Confucianist, Taoist
Gross national product (1976): $5.8 billion

Geography. The Republic of Singapore consists of the main island of Singapore, off the southern tip of the Malay Peninsula between the South China Sea and the Indian Ocean, and 60 nearby islands.

There are extensive mangrove swamps extending inland from the coast, which is broken by many inlets.

SOLOMON ISLANDS

Area: 10,983 sq mi. (28,446 sq km)
Population (est. 1978): 200,000
Capital and largest city (est. 1977): Honiara (on Guadalcanal), 15,600
Languages: Pidgin English, English, Melanesian dialects

Geography: Lying east of New Guinea, this island nation consists of the southern islands of the Solomon group: Guadalcanal, Malaita, Santa Isabel, San Cristóbal, Choiseul, New Georgia, and numerous smaller islands.

SOMALIA

Somali Democratic Republic
Area: 246,201 sq mi. (637,657 sq km)
Population (est. 1978): 3,440,000
Capital and largest city (est. 1976 by U.N.): Mogadishu, 286,000
Monetary unit: Somali shilling
Language: Somali
Religion: Islam
Gross national product: (1976): $370 million
National name: Al Jumhouriya As-Somalya Dimocradia

Geography. Somalia, situated in what is known as the Horn of Africa, lies along the Gulf of Aden and the Indian Ocean. It is bounded by Djibouti in the northwest, Ethiopia in the east, and Kenya in the southwest. In area it is slightly smaller than Texas.

Generally arid and barren, Somalia has two chief rivers, the Shebeli and the Juba.

SOUTH AFRICA

Republic of South Africa
Area: 440,521 sq mi. (1,140,943 sq km)[1]
Population (est. 1977): 26,765,000 (Bantu, 71%; white, 17%; colored (mixed), 9%; Asian, 3%
Administrative capital: Pretoria
Legislative capital: Cape Town
Judicial capital: Bloemfontein
Largest cities (est. 1976): Johannesburg, 1,371,000; Cape Town, 842,600; Pretoria, 634,400; Bloemfontein, 234,900; **(est. 1975):** Durban, 837,000; Port Elizabeth, 468,800
Monetary unit: Rand
Languages: English, Afrikaans, Bantu languages
Religions (1970): Dutch Reformed, 16%; Methodist, 10%; Roman Catholic, 9%; Anglican, 8%; other Christian, 55%
Gross national product (1976): $31.9 billion
National name: Republiek van Suid-Afrika

Geography. South Africa, on the continent's southern tip, is washed by the Atlantic Ocean on the west and by the Indian Ocean on the south and east. Its neighbors are South-West Africa (Namibia) in the northwest, Rhodesia and Botswana in the north, and Mozambique and Swaziland in the northeast. Lesotho, Bophuthatswana, and Transkei are independent enclaves within South Africa, which occupies an area three times that of California.

The country has a high interior plateau, or veld, nearly half of which averages 4,000 feet (1,219 m) in elevation.

There are no important mountain ranges, although the Great Escarpment, separating the veld from the coastal plain, rises to over 11,000 feet (3,350 m) in the Drakensberg Mountains in the east. The principal river is the Orange, rising in Lesotho and flowing westward for 1,300 miles (2,092 km) to the Atlantic.

The southernmost point of Africa is Cape Agulhas, located in Cape Province about 100 miles (161 km) southeast of the Cape of Good Hope.

1. Excluding South-West Africa (Namibia), Transkei, and Bophuthatswana.

BOPHUTHATSWANA

Republic of Bophuthatswana
Area: 15,610 sq mi. (40,430 sq km)

Population (est. 1976): 1,039,000 (Bantu 99.6%)
Capital: Mmabatho
Largest city (est. 1973): Ga-Rankuwa, 64,200
Monetary unit: South African rand
Languages: Central Tswana, English, Afrikaans

Geography. Bophuthatswana consists of half a dozen discontinuous areas within the boundaries of South Africa, most of them in the northern sector near Botswana.

SOUTH-WEST AFRICA (NAMIBIA)

Status: Mandate
Area: 318,251 sq mi. (824,292 sq km)
Population (est. 1977): 920,000
Capital (est. 1975): Windhoek, 77,400
Summer capital: Swakopmund (est. 1975): 13,700
Monetary unit: South African rand
National name: Suidwes-Afrika

Geography. The mandate, bounded on the north by Angola and Zambia and on the east by Botswana and South Africa, was discovered by the Portuguese explorer Diaz in the late 15th century. It is for the most part a portion of the high plateau of southern Africa with a general elevation of from 3,000 to 4,000 feet.

TRANSKEI

Republic of Transkei
Area: 15,831 sq mi. (41,002 sq km)
Population (est. 1976): 2,050,000
Capital (est. 1977): Umtala, 30,000
Monetary unit: South African rand
Languages: English, Xhosa, Southern Sotho
Religions: Christian, tribal

Geography. Transkei occupies three discontinuous enclaves within southeast South Africa that add up to twice the size of Massachusetts. It has a 270-mile (435 km) coastline on the Indian Ocean but no port. The capital, Umtata, is connected by rail to the South African port of East London, 100 miles (160 km) to the southwest.

SOVIET UNION

Union of Soviet Socialist Republics
Area: 8,649,489 sq mi. (22,402,200 sq km)

Population (est. 1978): 260,750,000 (Russian, 53%; Ukrainian, 17%; Byelorussian, 4%; Uzbek, 4%; Tatar, 2%; others, 20%)
Capital: Moscow
Largest cities (est. 1976 by U.N.): Moscow, 7,734,000; Leningrad, 4,372,000; Kiev, 2,013,000; Tashkent, 1,643,000; Baku, 1,406,000; Kharkov, 1,385,000; Gorky, 1,305,000; Novosibirsk, 1,286,000; Minsk, 1,189,000; Kuibyshev, 1,186,000; Tblisi, 1,030,000; Odessa, 1,023,000; Chelyabinsk, 989,999; Dnepropetrovsk, 976,000; Donetsk, 967,000
Monetary unit; Ruble
Languages: *See* Population, above
Religions: Russian Orthodox (predominant), Islam, Roman Catholic, Jewish, Lutheran
Gross national product (1976): $708.2 billion
National name: Soyuz Sovyetskikh Sotsialisticheskikh Respublik

Geography. The U.S.S.R. is the largest unbroken political unit in the world, occupying more than one seventh of the land surface of the globe. The greater part of its territory is a vast plain stretching from eastern Europe to the Pacific Ocean. This plain, relieved only occasionally by low mountain ranges (notably the Urals), consists of three zones running east and west: the frozen marshy tundra of the Arctic; the more temperate forest belt; and the steppes or prairies to the south, which in southern Soviet Asia become sandy deserts.

The topography is more varied in the south, particularly

Republics of the U.S.S.R.

Republic and capital	Area sq mi.	Population est. 1977 (thousands)
Russian S.F.S.R. (Moscow)	6,593,391	135,600
Ukraine (Kiev)	233,089	49,300
Kazakhstan (Alma-Ata)	1,064,092	14,498
Byelorussia (Minsk)	80,154	9,414
Uzbekistan (Tashkent)	158,069	14,474
Georgia (Tbilisi)	26,872	4,999
Azerbaijan (Baku)	33,475	5,776
Lithuania[1] (Vilnius)	25,174	3,342
Moldavia (Kishinev)	13,012	3,885
Latvia[1] (Riga)	24,595	2,512
Kirghizia (Frunze)	76,641	3,443
Tadzhikistan (Duschambe)	55,019	3,591
Armenia (Erevan)	11,506	2,893
Turkmenistan (Ashkhabad)	188,417	2,650
Estonia[1] (Tallinn)	17,413	1,447

1. Soviet jurisdiction not recognized by the United States.

in the Caucasus between the Caspian and Black Seas, and in the Tien-Pamir mountain system bordering Afghanistan, Sinkiang, and Mongolia. Mountains (Stanovoi and Kolyma) and great rivers (Amur, Yenisei, Lena) also break up the sweep of the plain in Siberia.

In the west, the major rivers are the Volga, Dnieper, Don, Kama, and Southern Bug.

SPAIN

Spanish State
Area: 194,897 sq mi. (504,782 sq km)
Population (est. 1978): 36,730,000 (Spanish, Basque, Catalan)
Capital: Madrid
Largest cities (est. 1977): Madrid, 3,870,900; (est. 1976): Barcelona, 1,846,250; Valencia, 748,730; Seville, 612,900; Zaragoza, 589,600; Bilbao, 486,600
Monetary unit: Peseta
Languages: Spanish, Basque, Catalan, Galician
Religion: Roman Catholic
Gross national product (1976): $104.1 billion
National name: Estado Español

Geography. Spain occupies 85% of the Iberian Peninsula in southwestern Europe, which it shares with Portugal; France is to the northeast. It is touched by the Bay of Biscay in the north, the Atlantic Ocean in the west, and the Mediterranean Sea in the south and east.

Spain, less than 10 miles (16 km) from Africa at the Strait of Gibraltar, is separated from France by the Pyrenees. The country is generally a broad plateau sloping to south and east and crossed by a series of mountain ranges and river valleys.

Principal rivers are the Ebro in the northeast, the Tagus in the central region, and the Guadalquivir in the south.

Off Spain's east coast in the Mediterranean are the Balearic Islands (1,936 sq mi.; 5,014 sq km), the largest of which is Majorca. Sixty miles (97 km) west of Africa are the Canary Islands (2,808 sq mi.; 7,273 sq km).

SRI LANKA

Republic of Sri Lanka
Area: 25,332 sq mi. (65,610 sq km)
Population (est. 1978): 14,200,000 (Sinhalese, 72%; Tamil, 21%; Moors, 7%)
Capital: Colombo

Largest cities (est. 1976): Colombo, 607,000; Dehiwela, 166,000; Jaffna,
  117,000
Monetary unit: Sri Lanka rupee
Languages: Sinhalese, Tamil, English
Religions: Buddhist, 67%; Hindu, 18%; Christian, 8%; Islam, 7%
Gross national product (1976): $3.1 billion

Geography. An island in the Indian Ocean off the southeast
tip of India, Sri Lanka is about half the size of Alabama.
Most of the land is flat and rolling; mountains in the south
central region rise to over 8,000 feet (2,438 m).

SUDAN
Democratic Republic of the Sudan
Area: 967,494 sq mi. (2,505,813 sq km)
Population (est. 1977): 16,550,000
Capital: Khartoum
Largest cities (est. 1973): Khartoum, 321,700; Omdurman, 250,000; Port
  Sudan, 130,000
Monetary unit: Sudanese pound
Languages: Arabic, English, tribal dialects
Religions: Sunni Moslem, Christian, Animist
Gross national product (1976): $4.6 billion
National name: Jamhuryat es-Sudan Al-Democratia

Geography. The Sudan, in northeast Africa, is the largest
country on the continent, measuring about one fourth the
size of the United States. Its neighbors are Chad and the
Central African Empire on the west, Egypt on the north,
Ethiopia on the east, and Kenya, Uganda, and Zaire on the
south. The Red Sea washes about 500 miles of the eastern
coast.

The country extends from north to south about 1,200
miles (1,931 km) and west to east about 1,000 miles (1,609
km). The northern region is a continuation of the Libyan
Desert. The southern region is fertile, abundantly watered,
and, in places, heavily forested. It is traversed from north
to south by the Nile, all of whose great tributaries are partly
or entirely within its borders.

SURINAM
Republic of Surinam
Area: 63,037 sq mi. (163,265 sq km)
Population (est. 1978): 460,000 (approx.: Hindustani, 37%; Creole, 30.8%;
  Indonesian, 15.3%; Bush Negro, 10.3%)

Capital and largest city (est. 1973): Paramaribo, 150,000
Monetary unit: Surinam guilder
Language: Dutch, Taki-taki (lingua franca)
Religions: Protestant, Roman Catholic, Hindu, Islam

Geography. Surinam lies on the northeast coast of South
America, with Guyana to the west, French Guiana to the
east, and Brazil to the south. It is about one tenth larger
than Michigan. The principal rivers are the Courantyne on
the Guyana border, the Maroni in the east, and the Suri-
name, on which the capital city of Paramaribo is situated.
The Tumuc-Humac Mountains are on the border with Brazil.

SWAZILAND

Kingdom of Swaziland
Area: 6,704 sq mi. (17,363 sq km)
Population (est. 1978): 520,000
Capital and largest city (est. 1975): Mbabane, 24,000
Monetary unit: Lilangeni
Languages: English and siSwati (official)
Religions: Christian, 60%, and Animist.
Gross national product (1976): $240 million

Geography. Swaziland, 85% the size of New Jersey, is surrounded by South Africa and Mozambique. The country
consists of a high veld in the west and a series of plateaus
descending from a maximum of 6,000 feet (1,829 m) to a
low veld of 1,500 feet (457 m).

SWEDEN

Kingdom of Sweden
Area: 173,732 sq mi. (449,964 sq km)
Population (est. 1978): 8,300,000
Capital: Stockholm
Largest cities (est. 1977): Stockholm, 661,300; (est. 1976): Göteborg,
    442,500; Malmö, 240,300
Monetary unit: Krona
Language: Swedish
Religion: Swedish Lutheran, 95%
Gross national product (1976): $71.3 billion
National name: Konungariket Sverige

Geography. Sweden occupies the eastern part of the Scandinavian peninsula, with Norway to the west, Finland and
the Gulf of Bothnia to the east, and Denmark and the

Baltic Sea in the south. It is one tenth larger than California.

The country slopes eastward and southward from the Kjólen Mountains along the Norwegian border, where the peak elevation is Kebnekaise at 6,965 feet (2,123 m) in Lapland. In the north are mountains and many lakes. To the south and east are central lowlands and south of them are fertile areas of forest, valley, and plain.

Along Sweden's rocky coast, chopped up by bays and inlets, are many islands, the largest of which are Gotland and Öland.

SWITZERLAND

Swiss Confederation
Area: 15,941 sq mi. (41,288 sq km)
Population (est. 1978): 6,310,000 (Swiss, 85%; Italian, 8%; German, 2%; Spanish, 2%; French, 1%—figures by place of birth)
Capital: Bern
Largest cities (est. 1976 by U.N.): Zurich, 389,600; Basel, 192,800; Geneva, 155,800; Bern, 149,800; Lausanne, 134,300
Monetary unit: Swiss franc
Languages: German, 65%; French, 18%; Italian, 12%; Romansch, 1%
Religions: Roman Catholic, 49.4%; Protestant, 47.8%
Gross national product (1976): $58.4 billion
National name: Schweiz/Suisse/Svizzera

Geography. Switzerland, in central Europe, is the land of the Alps. The tallest peak in Switzerland is the Dufourspitze at 15,203 feet (4,634 m) on the Swiss side of the Italian border, one of 10 summits of the Monte Rose massif in the Pennine Alps. The tallest peak in all of the Alps, Mont Blanc (15,771 ft; 4,807 m), is actually in France.

Most of Switzerland comprises a mountainous plateau bordered by the great bulk of the Alps on the south and by the Jura Mountains on the northwest. About a fourth of the total area is covered by mountains and glaciers.

The country's largest lakes—Geneva, Constance (Bodensee), and Maggiore—straddle the French, German-Austrian, and Italian borders, respectively.

The Rhine, navigable from Basel to the North Sea, is the principal inland waterway. Other rivers are the Aare and the Rhône.

Switzerland, twice the size of New Jersey, is surrounded by France, West Germany, Austria, Liechtenstein, and Italy.

SYRIA

Syrian Arab Republic
Area: 71,498 sq mi. (185,180 sq km)
Population (est. 1978): 8,000,000
Capital: Damascus
Largest cities (est. 1976): Damascus, 1,054,000; (est. 1975): Aleppo, 778,500; Homs, 267,100; Hama, 162,000
Monetary unit: Syrian pound
Languages: Arabic (official), Kurdish, Armenian, Turkish, Circassian
Religions: Islam, 83%; Christian, 17%
Gross national product (1976): $6.0 billion
National name: Al-Jamhouriya al Arabiya As-Souriya

Geography. Slightly larger than North Dakota, Syria lies at the eastern end of the Mediterranean Sea. It is bordered by Lebanon and Israel on the west, Turkey on the north, Iraq on the east, and Jordan on the south.

Coastal Syria is a narrow plain, in back of which is a range of coastal mountains, and still farther inland a steppe area. In the east is the Syrian Desert, and in the south is the Jebel Druze Range. The highest point in Syria is Mt. Hermon (9,232 ft.; 2,814 m) on the Lebanese border.

TANZANIA

United Republic of Tanzania
Area: 364,900 sq mi. (945,087 sq km)[1]
Population (est. 1978): 16,450,000
Capital and largest city (est. 1977): Dar es Salaam, 460,000
Monetary unit: Tanzanian shilling
Languages: Swahili, Bantu, Arabic, English
Religions: Animist, 34.6%; Christian, 30.6%; Islam, 30.5%
Gross national product (1976): $2.7 billion

Geography. Tanzania is in East Africa on the Indian Ocean. To the north are Uganda and Kenya; to the west, Burundi, Rwanda, and Zaire; and to the south, Mozambique, Zambia, and Malawi. Its area is three times that of New Mexico.

Tanzania contains three of Africa's best-known lakes—Victoria in the north, Tanganyika in the west, and Nyasa in the south. Mount Kilimanjaro in the north, 19,340 feet (5,895 m), is the highest point on the continent.

1. Including Zanzibar.

THAILAND

Kingdom of Thailand
Area: 198,455 sq mi. (514,000 sq km)
Population (est. 1978): 45,380,000 (incl. 2.5 million of Chinese descent born in Thailand; Chinese 1.6%; others, 0.2%)
Capital and largest city (est. 1977): Bangkok, 4,545,600
Monetary unit: Baht
Languages: Thai (Siamese), Chinese, English
Religions: Buddhist, 95%; Islam, 4%
Gross national product (1976): $16.2 billion
National name: Muang Thai

Geography. Thailand occupies the western half of the former Indochinese peninsula and the northern two thirds of the Malay peninsula in southeast Asia. Its neighbors are Burma on the north and west, Laos on the east, and Cambodia and Malaysia on the south. Thailand is about three fourths the size of Texas.

Most of the population is supported in the fertile central alluvial plain, which is drained by the Chao Phnaya River and its tributaries.

TOGO

Republic of Togo
Area: 21,622 sq mi. (56,000 sq km)
Population (est. 1978): 2,410,000
Capital and largest city (est. 1976): Lomé, 229,400
Monetary unit: Franc CFA
Languages: Ewé, Mina (south), Kabyé, Cotocoli (north), French (official), and many dialects
Religions: Animist, Christian, Islam
Gross national product (1976): $600 million
National name: République Togolaise

Geography. Togo, twice the size of Maryland, is on the south coast of West Africa bordering on Ghana to the west, Upper Volta to the north and Benin to the east.

The Gulf of Guinea coastline, only 32 miles long (51 km), is low, sandy, and without harbors. The Togo hills traverse the central section.

TONGA

Kingdom of Tonga
Area: 270 sq mi. (699 sq km)
Population (est. 1978): 100,000

Capital (est. 1976): Nuku'alofa, 18,400
Monetary unit: Pa'anga
Languages: Tongan, English
Religion: Christian

Geography. Situated east of the Fiji Islands in the South
Pacific, Tonga (also called the Friendly Islands) consists of
some 150 islands, of which 36 are inhabited.

Most of the islands contain active volcanic craters; others
are coral atolls.

TRANSKEI

See South Africa

TRINIDAD AND TOBAGO

Republic of Trinidad and Tobago
Area: 1,980 sq mi. (5,128 sq km)
Population (est. 1977): 1,120,000 (black, 43%; East Indian, 40%; mixed, 14%)
Capital and largest city (est. 1973): Port-of-Spain, 60,400
Monetary unit: Trinidad and Tobago dollar
Languages: English (official); Hindi, French, Spanish
Religions: Christian, 64%; Hindu, 25%; Islam, 6%
Gross national product (1976): $2.4 billion

Geography. Trinidad and Tobago lies in the Caribbean Sea
off the northeast coast of Venezuela. The area of the two
islands is slightly less than that of Delaware.

Trinidad, the larger, is mainly flat and rolling, with
mountains in the north that reach a height of 3,085 feet
(940 m) at Mount Aripo. Tobago is heavily forested with
hardwood trees.

TUNISIA

Republic of Tunisia
Area: 63,170 sq mi. (163,610 sq km)
Population (est. 1978): 6,400,000
Capital and largest city (est. 1976): Tunis, 960,000
Monetary unit: Tunisian dinar
Languages: Arabic, French
Religions: Predominantly Islam; Roman Catholic, Jewish, Greek Orthodox
Gross national product (1976): $4.4 billion
National name: Al-Djoumhouria Attunusia

Geography. Tunisia, at the northernmost bulge of Africa, thrusts out toward Sicily to mark the division between the eastern and western Mediterranean Sea. Twice the size of South Carolina, it is bordered on the west by Algeria and Libya on the east.

The country is covered by plains in the east and projects southward to the Sahara. In the north, the Atlas Mountains continue from Algeria but do not attain great altitude.

TURKEY

Republic of Turkey
Area: 301,380 sq mi. (incl. 9,121 in Europe) (780,576 sq km)
Population (est. 1978): 43,120,000
Capital: Ankara
Largest cities (1975 census): Istanbul, 2,500,000; Ankara, 1,700,000; Izmir (Smyrna), 640,000; Adana, 470,000; Bursa, 350,000; Gaziantep, 300,000
Monetary unit: Turkish lira
Language: Turkish
Religion: Islam
Gross national product (1976): $41.4 billion
National name: Türkiye Cumhuriyeti

Geography. Turkey is at the northeastern end of the Mediterranean Sea in southeast Europe and southwest Asia. To the north is the Black Sea and to the west the Aegean Sea. Its neighbors are Greece and Bulgaria to the west, the U.S.S.R. to the north, Iran to the east, and Syria and Iraq to the south. Overall, it is more than twice the size of Montana.

The country is divided into two natural areas by the historic waterway formed by the Dardanelles, the Sea of Marmara, and the Bosporus.

Turkey in Europe comprises an area about equal to the state of Massachusetts. It is hilly country drained by the Maritsa River and its tributaries. Almost all the population is concentrated in and near the three important towns, Istanbul (Constantinople), Ankara, and Edirne (Adrianople).

Turkey in Asia, or Anatolia, about the size of Texas, is roughly a rectangle in shape with its short sides on the east and west. Its center is a treeless plateau rimmed by mountains.

UGANDA

Republic of Uganda
Area: 91,134 sq mi. (236,036 sq km)

Population (est. 1978): 12,775,000
Capital and largest city (est. 1975 by U.N.): Kampala, 542,000
Monetary unit: Ugandan shilling
Languages: English (official), Swahili, Luganda, Ateso, Luo
Religions: Christian, Islam
Gross national product (1976): $2.8 billion

Geography. Uganda, twice the size of Pennsylvania, is in east central Africa. It is bordered on the west by Zaire, on the north by the Sudan, on the east by Kenya, and on the south by Tanzania and Rwanda.

The country, which lies across the Equator, is divided into three main areas—swampy lowlands, a fertile plateau with wooded hills, and a desert region. Lake Victoria forms part of the southern border.

UNION OF SOVIET SOCIALIST REPUBLICS
See Soviet Union

UNITED ARAB EMIRATES
Area: 32,278 sq mi. (83,600 sq km)
Population (est. 1978): 656,000
Capital and largest city (est. 1975): Abu Dhabi, 95,000
Monetary unit: Dirham
Language: Arabic
Religion: Islam
Gross national product (1976): $9.7 billion

Geography. The United Arab Emirates, in the eastern part of the Arabian Peninsula, extend along part of the Gulf of Oman and the southern coast of the Persian Gulf. They are the size of Maine. Their neighbors are Saudi Arabia in the west and south, Qatar in the north, and Oman in the east. Most of the land is barren and sandy.

UNITED KINGDOM
United Kingdom of Great Britain and Northern Ireland
Area: 94,250 sq mi. (244,108 sq km)[1]
Population (est. 1978): 55,800,000[1] (English, Scottish, Welsh, Northern Irish)
Capital: London, England

1. Including the Channel Islands and the Isle of Man.

Largest cities (est. 1976): London (Greater), 7,028,200; Birmingham, England, 1,058,800; Glasgow, Scotland, 856,000; Leeds, England, 744,500; Sheffield, England, 558,000; Liverpool, England, 539,700; Manchester, England, 490,000; Edinburgh, Scotland, 467,100; Bradford, England, 458,900
Monetary unit: Pound sterling (£)
Languages: English, Welsh, Gaelic
Religions: Church of England (established church); Church of Wales (disestablished); Church of Scotland (established church—Presbyterian); Church of Ireland (disestablished); Roman Catholic; Methodist; Congregational; Baptist; Jewish
Gross national product (1976): $222.2 billion

Geography. The United Kingdom, consisting of England, Wales, Scotland, and Northern Ireland, is twice the size of New York State. England, in the southeast part of the British Isles, is separated from Scotland on the north by the granite Cheviot Hills; from them the Pennine chain of uplands extends south through the center of England, reaching its highest point in the Lake District in the northwest. To the west along the border of Wales—a land of steep hills and valleys—are the Cambrian Mountains, while the Cotswolds, a range of hills in Gloucestershire, extend into the surrounding shires.

The remainder of England is plain land, though not necessarily flat, with the rocky sand-topped moors in the southwest, the rolling Downs in the south and southeast, and the reclaimed marshes of the low-lying Fens in the east central districts.

Scotland is divided into three physical regions—the Highlands, the Central Lowlands, containing two-thirds of the population, and the Southern Uplands. The western Highland coast is intersected throughout by long, narrow sea-lochs, or fiords. Scotland also includes the Outer and Inner Hebrides and other islands off the west coast and the Orkney and Shetland Islands off the north coast.

Wales is generally hilly; the Snowdon range in the northern part culminates in Mt. Snowdon (3,560 ft, 1,085 m), highest in both England and Wales.

Important rivers flowing into the North Sea are the Thames, Humber, Tees, and Tyne. In the west are the Severn and Wye, which empty into the Bristol Channel and are navigable, as are the Mersey and Ribble.

NORTHERN IRELAND

Status: Part of United Kingdom
Area: 5,452 sq mi. (14,121 sq km)

Population (est. 1977): 1,537,000
Capital and largest city (est. 1976): Belfast, 363,000
Monetary Unit: British pound sterling
Languages: English, Gaelic
Religions: Roman Catholic, 34.9%; Presbyterian, 29%; Church of Ireland, 24.2%; Methodist, 5%

Geography. Northern Ireland comprises the counties of Antrim, Armagh, Down, Fermanagh, Londonderry, and Tyrone, which make up predominantly Protestant Ulster and form the northern part of the island of Ireland, westernmost of the British Isles. It is slightly larger than Connecticut.

Dependencies of the United Kingdom

ANGUILLA, ANTIGUA

See West Indies Associated States

BELIZE

Status: Self-governing dependency
Area: 8,867 sq mi. (22,965 sq km)
Population (est. 1978): 150,000
Capital: (est. 1975): Belpoman, 5,300
Monetary unit: Belize dollar

BERMUDA

Status: Self-governing dependency
Area: 20 sq mi. (52 sq km)
Population (est. 1978): 65,000
Capital (1970 census): Hamilton, 2,100
Monetary unit: Bermuda dollar

BRITISH ANTARCTIC TERRITORY

Status: Dependency
Area: 500,000 sq mi. (1,395,000 sq km)
Population (1972): 79

BRITISH INDIAN OCEAN TERRITORY

Status: Dependency
Administrative headquarters: Victoria, Seychelles
Area: 85 sq mi, (220 sq km)

BRITISH VIRGIN ISLANDS

Status: Dependency
Area: 59 sq mi. (153 sq km)
Population (est. 1977): 12,000
Capital (est. 1975): Road Town (on Tortola): 3,500
Monetary unit: U.S. dollar

BRUNEI

Status: Independent state
Area: 2,226 sq mi. (5,765 sq km)
Population (est. 1977): 185,000
Capital (est. 1976): Bandar Seri Begawan, 48,000
Monetary unit: Brunei dollar

CAYMAN ISLANDS

Status: Dependency
Area: 118 sq mi. (306 sq km)
Population (est. 1977): 14,000
Capital (1970 census): Georgetown (on Grand Cayman), 3,800
Monetary unit: Cayman Islands dollar

CHANNEL ISLANDS

Status: Crown dependencies
Area: 75 sq mi. (194 sq km)
Population (est. 1977): 125,000
Capital of Jersey: St. Helier
Capital of Guernsey: St. Peter Port
Monetary units: Guernsey pound; Jersey pound

DOMINICA

See West Indies Associated States

FALKLAND ISLANDS AND DEPENDENCIES

Status: Dependency
Area: 6,270 sq mi. (16,239 sq km)
Population: est. (1977): 2,000
Capital (est. 1976): Stanley (on East Falkland), 1,100
Monetary unit: Falkland Island pound

GIBRALTAR

Status: Self-governing dependency
Area: 2.25 sq mi. (5.8 sq km)
Population (est. 1978): 30,000
Monetary unit: Gibraltar pound

GILBERT ISLANDS

Status: Territory
Area: 102 sq mi. (264 sq km)
Population (est. 1978): 60,000
Seat of government (est. 1974): Bairiki (on Tarawa Atoll), 17,100
Monetary unit: Australian dollar

HONG KONG

Status: Dependency
Area: 404 sq mi. (1,045 sq km)
Population (est. 1978): 4,580,000
Capital (est. 1971): Victoria (Hong Kong Island), 520,900
Monetary unit: Hong Kong dollar

ISLE OF MAN

Status: Dependency
Area: 227 sq mi. (588 sq km)
Population (est. 1977): 60,500
Capital (1971 census): Douglas, 20,389
Monetary unit: Isle of Man pound

LEEWARD ISLANDS

See British Virgin Islands; Montserrat; West Indies Associated States

MONTSERRAT

Status: Dependency
Area: 40 sq mi. (104 sq km)
Population (est. 1977): 13,500
Capital (est. 1974): Plymouth, 3,000
Monetary unit: East Caribbean dollar

PITCAIRN ISLAND

Status: Dependency
Area: 18 sq mi. (47 sq km)
Population (1976 census): 74
Capital: Adamstown

ST. HELENA

Status: Dependency
Area: 47 sq mi. (122 sq km)
Population (est 1978): 5,200
Capital (est. 1974): Jamestown, 1,600
Monetary unit: Pound sterling

ST. KITTS-NEVIS, ST. LUCIA, ST. VINCENT

See West Indies Associated States

TURKS AND CAICOS ISLANDS

Status: Dependency
Area: 166 sq mi. (430 sq km)
Population (est. 1978): 6,200
Capital (est. 1970): Grand Turk, 2,300
Monetary unit: U.S. dollar

TUVALU

Status: Dependency
Area: 10 sq mi. (26 sq km)
Population (est. 1978): 6,600
Seat of government: (est. 1976): Funafuti, 1,300
Monetary unit: Australian dollar

VIRGIN ISLANDS

See British Virgin Islands

WEST INDIES ASSOCIATED STATES

Status: Self-governing territories in free association with the United
  Kingdom, which is responsible for defense and external affairs. The British
  Government conducts its affairs with the West Indies Associated States
  through an official representative, whose office is in Bridgetown, Barbados.
Area: Antigua, 171 sq mi. (443 sq km); Dominica, 290 sq mi. (751 sq km);
  St. Christopher (Kitts)-Nevis-Anguilla, 153 sq mi. (397 sq km); St. Lucia,
  238 sq mi. (616 sq km); St. Vincent, 150 sq mi. (389 sq km).
Population (est. 1978): Antigua, 75,000; Dominica, 80,000; St. Christopher
  (Kitts)-Nevis-Anguilla, 70,000; St. Lucia, 113,000; St. Vincent, 111,000
Capitals: Antigua: St. Johns, 23,500; Dominica: Roseau, 10,200; St.
  Christopher (Kitts)-Nevis-Anguilla: Basseterre (on St. Kitts), 15,900; St.
  Lucia: Castries, 3,600; St. Vincent: Kingstown, 22,000
Monetary unit: East Caribbean dollar

WINDWARD ISLANDS

See West Indies Associated States

UPPER VOLTA

Republic of Upper Volta
Area: 105,870 sq mi. (274,200 sq km)
Population (est 1978): 6,480,000
Capital and largest city (est. 1975): Ouagadougou, 168,600
Monetary unit: Franc CFA
Ethnic groups: Mossis, Bobos
Languages: French, African languages
Religion: Animist, 75%; Islam, 20%; Christian, 5%
Gross national product (1976): $710 million
National name: République de Haute-Volta

Geography. Slightly larger than Colorado, Upper Volta is a landlocked country in West Africa. Its neighbors are the Ivory Coast, Mali, Niger, Benin, Togo, and Ghana. The country consists of extensive plains, low hills, high savannas, and a desert area in the north.

URUGUAY

Oriental Republic of Uruguay
Area: 68,037 sq mi. (176,215 sq km)
Population (est. 1978): 2,825,000
Capital and largest city (est. 1975): Montevideo, 1,229,700
Monetary unit: New peso
Language: Spanish
Religion: Roman Catholic
Gross national product (1976): $3.9 billion
National name: República Oriental del Uruguay

Geography. Uruguay, on the east coast of South America south of Brazil and east of Argentina, is comparable in size to the State of Washington.

The country consists of a low, rolling plain in the south and a low plateau in the north. It has a 120-mile (193 km) Atlantic shore line, a 235-mile (378 km) frontage on the Rio de la Plata, and 270 miles (435 km) on the Uruguay River, its western boundary.

VATICAN CITY STATE

Area: 0.17 sq mi. (0.44 sq km)
Population (est. 1978): 1,000 (Italian, 85%; Swiss and others, 15%)
Monetary unit: Lira
Languages: Latin, Italian
Religion: Roman Catholic
National name: Stato della Città del Vaticano

Geography. The Vatican City State is situated on the Vatican hill, on the right bank of the Tiber River, within the commune of Rome.

VENEZUELA

Republic of Venezuela
Area: 352,143 sq mi. (912,050 sq km)
Population (est. 1978): 13,150,000 (mestizo, 69%; white, 20%; black, 9%; Indian, 2%)
Capital: Caracas
Largest cities (est. 1977): Caracas (metropolitan area): 2,664,000; (1971 census): Maracaibo, 651,574; Valencia, 366,154; Barquisimeto, 334,333
Monetary unit: Bolívar
Language: Spanish
Religion: Roman Catholic
Gross national product (1976): $31.1 billion
National name: República de Venezuela

Geography. Venezuela, a third larger than Texas, occupies most of the northern coast of South America on the Caribbean Sea. It is bordered by Colombia to the west, Guyana to the east, and Brazil to the south.

Mountain systems break Venezuela into four distinct areas: (1) the Maracaibo lowlands; (2) the mountainous region in the north and northwest; (3) the Orinoco basin, with the llanos (vast grass-covered plains) on its northern border and great forest areas in the south and southeast; (4) the Guiana Highlands, south of the Orinoco, accounting for nearly half the national territory. About 80% of Venezuela is drained by the Orinoco and its tributaries.

VIETNAM

Socialist Republic of Vietnam
Area: 127,242 sq mi. (329,556 sq km)
Population (est. 1978): 49,275,000
Density per square mile: 387.3
Capital: Hanoi
Largest cities (est. 1976): Ho Chi Minh City (Saigon),[1] 3,460,500; Hanoi, 1,443,500; (est. 1973): Da Nang, 492,200; Na Trang, 216,200; Qui Non, 213,750; Hue, 209,000; (1960 census): Haiphong, 182,490
Monetary unit: Dong
Languages: Vietnamese, French, Chinese
Religions: Buddhist, Roman Catholic, Cao-Dai, Hoa-Hao, Confucian
National name: Công Hòa Xa Hôi Chú Nghia Viêt Nam

Geography. Vietnam occupies the eastern and southern

1. Includes suburb of Cholon.

part of the former Indochinese peninsula in Southeast Asia, with the South China Sea along its entire coast. China is to the north and Laos and Cambodia to the west. Long and narrow on a north-south axis, Vietnam is about twice the size of Arizona.

The Mekong River delta lies in the south and the Red River delta in the north. Heavily forested mountain and plateau regions make up most of the country.

WESTERN SAMOA

Area: 1,097 sq mi. (2,842 sq km)
Population (est. 1978): 155,000
Capital and largest city (1976 census): Apia, 32,100
Monetary unit: Tala
Languages: Samoan and English
Religions: Congregational, 51%; Roman Catholic, 22%; Methodist, 16%
Gross national product (1976): $50 million
National name: Samoa i Sisifo

Geography. Western Samoa, the size of Rhode Island, is in the South Pacific Ocean about 2,200 miles south of Hawaii midway to Sydney, Australia, and about 800 miles northeast of Fiji. The larger islands in the Samoan chain are mountainous and of volcanic origin. There is little level land except in the coastal areas, where most cultivation takes place.

YEMEN

People's Democratic Republic of Yemen
Area: 111,074 sq mi. (287,683 sq km)[1]
Population (est. 1978): 1,850,000
National capital and largest city (est. 1973 by U.N.): Aden, 264,300
Administrative capital: Madinat ash Sha'b
Monetary unit: Yemen dinar
Language: Arabic
Religion: Islam
Gross national product (1976): $480 million
National name: Jumhurijah al-Yemen al Dimuqratiyah al Sha'abijah

Geography. Formerly known as Southern Yemen, the People's Democratic Republic of Yemen extends along the southern part of the Arabian Peninsula on the Gulf of Aden and the Indian Ocean. It is comparable in size to Nevada.

1. Excluding Perim and Kamaran islands.

The Yemen Arab Republic is to the northwest, Saudia Arabia to the north, and Oman to the east.

A 700-mile (1,130-km) narrow coastal plain gives way to a mountainous region and then a plateau area.

YEMEN ARAB REPUBLIC

Area: 75,290 sq mi. (195,000 sq km)
Population (est. 1978): 7,300,000
Capital and largest city (est. 1975): San'a', 134,600
Monetary unit: Rial
Language: Arabic
Religion: Islam
Gross national product (1976): $1.5 billion
National name: Al Jamhuriya al Arabiya Yamaniya

Geography. The Yemen Arab Republic occupies the southwestern tip of the Arabian Peninsula, with its western coast on the Red Sea opposite Ethiopia. Its neighbors are Saudi Arabia to the north and east and the People's Democratic Republic of Yemen to the south. Its area is slightly less than that of South Dakota.

A north-south coastal plain 20–50 miles wide lies in the west; eastward, there are the interior highlands, which attain a height of 12,000 feet (3,660 m), and the expanse of the Rub 'al-Khali Desert.

YUGOSLAVIA

Socialist Federal Republic of Yugoslavia
Area: 98,766 sq mi. (255,804 sq km)
Population (est. 1978): 21,900,000 (Serbian, 42%; Croatian, 24%; Slovene, 9%; Macedonian, 5%; Albanian, 4%)
Capital: Belgrade
Largest cities (est. 1975 by U.N.): Belgrade, 870,000; (1971 census): Zagreb, 566,224; Skopje, 312,980; Sarajevo, 243,980; Ljubljana, 173,853; Split, 152,905
Monetary unit: Dinar
Languages: Serbo-Croatian, Slovene, Macedonian (all official)
Religions: Greek Orthodox, 41%; Roman Catholic, 32%; Islam, 12%
Gross national product (1976): $36.2 billion
National name: Socijalisticka Federativna Republika Jugoslavija

Geography. Yugoslavia fronts on the eastern coast of the Adriatic Sea opposite Italy. Its neighbors are Austria, Italy, and Hungary to the north, Romania and Bulgaria to the east, and Greece and Albania to the south. It is slightly larger than Wyoming.

About half of Yugoslavia is mountainous. In the north, the Dinaric Alps rise abruptly from the sea and progress eastward as a barren limestone plateau called the Karst. Montenegro is a jumbled mass of mountains, containing also some grassy slopes and fertile river valleys. Southern Serbia, too, is mountainous. A rich plain in the north and northeast, drained by the Danube, is the most fertile area of the country.

ZAIRE

Republic of Zaire
Area: 905,562 sq mi. (2,345,409 sq km)
Population (est. 1978): 27,150,000
Capital: Kinshasa
Largest cities (1974 by U.N.): Kinshasa, 2,008,250; Kananga, 601,250; Lubumbashi, 403,600
Monetary unit: Zaire.
Languages: French; Bantu dialects, mainly Swahili, Lingala, Ishiluba, and Kikongo
Religions: Animist, 50%; Roman Catholic, Protestant, Islam
Ethnic groups: Bantu, Sudanese, Nilotics, Pygmies, Hamites
Gross national product (1976): $3.5 billion
National name: République du Zaïre

Geography. Zaire is situated in west central Africa and is bordered by the Congo, the Central African Empire, the Sudan, Uganda, Rwanda, Burundi, Tanzania, Zambia, Angola, and the Atlantic Ocean. It is one quarter the size of the U.S.

The principal rivers are the Ubangi and Bomu in the north and the Zaire (Congo) in the west, which flows into the Atlantic. The entire length of Lake Tanganyika lies along the eastern border with Tanzania and Burundi.

ZAMBIA

Republic of Zambia
Area: 290,586 sq mi. (752,614 sq km)
Population (est. 1978): 5,500,000
Capital: Lusaka
Largest cities (est. 1976 for urban agglomeration): Lusaka, 483,000; (est. 1972 by U.N.): Ndola, 350,000; Kitwe, 290,100; Chingola, 181,500
Monetary unit: Kwacha
Languages: English and Bantu
Religion: Animist
Gross national product (1976): $2.4 billion
Member of Commonwealth of Nations

Geography. Zambia, a landlocked country in south central Africa, is about one tenth larger than Texas. It is surrounded by Angola, Zaire, Tanzania, Malawi, Mozambique, Rhodesia, and South-West Africa (Namibia). The country is mostly a plateau that rises to 8,000 feet (2,434 m) in the east.

International Treaties, Agreements, and Organizations

Alliance for Progress Agreement

Embodied in the Declaration of Punta del Este, adopted Aug. 17, 1961, by the U.S. and 19 other American republics, Cuba abstaining. The U.S. agreed to provide most of $20 billion needed over the next 10 years for Latin-American economic development. The other nations pledged themselves to increase their own contributions to economic and social development and to make the reforms necessary for all to share fully in the benefits gained under the Alliance for Progress.

Arab League

Formed at Cairo on March 22, 1945, as a loose confederation of Arab states seeking Arab unity. Founding members were Egypt, Iraq, Jordan, Lebanon, Saudi Arabia, Syria, and the Yemen Arab Republic, joined later by Algeria, Bahrain, Djibouti, Kuwait, Libya, Mauritania, Morocco, Oman, Qatar, Somalia, the Sudan, Tunisia, the United Arab Emirates, the Yemen People's Democratic Republic, and the Palestine Liberation Organization. Military cooperation has been hampered by differences among the members, except in the Suez Canal crisis of 1956. The league has proved more effective in economic and cultural affairs. A permanent secretariat was set up at Cairo.

Central Treaty Organization (CENTO)

Created in 1955 to provide a defense shield on the northern tier of the Middle East against Soviet penetration. Its original members were Turkey, Iran, U.K., Pakistan, and Iraq (which withdrew in 1959). In 1958, the U.S. signed a declaration of collective security to cooperate with the member states. CENTO was known as the Baghdad Pact until 1958, when its headquarters were moved to Ankara, Turkey.

Commonwealth of Nations

An association of equal and independent nations and subordinate areas formerly part of the old British Empire and united by their symbolic allegiance to the Crown. Member nations gained equal status with the U.K. under the Statute of Westminster of 1931, which formally initiated the Commonwealth. Its members consult and cooperate and share trade and other economic benefits. For a list of members, *see* Countries of the World by Groupings.

Economic Community of West African States (ECOWAS)

Formed at Lagos, Nigeria, in 1975 to link English- and French-speaking states for commerce, transport, industry, monetary and financial questions, energy and telecommunications, and to coordinate common services. A treaty with the EEC provides technical and other cooperation. The community's members are Benin, Cameroon, Chad, Gambia, Ghana, Guinea, Guinea-Bissau, Ivory Coast, Liberia, Mali, Mauritania, Niger, Nigeria, Senegal, Sierra Leone, Togo, and Upper Volta.

The European Community

In 1950, the then French Foreign Minister, Robert Schumann, proposed a "Community" of the French and German coal and steel industries, with membership open to other European countries. The *European Coal and Steel Community (ECSC)* was established in 1952; it eliminated customs duties and reduced currency and trade restrictions on coal, iron ore, and scrap. Original members were France, Germany, Italy, Belgium, the Netherlands, and Luxembourg.

By 1955, discussions began on other ways of increasing European economic integration. The *European Economic Community* (the *Common Market* or *EEC*) was established by a treaty, signed in Rome in 1957, by the original members of the ECSC. In 1970, the U.K., Ireland, Denmark, and Norway were invited to join. All except Norway did so in 1972; the enlarged "Community of the Nine" formally came into existence on January 1, 1973.

The purposes of the EEC include the removal of trade barriers, coordination of economic policies, and increased mobility of labor and capital among its members—much of which had been achieved by 1978. Its aim is eventual economic union of the member nations and ultimate political confederation.

A second treaty was signed in Rome in 1957 establishing the *European Atomic Energy Community (Euratom)* to integrate activities of member nations concerned with nuclear power and technology.

The three Communities (ECSC, EEC, and Euratom) make up the *European Community*, with a Council of Ministers and a European Parliament. A European Court of Justice and the European Investment Bank also function within the European Community. (*See* R.C. Mowat, *Creating the European Community*, 1973.)

European Free Trade Association (EFTA)

Formed in 1959 (formally begun 1960) to promote economic growth and fair competition, equalize the supply of raw materials among the member states, and to expand world trade. Members now include Austria, Iceland, Norway, Portugal, Sweden, Switzerland, and Finland (associate). Denmark and the U.K., originally members, withdrew before becoming members of the EEC in 1973; at that time a new trade agreement was made between the EFTA and the Common Market. By 1966, custom duties between members had virtually been eliminated. The EFTA is based in Geneva.

Marshall Plan (European Recovery Program)

Proposed in June 1947 by Gen. George C. Marshall, U.S. Secretary of State, to meet the need for integrated recovery efforts against "hunger, poverty, desperation, and chaos" in Europe. A July conference of 16 nations (the U.S.S.R. and its satellites refusing to participate) estimated four-year-aid requirements at $22.4 billion. In April 1948, Congress appropriated $5.4 billion. The U.S. established the Economic Cooperation Administration; European nations set up the Organization for European Economic Cooperation (OEEC). Each participating country set aside, in its own currency, sums matching the aid it received. The ERP ended in December 1951, a year ahead of schedule, with a total cost of $11 billion. Emphasis by then had been shifted to rearmament. (*See* S.E. Harris, ed., *Foreign Economic Policy for the U.S.*, 1948, 1968.)

North Atlantic Treaty Organization (NATO)

Set up April 4, 1949, under a regional defense treaty for the North Atlantic area stating that "an armed attack against one . . . shall be considered an attack against . . . all" and that participating nations will take necessary joint counteraction under the United Nations Charter, including the use of armed force. The founding members were the U.S., Canada, Iceland, Norway, Great Britain, the Netherlands, Denmark, Belgium, Luxembourg, Portugal, France, and Italy. Greece, Turkey, and West Germany were added later. NATO marked the first time that the United States pledged to go to war to support allies before the outbreak of hostilities. The member nations are represented on the governing NATO Council. Its organization comprises their top foreign, economic, defense, and financial ministers. Its major military commands are SACEUR for Europe and SACLANT for the Atlantic Ocean area. (*See* James Huntley, *The NATO Story*, 1969.)

Organization for Economic Cooperation and Development (OECD)

Founded in 1961 to encourage world trade and economic progress and aid underdeveloped nations. The OECD superseded the Organization for European Economic Cooperation, which had been established under the Marshall Plan in 1948. Members are Austria, Belgium, Canada, Denmark, Finland, France, West Germany, Greece, Iceland, Ireland, Italy, Japan, Luxembourg, the Netherlands, New Zealand, Norway, Portugal, Spain, Sweden, Switzerland, Turkey, the U.K. and the U.S. (Australia and Yugoslavia have a special association). Its structure is consultative; its decisions, not binding.

Organization of African Unity (OAU)

Founded in May 1963 by 32 African countries, the OAU has grown to include most independent African countries; Rhodesia and South Africa are specifically excluded. Its charter reflects historical Pan-African concern for the political sovereignty, economic advancement, and cultural cooperation of all African peoples. The charter affirms allegiance to United Nations principles; its key section emphasizes the eradication of colonialism and promotion of international cooperation. The OAU has assisted in the relaxation or settlement of border disputes and helped resolve internal crises. In economic cooperation, it has stressed transportation and telecommunications. It maintains a close relationship with the U.N. OAU headquarters are at Addis Ababa, Ethiopia.

Organization of Petroleum Exporting Countries (OPEC)

Founded in 1960 at Baghdad, Iraq, to advance its members' interests in trade and development and in relations with other oil-producing nations. Venezuela took the initiative; other founders were Iran, Iraq, Kuwait, and Saudi Arabia. They were joined by Algeria, Ecuador, Gabon, Indonesia, Libya, Nigeria, Qatar, and the United Arab Emirates. Through such practices as the 1973–74 embargo, OPEC has maintained high oil prices and has generally fixed the price of oil in international trade.

Organization of American States (OAS)

Created in April 1948 as a regional agency working with the UN to promote peace, justice, hemispheric solidarity, and economic development; and to defend the sovereignty of member nations. Original members were Argentina, Bolivia, Brazil, Chile, Colombia, Costa Rica, Cuba, the Dominican Republic, Ecuador, El Salvador, Guatemala, Haiti, Honduras, Mexico, Nicaragua, Panama, Paraguay, Peru, the U.S., Uruguay, and Venezuela. Barbados, Grenada, Jamaica, Surinam, and Trinidad and Tobago were admitted later. In 1962 Cuba was suspended. The permanent body of the OAS is the General Secretariat, formerly the Pan-American Union Headquarters, Washington, D.C.

Panama Canal Treaties

Approved by the U.S. Senate in March and April of 1978. The basic treaty provides for turning the canal over to Panama by the year 2000. Until noon Dec. 31, 1999, the canal will be operated by a new U.S. agency, the Panama Canal Commission, with five Americans and four Panamanians on the board. Until 2000 the U.S. will have primary responsibility for defending the canal; Panama will assume jurisdiction over the 533-square-mile Canal Zone.

The Neutrality Treaty, also effective Dec. 31, 1999, provides that the U.S. and Panama will each have the right to defend the canal against threats to its neutrality or the peaceful passage of ships. A Senate reservation gave the U.S. the unilateral right to use force if necessary to reopen the canal or restore its operations. The Senate specified that any intervention would be only to keep the canal open, not to interfere in Panama's internal affairs. (See *Panama*, also *Canal Zone*, under States and Territories in the United States section.)

Treaty for a Partial Nuclear Test Ban

Agreement, effective Oct. 10, 1963, signed in Moscow Aug. 8, 1963, by the U.S., U.K., and the U.S.S.R. Although over 100 nations have since signed, France and China have not. The treaty banned nuclear testing in the atmosphere, in outer space, or under water. The signatories can withdraw under certain conditions.

The Potsdam Declaration

Issued at Potsdam, Germany, July 26, 1945, after a conference of President Truman, Prime Minister Churchill (later, Clement Attlee), and Prime Minister Stalin. Pending entry of the U.S.S.R. into the war against Japan, it was issued in the names of Truman, Churchill, and Chiang Kai-shek (reached by radio). The declaration, designed to clarify and implement the Yalta Agreement, demanded unconditional surrender of Japan and outlined surrender terms. It called for elimination of "irresponsible militarism" and for Allied occupation until Japan's war-making power was destroyed. Other major points included "stern justice" for war criminals, democratic reforms, and respect for fundamental human rights. Successful U.S. testing of the atom bomb was revealed to Stalin at Potsdam.

Strategic Arms Limitation Talks (SALT)

Two agreements limiting American and Soviet nuclear weapons were signed in Moscow in 1972 after three years of negotiations. One was a five-year interim pact limiting some offensive strategic weapons and the number of launchers for intercontinental ballistic missiles carrying nuclear warheads. The other, a treaty of indefinite duration, restricted antiballistic or defensive missiles to 200 on each side. The agreements were signed by President Richard M. Nixon and Leonid I. Brezhnev, the Soviet Communist Party leader. The talks originated with discussions at Glassboro, N.J., in 1967 between President Lyndon B. Johnson and the Soviet Prime Minister, Aleksei N. Kosygin. On Nov. 24, 1974, President Gerald R. Ford reached agreement in principle with Mr. Brezhnev at Vladivostok on limiting the numbers of all offensive strategic weapons and delivery systems until Dec. 31, 1985.

Warsaw Pact

Signed May 14, 1955, by Albania, Czechoslovakia, East Germany, Hungary, Poland, Romania, and the U.S.S.R. Albania, barred from meetings in 1962, withdrew in 1968 after ideological differences. The pact is the Communist equivalent of NATO, providing that an attack on one shall be regarded as an attack on all.

The Yalta Agreement

Signed Feb. 11, 1945, at conference of President Roosevelt and Prime Ministers Churchill and Stalin. The U.S., U.K., and the U.S.S.R. agreed to require Germany's unconditional surrender and on dividing Germany into separate zones for occupation, with France invited to join as the fourth occupying power. The agreement pledged disarmament of Germany, breakup of the arms industry, punishment of war criminals, reparations for destruction by the Germans, and the wiping out of nazism and militarism. The conference also agreed on terms for Russia to enter the war against Japan. (See R.F. Fenno, ed., *The Yalta Conference,* 2nd ed., 1972.)

Largest Cities of the World

Census figures and population estimates in the following table are based on most recent available data reflecting different years. Some cities include metropolitan areas or contiguous suburbs, while others report only those residing within precise geographical or physical boundaries. Therefore, the ratings in this listing must be considered approximate.

City	Population	City	Population
Shanghai, China	10,888,000	Jakarta, Indonesia	6,178,500
Mexico City	8,941,900	Cairo	6,133,000
Tokyo	8,643,000	Bombay	5,970,575
Peking	8,487,000	Rio de Janeiro	4,857,500
Manila	7,800,000	Bangkok, Thailand	4,545,600
Moscow	7,734,000	Karachi, Pakistan	4,465,000
New York	7,481,600	Leningrad	4,372,000
São Paulo, Brazil	7,198,000	Tientsin, China	4,280,000
London	7,028,200	Teheran, Iran	4,000,000
Seoul, South Korea	6,899,470	Lima, Peru	3,901,000

Source: United Nations' *Demographic Yearbook, 1976,* and official estimates.

World Population, Land Areas, and Elevations

Area	Estimated population, in thousands, 1976	Approximate land area, in thousands of sq mi.	Percent of total land area	Elevation, feet — Highest	Elevation, feet — Lowest	Dimensions, miles — East–West	Dimensions, miles — North–South
WORLD	4,044,000	58,473	100.0	Mt. Everest, Asia, 29,028	Dead Sea, Asia, 1,290 below sea level	24,902	24,860
ASIA	2,304,000	10,678	18.2	Mt. Everest, Tibet-Nepal, 29,028	Dead Sea, Israel-Jordan, 1,290 below sea level	5,400[1]	5,300[1]
AFRICA	412,000	11,707	20.0	Mt. Kilimanjaro, Tanzania, 19,340	Qattara Depression, Egypt, 440 below sea level	4,600	5,000
NORTH AMERICA[3]	348,000	9,362	16.0	Mt. McKinley, Alaska, 20,320	Death Valley, Calif., 282 below sea level	3,200[4]	4,000[4]
SOUTH AMERICA	224,000	6,885	11.8	Mt. Aconcagua, Arg.-Chile, 23,034	Sea level	3,200	4,600
ANTARCTICA	—	6,000	10.3	Vinson Massif, Sentinel Range, 16,863	Sea level	—	—
EUROPE	476,000	1,906	3.3	Mont Blanc, France, 15,781	Sea level	3,300[2]	2,400[2]
OCEANIA	21,700	3,286	5.6	Mauna Kea, Hawaii, 13,796	Lake Eyre, Australia, 38 below sea level	—	—
U.S.S.R., both European and Asiatic	258,000	8,649	14.8	Communism Peak, Pamir, 24,547	Caspian Sea, 96 below sea level	5,000	2,500

1. Including Asiatic U.S.S.R. 2. Including European U.S.S.R. 3. Although Hawaii is geographically part of Oceania, its population is included in the population figure for North America. 4. Excludes Hawaii.

ALSO

Foreign Words and Phrases

(The English meanings given are not necessarily literal translations.)

ab ovo: from the beginning
à bon marché: good bargain; cheap
à deux: for two; between two
a priori: from something previous
à votre santé: to your health
ad infinitum: to infinity; with no end
ad valorem: according to its value
al fresco: outdoors
alma mater: one's college or school
alter ego: other self
amicus curiae: friend of the court
ancien regime: the old order
anno Domini: year of our Lord
ante bellum: before the war
au contraire: on the contrary
au courant: current; up-to-date
auf Wiedersehen: goodbye
bête noire: particular nemesis
bienvenue: welcome
bon mot: a funny or witty saying
bon vivant: a gourmet, an epicure
bona fide: in good faith; genuine; honest
carpe diem: enjoy today; seize the day
carte blanche: unlimited authority
cause célèbre: a cause that generates wide interest
caveat emptor: buy at your own risk; let the buyer beware
circa: about; approximately
chacun à son goût: each to his own taste
combien: how much?
corpus delicti: fundamental fact or facts about the commission of a crime
coup de grâce: finishing blow
cum grano salis: with a grain of salt
d'accord: in accord; agreement

456

de facto: as a matter of fact; actual
de profundis: out of the depths
Deo gratias: thanks be to God
Deo volente: God willing
deus ex machina: artificially produced to bring a solution to some extreme difficulty
dramatis personae: characters in a play
ecce homo: this is the man
en masse: all together
en passant: in passing
fait accompli: an accomplished fact
faux pas: a false step; a mistake
flagrante delicto: caught in the act
Gesundheit: good health (God bless you)
habeas corpus: common-law writ to bring a person before a court or judge
hoi polloi: the common people
honi soit qui mal y pense: evil to him who thinks evil of it
hors d'oeuvre: appetizer
idée fixe: fixed idea; obsession
in loco parentis: in place of a parent
ipso facto: by the very fact
je ne sais quoi: I don't know what; an elusive quality
jeunesse dorée: gilded youth
laissez faire: noninterference
l'chaim: to life
maven: an expert; connoisseur
mea culpa: I am to blame
mirabile dictu: wonderful to relate
modus operandi: method of operation; way of working
nom de plume: pen name
non compos mentis: not of sound mind
non sequitur: it does not follow
O tempora! O mores!: What sad times and customs
omnia vincit amor: love conquers all
per annum: by the year
per capita: by the head; individually
per diem: by the day; daily
persona non grata: an unwelcome or unacceptable person
plus ça change, plus c'est le même chose: the more things change, the more they remain the same
post mortem: after death
pro bono publico: for the public good
pro tempore (pro tem): for the time being; temporary

quid pro quo: something done or given in exchange for something else

repondez s'il vous plait: please reply; please answer (abbr. R.S.V.P.)

requiescat in pace: rest in peace

sans souci: without worry or care

savoir faire: know-how; manners for all occasions

semper fidelis: always faithful

shalom: peace

sic transit gloria mundi: so passes the glory of the world

s'il vous plait: if you please; please

sine die: with no day set for the next meeting

sine qua non: indispensable

status (in) quo: state in which anything is

sui generis: in a class by itself

tempus fugit: time flies

tout de suite: immediately

veni, vidi, vici: I came, I saw, I conquered

vis-à-vis: face-to-face

Nobel Prizes

The Nobel prizes are awarded under the will of Alfred Bernhard Nobel, Swedish chemist and engineer, who died in 1896. The interest of the fund is divided annually among the persons who have made the most outstanding contributions in the fields of physics, chemistry, and physiology of medicine, who have produced the most distinguished literary work of an idealist tendency, and who have contributed most toward world peace.

In 1968, a Nobel Prize of economic sciences was established by Riksbank, the Swedish bank, in celebration of its 300th anniversary. The prize was awarded for the first time in 1969.

The prizes for physics and chemistry are awarded by the Swedish Academy of Science in Stockholm, the one for physiology or medicine by the Caroline Medical Institute in Stockholm, that for literature by the academy in Stockholm, and that for peace by a committee of five elected by the Norwegian Storting. The distribution of prizes was begun on December 10, 1901, the anniversary of Nobel's death. The amount of each prize varies with the income from the fund and currently is about $165,000. No Nobel prizes were awarded for 1940, 1941, and 1942; prizes for Literature were not awarded for 1914, 1918, and 1943.

PEACE

1901	Henri Dunant (Switzerland); Frederick Passy (France)
1902	Elie Ducommun and Albert Gobat (Switzerland)
1903	Sir William R. Cremer (England)
1904	Institut de Droit International (Belgium)
1905	Bertha von Suttner (Austria)
1906	Theodore Roosevelt (U.S.)
1907	Ernesto T. Moneta (Italy) and Louis Renault (France)
1908	Klas P. Arnoldson (Sweden) and Frederik Bajer (Denmark)
1909	Auguste M. F. Beernaert (Belgium) and Baron Paul H. B. B. d'Estournelles de Constant de Rebecque (France)
1910	Bureau International Permanent de la Paix (Switzerland)
1911	Tobias M. C. Asser (Holland) and Alfred H. Fried (Austria)
1912	Elihu Root (U.S.)
1913	Henri La Fontaine (Belgium)
1915	No award
1916	No award
1917	International Red Cross
1919	Woodrow Wilson (U.S.)
1920	Léon Bourgeois (France)
1921	Karl H. Branting (Sweden) and Christian L. Lange (Norway)
1922	Fridtjof Nansen (Norway)
1923	No award
1924	No award
1925	Sir Austen Chamberlain (England) and Charles G. Dawes (U.S.)
1926	Aristide Briand (France) and Gustav Stresemann (Germany)
1927	Ferdinand Buisson (France) and Ludwig Quidde (Germany)
1928	No award
1929	Frank B. Kellogg (U.S.)
1930	Lars O. J. Söderblom (Sweden)
1931	Jane Addams and Nicholas M. Butler (U.S.)
1932	No award

1933 Sir Norman Angell (England)
1934 Arthur Henderson (England)
1935 Karl von Ossietzky (Germany)
1936 Carlos de S. Lamas (Argentina)
1937 Lord Cecil of Chelwood (England)
1938 Office International Nansen pour les Réfugiés
     (Switzerland)
1939 No award
1944 International Red Cross
1945 Cordell Hull (U.S.)
1946 Emily G. Balch and John R. Mott (U.S.)
1947 American Friends Service Committee (U.S.) and British
     Society of Friends' Service Council (England)
1948 No award
1949 Lord John Boyd Orr (Scotland)
1950 Ralph J. Bunche (U.S.)
1951 Léon Jouhaux (France)
1952 Albert Schweitzer (French Equatorial Africa)
1953 George C. Marshall (U.S.)
1954 Office of U.N. High Commissioner for Refugees
1955 No award
1956 No award
1957 Lester B. Pearson (Canada)
1958 Rev. Dominique Georges Henri Pire (Belgium)
1959 Philip John Noel-Baker (England)
1960 Albert John Luthuli (South Africa)
1961 Dag Hammarskjöld (Sweden)
1962 Linus Pauling (U.S.)
1963 Intl. Comm. of Red Cross; League of Red Cross
     Societies (both Geneva)
1964 Rev. Dr. Martin Luther King, Jr. (U.S.)
1965 UNICEF (United Nations Children's Fund)
1966 No award
1967 No award
1968 René Cassin (France)
1969 International Labour Organization
1970 Norman E. Borlaug (U.S.)
1971 Willy Brandt (West Germany)
1972 No award
1973 Henry A. Kissinger (U.S.); Le Duc Tho (North Vietnam)[1]
1974 Eisaku Sato (Japan); Sean MacBride (Ireland)
1975 Andrei D. Sakharov (U.S.S.R.)

1. Le Duc Tho refused prize, charging that peace had not yet been really established in South Vietnam.

1976 Mairead Corrigan and Betty Williams (both Northern Ireland)
1977 Amnesty International
1978 Anwar Sadat (Egypt); Menachem Begin (Israel)

LITERATURE

1901 René F. A. Sully Prudhomme (France)
1902 Theodor Mommsen (Germany)
1903 Björnstjerne Björnson (Norway)
1904 Frédéric Mistral (France) and José Echegaray (Spain)
1905 Henryk Sienkiewicz (Poland)
1906 Giosuè Carducci (Italy)
1907 Rudyard Kipling (England)
1908 Rudolf Eucken (Germany)
1909 Selma Lagerlöf (Sweden)
1910 Paul von Heyse (Germany)
1911 Maurice Maeterlinck (Belgium)
1912 Gerhart Hauptmann (Germany)
1913 Rabindranath Tagore (India)
1915 Romain Rolland (France)
1916 Verner von Heidenstam (Sweden)
1917 Karl Gjellerup (Denmark) and Henrik Pontoppidan (Denmark)
1919 Carl Spitteler (Switzerland)
1920 Knut Hamsun (Norway)
1921 Anatole France (France)
1922 Jacinto Benavente (Spain)
1923 William B. Yeats (Ireland)
1924 Wladyslaw Reymont (Poland)
1925 George Bernard Shaw (England)
1926 Grazia Deledda (Italy)
1927 Henri Bergson (France)
1928 Sigrid Undset (Norway)
1929 Thomas Mann (Germany)
1930 Sinclair Lewis (U.S.)
1931 Erik A. Karlfeldt (Sweden)
1932 John Galsworthy (England)
1933 Ivan G. Bunin (Russia)
1934 Luigi Pirandello (Italy)
1935 No award
1936 Eugene O'Neill (U.S.)
1937 Roger Martin du Gard (France)
1938 Pearl S. Buck (U.S.)

1939 Frans Eemil Sillanpää (Finland)
1944 Johannes V. Jensen (Denmark)
1945 Gabriela Mistral (Chile)
1946 Hermann Hesse (Switzerland)
1947 André Gide (France)
1948 Thomas Stearns Eliot (England)
1949 William Faulkner (U.S.)
1950 Bertrand Russell (England)
1951 Pär Lagerkvist (Sweden)
1952 François Mauriac (France)
1953 Sir Winston Churchill (England)
1954 Ernest Hemingway (U.S.)
1955 Halldór Kiljan Laxness (Iceland)
1956 Juan Ramón Jiménez (Spain)
1957 Albert Camus (France)
1958 Boris Pasternak (U.S.S.R.) (declined)
1959 Salvatore Quasimodo (Italy)
1960 St.-John Perse (Alexis St.-Léger Léger) (France)
1961 Ivo Andric (Yugoslavia)
1962 John Steinbeck (U.S.)
1963 Giorgios Seferis (Seferiades) (Greece)
1964 Jean-Paul Sartre (France) (declined)
1965 Mikhail Sholokhov (U.S.S.R.)
1966 Shmuel Yosef Agnon (Israel) and Nelly Sachs (Sweden)
1967 Miguel Angel Asturias (Guatemala)
1968 Yasunari Kawabata (Japan)
1969 Samuel Beckett (France)
1970 Aleksandr Solzhenitsyn (U.S.S.R.)
1971 Pablo Neruda (Chile)
1972 Heinrich Böll (Germany)
1973 Patrick White (Australia)
1974 Eyvind Johnson and Harry Martinson (both Sweden)
1975 Eugenio Montale (Italy)
1976 Saul Bellow (U.S.)
1977 Vicente Aleixandre (Spain)
1978 Issac Bashevis Singer (U.S.)

PHYSICS

1901 Wilhelm K. Roentgen (Germany), for discovery of Roentgen rays
1902 Hendrik A. Lorentz and Pieter Zeeman (Netherlands), for work on influence of magnetism upon radiation
1903 A. Henri Becquerel (France), for work on spontaneous

radioactivity; and Pierre and Marie Curie (France), for study of radiation

1904 John Strutt (Lord Rayleigh) (England), for discovery of argon in investigating gas density

1905 Philipp Lenard (Germany), for work with cathode rays

1906 Sir Joseph Thomson (England), for investigations on passage of electricity through gases

1907 Albert A. Michelson (U.S.), for spectroscopic and metrologic investigations

1908 Gabriel Lippmann (France), for method of reproducing colors by photography

1909 Guglielmo Marconi (Italy) and Ferdinand Braun (Germany), for development of wireless

1910 Johannes D. van der Waals (Netherlands), for work with the equation of state for gases and liquids

1911 Wilhelm Wien (Germany), for his laws governing the radiation of heat

1912 Gustaf Dalén (Sweden), for discovery of automatic regulators used in lighting lighthouses and light buoys

1913 Heike Kamerlingh-Onnes (Netherlands), for work leading to production of liquid helium

1914 Max von Laue (Germany), for discovery of diffraction of Roentgen rays passing through crystals

1915 Sir William Bragg and William L. Bragg (England), for analysis of crystal structure by X rays

1916 No award

1917 Charles G. Barkla (England), for discovery of Roentgen radiation of the elements

1918 Max Planck (Germany), discoveries in connection with quantum theory

1919 Johannes Stark (Germany), discovery of Doppler effect in Canal rays and decomposition of spectrum lines by electric fields

1920 Charles E. Guillaume (Switzerland), for discoveries of anomalies in nickel steel alloys

1921 Albert Einstein (Germany), for discovery of the law of the photoelectric effect

1922 Niels Bohr (Denmark), for investigation of structure of atoms and radiations emanating from them

1923 Robert A. Millikan (U.S.), for work on elementary charge of electricity and photoelectric phenomena

1924 Karl M. G. Siegbahn (Sweden), for investigations in X-ray spectroscopy

1925 James Franck and Gustav Hertz (Germany), for discovery of laws governing impact of electrons upon atoms

1926 Jean B. Perrin (France), for work on discontinous structure of matter and discovery of the equilibrium of sedimentation

1927 Arthur H. Compton (U.S.), for discovery of Compton phenomenon; and Charles T. R. Wilson (England), for method of perceiving paths taken by electrically charged particles

1928 In 1929, the 1928 prize was awarded to Sir Owen Richardson (England), for work on the phenomenon of thermionics and discovery of the Richardson Law

1929 Prince Louis Victor de Broglie (France), for discovery of the wave character of electrons

1930 Sir Chandrasekhara Raman (India), for work on diffusion of light and discovery of the Raman effect

1931 No award

1932 In 1933, the prize for 1932 was awarded to Werner Heisenberg (Germany), for creation of the quantum mechanics

1933 Erwin Schrödinger (Austria) and Paul A. M. Dirac (England), for discovery of new fertile forms of the atomic theory

1934 No award

1935 James Chadwick (England), for discovery of the neutron

1936 Victor F. Hess (Austria), for discovery of cosmic radiation; and Carl D. Anderson (U.S.), for discovery of the positron

1937 Clinton J. Davisson (U.S.) and George P. Thomson (England), for discovery of diffraction of electrons by crystals

1938 Enrico Fermi (Italy), for identification of new radioactivity elements and discovery of nuclear reactions effected by slow neutrons

1939 Ernest Orlando Lawrence (U.S.), for development of the cyclotron

1943 Otto Stern (U.S.), for detection of magnetic momentum of protons

1944 Isidor Isaac Rabi (U.S.), for work on magnetic movements of atomic particles

1945 Wolfgang Pauli (Austria), for work on atomic fissions

1946 Percy Williams Bridgman (U.S.), for studies and inventions in high-pressure physics

465

1947 Sir Edward Appleton (England), for discovery of layer which reflects radio short waves in the ionosphere

1948 Patrick M. S. Blackett (England), for improvement on Wilson chamber and discoveries in cosmic radiation

1949 Hideki Yukawa (Japan), for mathematical prediction, in 1935, of the meson

1950 Cecil Frank Powell (England), for method of photographic study of atom nucleus, and for discoveries about mesons

1951 Sir John Douglas Cockcroft (England) and Ernest T. S. Walton (Ireland), for work in 1932 on transmutation of atomic nuclei

1952 Edward Mills Purcell and Felix Bloch (U.S.), for work in measurement of magnetic fields in atomic nuclei

1953 Fritz Zernike (Netherlands), for development of "phase contrast" microscope

1954 Max Born (England), for work in quantum mechanics; and Walther Bothe (Germany), for work in cosmic radiation

1955 Polykarp Kusch and Willis E. Lamb, Jr. (U.S.), for atomic measurements

1956 William Shockley, Walter H. Brattain, and John Bardeen (U.S.), for developing electronic transistor

1957 Tsung Dao Lee and Chen Ning Yang (China), for disproving principle of conservation of parity

1958 Pavel A. Cherenkov, Ilya M. Frank, and Igor E. Tamm (U.S.S.R.), for work resulting in development of cosmic-ray counter

1959 Emilio Segre and Owen Chamberlain (U.S.), for demonstrating the existence of the anti-proton

1960 Donald A. Glaser (U.S.), for invention of "bubble chamber" to study subatomic particles

1961 Robert Hofstadter (U.S.), for determination of shape and size of atomic nucleus; Rudolf Mössbauer (Germany), for method of producing and measuring recoil-free gamma rays

1962 Lev D. Landau (U.S.S.R.), for his theories about condensed matter

1963 Eugene Paul Wigner, Maria Goeppert Mayer (both U.S.), and J. Hans D. Jensen (Germany), for research on structure of atom and its nucleus

1964 Charles Hard Townes (U.S.), Nikolai G. Basov, and Aleksandr M. Prochorov (both U.S.S.R.), for developing maser and laser principle of producing high-intensity radiation

1965 Richard P. Feynman, Julian S. Schwinger (both U.S.), and Shinichero Tomonaga (Japan), for research in quantum electrodynamics

1966 Alfred Kastler (France), for work on energy levels inside atom

1967 Hans A. Bethe (U.S.), for work on energy production of stars

1968 Luis Walter Alvarez (U.S.), for study of subatomic particles

1969 Murray Gell-Mann (U.S.), for study of subatomic particles

1970 Hannes Alfvén (Sweden), for theories in plasma physics; and Louis Néel (France), for discoveries in antiferromagnetism and ferrimagnetism

1971 Dennis Gabor (England), for invention of holographic method of three-dimensional imagery

1972 John Bardeen, Leon N. Cooper, and John Robert Schrieffer (all U.S.), for theory of superconductivity, where electrical resistance in certain metals vanishes above absolute zero temperature

1973 Ivar Giaever (U.S.), Leo Esaki (Japan), and Brian D. Josephson (U.K.), for theories that have advanced and expanded the field of miniature electronics

1974 Antony Hewish (England), for discovery of pulsars; Martin Ryle (England), for using radiotelescopes to probe outer space with high degree of precision

1975 James Rainwater (U.S.) and Ben Mottelson and Aage N. Bohr (both Denmark), for showing that the atomic nucleus is asymmetrical

1976 Burton Richter and Samuel C.C. Ting (U.S.), for discovery of subatomic particles known as J and psi

1977 Philip W. Anderson and John H. Van Vleck (both U.S.), and Nevill F. Mott (U.K.), for work underlying computer memories and electronic devices

1978 Arno A. Penzias and Robert W. Wilson (both U.S.), for work in cosmic microwave radiation; Leonidovich Kapitsa (U.S.S.R.), for inventions and discoveries in low temperature physics

CHEMISTRY

1901 Jacobus H. van't Hoff (Netherlands), for laws of chemical dynamics and osmotic pressure in solutions

1902 Emil Fischer (Germany), for experiments in sugar and purin groups of substances

1903 Svante A. Arrhenius (Sweden), for his electrolytic theory of dissociation

1904 Sir William Ramsay (England), for discovery and determination of place of inert gaseous elements in air

1905 Adolf von Baeyer (Germany), for work on organic dyes and hydroaromatic combinations

1906 Henri Moissan (France), for isolation of fluorine, and introduction of electric furnace

1907 Eduard Buchner (Germany), discovery of cell-less fermentation and investigations in biological chemistry

1908 Sir Ernest Rutherford (England), for investigations into disintegration of elements

1909 Wilhelm Ostwald (Germany), for work on catalysis and investigations into chemical equilibrium and reaction rates

1910 Otto Wallach (Germany), for work in the field of alicyclic compounds

1911 Marie Curie (France), for discovery of elements radium and polonium

1912 Victor Grignard (France), for reagent discovered by him; and Paul Sabatier (France), for methods of hydrogenating organic compounds

1913 Alfred Werner (Switzerland), for linking up atoms within the molecule

1914 Theodore W. Richards (U.S.), for determining atomic weight of many chemical elements

1915 Richard Willstätter (Germany), for research into coloring matter of plants, especially chlorophyll

1916 No award

1917 No award

1918 Fritz Haber (Germany), for synthetic production of ammonia

1919 No award

1920 Walther Nernst (Germany), for work in thermochemistry

1921 Frederick Soddy (England), for investigations into origin and nature of isotopes

1922 Francis W. Aston (England), for discovery of isotopes in nonradioactive elements and for discovery of the whole number rule

1923 Fritz Pregl (Austria), for method of microanalysis of organic substances discovered by him

1924 No award

1925 In 1926, the 1925 prize was awarded to Richard Zsigmondy (Germany), for work on the heterogeneous nature of colloid solutions

1926 Theodor Svedberg (Sweden), for work on disperse systems

1927 In 1928 the 1927 prize was awarded to Heinrich Wieland (Germany), for investigations of bile acids and kindred substances

1928 Adolf Windaus (Germany), for investigations on constitution of the sterols and their connection with vitamins

1929 Sir Arthur Harden (England) and Hans K. A. S. von Euler-Chelpin (Sweden), for research of fermentation of sugars

1930 Hans Fischer (Germany), for work on coloring matter of blood and leaves and for his synthesis of hemin

1931 Karl Bosch and Friedrich Bergius (Germany), for invention and development of chemical high-pressure methods

1932 Irving Langmuir (U.S.), for work in realm of surface chemistry

1933 No award

1934 Harold C. Urey (U.S.), for discovery of heavy hydrogen

1935 Frédéric and Irène Joliot-Curie (France), for synthesis of new radioactive elements

1936 Peter J. W. Debye (Netherlands), for investigations on dipole moments and diffraction of X rays and electrons in gases

1937 Walter N. Haworth (England), for research on carbohydrates and Vitamin C; and Paul Karrer (Switzerland), for work on carotenoids, flavins, and Vitamins A and B

1938 Richard Kuhn (Germany), for carotinoid study and vitamin research (declined the prize)

1939 Adolf Butenandt (Germany), for work on sexual hormones (declined the prize); and Leopold Ruzicka (Switzerland), for work with polymethylenes

1943 Georg Hevesy De Heves (Hungary), for work on use of isotopes as indicators

1944 Otto Hahn (Germany), for work on atomic fission

1945 Artturi Ilmari Virtanen (Finland), for research in the field of conservation of fodder

1946 James B. Sumner (U.S.), for crystallizing enzymes; John H. Northrop and Wendell M. Stanley (U.S.), for preparing enzymes and virus proteins in pure form

1947 Sir Robert Robinson (England), for research in plant substances
1948 Arne Tiselius (Sweden), for biochemical discoveries and isolation of mouse paralysis virus
1949 William Francis Giauque (U.S.), for research in thermodynamics, especially effects of low temperature
1950 Otto Diels and Kurt Alder (Germany), for discovery of diene synthesis enabling scientists to study structure of organic matter
1951 Glenn T. Seaborg and Edwin H. McMillan (U.S.), for discovery of plutonium
1952 Archer John Porter Martin and Richard Laurence Millington Synge (England), for development of partition chromatography
1953 Hermann Staudinger (Germany), for research in giant molecules
1954 Linus C. Pauling (U.S.), for study of forces holding together protein and other molecules
1955 Vincent du Vigneaud (U.S.), for work on pituitary hormones
1956 Sir Cyril Hinshelwood (England) and Nikolai N. Semenov (U.S.S.R.), for parallel research on chemical reaction kinetics
1957 Sir Alexander Todd (England), for research with chemical compounds that are factors in heredity
1958 Frederick Sanger (England), for determining molecular structure of insulin
1959 Jaroslav Heyrovsky (Czechoslovakia), for development of polarography, an electrochemical method of analysis
1960 Willard F. Libby (U.S.), for "atomic time clock" to measure age of objects by measuring their radioactivity
1961 Melvin Calvin (U.S.), for establishing chemical steps during photosynthesis
1962 Max F. Perutz and John C. Kendrew (England), for mapping protein molecules with X rays
1963 Carl Ziegler (Germany) and Giulio Natta (Italy), for work in uniting simple hydrocarbons into large molecule substances
1964 Dorothy Mary Crowfoot Hodgkin (England), for determining structure of compounds needed in combating pernicious anemia
1965 Robert B. Woodward (U.S.), for work in synthesizing complicated organic compounds

1966 Robert Sanderson Mulliken (U.S.), for research on bond holding atoms together in molecule

1967 Manfred Eigen (Germany), Ronald G. W. Norrish, and George Porter (both England), for work in high-speed chemical reactions

1968 Lars Onsager (U.S.), for development of system of equations in thermodynamics

1969 Derek H. R. Barton (England) and Odd Hassel (Norway), for study of organic molecules

1970 Luis F. Leloir (Argentina), for discovery of sugar nucleotides and their role in biosynthesis of carbohydrates

1971 Gerhard Herzberg (Canada), for contributions to knowledge of electronic structure and geometry of molecules, particularly free radicals

1972 Christian Boehmer Anfinsen, Stanford Moore, and William Howard Stein (all U.S.), for pioneering studies in enzymes

1973 Ernst Otto Fischer (W. Germany) and Geoffrey Wilkinson (U.K.), for work that could solve problem of automobile exhaust pollution

1974 Paul J. Flory (U.S.), for developing analytic methods to study properties and molecular structure of long-chain molecules

1975 John W. Cornforth (Australia) and Vladimir Prelog (Switzerland), for research on structure of biological molecules such as antibiotics and cholesterol

1976 William N. Lipscomb, Jr. (U.S.), for work on the structure and bonding mechanisms of boranes

1977 Ilya Prigogine (Belgium), for contributions to nonequilibrium thermodynamics, particularly the theory of dissipative structures

1978 Peter Mitchell (England), for contributions to the understanding of biological energy transfer

PHYSIOLOGY OR MEDICINE

1901 Emil A. von Behring (Germany), for work on serum therapy against diphtheria

1902 Sir Ronald Ross (England), for work on malaria

1903 Niels R. Finsen (Denmark), for his treatment of lupus vulgaris with concentrated light rays

1904 Ivan P. Pavlov (U.S.S.R.), for work on the physiology of digestion

1905 Robert Koch (Germany), for work on tuberculosis

1906 Camillo Golgi (Italy) and Santiago Ramón y Cajal (Spain), for work on structure of the nervous system

1907 Charles L. A. Laveran (France), for work with protozoa in the generation of disease

1908 Paul Ehrlich (Germany), and Elie Metchnikoff (U.S.S.R.), for work on immunity

1909 Theodor Kocher (Switzerland), for work on the thyroid gland

1910 Albrecht Kossel (Germany), for achievements in the chemistry of the cell

1911 Allvar Gullstrand (Sweden), for work on the dioptrics of the eye

1912 Alexis Carrel (France), for work on vascular ligature and grafting of blood vessels and organs

1913 Charles Richet (France), for work on anaphylaxy

1914 Robert Bárány (Austria), for work on physiology and pathology of the vestibular system

1915 No award

1916 No award

1917 No award

1918 No award

1919 Jules Bordet (Belgium), for discoveries in connection with immunity

1920 August Krogh (Denmark), for discovery of regulation of capillaries' motor mechanism

1921 No award

1922 In 1923, the 1922 prize was shared by Archibald V. Hill (England), for discovery relating to heat-production in muscles; and Otto Meyerhof (Germany), for correlation between consumption of oxygen and production of lactic acid in muscles

1923 Sir Frederick Banting (Canada) and John J. R. Macleod (Scotland), for discovery of insulin

1924 Willem Einthoven (Netherlands), for discovery of the mechanism of the electrocardiogram

1925 No award

1926 Johannes Fibiger (Denmark), for discovery of the Spiroptera carcinoma

1927 Julius Wagner-Jauregg (Austria), for use of malaria inoculation in treatment of dementia paralytica

1928 Charles Nicolle (France), for work on typhus exanthematicus

1929 Christiaan Eijkman (Netherlands), for discovery of the antineuritic vitamins; and Sir Frederick Hopkins (England), for discovery of growth-promoting vitamins

1930 Karl Landsteiner (U.S.), for discovery of human blood groups

1931 Otto H. Warburg (Germany), for discovery of the character and mode of action of the respiratory ferment

1932 Sir Charles Sherrington (England) and Edgar D. Adrian (U.S.), for discoveries of the function of the neuron

1933 Thomas H. Morgan (U.S.), for discoveries on hereditary function of the chromosomes

1934 George H. Whipple, George R. Minot, and William P. Murphy (U.S.), for discovery of liver therapy against anemias

1935 Hans Spemann (Germany), for discovery of the organizer-effect in embryonic development

1936 Sir Henry Dale (England) and Otto Loewi (Germany), for discoveries on chemical transmission of nerve impulses

1937 Albert Szent-Györgyi von Nagyrapolt (Hungary), for discoveries on biological combustion

1938 Corneille Heymans (Belgium), for determining importance of sinus and aorta mechanisms in the regulation of respiration

1939 Gerhard Domagk (Germany), for antibacterial effect of prontocilate

1943 Henrik Dam (Denmark) and Edward A. Doisy (U.S.), for analysis of Vitamin K

1944 Joseph Erlanger and Herbert Spencer Gasser (U.S.), for work on functions of the nerve threads

1945 Sir Alexander Fleming, Ernst Boris Chain, and Sir Howard Florey (England), for discovery of penicillin

1946 Herman J. Muller (U.S.), for hereditary effects of X rays on genes

1947 Carl F. and Gerty T. Cori (U.S.), for work on animal starch metabolism; Bernardo A. Houssay (Argentina), for study of pituitary

1948 Paul Mueller (Switzerland), for discovery of insect-killing properties of DDT

1949 Walter Rudolf Hess (Switzerland), for research on brain control of body; and Antonio Caetano de Abreu Freire Egas Moniz (Portugal), for development of brain operation

1950 Philip S. Hench, Edward C. Kendall (both U.S.), and Tadeus Reichstein (Switzerland), for discoveries about hormones of adrenal cortex

1951 Max Theiler (South Africa), for development of anti-yellow-fever vaccine

1952 Selman A. Waksman (U.S.), for co-discovery of streptomycin

1953 Fritz A. Lipmann (Germany-U.S.) and Hans Adolph Krebs (Germany-England), for studies of living cells

1954 John F. Enders, Thomas H. Weller, and Frederick C. Robbins (U.S.), for work with cultivation of polio virus

1955 Hugo Theorell (Sweden), for work on oxidation enzymes

1956 Dickinson W. Richards, Jr., André F. Cournand (both U.S.), and Werner Forssmann (Germany), for new techniques in treating heart disease

1957 Daniel Bovet (Italy), for development of drugs to relieve allergies and relax muscles during surgery

1958 Joshua Lederberg (U.S.), for work with genetic mechanisms; George W. Beadle and Edward L. Tatum (U.S.), for discovering how genes transmit hereditary characteristics

1959 Severo Ochoa and Arthur Kornberg (U.S.), for discoveries related to compounds within chromosomes, which play a vital role in heredity

1960 Sir Macfarlane Burnet (Australia) and Peter Brian Medawar (England), for discovery of acquired immunological tolerance

1961 Georg von Bekesy (U.S.), for discoveries about physical mechanisms of stimulation within cochlea

1962 James D. Watson (U.S.), Maurice H. F. Wilkins, and Francis H. C. Crick (England), for determining structure of deoxyribonucleic acid (DNA)

1963 Alan Lloyd Hodgkin, Andrew Fielding Huxley (both England), and Sir John Carew Eccles (Australia), for research on nerve cells

1964 Konrad E. Bloch (U.S.) and Feodor Lynen (Germany), for research on mechanism and regulation of cholesterol and fatty acid metabolism

1965 François Jacob, André Lwolff, and Jacques Monod (France), for study of regulatory activities in body cells

1966 Charles Brenton Huggins (U.S.), for studies in hormone treatment of cancer of prostate; Francis Peyton Rous (U.S.), for discovery of tumor-producing viruses

1967 Haldan K. Hartline, George Wald, and Ragnar Granit (U.S.), for work on human eye

1968 Robert W. Holley, Har Gobind Khorana, and Marshall W. Nirenberg (U.S.), for studies of genetic code

1969 Max Delbruck, Alfred D. Hershey, and Salvador E. Luria (U.S.), for study of mechanism of virus infection in living cells

1970 Julius Axelrod (U.S.), Ulf S. von Euler (Sweden), and Sir Bernard Katz (England), for studies of how nerve impulses are transmitted within the body

1971 Earl W. Sutherland, Jr., (U.S.), for research on how hormones work

1972 Gerald M. Edelman (U.S.), and Rodney R. Porter (U.K.), for research on the chemical structure and nature of antibodies

1973 Karl von Frisch and Konrad Lorenz (Austria), and Nikolaas Tinbergen (Netherlands), for their studies of individual and social behavior patterns

1974 George E. Palade and Christian de Duve (both U.S.) and Albert Claude (Belgium), for contributions to understanding inner workings of living cells

1975 David Baltimore, Howard M. Temin and Renato Dulbecco (all U.S.), for work in interaction between tumor viruses and genetic material of the cell

1976 Baruch S. Blumberg and D. Carleton Gajdusek (U.S.), for discoveries concerning new mechanisms for the origin and dissemination of infectious diseases

1977 Rosalyn S. Yalow, Roger C. L. Guillemin, and Andrew V. Schally (all U.S.), for research in role of hormones in chemistry of the body

1978 Daniel Nathans and Hamilton Smith (both U.S.) and Werner Arber (Switzerland), for discovery of restriction enzymes and their application to problems of molecular genetics

ECONOMIC SCIENCE

1969 Ragnar Frisch (Norway) and Jan Tinbergen (Netherlands), for work in econometrics (application of mathematics and statistical methods to economic theories and problems)

1970 Paul A. Samuelson (U.S.), for efforts to raise the level of scientific analysis in economic theory

1971 Simon Kuznets (U.S.), for developing concept of using a country's gross national product to determine its economic growth

1972 Kenneth J. Arrow (U.S.) and Sir John R. Hicks (U.K.), for theories that help to assess business risk and government economic and welfare policies

1973 Wassily Leontief (U.S.), for devising the input-output technique to determine how different sectors of an economy interact

1974 Gunnar Myrdal (Sweden) and Friedrich A. von Hayek (Austria), for pioneering analysis of the interdependence of economic, social and institutional phenomena

1975 Leonid V. Kantorovich (U.S.S.R.) and Tjalling C. Koopmans (U.S.), for work on the theory of optimum allocation of resources

1976 Milton Friedman (U.S.), for work in consumption analysis and monetary history and theory, and for demonstration of complexity of stabilization policy

1977 Bertil Ohlin (Sweden) and James E. Meade (U.K.), for contributions to theory of international trade and international capital movements

1978 Herbert A. Simon (U.S.) for research into the decision-making process within economic organizations

Reference Books And Other Sources

General References

Encyclopedias are a unique category, since they attempt to cover most subjects quite thoroughly. Two most valuable multivolume encyclopedias are the **Encyclopaedia Britannica** and the **Encyclopedia Americana**. Useful one-volume encyclopedias are the **New Columbia Encyclopedia** and the **Random House Encyclopedia**.

Dictionaries and similar "word books" are also unique: **Webster's New International Dictionary** (third edition, unabridged). **Random House Dictionary**. **Merriam Webster's Collegiate Dictionary** (eighth edition, abridged). **Oxford English Dictionary**. **Bartlett's Familiar Quotations**.

Roget's Thesaurus. Modern American Usage.

There are a number of useful **atlases: New York Times Atlas of the World,** a number of historical atlases (Penguin Books), **Oxford Economic Atlas of the World, Atlas of the Universe** (Rand McNally), **Atlas of the Historical Geography of the U.S.** (Carnegie Institution of Washington and the American Geographical Society), and contemporary road atlases of the U.S. (Rand McNally).

A source of information on virtually all subjects is the United States Government Printing Office. For information write: Superintendent of Documents, Washington, D.C. 20402.

For help on any subject, consult: **Subject Guide to Books in Print, The New York Times Index,** and the **Reader's Guide to Periodical Literature** in your library.

Specific References

America Votes (Congressional Quarterly, Inc.)

American Indian, Reference Encyclopedia of the (Todd Publications)

Amphibians of the World, Living (Doubleday)

Animal Life Encyclopedia (Van Nostrand Reinhold)

Antiques, Collectors Encyclopedia of (Crown)

Architecture, World (McGraw-Hill)

Art, Encyclopedia of World (McGraw-Hill)

Art, History of (Prentice-Hall)

Art, Oxford Companion to (Oxford University Press)

Art, Who's Who in American (R.R. Bowker)

Art Directory, American (R.R. Bowker)

Authors, 1000–1900, European (H.W. Wilson)

Authors, 1600–1900, American (H.W. Wilson)

Authors, Twentieth Century (H.W. Wilson)

Authors Before 1800 (H.W. Wilson)

Authors of the Nineteenth Century, British (H.W. Wilson)

Auto Racing, The New York Times Complete Guide to (Quadrangle)

Banking and Finance, Encyclopedia of (Bankers Publishing Co.)

Baseball Encyclopedia (Information Concepts/Macmillan)

(Baseball) **World Series Records** (The Sporting News)

Basketball, Modern Encyclopedia of (Four Winds Press)

Biographical Dictionary, Chambers (St. Martin's Press)

Biographical Dictionary, Webster's (G. & C. Merriam)

Biography Yearbook, Current (H.W. Wilson)

Birds of America (Audubon)

Book Review Digest, 1905— (H.W. Wilson)

Business Almanac, Dow Jones-Irwin (Dow Jones-Irwin)

Canadian History and Literature, Oxford Companion to (Oxford University Press)

Catholic Encyclopedia, New (Publishers Guild/McGraw-Hill)

Chemistry, Encyclopedia of (Van Nostrand Reinhold)

Chemistry and Physics, Handbook of (Chemical Rubber Co.)

Christian Church, Oxford Dictionary of the (Oxford University Press)

Church Annual, Episcopal (Morehouse-Barlow)

Churches, Yearbook of American and Canadian (Abingdon Press)

Climate and Man (U.S. Department of Agriculture)

Communist Affairs, Yearbook on International (Hoover Institution Press)

Composers, Great, 1300–1900; A Biographical and Critical Guide (H.W. Wilson)

Composers Since 1900; A Biographical and Critical Guide (H.W. Wilson)

Congressional Quarterly Directory (Congressional Quarterly, Inc.)

Consumer Sourcebook (Gale Research Co.)

Consumer Reports (Consumers Union)

Dance Encyclopedia (Simon & Schuster)

Drama, Crowell's Handbook of Classical (Crowell)

Ecology Information and Organizations, Guide to (H.W. Wilson)

Energy, Encyclopedia of (McGraw-Hill)

Environmental Quality Report (Council on Environmental Quality)

Environmental Science, Encyclopedia of (McGraw-Hill)

Europa Year Book (Europa Publications)

Facts, Famous First (H.W. Wilson)

Facts on File (Facts on File, Inc.)

Film, Oxford Companion to (Oxford University Press)

Filmgoer's Companion (Hill & Wang)

Fishing Encyclopedia, New Standard (Holt, Rinehart & Winston)

Football, Encyclopedia of (A.S. Barnes & Co.)

Foreign Terms, Dictionary of (Crowell)

Foundation Directory (Columbia University Press, dist.)

Game, Rules of the (Bantam Books)

Geographical Dictionary, Webster's New (G. & C. Merriam)

Geography, Dictionary of (Penguin Books)

Government Manual, U.S. (U.S. Office of the Federal Register)

History, Album of American (Charles Scribner's)

History, Atlas of American (Oxford University Press)

History, Dictionary of American (Charles Scribner's)

History, Documents of American (Appleton-Century-Crofts)

History, Encyclopedia of Latin American (Bobbs-Merrill)

History, Encyclopedia of World (Houghton-Mifflin)

History, Timetables of (Simon & Schuster)

Ice Hockey, Complete Encyclopedia of (Prentice-Hall)

Investments, American and Foreign, Manual of (Moody's Investors Service)

Jazz in the Seventies, Encyclopedia of (Horizon)

Judaica, Encyclopaedia (Macmillan)

Libraries, World Guide to (R.R. Bowker)

Library Directory, American (R.R. Bowker)

Literary History of the United States (Macmillan)

Literature, Oxford Companion to American (Oxford University Press)

Literature, Oxford Companion to Classical (Oxford University Press)

Literature, Oxford Companion to English (Oxford University Press)

Literature, Reader's Adviser to the Best in (R.R. Bowker)

Literature, Reader's Encyclopedia of American (Crowell)

Medical Adviser, Modern Home (Doubleday)

Museums, Directory of World (Columbia University Press)

Music, Handbook of American (Free Press, Div. of Macmillan)

(Music) ASCAP. Biographical Dictionary (American Society of Authors, Composers, and Publishers)

Music, Concise Oxford Dictionary of (Oxford University Press)

Music, Harvard Dictionary of (Harvard University Press)

Music and Musicians, Grove's Dictionary of (St. Martin's Press)

Musical Terms, Dictionary of (Gordon Press)

Mythology, (Larousse) World (G.P. Putnam's Sons)

Nations, Handbook of New (Crowell)

Nations, Worldmark Encyclopedia of the (Harper & Row)

Negro Reference Book, American (Prentice-Hall)

Newspapers and Periodicals, Ayer Directory of (Ayer Press)

Opera Book, Kobbe's Complete (G.P. Putnam's)

Periodicals Directory, International (Ulrich's)

Physics and Electronics, International Dictionary of (Van Nostrand Reinhold)

Poetry, Granger's Index to (Columbia University Press)

Politics, Almanac of American (Gambit, Inc.)

Politics, Who's Who in American (R.R. Bowker)

Private Schools, Handbook of (Porter Sargent)

Robert's Rules of Order (Morrow & Co.)

Science, American Men and Women of (R.R. Bowker)

Science and Technology, Asimov's Biographical Encyclopedia of (Doubleday)

Scientific Encyclopedia, Van Nostrand's (Van Nostrand Reinhold)

Scientific Terms, McGraw-Hill Dictionary of (McGraw-Hill)

Space, Encyclopedia of (McGraw-Hill)

Sports Dictionary, Webster's (G. & C. Merriam Co.)

Sports, Encyclopedia of (A.S. Barnes & Co.)

States, Book of (Council of State Governments)

Statesman's Yearbook (Burke's Peerage, Ltd.)

Tennis, Encyclopedia of (Viking Press)

Theater, Oxford Companion to the (Oxford University Press)

Theater, Who's Who in the (Gale Research Co.)

Trotting and Pacing Guide (U.S. Trotting Association)

United Nations, Demographic Yearbook (U.N. Publishing Service)

United Nations, Statistical Yearbook of the (U.N. Publishing Service)

United States, Historical Statistics of the (U.S. Department of Commerce)

(United States) Pocket Data Book, U.S.A. (Bureau of Census)

United States, Statistical Abstract of the (Government Printing Office)

Way Things Work (Simon & Schuster)

Weather Almanac (Gale Research Co.)

Wildlife, Atlas of World (Rand McNally)

Women, Notable American, 1607–1950 (Belknap Press)

Women's Movement, Practical Guide to the (Women's Action Alliance, Inc.)

Who's Who (British), (St. Martin's Press)

Who's Who in America (Marquis)

World, Harper Encyclopedia of the Modern (Harper & Row)

See the full range of publications of Dun & Bradstreet and Standard & Poor's for corporate financial and stockholder information.

For detailed information on American colleges and universities, see the many publications of the **American Council on Education.**

Also see the many specialized **Who's Who** volumes issued by Marquis for biographies of famous contemporaries in many fields.